To G   10 May '05

Happy Birthday
/(yet-again)
with love ⟶ J.

FISH,
FLESH
AND
GOOD RED
Herring

ALICE THOMAS ELLIS

FISH, FLESH AND GOOD RED Herring

Virago

To Josh, Taylor, Charlotte, Henrietta,
Jack, Isaac and Ruby
(and any others as yet unborn)

A *Virago* Book

First published in Great Britain by Virago Press 2004

Copyright © Alice Thomas Ellis 2004

The moral right of the author has been asserted.

A CIP catalogue record for this book
is available from the British Library.

ISBN 1 84408 085 4

Typeset in Fournier by M Rules
Printed and bound in Great Britain by
Clays Ltd, St Ives plc

Virago Press
An imprint of
Time Warner Book Group UK
Brettenham House
Lancaster Place
London WC2E 7EN

www.virago.co.uk

CONTENTS

PREFACE

I have dedicated this book to my grandchildren in the wistful hope that it might inspire them not so much to cook as to read. Their grandpapa, my late husband, and I differed in our attitude to this pursuit. He read, slowly and intently, works of scholarship from beginning to end, going so far as to lament the availability of the Public Library which, he held, encouraged the autodidact, the untrained enthusiast to wallow wildly in matters beyond his grasp, emerging with an undigested mass of factual error and proceeding, in his turn, to write books promulgating some daft theory about whatever had taken his fancy. I read quickly, flitting and sipping, skipping the boring bits and seizing on the oddities and inconsistencies which are often ignored by the scholar since they interfere with the measured and coherent approach to the matter in hand. I have done no ordered research but have sat amongst piles of old books – primary sources, books the ancestors wrote and read themselves without much concern for posterity, rather than later learned treatises on what they were up to – rapt in astonishment at what they did and said and what they had to eat. Many of these books were given to me by my husband as a sop when he had spent the housekeeping money on a stack of classical literature and it always worked. I would make some economical dish from plain but nourishing ingredients and settle down for a good read, calling my husband back from wherever he'd got to in the Peloponnesian War to learn that at some Victorian dinner parties there would be a maid stationed outside the dining room with jugs of hot water madly washing the used cutlery in preparation for the next course. There was some cultural give and take in the house: I suggested that Dacre Balsdon should write a book about Roman women, not from motives of ardent feminism, but because I would find it interesting, and my husband once followed a recipe and made some scones in order to prove that he couldn't. To his horror they emerged from the oven perfect and he never tried it again.

Most of my books date from the nineteenth and early twentieth centuries, and it is these that hold the greatest fascination because it is just possible to creep back along the frail bridge that separates us, identifying links and relationships with the present. At the far limits it is possible to peer into the eighteenth century, but further than that is a gulf and the people beyond move in a mist or, at best, an artificial light. I do not believe that I could find much in common with, say, Sir Theodore de Mayerne or the Vidame of Chartres, while I can imagine sharing a mid-morning glass of Madeira with Mrs Rundell or discussing the preparation of a ham with Dr Kitchiner.

Lest anyone should accuse the publishers of feckless editing, I admit that I insisted on retaining unfamiliar spellings and long esses when that's the way they were in the books. To remove them would have seemed like spraying great-grandmama with some anti-bacterial compound in order to make her fit with modern expectations. And sometimes I write receipt and sometimes recipe, and sometimes I forget to give the origin of a quote because the book I got it from has disappeared under a pile, and sometimes I lose the thread and myself disappear down a tributary. This is why the book is subtitled *Gallimaufry*, which means a hash of odds and ends . . . a hodge podge . . . a ridiculous medley. I hope that others who prefer the variety of the souk to the discipline of the department store will appreciate my intention and find something to amuse them among the odds and ends.

Alice Thomas Ellis

Powys, 2004

One

OFF THE BEETON PATH

$\mathcal{I}$n the 1930s and '40s when I was a child things were different, although not altogether in the way that many now suppose. We were not as indulged as the children of today but we had more freedom. In the Welsh village where we lived there remained traces of the Victorian era and we were not permitted to play out of doors on Sundays, but the rest of the time we knew few restrictions as long as we were home by nightfall. That was in the country with the mountains and the sea, but even in the towns where the streets were not then choked with traffic, children were always knocking on each other's doors with the words, 'Can Valerie – or Henry or whoever – come out to play?' We were not constantly supervised, but since mothers didn't work – outside the house, that is – we saw quite enough of them. We felt we had little in common with adults and the presently much vaunted family outing was regarded by many a reluctant child as more of a trial than a treat. We were not permitted to wear make-up before we were sixteen or thereabouts, were condemned to detention if apprehended in school uniform without our hats on our heads or seen eating in the street, and we would no sooner have addressed a teacher by her first name than have hanged her from the gym ropes: human nature being what it is we called them names behind their backs, but none of us swore or jutted out our lower jaws when reprimanded.

When in enemy territory (i.e. the company of adults, even those to whom we were closely related) we minded our manners, gave nothing away, kept our elbows off the table and never left it without asking if we might. 'Please may I leave the table?' was one of the earliest phrases we learned to lisp, and the sense of release when permission was granted is perhaps indicative of something distinctive in the English attitude to food. French *enfants*, I believe, seldom showed the same eagerness to escape from the *salle à manger*, but even before the Second World War, when eating became for everyone a question of survival rather than gourmandism, English cookery was, despite the expressions of nostalgia that some still utter, largely notable for mediocrity, bland monotony, adherence to the notion that native British produce was superior to all others, and a stubborn refusal to do anything with it that departed from the norm. The wealthy and sophisticated were not unduly discommoded by this attitude since they could buy the best and, with notable exceptions, generally employed people who brought a measure of *savoir faire* to what they were doing in the kitchen. For the vast majority, however, meal times offered nothing to look forward to with salivating expectation. Roast meat for Sunday lunch (cold with pickled beetroot for supper) was regarded as an essential aspect of civilised life. The cold meat appeared again on Monday (washday) and then was resurrected in various guises such as Cottage Pie or hash – 'that grey and slimy mass endured in too many an English home' as one writer put it – until mid-week.

This regime was considered by most British citizens to be sacrosanct.

Children had a particularly boring time of it. It was thought to be character as well as body building to make them eat up everything on the plate and the weekly menu was unvaried: the revenant Sunday joint in its differing manifestations, followed, as the week drew on, by stew, greyly thickened with flour; mince with triangles of toast; plaice steamed between two plates; and, to round it all off, stewed fruit and custard, cornflour shape, or milk or suet pudding. I remember the consistency of ground rice with a spoonful of cold slippery apricot jam as though it were yesterday. On the other hand, I also remember the flavour of chickens that had spent their brief span scratching for worms in open spaces, and potatoes straight from the earth and apples from the tree. My German immigrant godparents (Positivists who didn't actually believe in God) were early members of the newly formed Labour Party, belonged to the Church of Humanity and, cosmopolitan in their tastes, would serve exotic dishes like spaghetti and curry. I, of course, was not allowed these but I remember the heady aroma.

Teatime for children was largely unobjectionable. Gluttony was discouraged but after you had finished your bread and butter you were allowed cake. (I was also permitted a boiled sweet a day, after lunch.) Cake making held an inordinately important place in the cookery of the time and there were competitions at local shows and garden parties for the finest Victoria Sponge or the lightest scone. There still are cake competitions at church bazaars, agricultural fairs, etc., but they have a faintly anachronistic air and I don't think passions run so high as once they did. Looking back I remember that I then preferred bread and butter to cake, jelly and blancmange and occasioned my mother some embarrassment by refusing these treats at the numerous birthday parties to which children were subjected. I have always disliked parties but I have learned to appreciate cake. While at school I had been prejudiced against it since I detested the subject known as Domestic Science and much of it was devoted to the construction of confectionery. Our high-minded and scholarly headmistress held, quite correctly, that even a girl who might develop into a Senior Wrangler should have the basic elements of what was also known – though the term was already going out of style – as housewifery, at her fingertips, but since I had no intention of ever cooking anything as long as I lived, let alone sewing, washing, starching or ironing, I couldn't see the advantage. My intention then was to leave school as soon as was humanly possible, take off for Paris and, wearing black, grow white-faced and hollow-eyed on the *rive gauche*. The study of Domestic Science and the secrets behind Maids-of-Honour and Dundee Cake would not, I felt, play a large part in my future. I was in the habit of thinking of the housebound as cabbages, a term coined, I suppose, by the bright young things of the generation previous to mine in their own revolt against the confines of hearth and home. My opinion was not based on feminist conviction for I had no high ambition and found the lifestyle of the adult male equally lacking in sparkle. Starving in a garret seemed a more romantic option than either staying at home or going out to work, a course which held no appeal.

As one Flora Klickman had written in 1903, 'It does not follow that because a girl is at work in some office her mental and social outlook must be enlarged thereby: neither is it inevitable that the one upon whom Duty imposes household affairs must have her horizon entirely bounded by matters domestic.' No matter what her inclinations, says Flora, 'Religious and Philanthropic work lies at everyone's door, while [and here she seems to anticipate the internet] Literature, Art,

Music, Science, and a hundred other less hackneyed topics, are the motive-power of innumerable clubs and correspondence circles.'

She goes on in her faintly prescient fashion to state, 'This is the age of opportunities; but it is also the age of overwork, and many girls spurred on by ambition expect to reach the goal of their desire in about half the time a man would devote to the same end. Result: about seven out of every ten girls who take up such careers climax with a nervous breakdown.' And above all, the girl who stays at home 'escapes the annoyance of having to encounter undesirable people at times and is . . . safe from the disillusionments, petty jealousies, and disappointments with which the outside world is teeming'. What's more, 'No one who has not had the experience of a daily journey to and from town, in all weathers, can form any idea of the extra wear and tear this makes on a girl's clothes, hats, shoes, gloves, to say nothing of lunches and travelling expenses.' I can see what she meant about going out to work, but never cared for the notion of having Duty impose household affairs on me and spending my life wondering what to put on the table.

I grew up, went to Liverpool Art School and don't remember eating anything much, with a few exceptions, from the time I left home until the time I left the school. Students then didn't really expect to eat. One of my cousins and her earnest architect husband took cookery seriously and I have never forgotten their dry beef curry with its accompanying lentils, chutneys and copious draughts of lime juice, which they served for Sunday luncheon in their bohemian and unconventional fashion. Nor have I forgotten the 'Shanghai Rice' made by friends in The Cave, a sort of club that kept many a student from the brink of starvation. Very occasionally we could afford to go to the Far East, one of the first Chinese restaurants in the country, near my grandfather's old pub, The Nook in Nelson Street, where the food was a revelation; and sometimes a rich aunt took me to The Adelphi for a typically English lunch, though served in style, but we were driven mainly to subsist on things like Australian tinned tomato soup with Rice Krispies and tinned spaghetti with cream crackers. For the rest we filled up on currant buns from the art school canteen and instant coffee fortified with condensed milk. On trips to London, tea at the Ritz cost half a crown which represented excellent value for money – sandwiches, cake and a pot of Indian or China – and was more affordable than lunch anywhere.

In the convent where I stayed briefly I remember the compote made from the fruit in the surrounding orchards and gardens, and the fried liver which I had, under discipline to eat, cut up into minute bits which I swallowed whole. (Emily Post wrote in 1931, 'If food has been taken into your mouth, no matter how you hate it, you have got to swallow it.') I have written about that elsewhere and some fathead said I enjoyed eating things that made me sick. Having been firmly brought up I was used to such shifts, for it was taken as read that two or three times a week you would sit down and be expected to consume things you hated – chewy stew, boiled cod, Spotted Dick, etc. – which, at secular tables, children would attempt to palm surreptitiously to the dog. A work of 1685 says, 'If you happen to burn your Mouth, you must endure it if possible, if not you must convey what you have in your Mouth privately upon your Plate, and give it away to the Footman; For though Civility obliges you to be neat, there is no necessity you should burn out your Guts.'

Staying in the country with friends, I acquired the rudiments of pre-war, grown-up cookery – game and fish and frothy puddings. The man of the house found it more interesting to go by night and shoot his venison rather than buy it and this added an edge of excitement to the finished dish. Sometimes, frustrated in the chase, he would shoot a sheep.

Then, arriving in Chelsea in the pursuit of Art, I worked part-time for a French friend in her delicatessen and began to realise the extent of the gulf between the French and British attitudes to food. English food in the 1950s (prawn cocktail, Chicken Maryland and little cubes of cheese and pineapple sharing a toothpick were daring innovations) was less memorable than wartime food, with its attendant deprivations and enforced ingenuity, which had led to some macabre results, and it was startling to watch a Frenchwoman at work in the kitchen. Elizabeth David came to my notice since I frequently bumped into John Minton who illustrated her early books, but it never occurred to me to utilise her advice for I didn't have the time, the money or, admittedly, the inclination. It was from Françoise that I picked up, on the shop floor as it were, the methods of hand-making mayonnaise and cooking a *gigôt* with flageolet beans and no mint sauce, the mention of which brought a sneer to her features. She held that no good food ever came out of an immaculately tidy kitchen or a geometrically ordered counter, and took an aristocratically insouciant attitude to bourgeois values and pettifogging detail; retrieving and dusting, for instance, fallen roast chickens and consoling them with a decorative sprig of parsley.

It was here that I met my husband. He always claimed that he had wanted to buy an apple pie and I had sold him one with meat in it and he had gone home and put custard on it. Or it may have been the other way round and involved gravy. This is not impossible but I think it was one of his little jokes. At the time he was employed by his cousin (we were not then aware that this cousin, Cecil King, and Lord Mountbatten were planning to overthrow the government and run the country themselves), and was supposedly being groomed to take over his position as head of the Mirror Group, another bizarre idea which naturally came to nothing since he was more interested in translating Erasmus' *The Praise of Folly*. When, as was inevitable, he got the sack we were plunged into penury. Previous to this misfortune we had had a charlady called Mrs Biggs who had taken pity on my inexperience and given me a battered early copy of Mrs Beeton. I don't think I ever followed any of her recipes, but the picture that emerged of a vanished way of life was far more compelling than any of the history that I had been so painstakingly taught in school. I began collecting books on all household matters and particularly on cookery (from second-hand bookshops and Reg's junk stall in Camden market, all now gone), while having very little to cook. We lived on bread from the local bakery (now gone), the cheaper cuts of meat from the local butcher (now gone), fish from the local fishmonger (who has also gone), vegetables from our local market (now under threat) and I spent most of the evenings, after having made the soup, stew or salad which were our usual fare, reading a book called *The Dictionary of Daily Wants*.

This fascinating work ran to more than 1,140 closely printed pages and told the reader everything in extensive detail from Abatement, 'in commerce a deduction made in the price of goods either in consideration of the payment of prompt cash or . . . etc. etc.,' to Zinc Ointment, which is 'made by rubbing well together one oz. of oxide of zinc and 6 ozs of hog's lard. This ointment is useful for children . . .' and so on. *Daily Wants* tells you how to play golf, worm the dog, evaluate a diamond, kill rats, tame ravens, make a soufflé, grow tea, handle pails which are 'very roughly used by many persons letting them strike the stones heavily; this wears them out very fast, and may be easily avoided by moving from place to place more carefully', and how to recognise Death which is 'characterised by the universal coldness of the body, by a partially open mouth, closed eyelids and sunken eyes, by an extreme pallor of the face, sometimes assuming a greenish yellow tone: with lividity of the orbits and great flaccidity of all the joints . . .'

We could not afford to go to the theatre, cinema or restaurants – even if we had had a reliable babysitter. (We did have a series of au pair girls but they were, with two exceptions, more of a hindrance than a help and one was clinically insane.) These deprivations did not worry us in the least: my husband was fond of what he called sympathetic solitude and read and reread *The Decline and Fall of the Roman Empire*, his favourite book, while I was glued to *The Dictionary of Daily Wants* and learned that, 'The exercise of memory is an art within the compass of any person possessed of ordinary ability and intelligence. Forgetfulness is, in the majority of instances, another word for indifference since it is notorious that persons always continue to remember matters, however indefinite or remote, where self-interest is concerned . . .'

The 1960s were going on outside: celebrities appeared from nowhere to be met with cacophonous adulation, while the 'Me' culture began to infect the populace, starting the slide to the present victim/compensation state of affairs which would have been inconceivable to the sternly self-reliant writers of the nineteenth century. Having been an art student I had already gone through the anarchic stage and got it out of my system, so it was disconcerting, if mildly diverting, to see quite elderly, previously well-conducted people emulating the young in an unprecedented manner and suddenly going about in pink trousers and rat-skin tabards with flowers in their hair and defying convention, though I also felt the sort of irritation that a soldier might feel when confronted with a non-combatant, dressed up in uniform and blathering about some spurious campaign. I, after all, had been genuinely hard up, while a certain eccentricity in dress and demeanour had been *de rigueur* for the artistically inclined and regarded with nervous distaste by the ordinary citizen. When bohemianism was universally adopted by the unqualified it lost its point.

Every evening someone would take a jug to the nearby spit and sawdust (as it was known) department of the local pub and bring it back with three pints of bitter. ('The properties of beer as an ordinary beverage, if it be not too strong so as to disturb the brain or create over-excitement of the nerves of the stomach, are quite equal, if not superior to those of wine; and when the proportion of hop is sufficient to give a good bitter, beer is at once a tonic and a stimulant . . .') This, with a packet of Woodbines and a pile of books, constituted our entertainment. We had no TV and so I remained unaware of the first generation of semi-thespian cooks: Fanny Craddock and Graham Kerr were the most visible but I was in thrall to the past and out of sympathy with the present. The pub, the Good Mixer – it was rumoured that a cement mixer had somehow become entombed in its foundations – became fashionable in the late 1990s when a pop group took to frequenting it, followed by their fans, much to the discomfiture of the regulars who were residents of Arlington House, a refuge for homeless men. By day I cooked, did what housework as could not be avoided and pushed the children round in an old pram to second-hand bookshops and to small graveyards which were less crowded with the living than the adjacent parks.

Our circumstances improved again and when my seventh child was born I persuaded Janet to come and be her nanny. Janet's father then worked in a shop in the market and she had been helping out at weekends since she was eleven, so I already knew she was a competent girl. She has been with us for thirty years and could be described as general manager since she can do anything. When she was nine she won second prize for the best sponge cake at the church garden party, even beating her mum, but only, she says modestly, because her mum let her use the one available, appropriate tin to bake it in. Janet, as will be seen, took her Domestic Science lessons seriously, also learning a great deal from her mother who had been in service in the 1930s and was the most superb pastry cook I ever encountered. Even Janet cannot quite match her mother's hand with pastry. At about the same time, Alfred came into our lives, breaking in with a number of his little friends. They were all aged under ten and their main occupation – and recreation – was going round derelict houses (ours was undergoing refurbishment and lacked a wall or so) removing anything portable and selling it to an accommodating fence. I caught him and shook him but he expressed remorse and has been with us in one capacity or another ever since (he is my daughter's godfather), having proved from the outset to be a person of remarkable ability and application.

With the passing of the years I have perfected a ruse which I mention merely to deplore – a studied ineptitude which saves the practitioner much time and effort. I genuinely cannot type or drive or do sums, but I sometimes feign helplessness in the face of domestic tasks of which I am, in fact, capable, although not outstandingly so. An old friend, seeing through that, told me of a woman she had known who did not like shelling crabs; a fiddly, time-consuming business. The first time she tried it, her neighbour, watching, had swept her aside in exasperation and done it properly; thereafter, by always making sure there was someone present to witness her lack of skill in handling a crab she never, in all her life, had to empty one. In fact I don't mind shelling crabs – although as someone once put it, 'it is a slutt to kerve' – which is fortunate, as it is one of the things Janet refuses to do since they have too many extremities.

Mrs Rundell, a sensible person of the early nineteenth century whose book was frequently reprinted (she will appear often in these pages, sometimes identifying herself only as *A Lady*) wrote, 'In every rank those deserve the greatest praise, who best acquit themselves of the duties which that station requires. Indeed this line of conduct is not a matter of choice but of necessity, if we would maintain the dignity of our character as rational beings.' My husband, having bought Duckworth the publishers, immersed himself in the classics and I settled down to running the fiction list and cooking for writers, claiming that had he been a tailor I would have sewed on buttons. Most of my discoveries – and some were outstanding – went on to lusher pastures since my husband could never understand why they wanted money. He himself took very little interest in it. The Duckworth offices were eventually situated in the Old Piano Factory at the top of the Crescent where we lived, so unless my husband had elected to splash out in the local trattoria, he came home daily for lunch, usually with an author or two. He had the common unreasoning masculine prejudice against women who drink and lady novelists, but had to overcome it since I insisted on sometimes including my female friends in order to enliven these occasions. One of them always ended up under the table asleep on a large teddy bear that I kept solely for that purpose. I had early recognised that giving dinner parties was a mistake as they tended to go on until the following morning and I had often found distinguished people comatose in corners when I came downstairs. Most, though by no means all, luncheon guests left by suppertime.

We frequently gave large parties in the Old Piano Factory where we occupied a rotund area perfectly suited to the circulation of guests; although the ceiling-high racks of books were subjected to the hazards of spilled drinks and plates of salad, and offered more scope than is usual to the lecherously inclined who could indulge their proclivities in comparative isolation. It all added to the festive sense.

Once you know what you're doing, catering for a hundred or more people is easier than preparing an elaborate dinner party for six. My husband, evincing an untypical interest in culinary matters (whenever he dined out and I asked him what he had had to eat, it always transpired that he had not noticed), would hover anxiously around the kitchen asking if we were sure we were making an adequate quantity. He need have had no fear: a large ham baked in cider and a roasted turkey, together with rice, potato, green, bean and pasta salads, long loaves and a wheel of cheese provide a surprising amount of sustenance, while a roomful of people usually divides between those who expect to eat and do so, and those who have come for the drink and will be satisfied, if they bother at all, with whatever crumbs are left.

Jonathan Self, in his book *Self Abuse*, has written about one of our parties:

Will was, to my certain knowledge, in the janitor's cupboard snogging Beryl Bainbridge.

I was in the stationery cupboard snogging Sarah Thomson.

Our mother, when last spotted, had been sprawled on a chair with her feet up on a window sill trying to adjust her false teeth. One of her shoes was missing.

It was December 1977 and the occasion was the Duckworth Publishing Christmas Party . . . The quantity of drink ordered for this annual event can only be described as fantastic. The firm's proprietor, Colin Haycraft, spent the whole morning personally supervising its unloading and preparation. Then, at around midday, he would call his employees together and wish them a Merry Christmas. This was followed by a glass of champagne . . .

Jonathan, on the whole, describes the event accurately except that, as Janet points out indignantly, he suggests the employees contributed dishes of their own, which is not so. Our dear Gertrud would bring a delicious little German *quelque chose*, but everything else was prepared by Janet with assistance from myself. It was a challenge that we chose to accept and outside interference could only have diminished our achievement.

Two

FROM CRADLE TO GRAVY

$\mathcal{B}$uckmaster, who neglected to divulge his Christian name or date his work, dedicated his book 'By permission to H.R.H. Princess Louise, Marchioness of Lorne, as an active patroness of the National Training School of Cookery, and one who appreciates the importance of good cookery as an element of social and domestic happiness.' He observed that the history of cooking is the history of our manners and our civilisation, and the kitchen is a good place to keep in touch with the ancestors. A study of the ingredients boiled, fried or roasted and their manner of presentation in past eras serves to illustrate both similarities and differences and gives us an insight into bygone fashions and attitudes: accounts of the running of a household are more immediately interesting and less factually dubious than the historians' biased presentations of the past.

If, as Brillat-Savarin observed, we are what we eat, so we are, in a sense, what our ancestors ate: there is seldom a lot to be gained in lying about what you had for dinner, so we may trust

to their candour in that respect whilst not giving too much cre-
dence to their edicts. If they had faults in the culinary
department (apart from eating too often too much of what we
would now consider ill-judged), they arose from their habit of
plagiarising each other without attribution, often perpetuating
doubtful practice. In a revised and enlarged edition of her book,
Eliza Acton (a splendid person, wise and methodical, of whom
little is known) wrote in a plaintive though dignified tone:

> I must here obtrude a few words of personal interest to myself.
> At the risk of appearing extremely egotistic, I have appended
> *'Author's Receipt'* and *'Author's Original Receipt'* to many of the
> contents of the following pages; but I have done it solely in self-
> defence, in consequence of the unscrupulous manner in which
> large portions of my volume have been appropriated by con-
> temporary authors, without the slightest acknowledgement of
> the source from which they have been derived. I have allowed
> this unfairness, and much beside, to pass entirely unnoticed until
> now; but I am suffering at present too severe a penalty for the
> over-exertion entailed on me by the plan which I adopted for the
> work, longer to see with perfect composure strangers coolly
> taking the credit and the profits of my toil.

Brillat-Savarin's *Physiologie du Goût* was published eight
years after Dr Kitchiner's *The Cook's Oracle* in 1817 (the doctor
got his MD at Glasgow) and in several respects resembles it
remarkably closely, while I have found many of the same recipes
word for word in the works of less eminent authors. It is reminiscent of the way in which, in London, you meet people at
lunch only to encounter them again, unexpectedly, at the dinner
table of a different host in another district in the evening.

Victorian ladies who, one gets the impression, spent most of
their lives in what is now known as 'socialising', rarely set foot in

the kitchen except to have words with Cook, but were frequently found in hysterics, or high strikes as the condition was vulgarly known. When visitors came to call, a young woman had to know when to stay in the room or when to make herself scarce and while the writers on etiquette tried to be reassuring – 'A young girl with all the freshness of youth and the sweet dignity of woman-hood has a sure passport into society which assures her a warmth of welcome' (the proviso, as long as her papa has pots of money, was considered at once too obvious and too coarse to be stated) – it is no surprise that so many of them were reduced to lying on the floor drumming their heels and screaming. Hysteria, which was, according to *The Dictionary of Daily Wants*, 'more common in females than men', was characterised by 'low spirits, a feeling of depression and anxiety, sudden involuntary grief and tears, palpitation, sickness, a sense of suffocation and the apparent presence of a ball in the throat; these symptoms are or are not attended with sobs and sudden fits of laughter, convulsive twitches and contractions of the hands and arms, finally terminating, after more or less muscular contractions, in insensibility and coma'. If the patient was young and robust, she was bled, but in general it was thought sufficient to throw cold water on her. W. B. Tegetmeier, a lecturer in Domestic Economy, claimed that a fit of hysterics 'is generally increased by any expression of sympathy' and suggests 'a very effectual mode of cure' which 'consists of dipping a towel in cold water . . . and striking smartly with one end of it on the upper part of the chest'.

Women, according to *The Cook and Housewife's Manual* by Mrs Christine Isabel Johnstone, were also vulnerable to the dangers of open fires. 'So many fatal accidents arise from light dresses, catching fire, that every Manual intended for women should contain the following necessary cautions':

1. Let it be early and diligently impressed upon the mind of every girl, that flame uniformly tends upwards; that every article of her dress will consume much more rapidly if held upright, than if laid along the floor; and that her life may depend on her presence of mind, should her clothes unhappily catch fire. 2. Give instant alarm by pulling the bell, (which is generally near the fireplace) by screaming or any other means; but, if possible, avoid opening the door; for both the movement of the figure, and the current of air admitted, will increase the rapidity of the flames. 3. The alarm may be given while the female is at the same instant sitting down by the rug, attempting to tear off the articles of dress which are on fire, and rolling herself on a sofa or in the rug or carpet to smother the flame. If the latter is nailed down, she may easily when on the floor, tear it up. She may also catch at any piece of baize or vessel of water within reach; and, if very active, may even turn her clothes over her head and thus arrest the progress of the flames. 4. The most ready and effectual assistance a spectator in general can give will be to turn the clothes of the sufferer over her head, and hold them firm thus, till wrappers, cold water, &c., are procured. 5. A man may quickly strip off his coat and wrap it round the female. 6. Let the sufferer, even if she fail to pull away the burning articles, or to extinguish the fire by rolling on the floor, and wrapping herself on the hearthrug, (which is generally always ready) still protect her bosom and face, by lowering her face and crossing her hands and arms over her face and breast.

Gentlemen more commonly suffered from apoplexy, 'A disease which averts all voluntary motions and deprives a person of consciousness as though struck by a blow.' The victim would fall over and breathe heavily 'with a *snoring* kind of noise and considerable muscular action of the features. The face is red and swollen, the veins distended, the eyes protruding and blood shot . . . and a foam frequently forms about the mouth.' The 'predisposing causes' of apoplexy were given as 'the habitual indulgence of the appetite in rich and gross food, or stimulating drinks, coupled with luxurious and indolent habits, sedentary employments . . . and the habit of sleeping, especially in a recumbent posture after a full meal; and lying too long in bed'. The 'exciting causes' were 'excesses in eating and drinking; violent mental emotions; the suppression of piles, gout, rheumatism' or anything else that interfered with the circulation of blood.

Centuries earlier, Dr Andrew Borde (sometimes spelled Boorde), who also lived through changing times, had been one of the first to recognise the need to offer advice to his fellow citizens. He was born around 1490 into an old Catholic family, became a Carthusian monk but left the Order after twenty years and went abroad to study medicine. He took the Oath of Conformity and enjoyed the patronage of Thomas Cromwell, which did not save him from 'the rancour of the professors of the reformed religion' who viewed him with the suspicion so characteristic of the era and treated him roughly. Nonetheless, he found time to write several books, two of which, *The Dyetary* and *Brevyary of Helthe*, are remarkable for the way in which they depart from the received, mostly fantastic, wisdom of the time and anticipate the more relaxed approach that replaced the Victorian mode. He was keen on cleanliness, sunshine, fresh air and that 'minimal interference' that did not re-surface for several centuries, and seems to be out of style again as surgeries are overwhelmed by people suffering from stress, etc. He warned against the consequences of worry, 'Have a merry heart for pensifulness doth hurt the stomach,' he counselled.

And as for eating, 'two meals a day is sufficient for a rest man, and a labourer may eat three times a day, and he that doth eat after, liveth a beastly life . . . At dinner and supper use not to drink of sundry drinks and eat not of divers meats, but feed of two or three dishes at the most. At your supper use light meats of digestion and refrain from gross meats; go not unto bed with a full or empty stomach.'

It has been remarked that the longer we live, the more we worry about our health, which makes a sort of sense – when we all died young we didn't have much time to worry about anything. A bulletin from the medical profession states that taking a siesta is to dice with death. It has long been known, comes the sonorous pronouncement, that many strokes and heart attacks occur after sleeping. So, I imagine we are meant to conclude, to sleep twice in twenty-four hours is to double the risk. Dr Borde concurs, believing that, 'Healthy men should not sleep in the daytime . . . immoderate sleep and sluggishness doth humect and make light the brain; it doth engender reums and impostumes; it induceth and causeth obliviousness, and doth obnebulate the memory and the quickness of wit, and shortly, to conclude, it doth perturb the natural and animal and spiritual powers of man . . .' He sounds like one of those rare and curious creatures who think centuries ahead of their time.

Everything a Woman Ought to Know is not as enormously useful a work as it might sound since it was compiled in 1911 and is not nearly as comprehensive as *The Dictionary of Daily Wants* or the *Encyclopaedia of Domestic Economy*. Still, it offers some useful tips and insights. One learns from the section on holidays that travellers 'by being as circumspect in their behaviour' and, as far as the exigencies of travelling allow, 'as careful in their dress as when as at home, can do much to remove the bad impression made by the aggressive type of Britisher who so often frequents the Continent and does his best to earn for English people generally an unmerited measure of disapprobation'. It seems that the vacationing lager lout or football fan has his own specific ancestors and it wasn't only the young or the male, for 'there is no denying the fact that many women show a peculiar aggressiveness and intolerance when travelling . . .' One gathers that English ladies abroad wouldn't eat the food, made no attempt to speak the language, displayed their limbs and threw their weight about to the distress and annoyance of the natives. The author of my book found it necessary to remark magnanimously that 'though many of the customs of the foreigners are different from ours, yet they have a perfect right to practice them in their own country'. She was most insistent on this point. 'The cooking at foreign hotels and pensions may seem strange at first; but though it is different from what the English woman has been used to, it is nearly always very good, and she should not spoil her pleasure and that of others by grumbling at it, and wishing for some English dish not on the menu.' Those who now are so unfortunate or ill-advised as to stay in one of those vast international hotels will usually be provided with fare that the English woman of 1911 would have consumed without a murmur, that is, blandly inoffensive and characterless (it is sometimes poisonous but that is due to doubtful hygiene), while the English man continues to reveal his ignorance. A journalist in the spring of 2002 writing in a national daily was scornful of the delicious *Brandade de Morue*, 'a pasty cod and mash concoction from Nîmes' and of a pork dish 'swimming in fat' (that would be to preserve the meat) and calf cheeks and gizzards, the preparation of which demonstrates the skill of the chef and delights the knowledgeable diner.

The Victorians, in a way, are as strange to the British as are the Americans. So near and yet so far. They had implacably decided and, on the evidence, often fatally misguided views on health and nutrition. One text book advises that those left to care for an orphaned infant (mother was probably dead of puerperal fever, due to an insufficient understanding of basic hygiene – Mrs Beeton died in childbed at the age of twenty-seven) should give it, not milk, but water in which bread had been soaked. Toast and water was considered beneficial in many ways, 'Toast slowly a thin piece of bread till extremely brown and hard, but not the least black; then plunge it into a jug of cold water and cover it an hour before used. This is of particular use to weak bowels. It should be of a fine brown colour before drinking.' It could not have been long before mother and child were reunited in the grave.

Those who survived were brought up on a relentless diet of pap, progressing to meat, potatoes and suet pudding with a minimum of vegetables and fruit, which were considered indigestible. One directive reads, 'For a Child's Luncheon: Good sweet butter, with stale bread, is one of the most nutritious, at the same time the most wholesome articles of food, that can be given to children after they are weaned.' Another suggestion for tea was dumplings on toast. 'Boil the dumplings, then dip the toast in the same water and serve it up.'

To 'give pap with a hatchet' was a 'proverbial phrase for doing a kind thing in an unkind manner, as it would be to feed an infant with so formidable an instrument'. Privileged infants were lovingly fed from silver porringers, but for all the nutritional benefit they might as well have ingested their pap from the barrel of a loaded blunderbuss. I am sure the Victorians loved their children, but perhaps they were so aware of their potential or probable loss, that they had to psych themselves up in preparation, tell themselves that they had done all that science could advise and shroud all their lives in a miasma of sentimentality. Yet when, and if, they grew up, they had extraordinary vitality and went off to build the Empire, which was, to modern eyes, reprehensible, but makes one wonder whether pap, meat, potatoes, gravy and suet pudding had unsuspected properties.

Alexis Soyer, who was chef to various dukes and, most famously, at The Reform Club, gave himself airs, wore a silly hat when sitting for his portrait and could have been perceived as a figure of fun but was redeemed by his extraordinary energy and his efforts on behalf of the Irish in the famine and the troops in the sorry muddle of the Crimea. Amongst his other achievements, he wrote a book called *The Modern Housewife or Ménagère* in the persona of a lady called Hortense. She and her friend Eloise were in frequent correspondence about the vicissitudes of housekeeping, child rearing and the uncertain nature of our earthly tenure.

When her children (Hortense seems strangely real after a while) were eighteen months or two years old, she still kept them on bread and milk and porridge, but would give them a little tender meat, such as mutton, and broth. In the opinion of Buckmaster:

> As a rule, children, not only of the poorer classes, but of the middle classes, are often underfed, and many of their ailments arise from a debility of constitution brought about by under or improper feeding; and to give strength, quinine, cod-liver oil, port wine, and other stimulants are given instead of food. The diet of children should be a breakfast, with cocoa, milk, macaroni, or eggs; a dinner of meat, vegetables, and pudding; a substantial supper, like the breakfast, with cocoa or milk.

Lady Lyttleton, who was in charge of Queen Victoria's nursery, wrote in a letter, 'the Princess was over-watched and over-doctored: always treated with what is most expensive, cheaper and commoner food and ways being often wholesomer. She now lives on asses' milk, and arrowroot and chicken broth, and they measure it out so carefully for fear of loading her stomach, that I fancy she always *leaves off hungry*.' Asses' milk, in which the Ancients bathed, 'far surpasses,' said *A Lady*, 'any imitation of it that can be made . . . The fixed air that it contains gives some people a pain in the stomach. At first a teaspoonful of rum may be taken with it, but should only be put in the moment it is to be swallowed.'

A copy of the popular and frequently republished *Enquire Within Upon Everything* advises against permitting children to drink during their meals: 'Inundations of the stomach during the mastication and maceration of the food, not only vitiate digestion,' but cold drinks 'brought in contact with the teeth previously heated, may easily occasion cracks or chinks in these useful bones and pave the way for their carious dissolution.'

We tell ourselves complacently that babies now have a better time of it as we open a jar of organic, farm-fresh, vitamin reinforced, pre-digested something or other, but any adult who has tasted a spoonful will have concluded that the manufacturers of canned baby food hate either food or babies or both. It cannot be wondered at if children who are brought up from earliest infancy on their own exclusive servings of commercial fare rather than home-cooked produce go on to prefer commercial hamburgers, chips and pizzas to whatever the rest of the family is eating. If the rest of the family is also eating hamburgers, chips and pizzas, then all is lost. Nobody seems to know why allergies, asthma, eczema, etc. are now so common, but when pollution, smoking, the dust mite, the superbug, etc. are out of the frame, the finger of suspicion points at E numbers, additives, food colouring and the overall dog's breakfast that the Industry has made of food in the developed world.

There were, in the past, those who after one unfortunate collision with a bad oyster could never thereafter tolerate shellfish, but there were few who could not eat a peanut with impunity – at least as far as we know. The cook in Dorothy L. Sayers' *Strong Poison* published in 1930 said, 'Not but there's people as can't relish eggs in any form, my own mother was just the same, give her so much as a cake what had bin made with an egg in it and she'd be that sick and come out all over with spots like nettle-rash, you'd be surprised.' This reaction was sufficiently unusual to be worthy of remark and a measure of pride.

If the nursery in times gone by cannot have been the scene of great gustatory excitement the sick room was possibly worse, adding disgust to indisposition. Hortense wrote, 'Having here terminated my remarks upon the Nursery, I shall leave this scene of romp and confusion, to walk on tip-toe to the *sick-room door* and carefully enter, without noise, into the mournful abode of human suffering and captivity,' conceding that food for children and for invalids was more or less the same. According to advice from *A Lady* in *A New Work For Private Families Containing a Great Variety of Valuable Receipts With Directions For The Preparation Of Food For Invalids And For Children &c. &c.*, 'One of the loveliest accomplishments of a lady is to understand how to make the invalid in her family comfortable. Food prepared by the kind hand of a wife, mother, sister, friend has a sweeter relish than the mere ingredients can give, and a restorative power which money cannot purchase.'

Then come receipts for gruel, caudle, milk puddings, whey, calf's-foot jelly, beef tea, chicken soup and 'Suet Milk: Cut one ounce of mutton or veal suet into shavings, and warm it slowly over the fire in a pint of milk, adding a little grated lemon peel, cinnamon and loaf-sugar'; while 'Luncheon For An Invalid' reads, 'Put bread crumbs and red currant, or any other jelly, alternately into a tumbler, and when nearly half full, fill it up with milk.' Buttermilk, it is held, in the case of Consumptive Patients (TB was rife – and seems to threaten to be so again) should 'form the whole of the patient's drink; the food should be biscuits and rusks, ripe and dried fruits of various kinds, when a decline is apprehended'. Faced with a diet of such unremitting blandness, death must often have come as a happy release.

Baron Liebig had earned himself gratitude, deference, fame and probably a vast fortune by patenting, bottling, advertising and marketing his Extract of Beef. The producers of processed flours, oils, margarines, sauces, extracts and condiments, when they were new and exciting time-savers, persuaded the cookery writers of the day to turn out yet more little booklets sponsoring their products with ingenious suggestions on how to include them in everything from casseroles to cakes. Baron Liebig was early on the scene in 1897 with the *Lemco* [Liebig's Extract of Meat Co.] *Cookery Book* compiled by Miss H. M. Young (Diplomé Liverpool, London, Paris, Medalliste, etc.). It has a romantic picture of the company's factories in Uruguay, chimneys belching forth smoke and ships waiting in the bay to carry the substance all round the world, and announces with a pride which would be seen today as disastrously misplaced, that forty pounds of prime lean beef are used in South America to make one pound of Extract. The Baron also invented Marmite, for the then few non-meat-eaters to use up the yeast left over from the brewing process.

Miss Eliza Acton gives his recipe, summing it up in a subheading as 'Very Strong Plain Beef Gravy Soup'. She observes, 'This admirable preparation is not only most valuable as a restorative of the best kind for invalids who require a light but highly nutritious diet, it is also of the utmost utility for the general purposes of the kitchen and will enable a cook who can take skilful advantage of it, to convert the *cold meat* which often abounds in the English larder . . . into good nourishing dishes, which the hashes and minces of our common cookery *are not . . .*' Miss Acton states, 'Of its value in illness it is impossible to speak too highly,' and the economist who considers it expensive should bear in mind the cost of drugs and medical advice and remember the benefit derived from it in cases of 'extreme debility'. Florence Nightingale disagreed: 'Give a pint of beef tea and you have given scarcely a teaspoonful of nourishment.'

Miss Acton relays the method: you take a pound of good juicy beef and chop it up as small as sausage meat, mix it thoroughly with an exact pint of cold water and place it on the side of the stove to heat 'very slowly indeed', giving it an occasional stir. You leave it there for two or three hours before it is allowed to simmer and then it 'requires at the utmost but 15 minutes of gentle boiling'. Since the general opinion now is that meat must be initially subjected to intense heat in order to destroy whatever unwholesome element might be present, this substance, left as it was to slowly fester, must have seen off many an invalid by adding food poisoning to his infirmities.

As late as the 1930s, faith in the efficacy of beef tea persisted. In *The Doctor in the Kitchen*, Mrs Arthur Webb recommends 'Red Beef Tea', which was prepared by shredding lean raw beef, putting it in a cup with cold water and leaving it for two hours. 'If you have a ruby-coloured glass,' she suggests craftily, 'use it to put the red beef tea in so that the invalid will not see the colour of the liquid.' Cooked beef tea, she insists in italics, *'must not boil or even approach boiling point,'* nor should 'Mutton Tea', which she considered more nourishing than beef for the invalid. A hint of onion was permissible in mutton tea since, 'Later on as the patient is coaxed by good feeding to take a little more interest in the food business, you will have to think of all sorts of good ways of varying the flavour and appearance of items for the invalid's tray.' A concoction which, I imagine, the invalid would refuse with his dying breath, she called 'Liver Cocktail'. It consisted of half-cooked, sieved liver mixed with the juice of an orange and lemon and a pinch of sugar. 'It is helpful to drink water after each dose, to remove any after taste.'

Hortense, towards the end of her book, offers 'Soyer's Anti-Cholera Diet', begging Eloise not to alarm herself respecting the present epidemic, although it 'might affect you, being rather a nervous subject'. (Hortense is confident the motto 'Live well, fear not' is one of the most efficacious remedies.) If suffering symptoms such as 'weakness at the pit of the stomach, uneasiness, coldness, and giddiness, but especially sickness', the patient should take a dose of lovage and brandy, cut down on vegetables, fruit and fish and eat more boiled rice and curry. Those afflicted with cholera need 'altogether a more astringent diet than is generally necessary for this time of the year, thus enriching the blood, which is less likely to decompose by the want of the proper equalization in the electricity of which the atmosphere has latterly been deprived'. It took some time before it was understood that cholera was a water-borne disease.

For a while 'electricity' was fashionable in medical circles. A work called *Things a Lady Would Like To Know* recommends for the Cramp, 'Be electrified through the part which uses to be affected, or hold a roll of brimstone in your hand. For Deafness: Be electrified through the ear, and use a cold bath.' For a Cut it regresses somewhat, suggesting: 'Bind on toasted cheese,' while for a Relaxed Uvula, 'Bruise the veins of a cabbage leaf, and lay it on the crown of the head; repeat, if needed, in two hours.' Another book suggests a 'homely remedy' for an abscess: 'Boil a fair-sized parsnip to a pulp. Bathe the infected area with the water in which the parsnip has been boiled and then apply the parsnip itself as hot as can be borne.'

But if Victorian remedies were of doubtful efficacy, things were sometimes worse in earlier times. At one time a decoction of slugs was recommended as a cure for roughness in the chest; cobwebs were swallowed in case of ague or applied to open wounds (apparently this worked), while for 'Spitting of Blood' it was suggested that you 'take the Dung of Mice, beat it to a Powder, put as much as will lie upon a sixpence in a quarter pint of juice of Plantane, and sweeten with a little sugar. Give it in a morning, fasting, and at night going to Bed. Continue this for some time and it will complete the cure.' I don't know what it was about mice that struck people as so beneficial, but there is evidence of the continuous use of 'mouse medicine' over a period of at least 6,000 years. It was believed for centuries that they were spontaneously generated in the mud of the Nile and must, therefore, have magical properties. In 1901 during excavations in Upper Egypt, a number of bodies dating from about 3,400 BC were discovered in a remarkable state of preservation, due to their interment in the dry desert sand. Remains of mice were found in the alimentary canals of some of the children and when the archaeologists, medical men and historians of the time got to talking about it, they shared many interesting items of information.

Dr Netolitzky confided that the body of a mouse was the last resort of medical practitioners in the East several millennia later as a remedy for children *in extremis*, as it still was in Europe. Another said that in the ancient Egyptian medical papyri, there was a piece of advice on how to improve the hair – take a 'cooked mouse put in fat until it is rotten' and anoint the head with it. Dioscorides had written, 'It is well known that mice which run about houses can be very usefully cut up and applied to scorpion stings. If children eat them roasted, it helps to stop dribbling at the mouth.' Sixteen centuries later Abd-ar-Razzaq gave the same advice, while Pliny's *Natural History* is full of references to the therapeutic use of the creatures, the whole mouse or bits of it, its blood or its dung. Ibn el-Beithar of Malaga said they were good for warts and scrofula, Galen used their blood for cataract, in Syriac medicine the mouse was used for scabies and diuretic purposes, and Hildegard of Bingen recommended it for epilepsy. Theophrastus Bombast von Hohenheim who, rather sensibly, called himself Paracelsus, said it was 'a great Secret for the ptisick' and Culpeper said a 'flea'd [skinned] mouse dried and beaten into a powder' was good for incontinence and diabetes. And a work published in 1711 contained a remedy 'To stop the urine of those that piss in bed,' which included the torso of a mouse 'washed in white wine, and dried in an Oven'.

Nearly half a century later, prescriptions for mouse were still appearing in 'Dispensatories', recommended for virtually all the ills that flesh is heir to. Lady Evelina Camilla Gordon wrote that in 1893 in Suffolk, 'Fried mice are relied on as a specific for the small-pox, and I am afraid that it is considered necessary that they should be fried alive.' They were still being used in the 1930s and I once received the following letter:

> You throw doubt, tinged with scorn, on the efficacy of mice as a specific for children. In 1920 when I was four years old an old woman who lived near my family in Radlett and whom I used to visit on every occasion I could find, would give me sugar mice to eat. These were made by skinning mice, which she had caught in an ordinary mousetrap, emptying them and then tying them by the tail to a wooden spoon where they were suspended into a strong sugar syrup in a cast iron saucepan over a slow heat. After some hours (or days) the mice became crystallised and, when they were cold, she would give me one to eat. They were *delicious* and even the bones were crisp and edible (not unlike the bones in a mature tin of sardines). I remember her saying that I would never have chest trouble if I ate these 'sweetmeats'. I am now over seventy and have had little to complain about, health-wise as one says these days, in the years between these delightful treats and now.

Three

THE SCIENTIFIC APPROACH

*I*n the nineteenth century, intellectuals as well as medical men began seriously to take an interest in food, not in any cheerful sense of gustatory enjoyment, but as a subject for research, and managed to make the whole business sound most unappetising, despite the observation that

> The preservation of health depends so much upon a judicious selection of food as well as on the modes of preparing it . . . *It is only by resorting to the sciences of physiology and chemistry* in aid of experience, that the subject of food can be successfully investigated. The first makes us acquainted with the anatomical structure of the animal frame, and the nature of those functions upon which nutrition depends. The second teaches what are the component parts of the various substances usually employed as nutriment, and enables us to perceive substantial reasons why one species of food is preferable to another. Unless the subject be viewed in a scientific manner, it is impossible to acquire any other than the most vague notions respecting it.

So said the *Encyclopaedia of Domestic Economy*.

The 'experienced physician' Andrew Combe sought in a round-about way to remind his readers that they should chew their victuals: some eminent and earnest Victorians including, I believe, Mr Gladstone, chewed each mouthful sixty times before permitting themselves to swallow, which must by that time have rendered the morsel entirely tasteless and been irritating for any fellow diners eager for the next course. Nor could dining-room conversation have been noted for its animation. My husband had an occasional habit of closing his eyes as he lingered over a dish of broad beans, composing Greek epigrams in his head. I used to tell him not to.

The Girl's Own Indoor Book of about 1880, edited by Charles Peters, notes, 'Having been well cooked, the food ought to be thoroughly masticated.' Fanny Burney was also obsessed with mastication: 'Certain substances, of various sorts . . . are put between the Lips, where, by the aid of the Teeth, the Divisions are made yet more delicate, till, diminishing almost insensibly they form a general *mash*, or *wad* & are then swallowed.'

The Victorians prided themselves highly on their scientific skills and awareness, but then most eras have done so. Experts flourish in every generation and strive to convince the populace that their modern, up-to-date approach to the problems of surviving on earth supersedes all that has gone before, is the last word on the subject and will never be improved upon. In the nineteenth and early twentieth centuries the expert assumption was that the Great Unwashed had no notion of what was good or bad for them and needed direction on every point. Charles Peters concedes that, 'Guided by moderation and common sense, persons of ordinary intelligence do not usually violate scientific laws in regard to their food.' Still, 'A knowledge of the chemistry of the subject would tend to correct some common errors, and conduce to the invention of new, tasteful, and easily digested dishes.'

The books on household management and cookery were addressed to the rising middle class, but the expectation was that enlightened ideas and good practice would filter down through society and all would benefit (a version of the capitalist claim that the wealth of the few will enrich the many). One author held, on the 'vexed question of alcohol', that 'a very little will go a long way for useful results with ordinarily healthful persons', and Peters observes that tea and coffee are 'very apt to be abused and to be drunk at wrong times'. They were, he insisted, detrimental to the health of children and, taken with meat, greatly retarded digestion since 'their tannin forms with the gelatin of meat a leathery mass in the stomach, which produces dyspepsia and other unpleasant symptoms'. The proper time to take them, he advised, was with bread or starchy bodies, or, as in the East, between meals. 'Cocoa is much better than either, but most persons quickly get tired of it, and it disagrees entirely with many delicate stomachs.' He goes on to say that the functions and properties of the different kinds of foods enable us to select those which will supply suitable proportions of the various constituents necessary for building up our bodies.

Food, like sex, is susceptible to differing approaches: some treat it with earnest humourlessness while others take the matter far too lightly. Yet others, of course, simply indulge themselves without thought of the consequences. In 1891 Sir Henry

Thompson FRCS, MB Lond., etc., wrote a book baldly entitled *Food and Feeding*, in which he addressed himself to the question of the English diet. 'Our forefathers,' he observes, 'in their wisdom have provided, by ample and generously endowed organisations, for the dissemination of moral precepts in relation to human conduct, and for the constant supply of sustenance to meet the cravings of religious emotions common to all sorts and conditions of men . . . But it is not a sign of ancestral wisdom that so little thought has been bestowed on the teaching of what we should eat and drink . . .' Turn that upside down and we have the present state of affairs. In our permissive and inclusive society few are so foolhardy as to attempt to disseminate moral precepts for fear of incurring the righteous wrath of the liberal establishment, while government bodies are endlessly telling us what we should or should not eat, and you cannot turn on the TV or open a paper or magazine without finding some aficionado busily engaged in demonstrating dramatic new ways of preparing almost anything you can think of that will fit on a plate.

Sir Henry's chapter on the food of the English peasant and artisan has terse little observations in the margin. 'Food consumed by the labouring classes is often ill-selected' and 'wastefully prepared', It seems that at the time, 'The one idea which the working classes possess in relation to improvement in diet, and which they invariably realise when wages are high, is an abundant supply of butcher's meat.' Sir Henry notes grimly, 'Englishmen consume too much animal food,' and goes on to recommend more vegetables, haricots, lentils and rice, maize, macaroni and potato. He is sound on soup, although he cannot quite rid himself of the notion that most should be based on decoctions of beef, veal, game, fowl or fish. He did, however, possess a more frivolous side. Sir Henry gave dinners known as

Octaves at his house at Wimpole Street: they consisted of eight courses and were served at eight o'clock to eight persons.

In a book with the somewhat unalluring title *Sensible Food for All* written in 1939, the author, Edgar J. Saxon, tells us that, with the passing of time, the nation's palate had been confused, dulled and degraded by a hundred and fifty years of food sophistication and processing and by years of 'ever intensifying and misleading publicity for time-saving substitutes, palate ticklers and pre-digested or factory-compounded mixtures'. And what's more, he wrote, the adverts of the time, striving alternately to coax, flatter or hypnotise the people into spending money, used anything they could think of: 'Vitamins, germs, constipation, night-starvation, financial anxiety, domestic strife, strip stories by eminent novelists, pictures of puddings, portraits of film stars, rhyming slogans, recommendations by ten or twenty thousand doctors – in order to make us buy and put down our throats this, that or the other substitute for the fresh products of the living earth.'

Nothing much has changed except for further confusion and intensification and a hugely increased reliance on sex to sell food and drink of all kinds, as well as everything else. Freudians, of course, held that the baby's motive in suckling was primarily sexual: others had protested that if the baby failed to suckle it would starve, thus losing its breeding potential, but they were dismissed as fuddy-duddy. Freud, although now out of style in most psychiatric circles, is still influencing the advertising industry, which believes that no one would ingest a bar of chocolate or sink a pint of beer if it were not associated in their minds with the possibility of carnal intercourse.

The promise of health, youth, beauty and social success has always been held out by the manufacturers. An irresistible advert from 1925 reads:

ARE YOU FATIGUED?
GROWING OLD?
WRINKLES COMING?

Are you suffering from indigestion, malnutrition?
Are you too heavy or too thin?
Is your husband a social or business failure?
Are your children stupid, cross, not growing?
Do you realise you are living in an age of denatured food?
Your husband, children, and yourself are

– WHAT YOU EAT –

Your family needs Pro-ton-o the Rejuvenator, a concentrated
food, not a medicine.
It contains vitamins, cell salts and gland substance.
Pro-ton-o *can* help you – write for the Pro-ton-o book –
it is free

Sixty years ago, 'the creeping fungus of ignorance and publicity-conditioned credulity' had already crept from the towns into the remotest villages and I remember outlying farms where a treat for tea would consist of tinned salmon followed by tinned peaches, while the trout leapt in the stream running past the back door and blackberries burgeoned in the surrounding hedge. These were still eaten if anyone could be bothered to catch or pick them, but they were regarded as old-fashioned and therefore inferior. Mr Saxon held that 'sub-health' was accepted as the norm and 'Colds, catarrh, constipation ['Of course I take a laxative,' smiles the bright young lady in the advertisement], rheumatism, indigestion, headaches, flatulence, inflamed tonsils, dull skins, unhealthy teeth, defective sight' were commonly regarded as unavoidable. It was his contention that a 'sensible' diet would preclude these conditions: he accepted that there probably never was a Golden Age when everyone instinctively ate what was good for them, but rejects the 'all-too-easy view of human history as one long and unbroken climb from little running lemurs up to Mr H. G. Wells'.

There were rises and falls in 'progress' but 'human patience, skill and industry led to husbandry and thence intellectual development'. We would not be here today had our ancestors been content to roam the forests eating the fruit off the trees and following their instincts, but progress led to de-natured food and the consequent problems, and it's now too late for all to go back to the 'home-baked wheaten bread and oatcake, honey from the hive, eggs, cheese, butter and raw milk from the farm, fresh fish from the river and sea' of which Mr Saxon writes so wistfully. E coli, salmonella and listeria might be the result, but nor does anyone have to eat Pot Noodles, roast-beef flavour crisps or multi-coloured breakfast cereal.

There is always a tendency to romanticise the past but in the nineteenth century the unscrupulous Victorian baker added crushed human bone from the charnel house to bulk out his bread, sweeties were coloured green with lead, milk was watered down with the runnings from the gutters, while a report of 1856 records that cayenne was composed of red lead, mustard seed, brickdust, salt, ground rice and deal sawdust. They put sulphuric acid in the vinegar, and pepper in the cheaper establishments consisted of the sweepings off the floors of the warehouses. The same was said of tea and many people must have died of poisoning before the existence of allergies was even suspected. *A Lady* explained how to detect whether bakers' bread had been adulterated with whiting, chalk, bones, jalap, ashes, etc. For the first two you mixed it with lemon juice or strong vinegar to see if it fermented and for the rest you 'let it boil gently a long time in water' and then checked out the sediment.

Enquire Within Upon Everything advises the housewife on how to detect adulteration in dozens of commodities, but warns that she could drive herself mad. 'Somebody has written a little book to inform people *How to Detect Adulterations in our Daily Food and Drink*, and there is room for someone to write a key to the said little book, entitled, *How to Understand the Instructions in How to Detect Adulterations in our Daily Food and Drink*.' It seems that the means suggested are impracticable and sometimes dangerous and the housewife, by 'the upsetting of a bottle of sulphuric acid, or the explosion of a receiver of gas' might 'do herself more injury than she would suffer from adulteration in a lifetime'. *Enquire Within* comes to the rescue with a simpler set of tests. 'Our instructions will neither burn holes in her dress, stain her mahogany table, blacken her nails, make smarting chaps in her hands, nor fill her with monomaniacal fears that she is being ossified by bone dust, or that in a little while she will be crystallized all over like an alum-basket . . .'

As for instinct, a man called Katz experimented with his fussy children by presenting them with an assortment of dishes and telling them to eat what they liked: sardines and chocolate together if they felt so inclined. My informant does not reveal the result, whether they flourished or did not live to tell the tale, but the latest news from the experts who investigate these matters is that children who are free to eat whatever they fancy fall ravenously on junk food, putting themselves at risk of cancer and heart disease in later life, having missed out on all those vital nutrients. I could have told them that. Mr Katz was offering yet another example of the optimistic idea that human beings left to themselves and freed from constraint – civilisation, morality, law, religion, eat-up-your greens, etc. – will choose the correct course.

In *Health Foods: Facts and Fakes* (1973) Sidney Margolius writes, 'Many times the confused are leading the bewildered, as in the case of a health food clerk who advised a researcher that to produce fertile eggs "you need a happy rooster in each flock, and such eggs contain equal amounts of lecithin and cholesterol, helping the body to assimilate the cholesterol in eggs".' It has recently been declared that eggs don't contain much cholesterol anyway and we don't need to worry.

The macrobiotic diet was once hailed as a cure-all. Mr Margolius quotes the book *Zen Macrobiotics* by Ohsawa who said that 'thousands of incurable diseases could be cured in ten days or a few weeks', He further explained that baldness is caused by too much Yin (feminine) food; that no macrobiotic person can be affected by gonorrhea or any other venereal disease; that aspirin is suicidal, and 'that even the microbe is his own doctor', Mr Ohsawa prescribed various levels of diet, the highest consisting only of cereals, mostly brown rice: a twenty-four-year-old woman subsisting on this died of starvation in 1965 weighing seventy pounds. In 1999 a woman who had attempted to live on light was found dead by a river; the person who inspired her still claims to be thriving by the same means. Such non-eaters occur throughout history: the Welsh Fasting Girl, famous in the nineteenth century, was eventually exposed as a fraud when a snooper observed her parents smuggling tit-bits to her room under cover of darkness. When they stopped, she died. The food faddist and fanatic, the advertising industry and the mad scientist refuse to go away and will doubtless be with us till the end.

Perhaps this is the moment to drag in the monumentally obese Mr W. Banting, a London cabinet maker whose name for a time was used as a synonym for slimming as the stout declared their intention 'to bant'.

> We gather from Mr Banting the following diet and regimen for reducing too much flesh, and by which he reduced himself from 202 pounds to 156 in twenty days: For breakfast, four or five ounces of beef, mutton, kidneys, bacon, or cold meat of any kind with the exception of fresh pork; a large cup of tea without sugar or milk, a small biscuit or an ounce weight of toast – no butter. For dinner: five or six ounces of fish (no salmon) or meat (no fresh pork), all kinds of vegetables except potatoes; an ounce of toast, the fruit but not the paste of a tart, poultry, game, two or three glasses of good claret, sherry, or Madeira, but no champagne, port or beer. For tea: two or three ounces of fruit, about an ounce of toast, and a cup of tea without sugar or milk. For supper: three or four ounces of such meat or fish as at dinner, with one or two glasses of claret or sherry. Before going to bed, a glass of claret or sherry. This plan of Mr Banting's has been tried again and again with advantage.

And still is, not least in the Atkins diet, which is the subject of both fanatical enthusiasm and dire warnings. The diet as above was recommended to the public in 1863 and, in his poem 'A Day for Wishing' from around the same date, Henry S. Leigh wrote:

> If you wish to grow thinner, diminish your dinner,
> And take to light claret instead of pale ale;
> Look down with an utter contempt upon butter,
> And never touch bread till it's toasted – or stale.

When the great Church feasts, with the preceding fast days, were usual they would have had a beneficial effect on the wealthier members of the population who now have to have recourse to dieting in order to lose weight and stay fit. Some of my uncles, who were blamelessly devout, admitted that the observance of Lent went a considerable way towards getting them into shape for the cricket season. One other intriguing detail from the annals of slimming has stayed in my mind: there was in the 1930s or '40s a famous film star who made her salad dressings with liquid paraffin.

In a review of a biography of Elizabeth David a man observed that, after the Second World War, 'It was as much disgust with the ingredients rationing made us put up with, as an innate love of good cooking that made her turn her face to the Mediterranean.' Then he says, 'When someone mentions this, there is always some twerp on hand to say that actually the British were never as healthily nourished as they were during rationing. Do such people, I wonder, still insist on powdered egg and snoek in restaurants?' In a contest to see who could miss the point by the widest possible margin, this would be the one to back. No one, so far as I know, has ever suggested that the food tasted 'nice' during the War, they say it was *healthy*. And so it was: horrible but healthy.

Charles Elmé Francatelli in 1861 thoughtfully compiled a *Plain Cookery Book for the Working Classes* that was undeniably *de haut en bas*. He declared his intention in the introduction, 'My object in writing this little book is to show you how you may prepare and cook your daily food, so as to obtain from it the greatest amount of nourishment at the least possible expense; and thus by skill and economy, add, at the same time to your comfort and to your comparatively slender means.' He was presuming that the working classes to whom he addressed himself were sufficiently literate to avail themselves of his advice and makes a subtle distinction between these and the 'well-deserving poor' who, if they did not live in the 'immediate neighbourhood of noblemen and gentlemen's mansions in the country where the charitable custom of distributing wholesome and nutritious soup to poor families' already existed, were likely to have a rough time of it, 'especially in the winter months when their scanty means of subsistence but insufficiently yield them food adequate in quantity to sustain in them the powers of life in a condition equal to their hard labour.'

He gave a list of useful cooking appliances and utensils, followed by the recipes. These are similar to those for the middle classes but without the frills – sheep and calf's head, cod's head, the cheaper cuts of meat, and potatoes, cabbages, onions, carrots and parsnips, with soused mackerel or red herrings and such for a change. He also placed much reliance on tapioca, sago, barley, oats, ground rice and arrowroot, and advised on how to feed infants and the sick in the usual Victorian fashion which, looked at dispassionately, was more a form of euthanasia than a system of cure.

Because of the exigencies and the levelling effects of rationing during the war, the very poor, the survivors of the Depression, for the first time, had an adequate diet: awful but adequate; while the dyspeptic rich, deprived of all they had been used to were impelled to live more sensibly – and longer – provided, of course, they were not directly in the firing line. No more barons of beef or saddles of mutton or legs of pork, just scrappy little bits that would shrivel away if subjected to roasting heat. There was also a shortage of foreign fruit but everyone turned to the home-grown varieties, while school children picked rose hips so the government could pass round the syrup laden with Vitamin C; and rhubarb, another source of Vitamin C and one which I, personally, cannot bear even to think about, seemed to grow like a weed wherever there was a vacant inch of ground and an adjacent horse.

Those who had been in service in their youth would not have been as astonished as their employers by the deprivations. Mrs Beeton had recommended as their provisions:

Vegetables chiefly potatoes and greens.
Ale or stout: men 1 quart; maids, 1 pint per diem.
Washing, from 1s. to 1s. 6d.
Tea, a quarter-pound per week.
Sugar, a half-pound per week.
Butter, a half-pound per week.
Meat, three and a half pounds per week.
Bread, 1 pound per diem; quarter-pound cheese per week.
Soap, 1 pound per week for house cleaning, and 1 cake for
    personal use.

Tea and bread and butter, or bread and preserve, are the ser-
    vants' ordinary breakfast.
    Dinner, hot meat and vegetables, alternately with cold meat
and pudding; but a considerate mistress will consult her servants' health and her own interest, by giving them an agreeable
change of food.
    Tea and bread and butter for tea.
    Supper, bread and meat or bread and cheese.
    Coffee makes an agreeable change with tea, and should occa-
sionally be allowed in the proportion of a half-pound per head
per week.

And 'of course' they had their own crockery, cutlery, table-cloths, bedclothes, etc., all 'inexpensive' and on no account to be confused with the things used by the family.

In grander households the servants had not been permitted to finish off the leftovers and there are tales of the lobster salads, the Nesselrode Pudding, the remains of the baron of beef and anything else left uneaten by the Quality being thrown into a cart and wheeled off – by the servants, of course – to nourish the pigs. In more modest households there was less to waste but misunderstandings arose just the same. Mistress: What happened to the rest of the pie, Cook? Cook: Well, Mam, you told me to 'eat it up, so I het it.

Dr Kitchiner, in humorous vein, had written, 'To guard against *la gourmandise* of the second table provide each of your servants with a large pair of spectacles of the highest magnifying power and never permit them to sit down to any meal without wearing them; they are as necessary and useful in the kitchen as Pots and Kettles: they will make a *Lark* look as large as a *Fowl*, a *Goose* as big as a *Swan*, a *leg of Mutton* as large as a *Hind Quarter of Beef*, a *Twopenny loaf* as big as a *quartern*.' Another author, conceding that they need to be properly fed, warns, 'It does not answer, however, to give in too much to servants' whims about meals. If one does the whims and fancies will rapidly develop and become extremely numerous.'

Things were indeed hard in what was known as 'the Duration' but no one died from over-indulgence, although most people drank too much saccharine-sweetened tea and smoked Players and Woodbines, Senior Service and Craven A whenever they could get their hands on them. There was always the risk of food poisoning and some people perished in the heroic quest for different types of root or fungi; but there were terrifying posters depicting flies and descriptions of the harm they could wreak, so hygiene improved. (Now it seems we've gone too far with all the latest cleaning fluids and are so unaccustomed to germs that when

45

confronted by those we would once have shrugged off, we feebly succumb.) Everyone was exhorted to Dig for Victory, to Make Do and Mend, and waste was a crime. If you were caught throwing bread in the dustbin you were for it – 'A sailor's blood is on your head if you waste a scrap of bread' – and every newspaper and woman's magazine offered advice, not now on how to spend money or appeal to the opposite sex (for some reason it had never seemed to occur to anyone to extend this advice to men, who presumably, had no difficulty in this respect), but on what to do with an uneaten sprout or how to make the family's eyes light up at the prospect of a meatless, butterless, cheeseless and probably fruitless dinner, and how to stretch an egg. ('One scrambled egg will serve three people if the egg is mixed with more milk than usual, and a heaped tablespoonful of very fine breadcrumbs is added.')

The Depression had shocked the profligate into the practice of thrift but it was the War that brought leftovers into their own. As Christmas approached in 1941, *Good Housekeeping* observed, 'You will want to make the remains of your bird go as far as possible [put the bloody thing on the 10.45 to Fort William, went the mirthless jest]. One way is to use a little of the meat in *stuffed pancakes*. Mince the meat and any leftover vegetables, season well and bind with gravy. Fry some small thin pancakes and fill with the hot meat mixture. Serve with a green vegetable and the rest of the gravy.' This is actually a good idea and a better disguise for the bird than a curry or a *salmi*: it is disheartening to see again a slice of a bird that you've met before, foundering in sauce. The Christmas Pudding would have consisted largely of grated carrot with the minute quantity of dried fruit that you had saved up, unless you had seduced the grocer (suspicions and allegations were rife about women who appeared to have more than their fair share of such little luxuries), and to crown it you would make 'Mock Whipped Cream'.

The British then were consumed with envy of the American way of life, particularly of what they had to eat. The American soldier stationed in Britain was the object of contempt richly flavoured with sour grapes, while the masochistic dribbled over glossy American magazines full of gleaming portraits of cakes and roast meats. Now that we can travel and see the reality for ourselves, the vegetables in the supermarkets in the States look as though they are auditioning for a Still Life. They are regularly hosed down so that they gleam with that morning freshness so beloved of the advertisers and are all oversized and flawless, but it's perfectly true that they don't taste as you might hope. The flavour is somehow muted, falling just short of expectations. I think this is why some people over-eat; they go on chewing away hopefully just to see if the things on the plate might suddenly fulfil their yearnings for something delicious. The strange thing about parts of America is that the rich look near emaciated and the poor are enormous. There is a widespread terror of fat, salt and sugar and what they might do to the body, while commercial interests openly encourage the population to give themselves up to gluttony, 'All you can eat for $10 and then some.' The combination of poverty and waste is disconcertingly evident: what's thrown away would feed a small nation in perpetuity. Malnourishment takes differing forms. Should you go out to breakfast in the USA *un oeuf* is never considered sufficient and I recently ended up with two in the form of Eggs Benedict, which would have been alright, only they were flanked by a slice of melon, two quarters of an orange, half a huge apple and a raspberry, which also would have been alright if they'd been on a separate plate, but the flavour of fruit is not improved by immersion in Hollandaise Sauce and egg yolk.

Later we went out to lunch: all we wanted was a small Caesar Salad each and some halibut, but when they came each salad was such that I would have put it on the table for a party of four, and the halibut was supported by an entourage of mashed potato, red cabbage, green beans and broccoli and veiled in caper sauce. The capers, perhaps because of the marine connotations of the fish, were strongly reminiscent of the bobbing heads of drowning seafarers, and I realised again that a plate over-laden with assorted viands is more threatening than inviting.

Even in the UK with all the advice from the government on what to eat in order to stay healthy – five pieces of fruit per day, more oily fish, etc., etc. – the problem of obesity is increasing. The number of 'officially overweight' six-year-olds doubled in the ten years to 2003 and the proportion of fat fifteen-year-olds is trebling. In March 2000 a study found the proportion of over-weight British adults had risen from nineteen to twenty-three per cent in just two years. More than four and a half million men and five and a half million women were classed as dangerously over-weight – a statistic that alters upwards every year. Children have nowhere to play, are driven to school, and, when they go home, they watch TV or sit at their computers and eat junk food – or, conversely, they develop anorexia. Nor do many schools teach sensible cookery as they used to. A study by educational psychologists in February 2002 found that forty per cent of schoolgirls had never boiled an egg, while one – speaking for many – said cooking was a waste of time as you could buy 'those packets' ready prepared from the local supermarket.

Some haughty aristos of cuisine have mocked Delia Smith for showing the public how to boil an egg, but that is indeed not as simple as it may sound – a lot depends on whether you want it hard or soft for a start – and Delia's advice is not only useful but, in many cases, necessary. Her critics seem incapable of understanding that her practical approach is beyond computation of more value than all their flourishes: one of them describes her as the 'Volvo' of cookery, to which one can only say that anyone with an ounce of sense would choose this reliable vehicle in preference to some flibbertigibbet sports model when it comes to keeping body and soul together. One reviewer wrote by way of further criticism that she had a tendency to 'bang on about God'. There is another parallel here. On the evidence of history, there were a great many individuals in the nineteenth century who remained unmoved by the moral exhortations to which they were subjected, and recent statistical evidence seems to indicate that few people now, despite all the advice, spend more time in the kitchen than is required to pop the take-away pizza in the microwave. Once, the recreational approach to food was regarded as an improper subject for serious thought, and now it's The Almighty. The 'cravings of religious emotions' are largely catered for by the lunatic fringe, Christianity being unfashionable, and where once there were numerous preachers there are now countless cooks, not exactly haranguing us from street corners but appearing on all the TV channels.

Yet let no one suppose that the Domestic Goddess is entirely new upon the scene. A writer in the *Newcastle Chronicle* of 14 August 1887 enthused, 'We looked with a feeling akin to awe at the graceful kindly lady, who is rapidly raising cookery to a fine art. The most fastidious could watch Mrs A. B. Marshall [she would now doubtless be universally known merely as Agnes] with pleasure, and the highest compliment that I can pay her is to say that after seeing her cook one longs to partake of the viands she has prepared.' Mrs Marshall had demonstrated how to prepare 'many *recherché* dishes, which she classified together under the title "A Pretty Luncheon"' in front of an audience of six hundred. She worked 'without fuss and without stain. The aprons she and her assistants wore on Monday may do for any number of "Pretty Luncheons". They must have been worn for form's sake. Their protective value was wholly fanciful.' And at the end of the 'lecture, or performance, whichever it may be called, her labours elicited a unanimous outburst of applause.' Mrs Marshall is, perhaps, all things considered, the most demanding of Cook's advisers. She ran her own cookery schools and shops and marketed her own brand of food stuffs, utensils and kitchen appliances. (One of my copies of her much reprinted book contains the most poignant erratum slip ever. It reads: 'Page 272, Line 8, for "pint" read "pinch".' This refers to her own brand of Coralline Pepper.) An 1890s edition of her cookery book begins with a little list of quoted comments: '"Cooking has become more than ever a fine art," *Lancet*; "Cookery is not only an art but a master art," *Saturday Review*; "The man of sense and culture alone understands eating," Brillat-Savarin; "A dinner lubricates business," Boswell.' All of which was quoted, I imagine, to get Cook on her toes and bring her to a proper awareness of her responsibilities, which were great.

Home cooking, however, will never rise to the heights of restaurant cooking and quite right too. The traditions of 'bourgeois' and 'haute' cuisine are entirely separate and attempts to emulate restaurant methods in the private kitchen can only lead to frustration and impotent rage and cause people to buy their dishes ready-made. A piece in the *Evening Standard* in January 2001 mentioned the books put out by two highly esteemed restaurateurs which are 'infamous for containing recipes doomed to failure when prepared by anyone but the most professional of cooks'. One of the restaurant owners, it is alleged, said she never cooked anything anyway. The same cannot be said of Alexis Soyer, who himself wielded the wooden spoon and whose chief fault was never using a familiar word when he could dredge up an unfamiliar one ('geoponic' when he means agricultural, for instance, or the 'process of ebullition' when he means boiling). He kept referring to what he called the 'magiric' science and held that the new, high and elaborate system began in the seventeenth century. One of those responsible is probably Sir Theodore de Mayerne who, in 1658, wrote a book called *Archimagirus Anglo-Gallicus* consisting of 'Excellent and Approved Receipts and Experiments in Cookery, together with the best way of Preserving. As also Rare Formes of Sugar Works: According to the French mode and English manner.' They were off: the inventive chef had been given free rein. It is notable that although everyone was still eating roast meat, Sir Theodore gives only one recipe for a roast – a calf's head stuffed with oysters and Lord knows what. The rest of his recipes were for pies and pasties and everything else was boiled since this made it possible to include whatever combination of ingredients might occur to the cook. Even the calf's head was par-boiled to begin with.

It was once suggested to the Maréchal de Richelieu that he should marry a certain widow, whereupon he responded that they 'would quarrel continuously over salads with cream and spun-sugar sultanas that stick to the teeth; she is infatuated with this new cuisine that is utterly stupid and everything to eat in her house has so many frills that one has no idea what one is partaking of'. The Maréchal also declared, 'It is principally after the death of Louis XV that real gastronomical knowledge and, as a consequence, the science of the cook have gone to pieces.' He was bemoaning the loss of traditional or what might be loosely described as 'peasant' methods; not much changed, unless by circumstance, from medieval times – certainly not altered by conscious design – while Carême, for instance, despised the old ways and had not a good word to say for the cooks who preceded him. (It is a fact that many famous chefs display a touchiness of temperament, a vanity and a tendency to throw the furniture about, unmatched by any of the foremost practitioners of other, less demanding disciplines: painters, writers, musicians have their little ways but few are as given to envy, bigotry and rage as are chefs.) The argument over the differing approaches to cuisine had already boiled down at one point to home versus restaurant cooking; the supporters of the old ways staunchly refusing to eat anywhere but in their own dining rooms, while the opposing camp dined regularly in their favoured establishments: the one faction despising the effete nature of the ragouts, patés and sauced dishes on offer in the new eating houses and the other turning up its nose at the unimaginative simplicity of home cooking.

The debate continued for some time (my mother was suspicious of restaurants to the end of her days, always questioning the state of hygiene in the unseen kitchen), but now seems to have fallen silent as many people, intent on conspicuity, choose to entertain their colleagues, clients and even friends and family in some smart establishment rather than light the candles in their own dining room. Many well-intentioned observers lament the decline of the 'family dinner', but they forget how inharmonious these could be as Father (it was usually Father but could be anyone), seized the opportunity to let his views be known to a captive audience of his loved ones. Not to mention the growls of 'sit up straight', 'hold your knife properly', 'don't chew with your mouth open', etc. The domestic tyrant loses much of his (or her) power under the public gaze.

Even now, not being what you might call convivial by nature, I resort to several stratagems designed to avoid sitting down with company at the dining table. I might, for example, notice that I have forgotten the redcurrant jelly and go off to look for it, encouraging everyone to carry on eating as I might be some time; or, disregarding all well-meant advice to prepare in advance so as to be able to join your guests, I disappear to mix the salad. In truth, I prefer to eat alone, standing up with a book propped against the chopping board, and panic if I find myself in a restaurant without a copy of *The Times*. I don't mind talking to people, but have never overcome the sensation of despondency that descends when I'm confronted by some smug *hors d'ouevre* and an array of cutlery that indicates the imminence of many courses and hours of claustrophobic detention at the table; the glitter of spittle by candlelight as your neighbour utters a witticism before swallowing a mouthful of meat. I am aware that this reaction is inappropriate in a book intended partly to encourage the young to behave in a civilised fashion, but as long as they eat the right things at proper intervals I don't much care where they do it. I think I have the soul of a cook and the attitude of a kitchen maid: having cooked a meal, the last thing I want to do is look at it, let alone eat it.

And I'd rather wash all the dishes than suffer a 'banquet', followed by speeches.

Four

THE SERVANT PROBLEM

There was an ancient, widely quoted saying that 'God sends meat and the devil sends cooks', or as Milton put it rather less pithily, 'God sends meat and the cooks work their wills.'

'Until the art of cookery had arrived at the period of its perfection in the luxurious times of Greece and Rome, everybody was a cook,' wrote Charles Pierce, who had been for 'upwards of twenty years *maître d'hôtel* at the Russian Embassy and for some years at Chirk Castle in the family of Colonel Myddleton Biddulph, Master of the Queen's Household'. Pierce asserts that: 'The earliest cookery on record will be found in the history of the Hebrews and it is there stated that the collation set before the angelic visitants of Abraham, was prepared by Sarah; a proof of the superior science of the future mother of nations . . . So early as the mission of Moses, offerings of confectionery were ordained by law; and cakes of honey, flour and oil, evince the ingenuity and *savoir-vivre* of the fair descendants of Sarah.'

Alexis Soyer in his *Pantropheon* tells us breathlessly, 'The heroes of Homer prepared their repasts with their own hands – and what repasts, gods of taste! – and prided themselves on their culinary talents. Ulysses surpassed all others in the art of lighting the fire, and laying the cloth. Patroclus drew the wine, and Achilles very carefully turned the spit.' It is diverting to picture this charming domestic scene: 'Patroclus peeled onions! Achilles washed cabbages! and the wise Ulysses roasted with his own hands, a sirloin of beef.'

With the rise of civilisation such cheerful self-reliance came to a halt, for the later Greeks, affected by the introduction of that luxury which brings about an 'effeminate kind of existence which only permits certain men to be engaged in the painful or repulsive details of every-day life' relied on butchers and, by implication, cooks, and were too effete and spoiled to do it for themselves; while the Romans, who were deeply interested in food as well as other sensual pleasures, valued their cooks most highly, paying them eight hundred pounds per annum. Antony gave his chef a city 'in recompense' for a dinner which Cleopatra had much enjoyed – surely one of the earliest recorded instances of those intimate and expensive candle-lit occasions on which, through the ages, the would-be seducer has placed such reliance.

'With the Roman Empire, fell in Europe the great but unscientific kitchen of antiquity,' lamented Lady Morgan, a much-quoted celebrity of her time (1776–1859), while others mourned the abandonment of notions of hygiene as the bath disappeared for a few centuries – a development with inevitable and regrettable repercussions in the kitchen and dining room. On the revival of the culinary art in the seventeenth century, French cooks were raised to the rank of cavaliers and distinguished by being permitted to wear swords and 'embroidered dresses' and, observes Pierce, 'whilst on this point, it must not be forgotten, that in England the cook has never failed, in the first household in the Kingdom, to be in receipt of a large salary as an appreciation of his talent.' I'm not sure about this. I know a man who once worked as a chef in the royal kitchens and left because the pay was poor; the splendour of the position, he said, was considered remuneration enough. He became a builder.

Others have taken the matter more seriously. The chef Vatel was overwhelmed with inconsolable shame when, at a dinner given by the Prince de Condé for Louis XIV, the twenty-fourth and twenty-fifth tables from the royal board were 'indifferently supplied with roasts'. The next day, by four o'clock in the morning, only a few miserable sprats had arrived, though orders for fish had been placed at every port along the coast. Shattered, Vatel was convinced that no further supply could reach him in time. 'I never can survive this disgrace,' he exclaimed and, retiring to his quarters, he ran himself through with his own sword. The King observed that this evinced a nice sense of honour, and then 'from all parts the purveyors made their appearance with a profusion of magnificent fish'. It's always the way.

In 1815 the Prince of Wales offered Antonin Carême the sole, permanent control of the royal kitchens but the chef declined on the grounds that the Prince's establishment was lacking in *ton*. '*C'est que la cuisine de son altesse royale est trop bourgeois.*' Nor has royalty always been merciful to cooks. Under 'statute 22, Henry VIII' two of them, namely John Roose and Margaret Davy, were boiled to death. This seems an excessive response but bad cooks have always been the object of vituperation and despair while monarchs, given half a chance, are often ruthless. In an essay on Ivan the Terrible by Christopher Swann there occurs the memorable line, 'He was probably the only man of his time to fry a live man in a frying pan.'

An anonymous, choleric, clearly dyspeptic author wrote in 1862 in a work entitled *Dinners and Dinner Parties*: 'Among the whole tribe of women called cooks, there are not ten that are worthy of their salt.' He suggested that the dame of a man of independence, if unable to give instructions or read a cookery book, should engage a man cook from Belgium rather than 'the woman she employs to clean her street-door steps – a woman born in a shed, or under the lee of a brick-kiln, who, most probably, never tasted meat in the hole from whence she came. Common sense dictates that such a person ought not to be entrusted to cook anything beyond what is fitted for the pigsty.' This furious author, to whom I refer throughout as *Anon*, is perhaps my favourite.

Before the French Revolution it had been axiomatic among the 'fine gentlemen, the travelled men of the day' that to procure a good dinner in England, it was necessary to procure a good cook from France – male, one gathers – though according to one source the *Cordon Bleu* was 'an ancient distinction given to skilful female cooks since the time of Louis XV. It consists of a rosette made of dark blue ribbon, and was, and is, still much prized, as it shows that the cook is in the chef class.' Female cooks in England had been known as 'Cooky' or 'Cookess'. As time went by they were always given the honorary title Mrs no matter what their marital condition. Mrs Blackman, cook to Lady Diana Duff Cooper, said in 1943, 'You can learn a lot from a chef if you are observant and keep your eyes open, especially in the matter of decorating food – wonderful dishes in aspic and elaborate ices and so on – but a man will not teach you half so much as a woman; they haven't the same patience.' One of my neighbours tells of an old friend who employed a highly skilled Italian chef but constantly demanded things like bread and butter pudding and other such English nursery food, which is like setting a Derby contender to pull a milk float. I met a famous chef a few years ago: he was in philosophical and melancholy mood and said, shrugging his shoulders in his Gallic fashion, that while cooking was undoubtedly an art, it was the only one the products of which ended up in the sewer.

In 1847 the duties of the man cook who was 'found chiefly in the large establishments of princes and noblemen, or in those of very affluent families,' consisted in making out the bill of fare, knowing everything that was to be known about food, superintending the cooking generally and making, with his own hands, 'the rich sauces, ragouts, soups and other dishes of a complicated description not understood by ordinary cooks whose greater variety of business precludes their attainment of the highest degree of proficiency in the art'. Pierce observes, 'It is usual for the cook, when he has to present himself for orders, to do so in his full kitchen costume, with his jacket, apron, and cap, and not to remove his cap, even in the presence of Royalty. His dress should be the pattern of neatness and cleanliness, and his manners agree with his dress.' Writing of suitable dress for servants, the splendid Dr Kitchiner, who was directing his advice mainly to the rising middle class and not working on the assumption that his readers would be familiar with the basics of running a household, was the first cookery author to go into meticulous detail. He notes that, 'We often hear of really good servants objecting to wear caps . . . if it be because it is the insignia of office they dislike to wear it, we can only suggest that if they are not ashamed to *be* servants, they surely need not be ashamed to *look* like them.' The woman cook had to keep an eye on the kitchen maid and scullion and direct the whole business of the kitchen. 'She is responsible for the mode in which it is conducted and performed, and must, therefore, possess adequate skill; they on their part have only to be active, cleanly and obedient.'

Anon, still in a passion, recounts one of those stories that you wish you'd never heard: you know such things sometimes happen, perhaps now in the less salubrious restaurants, but you prefer not to dwell on it:

> The author was present with a young lady who had been educated in the usual nonsense, when the footman entered and asked her mother if he could say a word in private; the mother answered that she wished no secrets, and desired him to speak out; he hesitating, she bid him to say what he had to say. He replied, 'I think it right to tell you, mam, that cook was drunk last night, and, in pouring out the soup from the saucepan into the tureen, was ill, and before she could turn her head away from it, part of her illness went into the tureen.' Cook was immediately called up, but, of course, the brute stoutly denied it. However, there was no doubt of the fact; the footman said he did not like to disturb the party, so he wiped the edge of the tureen, and gave the soup a good stir. The lady, in great anguish, exclaimed, 'Good Heavens! I ate some of it!' and, being highly indignant, was not very gentle to William for stirring the soup, or the cook for her addition to it. The young lady listlessly exclaimed, 'I ate some of it; but what a fuss you are making, mamma! You know we must all eat a peck of dirt before we die.' This young woman had received a college education, and was finished at Brighton at 200 pounds a year, besides extras.

Kitchiner suggested more indulgently, though maybe with some enlightened self-interest, that the Master should treat his Cook with the tenderest care and 'especially be sure her taste does not suffer from her Stomach being deranged by Bilious Attacks'. Wyvern (Colonel Kenney Herbert) wrote a century later, 'Over and over again have revolting facts been discovered in connexion with the habits and customs of the cook-room,' and 'Though cognizant of the ingenious nastiness of our cooks, we shrug our shoulders, close our eyes, and ask no questions, accepting with resignation a state of things which we consider to be as inevitable as it is disgusting.' The problem in the nine-teenth century as *Anon* defined it, lay with the lack of culture of the rising middle class and the ignorance of the lower class employed as servants by the nouveau riche. No one knew how to behave: 'The offshoots of nobility with only empty titles for their fortunes; baronets who never ought to have had the honour; knights without means; aspiring merchants; aspiring barristers, who had been better with a trade; aspiring vulgarity of all sorts, ay, and all the other classes, jostle with the tradesman; they are all diseased with selfish vanity, and they all try to imitate the upper five thousand.' (It is noteworthy that people now who make enormous amounts of money – pop stars, footballers, TV celebrities – show little interest in crashing into the upper classes, but spend their money in their own way on things they like, which are often ghastly, but good luck to them.)

So much for *Anon*'s view of the employers, but as for the employees, 'The cooks are the sisters or cousins of the recruits of our army, who are paid one shilling per day, and no more, from which sevenpence is taken for their food. Not so with their sisters or cousins; they are paid by a different scale, and unhappily there are no corporals to drill them, or occasionally they would be treated with a flogging, and a taste of solitary confinement, and a stoppage of pay.' It is charitable to infer that *Anon*'s experiences of dining had brought him to the verge of madness. Another wrote, 'The majority of those who set up for Professors of this Art are of mean ability, selfish, and pilfering everything they can; others are indolent and insolent. Those who really understand their business (which are by far the smallest number) are too often either ridiculously saucy, or insatiably thirsty.'

A late nineteenth-century book, *Home Queries*, giving advice on dining, servants and the laying of tables, including seven ways – with diagrams – of folding 'serviettes' said: 'To see plates, from which you are going to eat, handled by a maid with grimy hands does not exactly act as an appetizer. Quietness is one of the qualities expected of a parlour-maid. Plates and dishes need not be packed together with a great deal of noise. They can be put down gently without any more bother. To slam plates together not only makes a most unpleasant clatter but is apt to chip the china.'

Ralph Nevill wrote of the 'inefficient attendance, the dirt, neglect, and wholesale fleecing to which an unwary bachelor used to be exposed . . .' He singled out for particular opprobrium 'the dirty, dowdy maid-of-all-work who often ruled the bachelors who had rooms in her mistress's house with a rod of iron' and quotes the response of one to some mild complaint from a lodger. 'Lawk sir, do you call these hands dirty? You should see my feet!' Most of these maids, says Nevill, 'were wholesale slaughterers of crockery; they seemed indeed to have sworn a war of extermination against china'.

Unlike the poor parlourmaid, Cook had 'perks'. One of these was permission to sell the household's surplus dripping and grease to the makers of cheap candles and such who called at the kitchen door. The householder was usually suspicious of these people, justifiably according to Buckmaster:

I have often spoken against *perquisites*. No invention of the devil has been a more fruitful source of dishonesty and waste among servants. The percentage of the tradesman, the sale of kitchen grease, which is often good dripping, the skimmings of saucepans, and fat meat most useful in the kitchen, ought to be discounted in every household. To sell fat at fourpence per pound and purchase lard at elevenpence; to purchase egg powders and charge for eggs, is simply dishonest. Better give your cooks two or three pounds a year more and encourage them to make the best of everything, than allow perquisites.

A Victorian High Court Statement records, 'To give away the master's property is to steal it. There is an old case recorded where a cook, out of compassion, gave a beggar bread and other things worth eightpence, the property of her master. She was convicted of larceny and so also was the person who received the articles.'

The wife of the Empire Builder had also been bombarded with advice and warnings. *Indian Domestic Economy and Cookery* states:

The misdeeds of Indian servants appear to be a general and unfailing source of complaint amongst all . . . laziness, dishonesty, falsehood, with a host of other vices, seem to be inherent in them. This need hardly be wondered at, when we consider the way in which they are brought up, taught from their earliest infancy to look for employment only in the particular calling of their parent, or the guardian by whom they have been adopted. Nor is the fault wholly on their side – much that is complained of, originates with the master, and is owing to him . . . servants have too often just cause for leaving their places suddenly, the slightest fault of a native servant being often visited with blows and such abuse as no respectable man will bear, very often too for no other fault than that of not understanding what the master has said, who has given his directions in some unintelligible stuff, from ignorance of the language, that no one could understand . . .

In some houses, besides the Khansumar or Butler, whose province appears to be merely superintending the concerns of the table, and of the servants attached to it, a sort of Jemadar of servants is also kept up, who takes charge of the purse and of all the out-of-door servants, pays all the expenses – in fact, superintends the household concerns in general. He is usually a Mussulman, but sometimes of the other class, answering in some degree to the Sircar in Calcutta. Very frequently, instead of a regular servant for the toilet, a Hindoo of the Bearer class is employed, and it seems the better plan; for being a dressing servant, he is in general too great a man to assist in carrying the palankeen . . .

A Furrash I suspect, is kept up in but few houses: his occupation is that of a Lascar or Khalassie; he sweeps the carpets, cleans the house and furniture, the care of which he has; also the beds, shades and lights, it being his duty to light the latter . . .

The Cook is usually a Native Christian or the lowest caste of Hindoos from Madras or the Coast; sometimes they are Mussulmen, but seldom in any proportion to the former. The bearers are a hard-working and very trusty class of people: you may leave articles of any value with them with perfect safety . . . Entrust money, jewels, clothes, &c., in fact, anything to their charge, and you will find them faithful. They will for years treasure up the smallest rags for you, though now and then you will see them appropriating articles, they have thought forgotten by their masters (from their never having been asked for), and if they can profit in any way from their intermedium in purchasing for you, you will find they will generally cheat you in over demands in some slight way or other. Should you become poor they will drop even this in a very great degree, or totally. In sickness they will take the greatest care of you, doing for you services that a European seldom ever will . . . They are in general sensitive of and grateful for kindness, and become active and zealous therefrom.

Their principal vice, besides what I have already given, is an intolerable habit of lying. In the way of tea, sugar, bread, milk, paper and such like articles, they will frequently, like European servants, appropriate a little for themselves . . . I think that you have only to treat natives well and kindly, and they will prove good servants to you. Sympathize in their griefs and joys, with the smallest words of kindness, speak kindly to them, and oblige them when you can, and they will serve you well, and will refuse to execute no sort of work how extraneous so ever from their regular duties . . .

Allowing for the limitations imposed by the Victorian version of prejudice and despite the critical tone, *Indian Domestic Economy and Cookery* gives the impression that, at least in some cases, relations between Sahibs, Memsahibs and staff were warmer than was customary at home in England, while the index has its own fascination. Scolloped Oysters is followed by Scorpion Sting or Bite of a Centipede, while Sirloin of Beef is closely followed by Smells, bad, to destroy, and Snake Bite, cure for – which describes what to do with a cupping glass, ligature, knife, hot iron, lunar caustic, *eau-de-luce* and spirits of hartshorn, and adds compassionately, 'A bottle of Madeira may be taken in draughts at a few minutes interval.' There are recipes for numerous dishes with names like *Kulleah Jogooranth*, *Doepeaza Pulwull*, *Bizah Sada*, all complex in both ingredients and preparation. One pictures the young English bride leaving Tunbridge Wells and having to master all that as well as cope with the many servants, learn new languages and possibly concern herself with the health of the horses. 'A cure for Mange: Fig leaves beat to a pulp, and soaked one night in Tyre will in three applications cure the most inveterate state of this disease.'

The English house might, if grand, have accommodated housekeeper, chef, butler, footmen, maids of many sorts, grooms, gardeners, scullions, boot boys, etc. and possibly a hermit for decorative purposes residing in the Folly, but on the whole they would have spoken the same language as their employer. (My husband's grandfather, a Cardiff dweller, once had his windows broken in consequence of inserting an advert for a parlourmaid in a newspaper reading, 'No Welsh need apply'.)

While most of the numberless cookery books and the reams of advice to the rising middle class on etiquette, dress and how to conduct a household that were published in the nineteenth and early twentieth centuries were deadly serious, some did attempt a more light-hearted, rueful approach. One T. S. Arthur in *Trials and Confessions of a Housekeeper* wrote, 'I had been married several years before I was fortunate enough to obtain a cook that could be trusted to boil a potato or broil a steak . . . moreover Margaret was good-tempered, a most remarkable thing in a good cook.' Unfortunately, the faultless cook eventually manifested a fault that vitiated all her good qualities: she drank and had to be 'let go'. The drunkenness and rage for which cooks were notorious is hardly surprising, given the prevailing conditions in the kitchen; down in the dark by the area steps with the range blazing or, not infrequently, sullenly smoking as the wind turned. As Dr Kitchiner expressed it, 'To say nothing of the deleterious vapours and pestilential exhalations of the charcoal, which soon undermine the health of the heartiest, the glare of a scorching fire, and the smoke so baneful to the eyes and the complexion which are continual and inevitable dangers; a Cook must live in the midst of them, as a soldier on the field of battle.'

When open fires were usual, before the concept of 'home' began to change and central heating altered all the old seated-around-the-fire arrangements, gentlemen would stand in the drawing room with their backs to the flames, thumbs hooked in their waistcoat pockets, and hold forth, keeping the warmth from the company. Women, as *The Cook and Housewife's Manual* advised (see Chapter Two), had to be rather more careful, but the instructions in the *Manual* were mainly intended for the daughters of gentlefolk while Cook remained at somewhat greater risk of burns and scalds in the kitchen. And it is in the kitchen that we now encounter fresh hazards as people struggle to liberate their 'convenience' foods from their patented packages: 37,000 ended up in casualty in 1998 having wounded themselves opening tins, cartons and those packets that defy the use of anything but a meat cleaver to prise them apart.

Another common disadvantage in times past was the presence of black-beetles: not just a few but carpets of them. Janet's grandmother worked as a cook in a restaurant kitchen and her father remembered going to collect her after working hours, walking into an unlighted room and hearing a horrid crunch. When the light was turned on the beetles had fled to the haven of the woodwork but the floor would show a line of black and bloody footprints. Janet adds musingly that her grandmother drank a lot of whisky.

Upstairs, even in quite modest establishments, the family demanded three meals a day all consisting of several courses, not to mention cakes for tea. There were terrible scenes below – not infrequently resulting in murder – as Cook fell out with the boot boy or scullery maid, while the Mistress was expected to combine the skills of Diplomat, Abbess and General and smooth over all the little difficulties. 'On entering the kitchen invariably say "Good morning, Cook,"' instructs Mrs Beeton, a recommendation that was otiose not many years later. She continues, 'Never listen to what one servant says of another; if angry voices and loud talk reach your ear, ring for the delinquents and before *both* say, "I have no wish to interfere with your quarrels, say and do what you please; but *I* must never hear a sound of dispute or anger in this house," and as this is a *tried* recipe for domestic *broils*, we give it verbatim. But it is only a gentlewoman who can say this – one who is never betrayed into an angry word or cross retort; example and precept must go hand in hand.' The counsel of perfection. (The heroine of *Trials and Confessions of a Housekeeper* had amongst her serial cooks one who 'had such a violent temper that I was actually afraid to show my face in the kitchen'.)

On the evidence, many young wives were frequently at the mercy of their cooks of whom they stood in terror. *Home Management*, 1904, admits, 'we shall never really understand servants. We often offend them when we mean to be kindest, out of pure ignorance of their own particular etiquette. The laws of which although unwritten are much more stringent than those of any other class of society.' Mrs Humphry, the author of this section, describes how an astonished mistress could find herself deprived of a cook because, all unwittingly, she had 'wounded Cook's dignity, made her look small before the tradespeople, or some servant in another family'. The cook of one lady of title immediately gave notice when her mistress opened a hat shop (a lot of ladies were doing this as times grew leaner), announcing that she had 'never served in a tradesman's family and never meant to'. One day she turned up at the shop, inspected the merchandise with a view to buying, remarked 'Wot trash', turned on her heel and left.

Mrs Pender Cudlip's *The Modern Housewife or How We Live Now* is largely concerned with the iniquities of the 'Queen of the Kitchen'. 'I hope the dinner will be delicious, but Cook's out of temper, and the chances are against it.' Dinner was not too good. The soup seemed to be composed of pepper, grease, hot water and bone in equal parts, the salmon was boiled to rags, the soles speckled and spotty and the chicken broiled to a cinder. Then, happily, came a magnificently roasted saddle of mutton with its accompaniments of jelly, asparagus, stewed mushrooms and mashed potatoes. Then followed ducklings and roast pigeons, some pastry and a soufflé. 'For dessert we had biscuits only, as the greengrocer had sent me nothing but cooking apples.'

Present at this dinner were just Mrs Pender Cudlip, her husband Arthur and an old family friend – bossy as old family friends often are. She it was who insisted that Cook should be spoken to and, 'Ere I had time to recover my nerve . . . Cook was in our midst.' Mrs Pender Cudlip had a moment merely to commence meekly that 'dinner was not altogether what I wished – and expected' when Cook launched into full flood. 'And the dinner wasn't at all what *I* wished and expected to be ast to cook in a lady's house who puts me to do it all at one small stove that ain't fit for nothing with an oven that won't bake and a boiler that won't keep the water at new milk 'eat and fellow-servants that is that disobliging that if I give way to them and demean myself to stay I shall have to gather and wash and I suppose in the end plant and cultiwate all the wegetables I want for the use of the 'ouse.'

I think there had been a misunderstanding here, for the constituents of this dinner sound like the provisions for a week. At grander tables more courses than the above would certainly make an appearance, but not usually at an everyday dinner for three. Perhaps Mrs Pender Cudlip had failed to make this clear to Cook for, 'The quantity was horful! horful!' said the odious woman with malignant satisfaction, going on to decry, 'what will always 'appen when ladies that know nothing about it think they're going to save theirselves by taking the work out of cook's 'ands and dealing straight with the tradesman.'

Mrs Humphry advises the inexperienced young mistress who has grasped the necessity of 'suavity towards inferiors' and is on amicable terms with Cook to take her along when she goes shopping, 'armed with as useful a basket as that superior person's notions of gentility will allow her to carry'. It was well to let shopkeepers know they were dealing with an informed adversary. Mrs Humphry also suggests, in total contradiction of received wisdom today, that the shopper should eschew breakfast and be hungry when she sets out. I think this unwise: even the usually thrifty buy too much on an empty stomach.

Buckmaster describes another sadly typical scene in the nineteenth century. Dining with a young couple who kept only a waiting maid and a 'very plain cook' (which he thought 'rather strong on 200 pounds a year'), he notes that dinner was three-quarters of an hour late, yet the fish was boiled to rags and the mutton burned to a crisp. Then came the potatoes, improperly boiled and the cabbage, raw. 'My friend,' says Buckmaster regretfully, 'now made use of language I had never heard him use before. "I wish," said he, "that the devil had the mutton and the cook."' His wife threw all the blame on the poor, untaught girl, the plain cook, who had probably never seen a leg of mutton before except in a butcher's shop. Buckmaster said pacifically that although the outside was burnt, 'the remainder will do for hash; I am told it is all the better for not being too much done.' The husband said his wife should have seen to the cooking, she said, 'Very complimentary to know that when you married me you thought you were marrying a cook.' He swore and she cried and left the room. Subsequently the young husband took to dining away from home, spent his evenings with sporting men and playing billiards, became a gambler and a drunkard, lost his job and died at thirty-one in a hospital, 'a cold, solemn death'. The wife tried to earn a living for herself and her child by teaching music, but the child died and shortly afterwards so did she.

In 1847 the brothers Mayhew wrote a book about the Servant Question called *The Greatest Plague of Life*, for which they adopted the persona of a lady called Caroline Skynaston. Mrs Beeton warned of the consequences of being too familiar with the servants, 'It is a bad plan, depend upon it, and often causes disagreeable liberties to be taken.' The consequences are exemplified in Caroline's account of her experience with her cook Norah Connor, who had represented herself as being of Cornish origin since the Irish were then regarded by English employers with extraordinary mistrust and contempt. In the US, advertisements frequently – and well into the twentieth century – carried the acronym N.I.N.A. (No Irish need apply). And so to Caroline and Norah:

Now, for instance, I remember, one morning about two months before little Annie was born, I rang the parlour bell, and when the woman came into the room, I said, in a quiet voice, 'I want a glass of water to drink, Norah.'

'You want to drink a glass of wather?' she replied. 'Well, I've no objection. Drink away, darlin'!!'

'Then,' I continued, blandly, 'I should feel obliged if you would be so good as to let me have one directly.'

'Let you have one?' she exclaimed. 'Faith, an' didn't I give you permission just now?'

This was past all bearing; but I restrained myself, and merely said, with becoming dignity, 'I didn't have you up stairs, Norah, to know whether *you* would permit *me* to drink a glass of water in my own house, or not.'

To which she replied, as familiarly as if she were speaking to the servant next door, 'Well, by my sowl, when I heard you ask me if I'd let you have that same, I thought you mighty stupid at the time. An' what is it you *do* want, then, mavourneen?'

'Why,' I returned, in measured terms, remembering my station, 'I want what I told you before, as plainly as a person could speak – a glass of water.'

'Well, then,' she cried, 'by the powers! if I were you, I'd get it! Isn't there plenty down stairs, honey?'

'But,' I continued, calmly, 'perhaps you will be kind enough, Norah, to bring me a glass up *here*.'

'Och,' she exclaimed, 'so an it's only a glass you're wantin' me to fetch you, afther all! A glass wid nothin' in it, is it you mane?'

'No,' I replied, almost losing my temper, 'A glass of *water*, woman, and *not* a glass without anything in it! Do you understand me *now*?'

'Out an' out,' she cried, with a nasty, low wink. 'You'd be havin' a glass of wather wid somethin' in it! Oh, go along wid you – wanting a drop on the sly, now! You're takin' to the bottle, though, betimes this mornin', I'm thinkin'.'

Norah, it transpires, was in that condition known as – not to say drunk, but having the drink taken – and despite her ensuing remorse was told to find another position. I am particularly fond of this book since it is set in Park Village, just up the road from my house in London, and at the time in which my own house was built. During the course of re-wiring the electrician found under our boards, on each floor, intricate tangles of wire and brass forming part of the bell-ringing paraphernalia which would have summoned the servant to attend on the family members. In the census of 1881 the occupants were listed as Henry

Ford, Surgeon and Head of the household, his wife, six daughters and Regina Hill, general servant.

She must have had her work cut out. Before we arrived and made a few improvements, the kitchen was effectively underground with very small windows, there were no bathrooms and in the time of Dr Ford, the only lavatory was in the back yard: thence would Regina have repaired each morning to empty the slops from the bedrooms before black-leading the grate, lighting the range and making the family's breakfast. Then would come the housework and preparation for the day's meals; an agenda enlivened by visits from the butcher, the baker and maybe the muffin man.

The Dictionary of Daily Wants described the duties of the Maid of All Work: 'A domestic servant who undertakes the whole duties of a household without assistance; her duties comprising those of cook, housemaid and various other offices, according to the exigencies of the establishment.' The subsequent outline of a typical day leaves her, as far as I can tell, with a few moments before tea to wash her face and comb her hair; the rest of the time being entirely accounted for. 'The situation is . . . usually filled by inexperienced servants or females who are so circumstanced that they are desirous only of securing a home or earning sufficient to keep themselves decently clad.'

'Caroline Skynaston' was in the habit of sending to Camden Town for 'Trifles' to crown her dinner parties, which must have saved some time and trouble, and it seems to have been general practice to hang pewter tankards on the railings for the itinerant brewer to fill with Porter. (There is a pale and distorted mirror image of this custom in the way passing drunkards now leave empty beer cans on the next-door wall.) She was further exasperated by a maid who entertained guardsmen from the still-existing local barracks, by having to wear pattens when venturing out on the streets of town in the winter months, ankle deep in mud and horse manure, and was tormented by the smuts and soot from the factories and newly constructed railway, which ruined the washing and blighted the vegetables in her neighbour's garden, but nothing compared with the Greatest Plague – the servants.

These were, in the nineteenth century, judging by my books, often far more trouble than they were worth and generally held in low esteem. It had not always been the case. In olden times the lower orders also ate in the Great Hall – though well below the salt – and in country districts the yeoman's family and workers gathered together in the evenings until the start of the twentieth century. A Carmarthenshire witness said before the Land Commission in 1895, 'There is now nothing of the kind; the servants are gradually losing their character as members of the family and do not remain so much in the farm kitchen. They have little or no domestic life.' In the *Encyclopaedia of Domestic Economy* 'by Thomas Webster FGS, assisted by Mrs Parkes, Author of *Domestic Duties*' (1847), the authors felt it necessary to point out that, 'Domestic servants are a class in society no less essential to its welfare and convenience than the equivalent in subsistence and money . . . In no era of time, nor in any state of social life, has man been able to dispense with the aid of his fellow creatures without losing ground in his progress towards civilization.' Charles Pierce wrote, on a defensive note, in 1863:

> The position of servants cannot be considered as that of under-lings compelled by poverty to bear the badge of painful servitude. Their position is of an enviable nature, if compared to that of soldiers or sailors, both of whom are compelled to endure every species of hardship, and to expose their lives for the smallest remuneration. The position of the servant appears

73

still more advantageous if compared to that of rustic labourers, or to that of many thousands who miserably curtail their span of life in the deadly atmosphere of manufactories.

But all the time more and more of the working classes were seeking other ways to make ends meet.

Around the turn of the century, getting a little desperate, people of the employer class were writing books with sections entitled 'How to make Domestic Service more Popular':

> Mistresses fail to move with the times, and to realize that the ideas and requirements of the working classes have altered considerably during the last few years . . . The young girl of today prefers to become a Board School mistress, and post-office clerk, a typewriter, a shop girl, or a worker in a factory – anything rather than enter domestic service because . . . she enjoys a higher social position: she is in point of fact 'a young lady' . . . Mistresses suffering, as they undoubtedly are, from a dearth of good servants, should endeavour to make domestic service more popular; and in no way can they do this so successfully as by making it more fashionable.

An uphill task.

In 1903, in *The Housewife's What's What*, Mary Davies reminded her readers that:

> All servants must be allowed some time in the day to themselves; they must also have time for fresh air and exercise, and a certain amount of liberty . . . In the present day, very many people complain that they can't get servants, and when they do come, they won't stay. Certainly far more girls go to mills, factories, etc., for work because they have their evenings and Sundays free. As a rule these girls are of a rougher, we may almost say a lower class, than the domestic servant. Mothers

nowadays are much to blame for the lack of good servants. Formerly a cottage girl was brought up to know she must go to service. Now the mother says, 'They may please themselves.'

By 1939, the 'famous and popular author' Dorothy Black was already writing in carefully respectful vein of her housekeeper. 'In days when it is fashionable to moan about how girls turn with horror from domestic work of all kinds – and to repeat sinister tales of unfortunate souls who, having acquired a house and furniture, are forced to jettison it because there is no one to clean and run same – let me point to my Miss Tait.' Dorothy B. feels it necessary to excuse her reliance on this paragon, familiarly known as Joan, by claiming that, 'The hand that writes the story does not guide the Hoover gladly. Or skilfully . . .' She insists that the term 'slavey' and 'skivvy' are utterly inappropriate in relation to Joan and reveals that 'She is mostly a lot better dressed than I am.' The middle classes had been shaken into acknowledging that all men are equal: even the charlady was becoming the 'lady help' and frequently felt entitled to throw her weight around and decide on the terms and conditions of her employment.

Five

AS GOOD COOKS GO . . .

'*T*he trouble about men is that they invariably require feeding and if you keep on giving them Irish stew and rice pudding they get mean and grumpy,' observed an author in the 1930s. This aspect of human nature had been acknowledged by earlier writers concerned that indifferent cookery might cause a rift in the family, imperil the fabric of society and signal the end of civilisation. 'The best-educated Englishwomen of the present day,' Pierce had written, 'scarcely know the *matériel* of an *entrée*, or the elements which give character to an *entremêt*; or can tell when an *hors d'oeuvre* should come in, or a *pièce de résistance* should go out . . .' Thus it was that the clubs arose, 'homes of refuge to destitute celibacy, chapels-of-ease to discontented husbands. There men could dine, like gentlemen and Christians, upon all the *friandises* of the French kitchen, much cheaper and far more wholesomely than at their own tables upon the tough, half-sodden fibres of the national roast and boiled . . .'

Another author addressing himself to the middle classes had

written in 1878, 'A popular idea exists that only those who can afford to give high salaries to their cooks can expect good dinners served at their own tables, and, as a consequence, many gentlemen are driven to dine at their Clubs rather than risk having both their temper and digestion spoiled by the incompetency of their cooks.' Buckmaster says, 'Hashed mutton drives men to dine at clubs and restaurants. It is the horror of most husbands . . .'

Mrs Beeton took up the cudgels on behalf of the 'tired man of business, who returning home after a harassing day . . . sorely needs a pleasant, well-cooked, comfortable meal to await him. If this be delayed, if hungry and as a natural consequence (unless he be superior to masculine failings) cross, small wonder is it if he makes those around him suffer for the fault of the one whose duty it should have been to have provided for his needs.' Having conjured up this chilling image of the man of business, mutton chop whiskers bristling with wrath, she goes on: 'Worse still, it often happens that a hardworking man thus tried, goes from his home to his club, or, in a lower social scale, to a public house . . .' 'How often,' *A Lady* had written in the late eighteenth century, 'the tavern is fled to as a welcome refuge from a comfortless home, and whole families go headlong to destruction.'

The temperance societies which flourished in the reign of Victoria were enraged by the way in which the entrepreneurial owners of the new public houses tempted out the working man, installing gas lighting, engraved glass and plush seating to create an ambience of warmth and colour, all of which contrasted remarkably with the conditions prevailing in the average slum dwelling.

The Victorians, who could never be said to have suffered from low self-esteem, would not have dreamed of questioning their attitude to servants, nor the rationale, whether medical, gustatory or patriotic, that lay behind their diet. Nor, with their high-minded Protestant image of themselves as the ultimate in civilisation and ethical awareness, could they bring themselves to allow that gentlemen might want to go out at night for any other reason than to ingest a well-cooked chop or beef steak. Easier to blame the cook and, in passing, the woman of the house. 'It must be acknowledged that at the present day most ladies of moderate income do not pay sufficient attention to their CUISINE.'

During the First World War and afterwards, with the huge changes in society, cooks had become scarce along with other domestic servants and there was a compensating flood of books aimed at people who would, perforce, mostly be doing it themselves. They had titles like *Kitchenette Cookery*, *Cookery for the Middle Classes*, *When the Cook is Away* and *When Madam Cooks*. In 1915, in her book *Learning to Cook: The book of 'how' and 'why' in the Kitchen*, Mrs C. S. Peel advises the housewife on how to instruct the 'cook-general', a form of hybrid who was expected to help out with the housework as well as prepare the meals. 'If English women of education and intelligence will learn to cook, become competent to teach, and then refuse to be put off with bad cooking, in time England will cease to be a country where the food is good, the amount spent on it great, and the cooking deplorable.' From the sound of it she borrowed her final observation from something said by Lord Chesterfield, altering the content to suit her purposes, which was dashing of her considering the nature of the original remark; but perhaps she thought the young housewives of the time wouldn't get the reference. (As far as I remember it went, 'The pleasure momentary, the position ridiculous and the expense damnable.') It is one of the peculiarities of human nature that when people tire momentarily of thinking of themselves as more virtuous than others, they like to see themselves as naughtier.

Mrs Peel was neither as patient nor as painstaking as the authors of the nineteenth century: 'I will not give more recipes for savouries, for if you use your brains (and unless you do you will never be a good cook) I have now taught you enough to enable you to concoct a great variety of savouries from the material which you have at hand.' The words 'you stupid things' hover, unwritten, over the page. She also gave an early warning about the inadvisability of using bottled Parmesan – it tastes 'only too strongly of rancid sawdust' – and was dismissive of a national institution: 'Personally the British breakfast is a meal which I fail to appreciate. In a large and rich and leisured household it may be a pleasant repast, but in the average small home, where the cook-general reigns, it has few attractions.' I think Mr Peel might have given her some trouble, for she observes acidly that, 'The man who wants two eggs, some fish or bacon and possibly cold ham or tongue cannot be catered for cheaply: either he must pay or go without.' There had been, one gets the impression, some ugly scenes at the breakfast table. I would back Mrs Peel: her overall style is that of a woman unaccustomed to defeat and it would be a brave man who persevered with his complaints. Nor would one readily accept the position of her cook-general. Mrs Peel was keen on thinking ahead. 'Thus the mistress says: "Stewed pears for Sunday. Well, do an extra quantity, and we can use them on Tuesday. And if you make a tart for Sunday, make some turnovers at the same time."' One can hear the unspoken words, 'And jump to it,' and Mr Peel muttering, 'Not stewed pears *again*' as he faces dinner on Tuesday.

Bad cooks were still around and the cause of much domestic strife. In 1931 Sir Francis Colchester-Wemyss wrote, in a book addressed to 'Those Charming Young Women At Cheltenham Ladies College':

Imagine an ordinary household at the end of a terrible dinner . . . the courses have ascended, in a crescendo of culinary crime, from tepid greasy soup to a soufflé like porridge. The mild individual who calls himself the head of the house breaks out at last. 'Araminta,' he says, 'this whole blessed dinner has been the absolute dog's body; you must set about that woman and tell her she's got to cook properly or go . . .' Poor Araminta creeps into the kitchen and after some ingratiating small talk, very coldly received, says in fear and trembling, 'Oh, and about dinner last night, Cook.' Cook, with the light of battle in her eye, demands to know whether she is to understand that there was anything wrong with last night's dinner, and is told, 'Oh no, Cook, dinner was very nice indeed; but Sir Marmaduke, when he was serving in Madras, got into the habit of liking his soufflé fluffy and standing up, so we must try and have them like that instead of the ordinary way.' With that Araminta makes her escape, just pausing *en route* to offer Cook another hour on her night out.

Sir Francis was as concerned as Mrs Peel to instruct young women in the culinary arts so that they could pass on their knowledge to the kitchen. 'To begin with, successful cooking is largely a matter of intelligence. There are born cooks, as there are gardeners born with a green thumb, and born poets. They are generally housemaids discovered as cooks by accident, and shortly afterwards they marry the chauffeur, but an ordinary intelligent person . . . can successfully accomplish quite a lot by means of recipes and cookery books.'

Sir Francis, my favourite representative of the twentieth

century, is as unlike *Anon* as chalk and cheese and exemplifies the remarkable change in masculine attitudes between the nineteenth and the following century. There were still, as there always will be, bigots and bullies, but there was a pleasant respite between the brutal pomposity of the Victorians and the brutish vulgarity of the present. Politeness, modesty and unassuming wit were then accepted as normal rather than as evidence of a poor self-image.

'She was a good cook, as cooks go and as good cooks go, she went.' This phrase, implicit with bitter resignation, was uttered with increasing frequency until Cook finally disappeared from the average household, together with the rest of the domestic staff. One might think that in view of the anxiety and heartache that had clearly been occasioned by the frequent misalliances of employer and employed, the overall feeling would be one of relief – a surprising number of couples suffered from the inability to quarrel satisfactorily when the servants were within earshot, while a lady said of a favourite maid, 'The first year she was an excellent servant; the second a kind mistress; the third an intolerable tyrant, at whose dismissal every creature about my house rejoiced heartily' – but the middle classes reacted as might a newborn herbivore in a threatening and unfamiliar environment: they were unsure of their ability to cope, timorous and tentative, in need of reassurance and advice. Just as they had had to learn how to cope with riches and servants, now they had to learn how to do without.

A booklet put about by Lea and Perrins (7th edition, 1933) begins, 'Hints on entertaining: The young and inexperienced housewife, anxious to entertain, should find the following suggestions helpful.' In a nutshell she should not attempt to do anything too fussy unless she had at least one experienced maid to wait at table. She should draw up one or two simple menus, 'if possible including the guest's favourite dish' (and all, naturally, containing Lea and Perrins Sauce), consider the capability of the maid, the equipment of the kitchen, the accommodation of the dining room and the extent of the table appointments. 'Even in the servantless house a dinner party may be a great success . . . Above all, the woman who is hostess, cook, and waitress must be natural and should not attempt to create an impression or to disguise the fact that she is single handed.' This suggests the possibility of high farce as the housewife darts in and out, variously accoutred as hostess, cook or maid, striving to alter her accent according to character while trying not to trip up with the soup tureen. One hundred years later, as people are forced to realise that even with the most modern of appliances they cannot do *everything* themselves, the need for help in the house is again beginning to be acknowledged – New Man has rather failed to rise to expectations – and apartments are built with extra accommodation for the butler and the maid, and of course the nanny, who can now command healthy wages and respect: the sensible person who needs assistance will seek out someone with an intelligence at least equal to her own and, where possible, with a more beautiful nature.

In 1925 *The Gentle Art of Cookery* by Mrs C. F. Leyel and Miss Olga Hartley appeared and was enthusiastically welcomed for what was considered to be its fresh, revolutionary approach to food and cooking. 'A great deal of the dullness of English meat dishes would be removed if we adopted the Continental and Eastern habit of serving them with purées and compôtes of fruit,' it said, and proceeded to give numerous recipes for hashed (that is, reheated) mutton and beef, brightened up with prunes, cherries, oranges, redcurrant jelly, etc. The authors, beginning their section on meat, announce frankly that they will give no recipes for 'plainly roasting or boiling' but add, daringly, 'though perhaps this is the place to remind people that every joint of mutton is improved by being roasted with a clove of garlic inserted in it'. When Alfred was still a little boy, he once persuaded his mother to put garlic in the Sunday joint of lamb; his brothers – all seven of them – said the lamb was off, the butcher was a crook, their mother had been cheated and they couldn't swallow a mouthful. Alfred neither explained nor apologised, but has progressed over the years to eating raw garlic sandwiches.

One of the more startling recipes in *The Gentle Art of Cookery* is described as 'An Italian Dish' and consists of 'Slices of tongue, raisins, almonds, candied peel, chocolate, vinegar, tomato, sugar, butter,' and begins, 'Fry some slices of onion . . .' It is a horrid parody of, I guess, bolito misto. The authors were greatly reliant on macaroons (which turn up in a reheated ham concoction), ratafias, almonds and anchovies; the last two coming together in a sandwich. Also recommended is a dish of prunes stuffed with smoked haddock. *Just William*'s juxtaposition of sardines and strawberry jam cease to seem so outlandish in this climate of reckless exploration and experiment, although the authors never quite let go of Grandmother's hand ('Many of the most famous dishes are quite old'), even while strewing her, as they did their spinach, with glacé cherries.

The Adventure Book of Cookery for Boys and Girls and for Anyone Interested in Cooking by Moira Meighn was published in 1937 and the author is hysterically, though quite innocently, snobbish. She begins by describing how Aunt Jessica, having seen Marie Antoinette's little house at Versailles decided she wanted one just like it, so Uncle Jasper built one for her. One day, writes our author, 'a boy who lived near the Big House and was a friend of mine caught his first really big trout'. So they cooked it and ate it in the little house and then Aunt Jessica said, 'What about the washing-up?' Our author confides, 'I hate washing-up, especially when it's greasy, fishy washing-up, and there's tobacco ash and old matches mixed with the butter and jam on the plates.' Don't we all? 'Can't Lizzie do it?' she asked (Lizzie was the kitchenmaid at the Big House), thus earning herself a gentle reproof and lecture. Aunt Jessica explained in a roundabout way that 'the reason why Marie Antoinette and so many of the French lords and ladies had their heads cut off during the Revolution, was that they had never troubled to think about saving people from having to do jobs they themselves disliked, like washing up one's own cooking things.' It is diverting to think that if the *ancien régime* had only thought to get on with the dishes they'd have been spared the Terror and the course of history would have been quite different. 'Afterwards Aunt Jessica let me wear her pearls that had once belonged to Marie Antoinette, and she and Uncle Jasper told us marvellous things about meals they had eaten in all sorts of places.'

'Talking of Royalty,' continues Moira Meighn, 'reminds me of a story I heard about Princess Elizabeth, our future Queen, and the real cooking she does in the kitchen of her little Welsh cottage. She always has to do her own washing-up after it! Think of this fact when you feel inclined to leave your dirty pots and pans for someone else to clean!' One might be justified in thinking Mrs Meighn slightly dotty on the subject of royalty ('the cooks at Buckingham Palace and Marlborough House, where Queen Mary lives, always make their sauces like Béchamel did . . .'), and on the less engrossing topic of washing the dishes – but one must make allowances. In the 1930s most people, apart from a few free-thinkers and Bolsheviks, revered royalty: very little was known about their private lives and the little princesses always had clean white socks and well-brushed curls which endeared them to adults. Children preferred *Just William* as a role model, but that's children for you.

On the subject of royalty, here are some of the regulations of the household of Henry VIII:

> His Highness's baker shall not put alums in the bread, or mix rye, oaten, or bean flour with the same: and if detected, he shall be put in the stocks. His Highness's attendants are not to steal any locks or keys, tables, forms, cupboards, or other furniture, out of noblemen's or gentlemen's houses, where they go to visit. Master cooks shall not employ such scullions as go about naked, or lie all night on the ground before the kitchen fire. No dogs to be kept in the Court, but only a few spaniels for the ladies. Dinners to be at ten, suppers at four. The officers of his privy chamber shall be loving together, no grudging nor grumbling, nor talking of the king's pastime. There shall be no romping with the maids on the staircase, by which dishes and other things are often broken. Care shall be taken of the pewter spoons, and that the wooden ones used in the kitchen be not broken or stolen. The pages shall not interrupt the kitchen-maids. Coal only to be allowed to the king's, queen's, and Lady Mary's chambers. The brewers are not to put any brimstone in the ale.

As for washing-up in the '30s, it *was* a nightmare. No machines and no efficient detergents. If you didn't have a kitchen maid you were left to cope with only the aid of hard brown soap and soda and boiling kettles of water, because in all probability you didn't have 'running hot and cold', as this luxury was then known. A dirty plate broken on the way to the sink was often known as one of God's little blessings to the person up to her elbows in scummy water, and the invention of the dishwashing machine has contributed significantly to the sum of human happiness. It also makes one sad to think of the time and effort wasted due to the conviction that dishes should be dried with a cloth as they emerged from the sink; the endless arguments as to who should wash and who dry, when it would have been so much more convenient and immeasurably more hygienic to rinse the plates in order to cleanse them of the foul soup to which the washing-up water had been reduced and leave them to drip in a simple rack. Even when there was a rack, slaves to convention would fondle the dishes with their damp and greasy cloths before stacking them in it.

The most basic advice of all that I have found comes in the *Official Handbook of the National Training School for Cookery* (1879):

1. We should wash the saucepan well in hot water and soda.
    NB – All the black should be removed from the outside and bottom.
2. We must soap the palm of one hand, and rub the inside of the saucepan.
    NB – In washing any greasy utensil it is best if possible to use the hand instead of a flannel, as the latter retains the grease and so keeps putting the grease on again instead of rubbing it off.
3. We mix some sand and powdered soda together, and then dip the soap into it and rub the inside of the saucepan until it is quite clean and bright.
4. We now rinse it in water and dry it with a cloth.
5. We should clean the lid in the same way.
    NB – A white enamelled stewpan is cleansed in the same way, great care should be taken to remove all the stains off the white enamel inside.

NB – Salt might be mixed with the sand and used to remove the stains from the enamel.

Now it is finished.

A book written in the '20s entitled *Silvester's Sensible Cookery* begins with 'Hints to the Servantless'. 'In the first place I hope to help by a few hints the many who in these days are servantless, or who have to leave their homes early for business and return in the evening and find a hot meal . . . Come down in dressing gown a quarter of an hour before breakfast and put a kettle and milk for coffee over a gently simmering burner and they will be ready by the time you are dressed.' You might think that anyone who needed advice in such detail would hardly be mentally equipped to go out to business, but it casts an interesting light on the wholly unprepared state of those suddenly and cruelly deprived of domestic help. 'The beds and windows should be opened before coming down. Place the water in an enamel bowl over the top of the milk saucepan and that will be found hot for washing up the breakfast things and save gas. After breakfast, wash up. To do this wash the silver and place in a small jug of hot water so that your washing-up water will not get cold while you are drying it, then wash the cups in boiling water with your dish washer [this was a little mop].' And so on, with helpful illustrations portraying the zinc-covered top of a kitchen table and a sink basket.

Then comes a dauntingly comprehensive list of 'Kitchen utensils required for a servantless house of about four persons.' This was far more elaborate than the *batterie de cuisine* of a bishop's kitchen in 1262, which consisted of 'a strong table for chopping and mincing herbs and vegetables; pots of brass and copper of divers sizes for divers use; trivets, tripods, an axe for chopping bones; a mortar and pestle, a mover, a pot stick for stirring, divers crooks and pot-hooks, two large cauldrons, a frying pan, two sauce-pans, a large dish [pewter], two large platters [pewter], a vessel for mixing sauces, a hand-mill for pepper, and an instrument for reducing bread to crumbs.' Having dealt with utensils, Mrs Silvester follows with a chapter on 'Food Values'. One begins to think she, too, was not merely not sensible but possibly unhinged with her obsessive compulsion to spell everything out. She was writing at the time when 'Many of us have had to come out of our old groove, and buy and cook for ourselves. The sooner we study the subject, and master it, the better for England – and our husbands.' All those spoilt flappers of the 1920s who had expected to lead lives of leisure, exerting themselves to no greater extent than was needed to paint their nails and do the Charleston, had suddenly to pull themselves together and battle through the Depression, learning how to make such things as 'Mince Souffle (Useful for Invalids)' and a 'Nice Way of Re-heating Mutton'.

In the 1920s and '30s there remained a few 'treasures', but if you had a good cook you lived in constant fear that your friends would try and entice her away with bribes and promises. In *When the Cook is Away*, written by Catherine Ives in 1928 to 'come to the rescue of people whose kitchens have been deprived of their cooks and who know nothing about cooking', instructions are given on how to break eggs and how to prepare fried bacon. Her main concern, however, seems to be to produce food 'to perfection without damage to the hands, complexion and temper of the cook'. She devotes several paragraphs to 'the hands of the cook [which] make continuous demands upon her attention', advises the use of lemon, pumice, tomato juice, oatmeal and a soothing lotion so that any stains or smells caused by fruits and vegetables, particularly the arch enemy, onions, 'are removed at the first possible moment . . . All these precautions are known to most women, but my excuse for repeating them here is that so many people forget to transplant them from the bedroom or bathroom where they live as a matter of course, to the kitchen where their presence is more imperative than anywhere else.'

In 1931, Eric Weir wrote a relentlessly jolly little book with an underlying hint of murderous desperation. He tells of Gladys and Edgar who married in haste as Edgar was leaving by the night boat for the 'most awkward part of Africa'. Gladys follows, and after showing her round the newly built bungalow Edgar asks what she means to cook him for supper. 'I don't know. What is there in Africa?' asked Gladys who hated cooking and kitchens. Edgar said there were eggs and Gladys said she couldn't cook eggs but would play him something from Chopin, whereupon Edgar threw her to the lions. Weir writes of rising prices and falling shares and states that his intention is to help harassed housewives to solve that awful, nerve-wracking eternal question, 'What are we going to have for dinner today?'

During the Second World War the question grew more, or perhaps less, pressing, depending on your point of view, for there was not much on offer and very little choice. The weekly ration allowance for an adult at one point during the War was one shilling's worth of meat, two ounces of cheese, eight ounces of sugar and two of tea, four ounces bacon or ham, eight ounces of fats, which included margarine and lard, and not more than two ounces of butter. Eggs were scarce as hen's teeth. Added to this were any vegetables and indigenous fruit that you could buy, beg or grow yourself as you Dug for Victory, and the National bread, despised – nay, loathed – for its greyish hue but the sort of thing people now visit *recherché* health shops to seek out. There was also the Black Market, and the ruse known as 'under the counter' whereby shopkeepers would surreptitiously pass extra treats to their favoured, or more open-handed, customers.

As rationing occasioned by the War went on, the older and erstwhile wealthier civilians looked back with nostalgia to the days when early morning tea, breakfast, elevenses, lunch (once known as 'noonings' or 'nuncheon'), tea, dinner and possibly a light supper were the norm. Even when the Victorians had gone to their graves, which many of them must – as the saying has it – have dug with their teeth, the general opinion remained that failure to ingest three substantial meals a day could only be deleterious to the health. Elizabeth Craig, in her 1933 masterpiece *Entertaining with Elizabeth Craig*, presumably had in mind those whose fortunes had remained unimpaired by world events since she made no allowance for a fall in standards: all her menus consisted of several courses, with all the trimmings and she offered no concessions. She supplies vignettes of an aspect of life enjoyed by the leisured classes by the time of the 1930s, although 'leisured' seems a misnomer in view of her demands. The hostess who might now be forced by circumstance to be her own cook and, if real misfortune was her lot, her own maid as well, was nevertheless expected to keep up appearances and to entertain morning, noon and night while maintaining a smart, cool and pleasant demeanour. She would, as well as giving luncheon parties, garden parties, tea parties, dinner parties, tennis parties, dance parties, card parties and supper parties, have people to stay (give them breakfast in bed to save time) and remember to do something special on Boat Race Day.

It might seem strange that the enlightened generation, which on the whole had striven to eliminate the more ponderous aspects of the Victorian era from the modern mode, should adhere so closely, if not quite in quantity yet in kind, to the culinary repertoire of their parents. The opulence, the extravagant wealth of ingredients were gone but the basic style remained, perhaps because there is truth in the observation that eating habits are the hardest to change. While some followed the dictates of such sophisticates as Mrs Craig, others clung to the ways their mothers had taught them and trusted to weightier tomes: Mrs Beeton had quietly borrowed much of her material not only from Eliza Acton but several others, and had been reprinted and updated. She lost much of her charm in the process, as divers hands added their own comments and the latest thinking on the subjects under consideration, and still the books kept coming.

In my earliest copy Mrs Beeton had directed, 'As soon as The Mistress hears her husband's step, the bell should be rung for the hot dish; and should he be, as business men usually are, rather pressed for time, she should herself wait upon him, cutting his bread, buttering his toast, &c. Also give standing orders that coat, hat, and umbrella shall be brushed and ready; and see that they are, by helping on the coat, handing the hat, and glancing at the umbrella.' This, I feel, was the real Isabella speaking, and I do not think that Elizabeth Craig would have gone along with her here: the smart woman of the 1930s was asserting herself in her own fashion long before the heavy mob – the American-inspired Sisterhood – lumbered on to the scene.

The human compulsion to press on others the fruits of one's own experience and to offer advice is timeless and eternal, but the cookery book is arguably less harmful than other *How To* volumes. Of all the millions of words written and spoken about cookery, some of the most revealing occur in the booklets put about by the makers of ovens and the various gadgets used in the preparation of food, intimating that no dish could aspire to the peak of perfection unless subjected to the particular processes offered by the appliance in question. The compilers have applied their minds, not only to what their product is capable of, but what the normal person usually eats. In the course of tidying up the attic, I found a manual for the Wee Baby Belling, admittedly of a certain age, but not so old as to be a mere curiosity. (The Baby Belling first appeared on the market in 1929 at the same time as the Aga.)

It begins with instructions on its installation in sensible, measured terms, assuming the words are addressed to an adult, and does not go into the frenzied detail of warnings and alarums now usual as the compensation culture increases its grip on the mentality of the populace. (I once spoke to an oven manufacturer who had been sued by a lady because she'd stood on the oven door to reach the nutmeg on a high shelf and the door had collapsed beneath her.) The section headed 'WARNING' reads with admirable economy, 'This appliance must be earthed.' Then comes information about the grommets and variously coloured wires, how to clean the cooker and the procedure to follow in order to 'expel any odours resulting from newness', which leads one to reflect for a moment, in philosophical vein, on the concepts of new and old and all foregone conclusions.

The recipe section begins with 'TOAST: Turn grill full on for 3 or 4 minutes. Remove deflector plate and toast bread on both sides on an oven shelf as close to the heat as possible.' As my mother would have said, even a man could follow that. Then comes advice on how to boil fish, meat, vegetables and eggs, with a fine disregard of the accepted wisdom that fish and meat react badly to boiling and should, preferably, be simmered.

Cauliflower Cheese ends simply, 'Proceed as for Macaroni Cheese but using the cauliflower instead of the macaroni.' Nevertheless, a beginner in the kitchen would find all this of more use than the present large, shiny volumes with the pictures of food bearing as little relation to reality as the models in fashion magazines. An innocent apprentice in the kitchen could turn suicidal trying to make his dish resemble the illustration.

There are menus for breakfast: Porridge, Bacon and Egg, Toast and Marmalade; Luncheon: Steak and Dumplings, Two Vegetables, Milk Pudding and Fruit; Tea: Buttered Toast, Toasted Teacakes or Crumpets, Small Cakes, Plain or Fruit Scones, etc.; Dinner: Soup, Mixed Grill, Two Vegetables, Steamed Pudding, Biscuits and Cheese, or (one assumes this would not be *and*) Supper: Macaroni Cheese, Toasted Sandwiches, Welsh Rarebit [*sic*], Grilled Sausages, etc. It is salutary to reflect that all this was, for many years, unthinkingly accepted as the norm in most households, even if you only had a Wee Baby Belling to do it on, and obesity was not then a problem. Perhaps the mere effort of preparing it all kept the weight off the cook, while the rest of the family had, at least, walked home from the station or bus stop. Nor were the family members filling themselves up with processed products. I note that the Belling company was 'By appointment to H.M. Queen Elizabeth II, Manufacturers of Electrical Appliances', which reminds one of those sweet rumours about the Queen making toasted cheese for her husband with her own hands.

In the early middle age of the twentieth century labour-saving was the watchword: it was smart and up-to-date to use commercially prepared items like curry, gravy and custard powders in packets and avoid spending laborious hours in the kitchen. The servants had disappeared, but the middle classes were certainly not going to let the side down by being observed doing things the menials would previously have done. With the decline in circumstances, standards inevitably fell, but the only course was to put a brave face on it and make use of all the available technology:

> If your home is installed with electricity, and there are few homes today which pride themselves on being up-to-date, which are not, you can have practically all the household work done for you by electricity. It will clean your rooms, cook the meals, do the washing and ironing and a host of other things without any demands upon you other than what is purely supervisory.
>
> In the interests of your health, your happiness and the welfare of yourself and those about you, as well as in the interests of your pocket, you should not fail to investigate what electricity can do for you.

The old-fashioned, practical apron with its connotations of servitude was out of style and the modern housewife went about her tasks in a fetching pinnie and a cheerful scarf tied, turban-wise, round her curls (lower down the social scale these would still be developing in curlers), indicative of the light and untroublesome nature of her work with vacuum cleaner and feather duster. The Victorian passion for ornamentation, knick-knacks and superfluity was dismissed with, possibly in some quarters, a slightly forced enthusiasm as minimalism came into vogue. Electricity is now taken for granted and earnest cooks have reverted to the old ways and use it to grind their own spices: the 'modern', which never really caught on with everyone, looks increasingly self-conscious and dated as the earnest cook insists on the advisability of rejecting patented, commercial aids to cookery and doing it yourself – if, that is, you do it at all.

In the olden days before all these conveniences were launched on the populace, before cooks even had watches and timing was by guess or by God, the pious would use prayers to time their dishes. One began,

> I fortify myself in this rod, and deliver myself into God's allegiance, against the sore sigh, against the sore blow, against the grim horror, against the mickle terror, which is to everyone loathly, and against all the loathly mischief which into the land may come: a triumphant charm I chant . . . let this avail me; let no nightmare mare me, nor my belly swink me; nor fear come on me ever for my life; but may the Almighty heal me and his son and the Paraclete Spirit; Lord worthy of all glory, as I have heard, heaven's creator . . .

It goes on, appealing, in passing, to prophets, saints, apostles and angels, and ends with a plea for protection against 'the loathsome one, who hunts me for my life'. I don't know what might have been simmering away while all this went on, but it seems certain that any interruption would have brought catastrophe in its wake.

An egg would be soft-boiled in the time it took to slowly say a *Pater Noster* – the old-fashioned version, not the one I saw quoted recently, which commenced 'Our Father and Mother, in whom is Heaven . . .' – while once people timed the infusion or drawing of the tea by the time it took to repeat the *Misere* (Psalm 67) 'very leisurely'.

Janet once said she'd been in the middle of her prayers and found she couldn't remember the lines, so I told her about an old method of testing a witch: you made her recite the Lord's Prayer without error or hesitation, which must have been difficult under the cold eye of the witch-finder. If she failed she was fried.

Six

A LOOK AT THE MENU

$\mathcal{I}$t depends upon your metabolism whether the first meal of the day causes you to feel re-invigorated or whether it induces in you the need to go and lie down. Some authorities insist that a good breakfast is essential if you are to face the morning with equanimity, while many people find that orange juice, cereal, bacon and eggs, toast, marmalade and coffee put them straight back to sleep. It is interesting how didactic people become on matters of food and drink, no matter how trivial. Elizabeth Craig, ever authoritative, goes into minute detail: 'If grapefruit be served, have it at each place with pointed spoon on the side before announcing breakfast.' Still, she was more moderate than Mrs Beeton and her peers whose suggestions, nay imperatives, range from Bacon and Macaroni, Minced Beef and Poached Eggs, through Bloater or Brain Fritters, Cod's Roe, Kedgeree, etc., to Curried Lobster, Devilled Game and Kidneys and Oysters. Rolls and butter, toast and marmalade, muffins, crumpets, fruit, tea, coffee and chocolate would also then have weighed down the sideboard.

Even that pales into insignificance beside the breakfast consumed by Peter the Great and his party at an inn in Godalming in the eighteenth century. They had half a sheep, a quarter of a lamb, ten pullets, twelve chickens, three quarts of brandy, six quarts of mulled wine and seven dozens of eggs with salad 'in proportion'. Admittedly no one 'lunched' in those days and they had to keep going until dinner. When the time for that came round they had five ribs of beef, one sheep, three quarters of a lamb, a shoulder and loin of veal boiled, eight pullets, eight rabbits, two dozen and a half of sack and one dozen of claret. There were twenty-one persons in the party, but it does seem like a lot. The Czar himself had a pint of brandy and a bottle of sherry for his regular morning draught and yet made himself 'an expert and active shipwright, sailor, pilot and commander' and 'changed the manners, customs and laws of the Russians'. He could mend watches too; you cannot help but warm to him. When he was taken to Westminster Hall he asked who 'all those busy people in black gowns and flowing wigs were and what were they about?' On being told that they were lawyers, he was much astonished, exclaiming, 'Lawyers! Why I have but two in my whole dominions and I believe I shall hang one of them the moment I get home.'

Before tea became both popular and affordable, the British started the day with draughts of small beer or, before the Reformation, ale. Hops and heresy grew together, 'With this same beer, came in heresy here' and ale was known as your Catholic drink. The sort that was drunk at breakfast was more or less non-alcoholic, having been through many waterings, like tea made from a much-used tea bag. In 1512 the eleven-year-old Lord Percy and his younger brother breakfasted on bread and butter, fish, salted and fresh, and a 'Potell of Bere', i.e. two quarts.

In the great country houses in the eighteenth century breakfasts were large and late, and no 'luncheon' was expected, although people might take a little something for their 'noonings'. Dinner was on the table by five or six. Round about the middle of the nineteenth century dinner got later and luncheon became more desirable. In the middle classes, even if Papa could not get back from the city and elected to eat in a chophouse, Mama might now take more than a glass of wine and a biscuit and sit down with the children to yesterday's dinner leftovers or she might invite guests and, as it were, make a meal of it. A typical summer luncheon: Fried fillets of plaice, beef roll, salad, gooseberry pudding, butter, cheese, bread, biscuits. A winter luncheon: Curry of cold meat, grilled steak, fried potatoes, apple dumplings, butter, cheese, bread, biscuits. Book after book offered suggestion after suggestion, but few small households would have followed these too closely; using, rather, what they had to hand, and not getting into a lather in pursuit of perfection.

Sir Francis Colchester-Wemyss, striving for the modern, common-sensical approach, discussed the question: 'Probably the best lunch one could have regularly would be a crust of bread and cheese and a pot of draught beer,' though he conceded that people sometimes had to sit down to a long, elaborate luncheon and would be better off with only a couple of courses: say an omelette, a slice of grilled ham and a piece of Camembert; or a half-lobster and a slice of pressed beef; a sole and a cheese omelette, perhaps; whitebait and a nicely cooked chop or a grilled kidney; or even half a grouse or partridge and a cheese soufflé followed by stewed fruit or a caramel custard. Anything more, he feared, might spoil dinner, still the important gastronomical happening of the day. I would now give Elizabeth Craig's views on luncheon and of what it should consist, but I also wish to reveal her ideas about tea – and there are limits to what the reader can digest.

In medieval times it seems that the rich ate huge heaps of meat and bread and the poor subsisted on bread and cheese. (Buckmaster says that the wealthy lived chiefly on wheaten bread, game, eels, fowls, pork and venison, while 'the chief food of the common people' was broth, barley and rye bread, milk, butter, eggs and cheese. The servants were called loaf-eaters.) The menus were not in themselves interesting and hardly worth the attempt to reproduce, merely being quantities of cooked animals and birds, but I once prepared a Roman meal to celebrate a Regius Professor's latest work and used Apicius (almost the only ancient Roman whose cookery book survives) as my guide. It took me a long time. There were numerous small dishes, rather like the present day Greek *meʒe*, and they all called for *garum*, otherwise known as liquamen. I made a substitute with anchovies, honey, herbs and white wine. I couldn't get hold of any asafoetida (also known as devil's dung), so used extra garlic in the dishes calling for it, and I reduced the number of herbs that Apicius seemed to consider necessary. And no small birds, sow's udder or dormice appeared amongst the finished dishes, although I have heard of people who have gone to these lengths in the cause of authenticity.

The Romans never sat down to a 'good square meal', but since they elected to eat in a reclining position leaning on one elbow, they ate those endless courses of morsels which needed no cutting up and could be conveyed to the mouth using one hand. I don't believe I have ever read an explanation of why they did this. It is more difficult to eat recumbent than in any other position except upside down, as the bedridden will attest. Those with spacious dining rooms staged gladiatorial contests during dinner, which seems perverse to the contemporary diner who prefers to eat in peace, requests that the volume of music be lowered, and complains to the management if there occurs unseemly rowdiness at neighbouring tables or children are permitted to riot unrebuked. Perhaps the Roman custom is echoed in the private house where the inhabitants relax on sofas with pre-prepared supermarket meals that need no cutting up as they watch – say – the *Jerry Springer Show* on TV.

At Trimalchio's Feast there were served olives, dormice in honey, sausages, damsons, pomegranate seeds, pork liver, wholemeal bread, cold tart and warm honey, chickpeas, lupins, nuts, apples, bear, cream cheese and boiled wine, snails, tripe, eggs, turnips, mustard and a bowl of cumin in vinegar. The Emperor Vitellus was noted for his appetite as well as his cruelty – he ate three or four times a day, often inviting himself out and costing his hosts a fortune. His favourite dish contained pheasant and peacock brains, pike livers, flamingo tongues and lamprey milt. It is said that he would bolt down meat snatched from the sacrificial altar or brought to him 'smoking hot' from wayside stalls and had frequent recourse to emetics. This type of behaviour was known as gluttony but would probably now be considered an eating disorder and called bulimia.

In olden times quantity was of greater significance than quality, a sign of power and wealth, and there are numerous accounts of enormous feasts, some of them detailed. In 1770, for example, the great Sir Watkin Williams Wynne gave an entertainment to celebrate the coming of age of his son. Here is the bill of fare:

30 bullocks, one roasted whole; 50 hogs, 50 calves, 80 sheep, 18

lambs, 70 pies, 51 guinea fowls, 37 turkeys, 12 turkey-poults, 84 capons, 24 pie-fowls, 300 chicken, 360 fowls, 96 ducklings, 48 rabbits, 15 snipe, 1 leveret, 5 bucks, 242 pounds of salmon, 50 brace of tench, 40 brace of carp, 36 pike, 60 dozen of trout, 108 flounders, 109 lobsters, 96 crabs, 10 quarts of shrimps, 200 craw-fish, 60 barrels of pickled oysters, 1 hogs-head of rock oysters, 20 quarts of oysters for sauce, 166 hams, 100 tongues, 125 plum-puddings, 34 rice-puddings, 7 venison pies, 60 raised pies, 80 tarts, 30 pieces of cut pastry, 24 pound cakes, 60 Savoy cakes, 30 sweet-meat cakes, 12 backs of bacon, 144 ice-creams, 18,000 eggs, 150 gallons of milk, 60 quarts of cream, 30 bushels of potatoes, 6,000 asparagus, 200 French beans, 3 dishes of green peas, 12 cucumbers, 70 hogs-heads of ale, 120 dozen of wine, brandy, rum and shrub rock-work shapes, landscapes in jellies, blancmange etc., a great quantity of small pastry, 1 large cask of ale which held 26 hogsheads.

In the eighteenth century, when people dined at what we would consider teatime, to our eyes they dined oddly. Mrs Raffald, who was born round about 1733 and was housekeeper to Lady Elizabeth Warburton of Arley Hall, Cheshire, gives the first and second courses of a typical repast, with illustrations:

First courſe (Fiſh Remove) – Tranſparent ſoup: Hare ſoup: Pigeonſ Comport: Fricaſ 'd Chickenſ: Marrow: Lambſ Earſ: Catſoupe: French Pye: Pork Griſkinſ: Fricaſaide Veal: Kidney Beanſ: Brocoli &c.: Boil'd Turkey: Mock Turtle: ſmall Ham: Boil'd Peaſ: ſallad: Larded Oyſterſ: ſheepſ Rumpſ & Kidney in Rice: ſweet Breadſ à la Royal: Ox Palateſ: Florendine of Rabbitſ: Beef Oliveſ: Duckſ à la Mode: (Remove Haunch of Veniſon).

ſecond Courſe – Pheaſant: ſnow ballſ: Crow fiſh on ſavory Jelly: Moonſhine: Fiſh Pond: Pickl'd ſmelts: Marblé Veal: Globeſ of gold web with mottoeſ in them: ſtew'd Cardoonſ: Pompadere Cream: Roaſt Woodcockſ:

Tranſparent pudding cover'd with a ſilver Web: Pea Chick with Aſparaguſ: Macaroni: ſtew'd Muſhroomſ: Piſtacho Cream: Collar'd Pig: Croerant with Hot Peppinſ: Floating Iſland: ſnipeſ in ſavory Jelly: Rocky Iſland: Burn't Cream: Roaſt'd Hare.

Everything was put on the table at the same time when, I suppose, the diners would indicate which dish they fancied at the moment and it would somehow be transported to their plates: a person sitting facing the Roast'd Hare and Snipes in savory Jelly flanked by Burn't Cream and Rocky Island (fish-shaped 'Stiff flummery' gilded and sprinkled with 'Silver bran and glitter mixed together' and accompanied by ducks and lambs – it would take too long to explain), might yearn for the Moonshine (flummery in moon and star shapes in lemon cream – 'It is proper for a corner diſh for a large table') at the other end; and whether he would reach for it or it would be passed to him by his fellow diners or whisked round by a servant, I do not know. The arrangement appears inconsistent with the Age of Reason.

According to Charles Pierce, the dinner *à la Russe* was first introduced into France and England at the Peace of 1814, 'out of compliment to the Emperor of Russia. There is no doubt but that the style is ancient, even dating as early as the Caesars, when it was the custom to send the dishes to the table as hot as possible.' He adds that the *hors d'oeuvres* – or provocatives – were also known in Ancient Rome and 'used to be partaken of early in the dinner, with the accompaniment of boiled wine etc.' (Provocatives is a more agreeable word than 'starters' and should perhaps have been retained.) Now everything was served from a side table in orderly progression: the steward, after the soup and *hors d'oeuvres* had gone round, would cut up the fish and hand it to each guest, while a second servant followed with the sauce and potatoes. Then the meat was carved, again at the side table, and presented in small dishes with gravy while the second servant tripped round with the vegetables.

Then came the *entrées* and the second course. Roasts with salad and 'the small pickled cucumber of Russia'; the *entreméts*, savoury and sweet; the jellies, the ices, the *fondue* and the cheese – accompanied by port and, occasionally, by bottled porter or ale. Three types of wine, champagne or punch had already been served. After that came the dessert of fresh fruits, followed by compotes, while the *bon-bons* were handed round last. Then more ices and liqueurs. Then back to the drawing room for coffee and more liqueurs. It was about this time that Liver Salts were introduced and I'm not surprised.

Captain Gronow, a Welshman and a friend of Shelley, described a dinner party held some time in the years after the Battle of Waterloo:

> Mulligatawny and turtle soups were the first dishes placed before you; a little lower the eye met with the familiar salmon at one end of the table and the turbot surrounded by smelts at the other. The first course was sure to be followed by a saddle of mutton or a piece of roast beef; and then you could take your oath that fowls, tongue and ham would as assuredly succeed as darkness after day.
>
> Whilst these never-ending *pièces de résistance* were occupying the table, what were called French dishes were, for custom's sake, added to the solid abundance. The French, or side dishes, consisted of very mild but very abortive attempts at Continental cooking; and I have always observed that they met with the neglect and contempt that they merited. The universally adored and ever-popular boiled potato, produced at the very earliest period of the dinner, was eaten with everything, up to the moment when sweets appeared.
>
> Our vegetables, the best in the world, were never honoured

by an accompanying sauce, and generally came to the table cold. A prime difficulty to overcome was the placing on your fork, and finally in your mouth, some half dozen eatables which occupied your plate at the same time. For example, your plate would contain, say, a slice of turkey, a piece of stuffing, a sausage, pickles, a slice of tongue, cauliflower and potatoes. According to habit and custom a judicious and careful selection from this little bazaar of good things was to be made, with an endeavour to place a portion of each in your mouth at the same time. In fact, it appears to me that we used to do all our compound cookery between our jaws.

The dessert – generally ordered at Grange's, or at Owen's in Bond Street – if for a dozen people, would cost at least as many pounds. The wines were chiefly port, sherry and hock; claret and even Burgundy being then designated 'poor, thin, washy stuff.' A perpetual thirst seemed to come over people, both men and women, as soon as they had tasted their soup; as, from that moment, everybody was taking wine with everybody else till the close of the dinner; and such wine as produced that class of cordiality which frequently wanders into stupefaction. How all this sort of eating and drinking ended was obvious, from the prevalence of gout, and the necessity of everyone making the pill box their constant bedroom companion.

In 1833, *A Lady* was still recommending the eighteenth-century style, adding:

In some houses, one dish at a time is sent up with the vegetables or sauces proper to it, and this in succession, hot and hot. In others, a course of Soups and Fish: then Meats and Boiled Fowls, Turkey, etc.: Made Dishes and Game follow: and lastly Sweet Dishes; but these are not the common modes.

It is worthy of observation here, that common cooks do not think of sending up such articles as are in the house unless ordered; though by doing so, the addition of a collared or pickled thing, some Fritters, fried Patties, or quick-made Dumplings would be useful when there happen to be accidental visitors . . . Vegetables are put on the side-table at large dinners, as likewise sauces, and servants bring them round: but some inconveniences attend this plan: and when there are not too many to wait, delay is occasioned, besides that by awkwardness the clothes of the company may be spoiled. If the table is of a due size, the articles alluded to will not fill it too much.

Dinner parties, in aristocratic circles, might last until dawn and Captain Gronow relates a tale of Twistleton Fiennes, Lord Saye and Sele who, returning home with the milk (as the saying has it) after dining out, instructed his manservant, 'Place two bottles of sherry by my bedside, and call me the day after tomorrow.'

Alexis Soyer offered advice on a truly massive scale; not neglecting the detail. To cook for a regiment of a thousand men you:

Place 20 stoves in a row, in the open air or under cover. Put 30 quarts of water in each boiler, 50 lbs of ration meat, 4 squares from a cake of dried vegetables – or if fresh mixed vegetables are issued, 12 lbs weight – 10 small tablespoonfuls of salt, 1 ditto of pepper, light the fire, simmer gently from two hours to two and a half, skim the fat from the top, and serve. It will require only four cooks per regiment, the provision and the water being carried to the kitchen by fatigue-parties; the kitchen being central, instead of the kitchen going to each company, each company sends two men to the kitchen with a pole to carry the meat.

He relied heavily on salt beef and pork which, of course, had to be soaked before use. 'I should advise, at sea, to have a perforated iron box made, large enough to contain half a ton or more of meat, which box will ascend and descend by pulleys . . . the meat being placed outside the ship on a level with the water, the night before using, the water beating against the meat through the perforations will extract all the salt.' I cannot believe sea water would do much to desalinate anything and, even if it were not a near saturated solution, at the scene of carnage it would be polluted with the bodies of the dead, men and horses. 'The picturesque harbour of Balaclava itself became a sewage pond, in which arms and legs amputated after the battle floated and stank,' as Cecil Woodham Smith put it.

Soyer, his tone resolutely upbeat, does not mention this. 'Amidst the most terrible discharges of cannon, the order for the general attack was announced to the troops for the following day. The news acted like an electric spark and inspired all hearts. Each soldier appeared to breathe more freely; hope, the enchantress, filled the hearts of the brave with enthusiasm; fear was unknown; all faces were radiant with lust of glory and vengeance.' Delight in slaughter seems to have been accepted as natural to the brutal and licentious soldiery until the First World War, when poets brought home a different perspective. Before then it was '. . . war! war! and glory at any risk. Bloodshed, epidemics, destruction, loss of life etc. were matters of little interest.' I like the 'etc.'

Nor did Soyer neglect the officer class. '"We have done fighting," said everyone, "so let us terminate the campaign by feasting, lay down our victorious but murderous weapons, and pick up those more useful and restorative arms – the knife and fork." All appeared to have caught a giving-parties mania . . .' Having been generously entertained, Soyer explained, 'I could do no less than return the compliment, which was of course expected from me, The Gastronomic Regenerator . . .' At the first dinner he gave were present a lord, three generals, three colonels, two majors and a captain, partaking of the following humble bill of fare:

Potage à la Codrington
Filet de turbot clouté à la Balaklava

—

Quartier de mouton à la bretonne
Poulets à la tartarine

—

Queues de boeuf à la ravigotte
Cotelettes de mouton à la vivandière
Rissolettes de volaille à la Pelissier
Filet de boeuf pique mariné, sauce poivrade

—

La mayonnaisse à la russe, garnis de cavea

—

Les plum-puddings à la Cosaque
Les haricots verds à la poulette
Les gelées de citron garni
Les coutes à l'abricot

—

La bombe glacé à la Sebastapol

—

Hors d'oeuvres
Les anchoix — sardines — lamproies à l'huile — Mortadelle de
Vérone — olives farcies — thon — cornichons à l'estragon — salade —
legumes — dessert — café — liqueurs

Why did the *hors d'oeuvres* come at the end with the 'legumes' and the 'dessert'? I don't know. This perhaps serves to illustrate my point about it being simpler to cook for hundreds of soldiers, or in my case, literary persons, rather than a few demanding aristocrats and military top brass, etc.

Francatelli's *The Modern Cook* was originally published in 1846 (my copy is of the twenty-seventh edition and appeared in 1883). The author describes his book as 'A Practical Guide To The Culinary Art – In All Its Branches' and himself as 'Pupil Of The Celebrated Carême And Maitre-D'Hotel And Chief Cook To Her Majesty The Queen'. He 'ventures to offer a few suggestions for the consideration of Epicures. In the first place the English custom of dividing a grand dinner into several courses is an error quite at variance with common sense and convenience. It is a needless complication that necessarily leads to useless profusion, and much additional trouble. Our neighbours across the channel – the best authorities in all gastronomic questions – allow of *two* courses only in the largest dinners.' Not that the word simplicity would leap to mind in connection with Francatelli: he was just being awkward – prey to that temptation to denigrate rival advisers and practitioners that bedevils the professional.

The Victorians, who took such elaborate pains in regard to all their social activities, were particularly concerned with dinner parties. A specimen menu for dinner for between ten and twelve persons compiled by Mrs Marshall went as follows: '*Hors d'oeuvre: Huitres Naturel* [which would at least have saved a bit of time]; *Potage: Tortue fausse claire*; *Poisson: Sole au Gratin*; *Entrée: is de Veau frit*; *Relevé: Côtelettes de Mouton à la Rothschild, Carottes braisées, Pommes de Terre frites*; *Rôt: Poulet au Cresson*; *Entremets: Fonds d'Artichauts à l'Estragon, Gelée à la Belgrave, Fondue au Parmesan*.' Everyone having swallowed their oysters, they addressed themselves to the soup which, in this case, was made of a calf's head that had been left to soak in running water for twenty-four hours. Cook had then boned it, removed the brains and tongue (to make another dish for tomorrow), wrapped it in a cloth, boiled it, skimmed it, washed it, put it in a pan with six quarts of gravy stock, assorted vegetables and spices and simmered it for three or four hours. This was by no means the end of it: there were four or five further stages until you came to cutting out some of the glutinous meat, stamping it in little rounds, skinning them, washing them and dusting them with cayenne before adding them to the soup.

The sole had to be skinned, beheaded, trimmed and cooked in buttered paper in a *bain marie* before being covered in a *gratin* sauce and baked. The veal sweetbread had to be blanched, pressed, stewed and basted, then fried in egg and breadcrumbs and served on a bed of fried parsley. The mutton cutlets you had to smite with a wet cutlet bat, trim and make an incision at the bottom in which to force *paté de foie gras*; then, put them in 'cutlet cases' with the sauce, cut out foolscap paper and grease it to cover the cases, and cook them for twelve to fifteen minutes. And, of course, braise the carrots and fry the potatoes. The chicken was roasted in front of a 'nice, clear fire', frequently basted and served with 'nice, crisp watercress', bread sauce and gravy, and then came the artichoke bottoms which were filled with asparagus points and a sauce made of butter, egg yolks and tarragon vinegar.

The *Gelée à la Belgrave* was made in a mould with lemon jelly flavoured with wine, and required the cook to put pipes in the mould until it set and then fill the spaces thus formed with differently flavoured creams – which could also be differently coloured 'if liked'. The *Fondue* turns out to be a dozen little *soufflés*, with the attendant anxieties about timing, etc. which that implies. After that the company would toy with dessert and then retire to the drawing room for coffee or tea (both were served), negotiating their way between the occasional tables, chiffoniers, stools, chairs and screens that were considered essential to the well-furnished home. The above was regarded as a fairly modest repast.

Mrs Pender Cudlip, in more ordinary circumstances, gave utterance to the eternal cry, 'A short time since I was reduced to the verge of despair by my husband bringing three gentlemen home to dinner one short half-hour before that meal had to be served.' All she had in the house was lentil soup, the remains of a small leg of mutton cold, half a cold boiled chicken, one uncooked sole, two or three lettuces, and some beetroot and a few eggs. The soup was heated, the sole stewed in milk, the mutton minced and half made into small balls and fried, with the rest served on toast and garnished with half a dozen poached eggs; and the chicken was diced, warmed in thickened milk and presented with celery sauce. Then the salad. Though not exactly tempting, this at least sounds realistic.

When it came to dinner in the 1930s, Sir Francis faced the facts, allowing that it would be satisfactory if everyone whose circumstances permitted could sit down to a carefully designed and well-cooked meal some time between eight and nine p.m., but that it seldom happened. 'Take this dinner,' he suggests gloomily: 'Soup, boiled white fish and so-called white sauce, roast leg or shoulder of mutton with boiled potatoes, a green vegetable, perhaps salad, and blancmange (i.e. cornflour shape) with tinned apricots and coffee. Scores of thousands of middle-class English families have a dinner like this every day.' He holds that dietetically it was adequate, '. . . a meal on which heroes may be brought up and flourish. All its constituents are probably of the best; but it is deadly dull, and it is extravagant, because so much more might be made of the materials employed,' but goes on to attack the treatment of each dish in detail, concluding that, 'The coffee is quite certainly dreadful beyond words.'

Sir Francis has, 'One final thought. One sometimes has the sad experience of finding that a guest – almost always a female – demands to smoke between the courses – or does so without asking permission. It is a horrible and disgusting habit, and decent food and wine are utterly wasted on such people. At the time one can only sit and suffer and resolve to put the names of such barbarians on one's black list, and so be safe from them in future. Smoking may be a pleasure, but it is not one of the Pleasures of the Table.' Of course he is right, but a number of my female friends regard eating as a tiresome distraction from smoking.

As the Millennium was approaching Janet was run over by a bicycle in Soho and had to spend some time lying down re-reading the *Forsyte Chronicles* because she'd read everything else. She finds the characters unsympathetic except for Soames and particularly hates Irene, but she did come across some interesting details. In the story, Uncle Lawrence and his niece Dinny, after a walk in the park and a light-hearted exchange about prostitution ('But really, why should these girls be arrested? That all belongs in the past when women were under-dogs'), come to a most absorbing topic – what to eat. They decide to dine in the station buffet at Paddington. 'We'll have a spot of the "boy",' says Uncle Lawrence. (Edward VII, when Prince of Wales, was once at a shooting party where the bucket of champagne was entrusted to a boy. When HRH felt the need for a drink, he would shout 'Where's the boy?', whereupon the Court and hangers-on adopted the phrase and it drifted down through Society). 'And for the rest, if I know our railway stations, oxtail soup, white fish, roast beef, greens, browned potatoes and plum tart – all good, if somewhat English.'

So you might have got a better dinner at the station than at home *and* the trains ran on time. But I think Paddington must have been exceptional: another opinion reads, 'In many of our public restaurants, hotels and railway stations, the greasy messes served as soups, the stuff called coffee, the oxidised pieces of cold meat under yellow gauze, the pyramids of sausage rolls, the skin and gristle between slices of bread and mustard called sandwiches, and the wedges of pork pie are sufficient to indicate the fewness of our resources and the barbarous condition into which we have fallen.' This outburst sounds more like my own memories of the things on offer at railway stations in the 1940s.

Reading *Five To A Feast* by T. A. Layton, a book published by Duckworth in 1948, I came across a chapter on Maurice Platnauer who had become Vice-Principal of Brasenose College in 1938. His was a name that in the early days of my marriage was on everyone's lips; everyone, that is, who had been to Oxford. I might even have met him but at that time I was mourning the lost Left Bank, old Chelsea, and the feckless layabouts who had previously made life so agreeable and I found dons unworthy of note; pale figures bound up in their own arcane diversions. Later I realised that many dons led cheerfully irregular lives and some did fuss about what they had to eat, although few could have boiled an egg, and we might have idled away hours arguing about food. Canon Kelly, I remember, liked his omelette well done, not damp and fluffy but resistant to force.

Layton gives the menu of a dinner Maurice Platnauer had with Harold Cox in his private room at Lincoln. It is an example of the sort of thing that I found exasperating in those early days of marriage – since I now had to cook I favoured the no-nonsense 'peasant' style. Platnauer's menu is pretentious, predictable, pedantic, greedy and not as smart as it makes out – slightly suburban and itsy-bitsy, although I suppose one must make allowances for the times, and there is always something irritating in the style exemplified here. A real man, the Town feels obstreperously, would have given the dinner to the dog and encouraged his guest to get stuck into the drink without scrutinising the labels: '*Bâtons de Foie Gras. Truite au Maître d'hôtel d'anchois. Grand Montrachet* 1929. *Mignonette de Veau Yvonne Arnaud. Château Mouton Rothschild* 1918. *Pluviers rôti. Salade d'orange Verte. Pommes Croquettes. Clos de Vougeot* 1919. *Soufflé Tosca. Rudesheimer Berg* 1920. *Petits beignets au Parmesan. Port Demelles* 1904.'

I know I met Harold Cox because we moved into the cottage he had rented in the Welsh hills when he grew tired of it. The scullery floor was entirely given up to empty bottles which took years to dispose of, but I still have his coal scuttle and I also remember dining with him in his rooms in Oxford because we had Sole Veronique, which means it had grapes in it; it struck me then as a bad idea and still does. Meat and fruit, yes. Fish and fruit, no. Except for the useful lemon and the *groseille de maque-rau* – although there were old recipes for fish with fruit preserve and cinnamon and I have a horrible feeling that someone in the 1930s suggested fried banana with plaice. (My editor has a copy of *May Byron's Pot Luck or The British Home Cookery Book*. Months after I wrote this I was leafing through the pages and out fell the back of an envelope with the handwritten recipe for fried plaice with banana, which leads me to suppose people must have eaten it.) Ah well, *autres temps, autre moeurs*.

Many years ago I read an article in a woman's magazine insisting that the single lady, living alone, should not eat sardines from the tin, standing up. On the contrary, she should go to great pains to eat not only sensibly but elegantly: she should cook herself nourishing little meals and eat them from a table (or possibly, if she was feeling a bit tired, sometimes a tray by the electric fire), laid with a pretty cloth, set out with the requisite cutlery, china and glass, adorned with a candle and a bunch of violets – or whatever she could pick up at the florist's on the way home from business (the article was aimed at the professional woman). In this way, should an acquaintance chance to call at dinner time, the single lady would be found not to have lowered her standards and would command respect for her dignified demeanour. I picture her opening the door of her bedsit, dabbing her lips with a damask napkin. It's the same spirit that was supposed to inform the explorer, dressing for dinner alone in the jungle with the wild beasts snuffling round his tent. The visiting acquaintance today would probably think she'd gone mad. Standards have changed and the solitary diner is usually eating a takeaway in front of the telly with a bottle of Chardonnay to hand. A recent survey tells us that many households now consist of single people: in Kensington, it seems, fifty per cent of the residents live alone.

In 1936, Marjorie Hillis – who was rather like an early version of Bridget Jones – in her book *Live Alone and Like It: A Guide for the Extra Woman*, was writing of 'solitary women (new-fashioned girls, subsisting mainly on old-fashioned cocktails) who seem only to appear at drinking parties and the popular night clubs and whose solitude is undoubtedly dedicated to sobering-up'. I have a strong impression that these girls also lived in Kensington. Miss Hillis did not necessarily approve whole-heartedly of them, but she bears witness to their existence, even suggesting how to take a lover – discreetly – which makes a nice change from the detailed revelations so popular now. She does not advise this move, but acknowledges the possibility, mentioning the thousands of 'prosperous lady milliners, lady dress designers, decorators and agents of various sorts . . . the ten thousand other ladies of breeding who are scattered among the fashion magazines, small shops, travel bureaux, picture galleries, publishing houses and department stores'. If you forget the milliners – hats are out of everyday style – substitute wine bars for tea shops and ignore the 'breeding', there isn't much change.

Eating habits, however, are different now. Few women 'hope to disperse their melancholy by inviting unwary males to dinner at little tea-shops and feeding them on dainty repasts chiefly composed of water-melon, the lesser vegetables like lettuce and water-cress with a thin mayonnaise, stewed fruit and cream to top up with'.

Seven

TEA AND SYMPATHY

$\mathcal{T}$he custom of afternoon tea was inaugurated, so the story goes, by the Duchess of Bedford who arrived at Belvoir Castle bearing a packet of tea, then an expensive luxury. According to Lady de la Warr, she used to invite the other ladies staying in the castle to have tea with her, by turns, in her room. She continued the practice in town and, by slow degrees, the fashion for afternoon teas spread until they became indispensable – the habit begun in the eighteenth century was still cherished by the ladies of the 1930s. Some hold that Catherine of Braganza initiated the custom, while others maintain it is merely a refined version of the cottager's early evening meal and a novelty only in its delicacy and the chosen beverage.

Here is some advice given in 1664 to Sir Kenelm Digby by a Jesuit priest who brought some of the first tea from China:

> . . . beat up the yolks of two new-laid eggs with a dessertspoonful of fine sugar and then mix them with a pint of hot (but not

boiling hot) China tea that has been poured off the leaves. This . . . when you come home from attending abroad, and are very hungry, and yet have not convenience to eat presently a competent meal; this presently discusseth and satisfieth all rawness and indigence of the stomack, flying over the whole body into the veins, and strengtheneth exceedingly and preserves one a good while from the necessity of eating.

Cobbett believed that the poor should stick to small beer and that tea would be the ruin of the working classes. He was not, like some, perturbed to think they were aping their betters but was concerned for their welfare, maintaining that beer carried more nutrients – which is probably true. Soyer took the opposite view: 'Tea is without doubt, one of the most useful herbs ever introduced into this country; it was in the year of the Fire of London, 1666, and has displaced an unwholesome and heavy drink [ale] which used to be partaken of previously, and has created habits of sobriety.' When I was a child, some people used to pour their tea from the cup into the saucer in order to drink it, a custom frowned upon by the well-conducted.

The egregious Elizabeth Craig, who generally addressed herself to the more sophisticated, wrote in a booklet aimed at the rather less privileged:

There was a time when we took a pride in baking our own Bread and Scones, and in filling our own Cake Basket. In those not so distant days, no housewife would condescend to load her table with *bought* Bread and Cakes. Then it was our delight, when friends came to call, to present them with crisp loaves, dainty scones, and tea cakes light as a feather, rich fruit cakes groaning under a cap of frosted almond paste, biscuits, cheese-cakes, and sandwiches that made our name famous.

The making of most 'light as a feather' cakes that we think of as traditional can only have become possible in the late nineteenth century with the invention of the easily regulated oven. A typical receipt from 1834 went like this:

Wash two pounds and a half of fresh butter in water first, and then in rose-water, beat the butter to a cream; beat twenty eggs, yolks and whites separately, half an hour each. Have ready two pounds and a half of the finest flour, well dried and kept hot, likewise a pound and a half of sugar pounded and sifted, one ounce of spice in finest powder, three pounds of currants nicely cleaned and dry, half a pound of almonds blanched, and three quarters of a pound of sweetmeats cut not too thin. Let all be kept by the fire, mix all the dry ingredients; pour the eggs strained to the butter; mix half a pint of sweet white wine with a glass of brandy, put it to the butter and eggs, mix well, then have all the dry things put in by degrees; beat them thoroughly; you can hardly do it too much. Having half a pound of stoned jar raisins chopped as fine as possible, mix them carefully, so that there should be no lumps, and add a tea-cupful of orange-flower water. Beat the ingredients together a full hour at least. Have a hoop well buttered, or if you have none, a tin or copper cake-pan; take white paper, doubled and buttered, and put in the pan round the edge . . . fill it more than three parts, for space should be allowed for rising. Bake in a quick oven. It will require three hours.

General advice: 'Whether black or white plum cakes, they require less butter and eggs for having yest [*sic*] and eat equally light and rich . . . Cakes kept in drawers or wooden boxes have a disagreeable taste. Earthen pans and covers, or tin boxes preserve them best.'

Elizabeth Craig further tells us that:

Earlier still, when Banbury cakes, Bath buns, Chelsea buns, Eccles cakes, Cumberland ginger shortcakes, Pitcaithley bannock, Sally Lunns, Scotch buns, and Yorkshire parkin and many another tea-table delicacy – such as Devonshire splits and Northumbrian girdle cakes – were invented, the recipes were carefully written in manuscript Cookery books by housewives who took a pride in their table.

Let's be houseproud again!

It's not hard to do your own cooking. Given the proper equipment, good recipes, and ingredients required, *any woman can be a good cook if she'll take the trouble*.

I want you all to be good cooks.

Her tone is oddly but compellingly reminiscent of Moses addressing the Children of Israel.

Relating to the better circumstanced she also tells us that the hostess who wished to 'gain a reputation for giving smart afternoon bridge parties' should 'make a point of introducing a novelty every time you give one. The Continental hostess, for example, sends out her invitations on dainty cards emblazoned with four cards at each corner.' Whatever happened in the novelty department, coffee and liqueurs were served beforehand and you had to offer both Egyptian and Turkish cigarettes, as well as a box of Virginians for the many smokers 'who prefer these to the most exotic brands you can provide'. The coffee and the liqueurs were intended as a lure to persuade the guests to hasten to the bridge table from wherever they'd been lunching and by four thirty p.m. it was time for tea – a repast for which the hostess's friend instructs, 'Offer a variety of dainty cakes, *éclairs* and thinly-buttered walnut and raisin bread, and offer at the end tiny *canapés* of buttered toast spread with caviare, *foie gras*, or cream cheese moistened with cream and sharpened with minced pimento and tomato catsup.'

Oh, and tea – *à la Russe* or *à la Americaine* – China, Ceylon and Indian, and when the weather is very hot, iced coffee and cream and strawberries and, 'Improvise a dressing table near the card room for ladies to leave their hats (it is now the fashion to ask guests to remove their hats before sitting down to bridge) and supply a selection of face powder to suit all skins and tufts of cotton wool and pins and combs and . . .'

The list goes on. And you had to have ashtrays on each table and decorative *bonbonnières* with chocolates or other sweets that 'will not make the fingers sticky'. And after that everyone went off to dinner or possibly the theatre, in which case an elegant little supper would follow.

But it is her 'Tea in Heather Time' that ranks among the most frightening of Elizabeth Craig's suggestions:

> If you plan to give a tea in heather time, go out and rob the common of its purple glory, if you have not a garden planted with heather, then hold your party indoors under a chandelier hidden in a shower bouquet of heather, tied in place with tartan ribbon.
>
> There are many excuses for giving a heather tea. You could give one to honour a Scottish bride, someone about to leave for Scotland, or just for the fun of pretending you are somewhere near the moors. A Scottish debutante could give a heather tea for her girl friends. A young matron might change her usual once a month 'At Home' into a purple heather tea. You could, if you like, make such a tea just a golden hour *à deux*.
>
> If you wish yours to be a white heather party, send out your invitations on thick white notepaper. If a purple party, choose a notepaper as near the purple heather shade as possible. Or you could use white with your monogram, engraved in Continental fashion on the left top corner of your notepaper, and on the flap of your envelope, in purple. Only this is an extravagance unless you are willing to make notepaper of this kind your fad of the moment.

Then plan out your table. Use a white or purple linen tea cloth as you feel inclined, choosing tea serviettes to match, or select white linen embroidered with sprays of purple heather, or purple linen embroidered with sprays of white heather. It is best to have white china decorated with heather sprays.

Failing these, select self-coloured purple heather china, and use a silver tea service. Have everything required for the table silver, where china is not used. For example, serve hot buttered Scotch muffins in a silver muffin dish with boiling water in the lower compartment. Serve a Scotch bun, if you can make one, in a silver cake basket. Pipe in white icing a sprig of heather on a large cake of home-made shortbread or Pithcaithley bannock.

Then arrange to serve not only tea, a fragrant brew of muscat-flavoured Darjeeling or Russian Caravan, but iced tea, rolled bread and butter, with curls of young cress peeping out each end, a layer cake put together with butter icing flavoured with heather honey, and vanilla ices, served in scoops in tall glasses, with a hollow in the centre of each filled with run heather honey and masked with whipped cream.

If you are giving this tea in Scotland, serve either drop scones or white girdle scones with fresh butter and heather honey in the comb. If in England, offer any light tea cakes like Cornish splits and honey buns . . . If you want to keep up the purple heather note to the very end, offer purple-tipped cigarettes after tea.

She adds, unbelievably:

In America, the hostess who serves tea makes *more a rite of the function* [my italics] than we do to-day. You would not recognise our homely tea-time meal if you saw the blaze of flickering candles that oft accompany its service in the United States. Over there, too, they make much of the accessories. Not content with tea and sugar and cream, or even with a slice of lemon floating *à la Russe*, they serve with tea tiny plates of seeded lemon slices pricked with one or two cloves in the centre, or thick slices of seeded orange pricked with large Penang cloves.

We once had a most delicious tea in Mariposa County, California, seated at a dining table where the napery matched the china. There were smoked salmon and cucumber sandwiches and two sorts of cake, while outside cougars and bears roamed the primeval forest. Back over the Atlantic tea is not what it was and is found only in hotels or provincial Tea Shoppes. Most people are still at work at tea time and no longer do drawing rooms echo to the rattle of teaspoons and the clatter of fine china, which does not matter in the least: drawing-room tea was always uncomfortable and a challenge to the less deft, since juggling cup, saucer, spoon, plate, fork, milk, lemon, sugar tongs, tiny sandwiches and iced fancies carried the threat of disaster as the participants strove not to splutter crumbs over the vicar whilst striving simultaneously to make conversation.

Sorting through her loft, Janet found an old school book dating back to 1964 or '65. It contained all she had learned in her Domestic Science classes, from how to scramble an egg to how to wash, starch and iron table linen. She had obviously taken the subject seriously and her handwriting was already unusually neat, all of which contributes to its status as an Historical Document. The first page is headed 'To Make Tea' and begins, 'Method: 1) Fill the kettle with cold water, and put on to boil. 2) Lay the table, and see to the food . . .' Janet's tea table would have held, perhaps, Queen Cakes (two ounces margarine, two ounces caster sugar, three ounces self-raising flour, one egg, 1 tbsp milk, two ounces dried fruit), or Butterfly Cakes with icing, Scones and bread and butter. It might have sported a simple Cheese Salad, served 'fresh' with potatoes or bread. Thrift was also still in style in the early '60s and bread, the staff of life, was seldom wasted. Janet's mentors told her the following – to use *stale* bread for breadcrumbs (Cheese Pudding), and to make raspings with the crusts (Apple Charlotte, Stuffing, Rusks and Coating Fish For Frying).

This might all seem amusingly basic, but if children are not taught such things they won't do them and will watch the TV chefs in the same spirit as they watch Paul Daniels or David Copperfield: masters of the art transforming cookery into a spectator sport, and performing esoteric feats of culinary magic, which are not to be tried at home.

Tea shops too are scarcer than they were. I have a book dating from the 1930s explaining in detail how to run one, and even then publishers seldom produced books that perhaps only half a dozen people might buy. It is said that tea shops have been driven out of business by chains of coffee shops rather as the red squirrel has been dispossessed by the grey – not by overt aggression but by the grey's good fortune in finding itself more able to utilise the available resources.

I looked up the history of coffee shops and can tell you that the first English one opened in Cornhill, London, in 1652. I remember when the first 'coffee bars' appeared in the 1950s: a phrase I came across in a Victorian short story was applicable then, as it is now, almost everywhere you don't make the coffee yourself. A character stops at a stall offering refreshment and remarks on a beverage 'surprisingly known as coffee'. During the Second World War, American servicemen were unanimous in their contempt for the English failure to produce a decent cup, and we were shocked and disappointed to find, when we first went to the USA, that the coffee was weak and tasteless – just like the stuff in the American chains here. Arabs and Turks make the best coffee.

What used to be known as High Tea is still presented to children on their return from school in the afternoon only it takes a different form. To judge by the adverts on TV, oven chips and frozen hamburgers are usual, varied by commercial pizza. Once upon a time, high tea implied a boiled egg or sardines or cold ham with salad and pickles, followed by fruit cake and possibly a bowl of tinned fruit. On some tables would have stood a loaf and a dish of butter and on others a plate of bread and butter already sliced. The ancient way with bread was to break it and, if for some reason it was ready-cut, it seemed it was brought to the table in a basket. One knows without doubt that there must have been stringent rules of etiquette governing the presentation and consumption of bread but they are forgotten, perhaps because they appeared too obvious and unassailable to be written down. For instance, it is still held that only an oaf would cut, rather than break, his dinner roll. We are all supposed to know that without being told.

There were dozens of methods of bread-making. One was called *The Rev. Mr Hagget's Economical Bread*, which required five pounds of coarse bran flakes, four gallons of water and 'fifty-six pounds of flour, salt and yest [*sic*] . . . if this was adapted throughout the kingdom, it would make a saving of ten millions sterling a year, when wheat was at the price it stood in the scarcity . . . At the ordinary price of flour, four millions would be saved. When ten days old, if put into the oven for twenty minutes, this bread will appear quite new again.'

My mother used to terrify unaccustomed onlookers when slicing bread since she held the loaf to her chest and cut it inwards: this is the correct and courteous mode, for if she was to stab anyone it could only be herself. Why she didn't cut it on the breadboard I do not know, but I suspect the breadboard is a recent invention. Sliced bread is, as we all know, the most popular thing since . . . but I find it useless except for fairy toast. The slices are always too thick for elegant little sandwiches and more sustaining sandwiches are better made with half a baguette. One of my daughters-in-law saw in Paris a notice explaining the baguette: it seems that Napoleon did not want his troops to have their knapsacks weighed down by large, clumpy loaves, so designed the long, slim sort to fit down the legs of their trousers. I suppose it could be true.

It was said that John Montague invented the sandwich as fast food to sustain him at the gaming tables, slapping a slice of beef between two of bread to keep his fingers free of grease, but no. 'The sandwich is said to have been invented by a celebrated Earl of Sandwich, which is an error. Suetonius, in the life of Tiberius Claudius Caesar, mentions it under the name of offula.' Sandwiches once took pride of place, not only at picnics but also at tea, bridge and tennis parties, and had become an art in themselves rather than simply 'fast food' – as John Montague had intended them to be and is the condition to which they have reverted.

Back in the 1950s, Gretel Beer wrote a book about them, in the days before the proliferation of sandwich bars and before it was possible to buy packets of the things in supermarkets, garages, newsagents and chemists. 'Give a thought to savoury butters,' she advises. 'In their more usual setting – atop a nicely grilled steak, with fish – they are an accepted culinary asset. Yet in sandwiches, where their presence is equally desirable, their existence is often denied to them. They are left off altogether, or worse still, form the sole contents of those miserable little sandwiches which can be identified only by the flag which labels them, and curling at the edges with boredom.'

Those tiny sandwiches flying their flags are now seldom seen at parties, having been largely ousted by *canapés*, but if you're doing your own catering, they are simpler and cheaper and don't curl up at the edges if the savoury butter is lavishly applied.

Sandwiches ready-made for sale have ever aroused questions in the minds of the suspicious. Rightly so. In 2003 the British Sandwich Association (Montague and Suetonius would be surprised, as I was, to learn that there was such a thing) was horrified to hear that 'criminal gangs' supplying corner shops were extracting the fillings from between curling slices of bread, sliding them between fresh slices and returning them to the display counter. 'Oi, Crusher, scrape that fluff off o' that bit of ole cheese and bung it 'ere, will yer . . .' I have always maintained that anything could have happened inside a ready-made sandwich.

It is often said that food tastes better in the open air, but the country picnic is usually attended by cows, wasps (never drink out of the can on these occasions for a wasp might well have insinuated itself through the opening) and threatened by cloudbursts. Brewer gives a suggested origin for the term 'A pretty kettle of fish': 'An old Border name for a kind of *fête champêtre*, or riverside picnic, where a newly caught salmon is boiled and eaten. Sir Walter Scott wrote in *St. Ronan's Well*, "As the whole company go to the water-side today to eat a kettle of fish, there will be no risk of interruption." The discomfort of this sort of party may have led to the phrase describing an awkward state of affairs, a mess, a muddle.' Brewer was clearly another who took a jaundiced view of picnics.

The concept is so perverse that most people suppose it to be peculiarly English, for surely no other nationality would elect to eat in a field at the mercy of the elements and insects unless under duress – previously only beggars, gypsies, harvesting peasants or armies on campaign would have sat down and eaten without a roof over their heads. However, the origin of the word, we are told, is French: *pique-nique*. My informant has no idea where that originated from and nothing more to say on the subject, but then we remember the *fête champêtre* and think of Marie Antoinette and her court, all of them – men and women alike – wearing high heels, which go a long way towards adding to the discomfort of the picnic or garden party by sinking into the earth and upsetting the balance. Call for a tumbril, Jacques. Victorian picnics were huge, elaborate affairs with footmen and lobster patties, etc., etc., etc. They must have driven the servants mad.

The garden party still suggests the need for dressing-up, which incurs the risk of getting salad dressing on your chiffon as your hat blows away and your feet sink into the lawn. We were once asked to one at Buckingham Palace: the books of etiquette say this amounts to a Royal Command and you must have an iron-clad excuse for refusing the invitation. This seems high-handed and I threw away the card from the Comptroller of the Household. Post-lapsarian garden parties are folly, no fun for the daughters of Eve and hard on the herbaceous border.

And so to the cocktail hour: 'Here is a recipe for a delicious cocktail that is not too "heady". Mix together equal parts of gin, French vermouth and cointreau, and ice well,' says one sugges-tion. From Elizabeth Craig, writing at about the same time in

1933: a half portion each dry gin and French vermouth; two dashes each absinthe and Angostura bitters; four dashes Benedictine – to be served very cold. She calls this a 'Pen Club Cocktail', which suggests that the writers of the 1930s might have been rather more dashing than those of the following generation – the World of Books struck me as strait-laced after the society of painters; Dylan Thomas had gone away and died just before I arrived in Chelsea. Elizabeth adds, 'You can drink two and go home, but if you take three you won't want to go home.' Absinthe is made from wormwood and was invented in Switzerland in the late eighteenth century. *L'Absinthe Rend Fou*, and it certainly makes you fall over. 'The aperitif used to be drunk in large quantities in France. It is said to be extremely bad for the liver,' another writer notes, and, of course, absinthe makes the heart grow fonder.

In 1887, *Spons Household Manual* advised, 'When liqueurs are handed with the ices young ladies are not expected to take them, and, a young lady would not drink more than half a glass of sherry with soup or fish, one glass of champagne during dinner, or a glass of sherry if champagne is not given, a half a glass of sherry at dessert. A married lady would perhaps drink a glass and a half of champagne at dinner, in addition to a glass of sherry with fish or soup. Some ladies drink less than this, and others perhaps a little more . . .' So they do.

Marjorie Hillis entitled one of her chapters 'A Lady and her Liquor'. She writes, 'Practically anybody old enough to read these words can remember when few, if any, ladies drank . . . Today, the woman who doesn't drink is more apt to have high blood-pressure than moral prejudices . . . For breaking ice, mixing strangers and increasing popularity, alcohol is still un-rivalled, Mrs Grundy and all her willing workers to the contrary.' Sixty-odd years later the young are surprised to hear these cheerful sentiments, imagining that they are the first generation after Cromwell to have a good time. Some have gone too far and those who take it upon themselves to worry about these things, are concerned that the young female of today is doing herself a mischief by getting drunk at every conceivable (there is indeed a pun here) opportunity and ruining her chances of a healthy maturity. Commentators not known for prudishness noted, at Ascot Ladies' Day in June 2003, that many young women, apart from falling out of their frocks fore and aft, were hell-bent on getting legless and thereafter laid – just like the lads – which may be considered equality but looks more like foolishness.

Marjorie Hillis does sound a note of caution. Of Mrs E., 'an optimistic widow . . . [who] extemporizes in the matter of mixing odd bits from the vast array of bottles assembled by Mr E.,' she warns: 'The neighbours complain of occasional uproars disturbing the nights in the vicinity of her house. Her friends are beginning to talk about the run-down look caused by stains and cigarette burns on the furniture, and the police have been known to call and inquire into the commotion.' To avoid this embarrassment Marjorie Hillis gives a list of 'the essential bottles'. These contain sherry, gin, Scotch whisky, rye, French and Italian vermouth and bitters. 'While you are still learning, never buy anything but the best.' She adds, 'Don't think either, that it would be nice to have some unfamiliar cocktail for variety. Your guests won't agree with you.' She also warns her readers not to offer so many cocktails that the guests won't appreciate their dinner and concludes, 'Whatever you do, don't let the cocktail hour be a bore to you. Its purpose in life is to inject a little gaiety into a weary world, and if it doesn't do that for you, you might as well get your fun out of wearing a blue ribbon and making soap-box speeches for the temperance league.'

From *The Sons of Temperance and Cadet Songster* (circa 1890) comes a song:

> You may with safety, some folks think,
> Just take a little drop;
> But if you once commence to drink,
> Where are you going to stop?
>
> . . . We'll sing, yes, sing of Temp'rance sweet,
> And roll her praise along;
> While here we all together meet,
> A happy joyous throng.

The note of desperate gaiety is tragically unconvincing, but the question at the end of the first verse is a legitimate one and alcohol undoubtedly caused problems in the nineteenth century. The poor drank (mostly cheap gin) in an effort to distance themselves from the dreadfulness of their lives and many of the rich were alcoholics. The awful Helen Huntingdon in *The Tenant of Wildfell Hall* gave her child wine spiked with tartar emetic in order to put him off drink, which would, one imagines, have served rather to put him off his mother. Some people binged and some 'soaked' – that is, quietly drank from dawn till dusk without making too great a spectacle of themselves. In 1909, in *The Merry Past*, Ralph Nevill wrote of the early nineteenth century that, 'At that time drunkenness was not viewed with the same severity as it is today, when very rightly it has come to be regarded both as a social nuisance and a destructive malady. All classes were tainted with it . . .' A century earlier Queen Anne had been given the nickname 'Brandy Nan', and her statue which stood between St Paul's and a gin palace was adorned with some early graffiti:

Brandy Nan, Brandy Nan, left in the lurch,
Her face to the gin-shop, her back to the church.

Indian Domestic Economy and Cookery says Rum Fustian is prepared at Oxford as follows: 'Whisk up to a froth the yolks of six eggs and add them to a pint of gin and a quart of strong beer; boil up a bottle of sherry in a sauce-pan, with a stick of cinnamon or nutmeg grated, a dozen large lumps of sugar, and the rind of a lemon peeled very thin; when the wine boils, it is poured upon the beer and gin and drank hot.' I don't know why this beverage is called Rum unless the author intended it as an adjective in the sense of 'odd'. If he was searching for a term he might well have settled on pernicious. We once knew a man who habitually poured a tot of gin in his pint of mild, but I don't know what became of him. Gin tends to have a confusing effect, I find. Janet and I once celebrated New Year with friends of my fourth son in Mariposa. Our hostess gave us martinis with an oily viscous quality; the gin writhing visibly like a snake in the glass. We don't remember anything else.

Soyer, in the midst of war, suggests, *Crimean Cup à la Marmora*:

Proportions: Syrup of orgeat, one quart; cognac brandy, one pint; maraschino, half-a-pint; Jamaica rum, half-a-pint; champagne, two bottles; soda-water, two bottles; sugar, six ounces; and middling-sized lemons.

Thinly peal [*sic*] the lemons, and place the rind in a bowl with the sugar; macerate them well for a minute or two, in order to extract the flavour from the lemon. Next squeeze the juice of the lemons upon this, add two bottles of soda-water, and stir well till the sugar is dissolved; pour in the syrup of orgeat, and whip the mixture well with an egg-whisk in order to whiten the composition. Then add the brandy, rum, and maraschino; strain the whole into the punch-bowl, and just before serving add the champagne, stir well with the ladle: this will render the cup creamy and mellow.

Half the quantity given here, or even less may be made; this receipt being for a party of thirty.

The drink my husband himself prepared became known as 'Colin's Killer'. It was only a 'champagne' cocktail made with a lump of sugar, a few drops of Angostura, a measure of brandy and sparkling wine. I don't know quite why, but it was extraordinarily intoxicating. *The Dictionary of Daily Wants* notes,

> Though one of the most delicious wines, champagne ought to be indulged in with great caution. The piquancy of flavour and the sparkling brilliancy, are mainly derived from the presence of an acid, which, if not counteracted, is productive of deleterious consequences . . . and stimulates the stomach to a greater action than it can well bear. Habitual indulgence has a tendency to produce gout, apoplexy, &c., with all the accompaniments of a deranged digestion. A few grains of carbonate of soda thrown into the wineglass will obviate some of the ill effects, although it somewhat interferes with both the taste and appearance of the wine.

Another author, having remarked on 'the great and increasing intercourse between this country and the Continent' and the 'probable relaxation of the duty on foreign wines' goes on to foresee an increase in their consumption at the dinner table and 'cannot refrain from alluding to an injudicious habit, frequently adopted at English tables – that of introducing *sweet* champagne in the First Course'. He says Madeira, Sherry and Burgundy are better suited at this stage, 'Their stimulating and generous qualities tending considerably to aid digestion.' The French don't touch their champagne until 'the latter part of the Second Course', by which time 'the palate has become more fit to appreciate the delicate *bouquet* of this delicious and exhilarating beverage'. I confess I am not an oenophile and prefer beer, but the only clash of flavour I am personally aware of, the results of which are undeniably calamitous, is that between red wine and a globe artichoke.

The Dictionary of Daily Wants again:

> It is customary at dinner parties and other repasts among the higher classes, for the assembled guests to take wine with each other . . . When you are about to take wine with a person, you select a favourable moment and say to the person, 'Mr So-and-so, I should be happy to take wine with you'; the person thus addressed, replies 'With pleasure.' The challenger and the challenged then fill their glasses, raise them at the same moment, and bow towards each other in silence.

If you wish to get a lady tiddly (for this must often have been the consequence), you ask her what sort she would prefer and 'call upon the gentleman sitting next to her to see that her glass is replenished . . . Mutual acquaintances might ask permission to "join in" and each wait until the glasses are filled and bow to one another in due order . . . Certain laws are laid down which it would be considered very vulgar to break. For instance, a senior in age, or a superior in rank always claims the initiative . . .' And you had to think about 'the timing of the raising of the glass, the catching of the eye, the bow and the expression that accompanies it . . . to avoid the appearance of awkward and uncouth behaviour'.

He whom Janet calls Beloved is a member of a golf club where the custom was honoured. As the evening drew on and all the possible permutations got wilder, he says he waited in expectation of the inclusion of the greenkeeper's dog. He knows a bank robber who once, musing over a bottle, observed that as his knowledge of French led him to believe that *chat* meant cat and *eau* meant water; it gave him furiously to think. In the *Concise Household Encyclopaedia*, 'Chablis' follows 'Cesspool'. Nella Whitfield in the *Kitchen Encyclopaedia* provides the following on nightcaps:

> The idea of nightcaps, or soothing hot drinks with which to finish the evening, seems to be quite an English one and probably originated from the fact that our bedrooms were once so cold that it was necessary to take a warming drink to induce sleep – otherwise one might lie awake and cold for a long time.
>
> The 'caps' varied from the ordinary hot toddy of rum and water, or home-made cordial and hot water, to the more elaborate drinks we usually call punch. Several of these drinks still have ecclesiastical names:
>
> *Bishop* is made with port wine, an orange stuck with cloves and roasted until the skin is brown and shrivelled (giving a lovely perfume), with other spices and with a little hot water, the whole brought almost to boiling point, but never allowed to boil.
>
> *Lawn Sleeves* is another version of bishop, made with sherry, a lemon and calves' foot jelly, rich enough for an invalid as well as a bishop.
>
> *Cardinal* is the same, but a rich red claret is used instead of port or sherry.
>
> *Pope* is luxurious, but not as heartening, since champagne and no calves' foot jelly is used.

Eight

IN THE SOUP

In the sixteenth century Andrew Borde explained simply that, 'potage is made of the liquor in which flesh is sodden, [which] with putting to it chopped herbs, if they be pure, good and clean, not worm eaten, nor infected with the corrupt air descending upon them, doth comfort many men, ventosity notwithstanding. Pease potage and bean potage doth replete a man with ventosity, albeit they be competent of nourishment.'

Dr Kitchiner wrote:

The cook must pay continual attention to the condition of her Stew-pans and Soup-kettles, &c. – which should be examined every time they are used. *The prudent housewife will carefully examine the condition of them herself at least once a month.* Their covers also must be kept perfectly clean and well tinned, and the Stew-pans not only on the inside, but about a couple of inches on the outside: – many mischiefs arise from their getting out of repair: and *if not kept nicely tinned, all your good work will be in vain*: the Broths and Soups will look green and dirty, taste bitter and poisonous, and will be spoiled both for the Eye and the Palate, and your credit will be lost. The Health, and even the Life of the Family depends upon this . . . Though we do not suppose our Cook to be such a naughty Slut as to wilfully neglect her Broth-Pots &c. yet we may recommend her to wash them immediately and make sure they are thoroughly dried at the fire before they are put by . . .

He was not exaggerating: many people were poisoned by the copper in insufficiently tinned utensils, and quite recently a letter was published in a newspaper from a lady concerned that her pans were making certain foodstuffs turn out a funny greenish colour. The chef to whom she had addressed herself responded breezily that it didn't matter. I hope she's alright. It is all very fine and large to cook in traditional ways using traditional articles but you have to know what you are doing. For instance, it is unwise to start the pickling process by putting the thing to be pickled in an old earthenware crock and pouring in vinegar: the acid, I am told, can release the arsenic from the glaze. As *A Lady* warned in her oft-reprinted *A New System Of Domestic Cookery. Formed Upon Principle of Economy And Adapted To The Use Of Private Families*, 'Vegetables soon sour, and corrode metals and glazed red ware, by which a strong poison is produced. Some years ago, the death of several gentlemen was occasioned at Salt-hill by the cook sending a ragout to the table which she had kept from the preceding day in a copper vessel badly tinned. Vinegar by its acidity does the same, the glazing being of lead or arsenic.' As for those Victorian cast-iron pans – I have six and can barely lift the largest when it's empty. God alone knows how Cook coped when it was brimming with scalding soup.

In 1827, Mrs Christian Isabel Johnstone published *The Cook and Housewife's Manual*, adopting the nom de plume of Mistress

Margaret Dods of the Cleikum Inn, St. Ronan's. It is a long story, but Meg Dods was a character in Sir Walter Scott's novel *St. Ronan's Well*, one of his less stirring tales, but notable for the portrayal of Meg, whose tongue 'when in full career, was audible from the Kirk to the Castle'. She was a no-nonsense type of old Scots hostess: 'In single blessedness and with the despotism of Queen Bess herself she ruled all matters with a high hand.' Sir Walter entered into the spirit of Mrs Johnstone's harmless deception with the relish for little games and conceits so typical of the time, and contributed an introduction to the second volume.

The section on soup is headed '*C'est la soupe qui fait le soldat*'. (This is one of Napoleon's *aperçus*.) Mrs Johnstone begins, 'Soup has been aptly termed the vestibule to a banquet. [The snooty still maintain that soup as a luncheon course is vulgar.] We call it the softest foundation to the principal repast of the day, whether it be a Cottage or a Cabinet dinner. With this belief we hold as maxims, that the French take the lead of all European people in *soups* and *broths*; that the Scotch rank second, the Welsh next; and that the English, as a nation, though with many honourable exceptions, are at the bottom of the scale.'

In 1903, in *The Young Woman*, Mary Halliday wrote about having seen a little book entitled *Every Man his own Lawyer* – I believe I have a copy – and suggests, 'Why not *Every Woman her own Cook*. Some day, doubtless, it will come to that, and even as things are now, the mistress herself does the cooking in most middle-class homes.' She goes on to deplore the 'wrong or foolish feeding' which is 'probably at the root of the delicacy prevailing among young children in the present day – either through ignorance (which can be remedied) or carelessness (which is unpardonable) they are often most unsuitably fed', and advises giving them oatmeal, since to her mind there was nothing to equal the old-fashioned porridge. Many reliable nutritionists favour oatmeal as a valuable part of the diet, and the races who once ate a lot of it grew hale and hearty before they were seduced by white bread, etc., so that is incontrovertible, but I wish I knew what she meant by 'unsuitably fed'. It might be that some reckless mothers were giving their children things other than pap — meat and vegetables — before they were two years old, in contravention of the current wisdom.

Mary Halliday then goes on to soup, remarking, again without risk of contradiction, that: 'The woman who wishes to be thrifty should certainly patronize soups as do the Scotch, the French and indeed most of our neighbours on the Continent.' She states that in England, at least among the middle-classes, soup seems to be regarded as a luxury and is rarely seen on the table: 'The average cook has but one, or at the most two, in her repertoire — a dirty brown fluid, slightly thickened with tapioca, and tasting only of pepper, is perhaps the most usual.' She then says, according to the mores of the time, that hardly anything comes amiss in the stock-pot, but redeems herself by recommending vegetable soups without any meat at all, although 'if one is not really a vegetarian on principle, dripping can be used instead of butter for the preliminary frying . . . The great objection to thick soups — from the busy woman's point of view — is that it is absolutely necessary to press them through a hair sieve.' I did that before I got a hand-operated Mouli and now we have a food processor, so in one small way life has got simpler.

In the view of the inimitable *Anon*: 'Thick soups are not to be tolerated; it is very well to give those kind of soups to cricketers, boat rowers, and the like, but it is not allowable to choke your guests off their dinner.' He gives a recipe for Hotch Potch (mutton and various vegetables) — 'If it should be too thick it may be thinned with a little hot water. N.B. I have seen this put on the table in Scotland with grouse soup, when every person refused the latter, but greedily partook of this.' My lawyer tells me that hotchpotch is also a term for some ungraspable legal something or other.

Milton, who wrote some of the most annoying and theologically unsound words ever penned (e.g. 'He for God only, she for God in him'), is quoted in *Things A Lady Would Like To Know*:

> Nothing lovelier can be found,
> In Woman, than to study household good,
> And good works in her husband to promote.

The opening section of the above work consists of similar reflections. It starts with Proverbs and ends with the views on women of the Rev. C. J. Vaughan, who 'inclines to think that, in grasping at power, she will lose influence; and that though the novelty may dazzle for a moment, in the end the performance will disappoint the promise.' Having got that out of the way, the author goes on to lay down the rules, beginning with cookery. Don't buy diseased meat, he advises, it has a 'sickly, cadaverous smell, and sometimes a smell of physic [which is] discoverable when the meat is chopped up and drenched with warm water.' The hint of the presence of 'physic' is interesting in view of our present worries about antibiotics, hormones, etc. in meat. He repeats the then general and frequently quoted opinion that, 'The chief art of making good soup lies in the judicious blending of the different flavours, so that nothing shall predominate' (his 'vegetable soups' were based on shin of beef, hock of ham, or some other part of an animal). *A Lady* states implacably: 'The perfection of soup is, that it should have no particular flavour.' Liebig wrote, 'Soup is the medicine of the convalescent. No one estimates its value more highly than the hospital physician, for whose patients soup, as a means of restoring the exhausted strength, cannot be replaced by any other article of the "Pharmacopoeia". Its vivifying and restoring action on the appetite, on the digestive organs, the colour and general appearance of the sick, is most striking.'

'The soup,' wrote an author in the 1920s, seemingly unaware of the views of Liebig (who anyway had a vested interest in soup), 'has up to within a few years been considered an accessory – something with little or no food value, to be used either as an adjunct to an elaborate meal or when there was nothing else in the house.' The anonymous author was American but was describing an English (not British – the Welsh and Scottish ate up their soup), post-Industrial Revolution attitude. Soup as a meal was, in the opinion of many, fit only for the Poor or foreigners. (Eliza Acton had written in a footnote, '. . . the popular taste in England, even at the present day [1868] is far more in favour of what is termed *substantial* food, than any kind of pottage.') Concerned observers visiting in rural cottages had wrung their hands and torn their hair at the spectacle of the woman of the house boiling a bit of meat and throwing out the liquor. 'To be sure,' continues our American, 'the familiar clear soup contains very little that is nutritive,' but if you add a little of the soup meat and some vegetables and 'toasted squares' of bread or dumplings, it becomes a 'balanced meal in itself, needing only a little fruit to round it out.'

She too was unable to rid herself of the conviction that no soup could be beneficial to the system unless it had a meaty basis and racked her brain for ways of using not the liquor, but the flesh that had flavoured it. 'Many have felt that the meat left from the making of soup stock or broth was not only tasteless, but that it had lost all its nutritive value.' Not so, she insists: mix it with a salad dressing or 'something of that nature' and eat it up.

Or turn it into Hungarian goulash, hash, meat cakes, meat loaf or croquettes. In France, with dishes like *pot au feu*, you can eat the soup and follow it up with the meat and vegetables nicely laid out on a plate: a mode the English never adopted in the right spirit. I once had a terrible dinner consisting of mutton broth followed by mutton. It was a long time ago but the memory lingers on. Anyway, meat soups are now largely out of style and few people derange themselves to the extent of making consommé or beef bouillon, let alone preparing a meat stock to serve as a vehicle for something else. Nicolas de Bonnefons in 1654 had the right idea: 'Let a cabbage soup smell and taste of cabbage; a leek soup of leeks, a turnip soup of turnips.' Eliza Acton's 'parsnep' soup calls for a quart of veal stock and is followed by the observation, 'We can particularly recommend this soup to those who like the peculiar flavour of the vegetable.' By peculiar she means, of course, distinctive, but it's more satisfyingly peculiar without the veal.

I was sixteen when I had vegetable *potage* for the first time. It was not long after the War in a place in the Haute-Savoie called Villard de Lans. We had stayed one night in Paris in a sort of youth hostel and been served an even nastier soup than those I was accustomed to. 'Brown Windsor', in hotels often seemingly composed of the dregs from the gravy boats which had graced the week's dinner tables, was much eaten in England at the time – it was never drunk: the former butler of the late Princess Diana, advising on matters of etiquette in a magazine, was asked by one correspondent whether soup was 'eaten' or 'drunk'. He responded that the royal family sometimes tackled theirs with a spoon and sometimes drank it out of cups – which was not what the questioner wished to know: she wanted to know which word was the one used in polite society. Even if they were drinking it they should, to be correct, say they were eating it, and they used to slurp it out of large tablespoons. Not that it matters much in the eye of eternity and, except for tinned tomato, most soups were still considered ineffectual if they didn't have some kind of meat stock in them to give them a bit of literal backbone, but the Parisian soup surpassed them all. It was thin and brown, an impossibly distant relation of consommé, and was served in tin bowls with tin spoons and tasted of tin; and then we arrived at a small, traditional inn on an Alp and found bowls of herb-flavoured, thick, potato soup steaming before us, something entirely different from anything we knew.

Why the British had never thought of treating the potato in this fashion must be due to something in the national character and can probably be traced back to the Reformation. Dr Borde had remarked, 'potage is not so much used in all Christendom as it is used in England' which, as a later commentator observed, is odd, since soup-making was, by his time (between the wars), seen as 'so essentially an accomplishment of the Continental housewife'. When the country was in need of recruits for the Boer War, sixty per cent were rejected as physically unfit, the main cause for this state of affairs being malnutrition. It was concluded that although the English working man earned more than his continental counterpart, he was worse fed. Sir John Gorst, MP, declared, 'Nothing is more deplorable than the general English labourer or labourer's wife in the presence of food. Where a Frenchwoman would make an excellent dinner an

Englishwoman would almost starve ... I have been in a great many poor people's homes in both England and France and I should say that, although an Englishwoman spends a great deal more on feeding her family than the Frenchwoman, the Frenchwoman gives them a great deal more food.' Indeed, the French had felt that their defeat in the Franco-Prussian War of 1871 had its roots in the malnutrition that was prevalent throughout nineteenth-century Europe. They introduced guidelines, which emphasised the need for good food for infants, children – including the introduction of school meals – and their mothers.

Buckmaster gives two versions of what he calls *Bonne Femme* soup: the posher one has lettuce, sorrel, tarragon, chervil, cucumber, butter, white stock, three egg yolks, cream and the crust of a French roll. For both soups he makes the observation, 'Great care must be taken to prevent the vegetables discolouring or burning and the soup must not boil after adding the *liaison*.' I was once given a green and leafy soup in Egypt (it is famous but I cannot remember the name of the herb) and was told that if I was Welsh I would undoubtedly appreciate it: I found this surprising, not having suspected this culinary link between the people of Alexandria and the people of Llanrheaedr Ym Mochnant. (My Egyptian surgeon and my friend Donna have since both reminded me that it is called Molukhia.) Janet makes cold tomato soup with a tin of tomatoes, fresh garlic, minced ice and whatever herbs, chopped, that she has to hand. This takes less time than *gazpacho*, which can be a nuisance to prepare. Just don't pretend that you are following the Spanish mode.

I once acquired, for a mere two pounds and fifty pence, five pounds of mutton, roughly chopped, with bones, from an East End stall and thought I'd do something exotic with it. Looking through *Indian Domestic Economy and Cookery* in search of a receipt for that famous Victorian stand-by, Mulligatawny soup, I found the Indian advice somewhat elaborate, so I looked elsewhere. Mutton, onion, carrot, apple, a small turnip, a tablespoonful of curry powder, and the juice of a lemon are called for. There are dozens of other versions, too numerous to detail, and on reflection there is not much point in making Mulligatawny since I don't think anyone would now truly appreciate it.

At the risk of contradicting Nicolas de Bonnefons, I must say that cabbage soup is best cooked in the oven with a lump of pork and/or some smoked sausage, and dried pea soup is not the same without ham stock. Janet always boils the carcass to make chicken soup – a practice left over from the time when chicken was an expensive treat for high days and holidays. It makes perfectly acceptable soup with added vegetables or pulses, and/or dumplings, but her Jewish friend Susy Fleischmann buys a kosher old boiler and starts from scratch. She says there are almost as many idiosyncrasies as there are cooks, but potato, carrot and leek are usually included, as are the unlaid egg yolks which should be found inside the bird, to be added with the *kneidlach* (dumplings made with matzo meal) towards the end of the cooking time. *Borsch* was originally made with any roots the Eastern European peasant could get hold of, but now implies beetroot. You can make it in virtually any way you like – it has the same sort of status as the kosher Chicken Soup.

I will never understand how people would rather serve in the office than reign in the kitchen. Even our senior executives, it seems, suffer dreadfully from stress, while preparing these peasant dishes is as soothing as meditation. Elaborate *haute cuisine* is another matter and should not be attempted by the tired since it usually results in hysterics, burned fingers, pans and expensive ingredients, and an all-round loss of appetite. At the opposite extreme, short cuts can also be counter-productive. One of my books has a recipe for tinned baked beans in soup, but since the flavour is unmistakable, one would be better advised to eat them on toast in the accepted fashion. Even if you rinse them from the surrounding juice the flavour persists, giving one the feeling that something is wrong somewhere. In an American cookbook in the section on soups we find, 'TRICK: Use cans of strained baby-food vegetables in place of the leftovers for a quick and easy soup. Use as many as you like. You'll find they taste wonderful.' I wouldn't even try this on the baby since I know beyond doubt that he'd spit it out. 'Tomato Supreme' is canned tomatoes with celery and onion and two tablespoons of margarine (which strikes me as not a good idea). 'TREAT: A No. 2 can of corn may be added to this recipe for variation', which also strikes me as not a good idea, since the ingredients would cancel each other out – *and* 'have no particular flavour' now I come to think of it.

Mrs Pender Cudlip says she was 'constantly met with the argument that "soup is too expensive for *us* to indulge in it very often."' But she maintains that it can be 'made most economically . . . Every scrap of fish, meat, or vegetable that would otherwise be wasted, can in soup be used up with greater advantage.' We, that is Janet and I – for my daughter, a modern girl, is over-cautious about things a day old – do make soup from leftover vegetables, but we give some thought to the elements of its composition: sprouts, for instance, lose their point if combined with red cabbage. Caroline Blackwood and I compiled a book about cheating in the kitchen called *Darling, You Shouldn't Have Gone to So Much Trouble*. Quentin Crisp, who was, as well as one of our authors, the godfather of my dear friend Crispin Kitto –

author, musician, and part-time chef to the grander film stars in Los Angeles – gave us a recipe that evinced an original attitude to the received idea. It was for a dish called Tibetan Workhouse Soup: 'Take a saucepan which has been used for a variety of purposes without ever being washed up, fill it with water and bring to the boil . . .' The last time I saw Quentin, he was sitting in my kitchen wearing Wellington boots because, he explained, he had to fly to New York and they were by far the most comfortable things to wear on your feet if you were compelled to get into an aeroplane. I said I had always been led to believe that it was unhealthy to leave your feet in Wellingtons for too long, but he said that was an old wives' tale and if they were sufficiently capacious there was no problem; it all depended on your requirements and your point of view. He died of old age.

A *Naturalist at the Dinner Table* remarks, 'Almost anything can be converted into soup, a course which is apt to be an enigma in the less reputable restaurants. Vile rumour has it that an eating establishment not a hundred miles from Soho preserves a dozen sets of ox-tail bones which have been in use for more than a quarter of a century.'

If they don't spend the spare time in the fridge, soups should be eaten on the day of preparation. Most people now hesitate to warm things up twice and throw other things out when they've been in the fridge a few days. We shrink from the danger of food poisoning as our better-conducted ancestors shrank from sin. They went regularly to Church but left the stockpot simmering at the back of the stove more or less continuously, since it was an article of faith that a powerfully flavoured stock was essential to numberless dishes.

Francatelli begins his book *The Modern Cook* (addressed to those in service to the wealthy) with a chapter on 'Common Stock, Stock Sauces and Grand Stock for General Purposes':

When about to prepare for the reception of company, it is advisable to begin, if there be sufficient time, two days beforehand in summer, or three days in winter, by getting ready the grand stock – an article so essential to all the after preparations, that it may be looked upon as the basis of operations . . . For a dinner of twelve *entrées*, two legs of white veal (about forty pounds weight), the same quantity of gravy beef, and forty pounds of leg of beef and knuckles of veal would be required.

You had to cut away the nicer bits of veal to be used for *fricandeaux*, *grenadins* or *noix*, for removes or *entrées* 'as the case may be' and then gently boil the bones, the beef, carrots, turnips, celery and leeks for seven hours. He gives a hundred and thirty-six recipes for soup and a similar number for sauces. Stock was needed for nearly all of them as well as for the entreés, ragouts and gravies, etc. It was customary to offer two soups at dinner parties – one thick and one clear.

Ida C. Bailey Allen – Author, Editor, Lecturer, International Authority on Foods and Cooking (with the passing of time the title *A Lady* had clearly come to be seen as insufficient) – wrote of stock preparation in 1925 that, 'One or two-gallon stock pots of aluminium or granite ware are excellent for the purpose.' She was unaware that aluminium was later to be suspected (and then cleared, as is usual with many scares put about by the experts) of contributing to the development of Alzheimer's. She says you can use 'odds and ends of food' left over but the stock should not at any time be allowed to 'boil furiously'. I have heard of people who added to the brew baked potato skins, kipper bones and the fat and gristle that the fastidious left on their plates. They claimed it made for a greater intensity of flavour, but once you start thinking along those lines there is really no limit to what you might do. Anyway, if you really feel the need of stock, which doesn't play much of a role in current domestic culinary modes, you can make it freshly or slip a vegetable stock cube or a spoonful of bouillon powder into whatever dish you feel might be improved by its addition. But not chicken stock cubes, for I have heard that they are made from live chicks, ground down and with the beaks, bones and feathers sieved out. I was loth to believe this, but having learned more about the conditions in which hens are intensively reared, it seems not impossible. And not beef stock cubes either, following the revelations about 'meat retrieval' systems and the BSE scare.

By 1932 two women, one the Head of a Household Arts department and one with a *Diplomée Cordon Bleu*, had reached the conclusion that it was 'really a mistaken idea that soup made with stock provided a definite food value in the diet'. They wrote horridly of extractives, gelatine, protein, calories, digestion and gastric juices, and warned that the stockpot should not be kept as a receptacle for unwanted scraps. Nevertheless, they insisted that 'well-made stock is the foundation of all good cooking', thereby indicating that if not soups, then entrées – 'made-dishes' – were a major item in the cuisine of the 1930s. Much of the book consists of pessimistic advice on what might go wrong in the kitchen ('Reasons for Common Failure') and deals with acidity, greasiness, curdling, lumpiness and collapse, and all the time the stockpot loured from the back-burner. If the stock was cloudy they cleared it with egg white, but all the authorities insisted that it should be meticulously and frequently skimmed. I once went to a wedding breakfast in a grand and famous riverside restaurant and, taking a mouthful of what the grand and famous chef would doubtless have called the *jus*, was overwhelmed by the aroma of Oxo. I assumed that he had contrived, for whatever reason, to arrive at this result by his own efforts with the stockpot, but learned later that his reliance on the commodity was well known. Oxo, like the baked bean, has a taste that cannot be disguised.

In times gone by, people made their own 'Portable Soup':

Boil one or two knuckles of veal, one or two shins of beef, and three pounds of beef in as much water only as will cover them. Take the marrow out of the bones, put any sort of spice you like, and three large onions. When the meat is done to rags strain it off, and put it into a *very* cold place. When cold take off the cake of fat (which will make crusts for servants' pies), put the soup into a double-bottomed tin sauce-pan, and set it on a pretty quick fire, but do not let it burn. It must boil fast and uncovered, and be stirred constantly for eight hours. Put it into a pan, and let it stand in a cold place a day, then pour it into a round soup china-dish, and set the dish into a stew-pan of boiling water in a stove, let it boil, and be now and then stirred, till the soup is thick and ropy, then it is enough. Pour it into the little round part at the bottom of cups or basons [*sic*] turned upside-down to form cakes, and when cold turn them out on flannel to dry. Keep them in tin canisters. When they are to be used melt them in boiling water, and if you wish the flavour of herbs, or anything else, boil it first, strain off the water, and melt the soup in it.

This is very convenient in the country or at sea, where fresh meat is not always at hand, as by this means a bason of soup may be made in five minutes.

Which is, I suppose, some sort of return if you'd spent eight hours stirring it 'constantly'.

An ancient soup receipt, dating from medieval times, called for roast chicken or partridge breasts, sweet almonds and the 'whitest bread' pounded together in a paste. Rich veal stock and cream were then added. Miss Acton gives a version 'without

149

any variation from the original, as the soup made by it – of which we have often partaken – seemed always much approved by the guests of the hospitable country gentleman from whose family it was derived and at whose well-arranged table it was commonly served'. She then goes on to advise a modification: 'but we would suggest the suppression of almond spikes, as they seem unsuited to the preparation, and also the taste of the present day'. Some people like bits in their soup and some don't. Mrs Raffald wanted her readers to 'ſtick' almonds all over the tops of French rolls and drop them in the tureen. 'When diſ hed up theſe rollſ look like a hedge-hog: ſome French cookſ,' she remarks, clearly appreciative of this piece of Gallic wit, 'give this ſoup the name of Hedge-hog ſoup.' She gave a second variant the title *Soup à la Reine* and someone else called it *Lorraine* soup, claiming it was introduced by the wife of James V. The truth is obscured in the mists of time.

Speaking of which, before the Clean Air Act, London fogs were known as pea-soupers, indicating, I believe, that this dish was once more widely known and consumed than it is now. I make it from dried peas, or the mushy sort which you can buy frozen, and add a great deal of chopped mint and a large spoonful of honey: it is my favourite soup but no one else likes it. In Victorian times both the air pollution and pea soup were known as London Particulars. I was living in Hampstead when the last fog fell on London: I had been to the corner shop and had to find my way home by feeling along the walls and railings and going up front steps until I got to the right house. Truly, you could not see your hand in front of your nose. It was oddly thrilling and although a lot of people died from inhaling fog, it added a touch of drama and mystery to the prosaic London scene.

Soyer's Hortense writes:

> It is unnecessary to state that, for many years past, turtle has been esteemed the greatest luxury which has been placed upon our tables. It was introduced into this country in the early part of the last century, and then only at the tables of the large West Indian proprietors, from whom it progressed to the city companies. During the time of the South Sea Bubble, when the female aristocracy partook of the prevalent feature, and flocked into the courts and alleyways surrounding the Exchange, turtle-soup was in the height of fashion, the cost being one guinea per plate.

By the nineteenth century, at grand dinners, Turtle Soup was inescapable and the Lord Mayor's Banquet could not have proceeded without it. The turtle – the so-called green sort – was imported from the tropical seas, especially from around Ascension Island, and was shipped over upside down since the underside was soft, and as it could weigh more than three hundredweight, if left right side up, 'the internal organs would suffer compression and death would speedily ensue'. They had no teeth but razor-edged jaws and 'Many an employee of a turtle soup factory has parted with one or more fingers.' One cannot regret this as much as one might, for somehow one's sympathies lie with the turtle. The Romans used turtle blood as shampoo, toothpaste and as a cure for earache when mixed with human milk. In the USA, freshwater turtle, or terrapins, were made into soup ('the female is the only one used for food, it is distinguished by a diamond-shaped marking on its shell'), or '*Terrapin à la Maryland*'; this was the principal article of diet of the slaves who eventually revolted against its monotony. Mrs Somerville's Turtle Soup is as follows:

Take the turtle from the water the evening before it is wanted, lay it on its back in the morning, tie its feet, cut off the head, and hang it up to bleed [*A Lady* gives the helpful tip 'hang it up by its hinder legs, and without giving time for it to draw in its neck, cut off its head], remove the scales and cut it open, take out all the meat, soak the white meat by itself in salt and water, cut off the fins, keep them separate, keep the *inside* or gut separate also, put all the refuse meat into a soup pot, with sufficient water, a turnip, carrot, celery, parsley, a few onions, and a bunch of sweet herbs, including a predominance of basil, a seasoning of mace, nutmeg, cloves, salt, and white pepper; boil them gently for three hours. The gut having been cut up and well washed is simmered until quite tender, and cut into narrow stripes [*sic*]; the white meat is stewed with the lungs and heart, cut into small square pieces, reserving a portion for cutlets. Add these to the strained soup, and also a portion of the green fat of the turtle, and thicken with arrowroot; add half a pint of wine, a dozen forcemeat balls, also a dozen egg balls. Turtle fins make a nice corner dish, as also the cutlets.

From *The Dictionary of Daily Wants* we take Mock Turtle Soup which was served by those who could not run to a turtle:

Procure a fresh calf's head with the skin on, take out the brains, wash the head several times in cold water, let it soak for about an hour in spring water, then lay it in a stewpan, and cover it with cold water, and half a gallon besides; remove the scum as it rises; let it boil gently for an hour, take it up, and when almost cold, cut the head into pieces about an inch and a half by an inch and a quarter, and the tongue into smaller pieces. When the head is taken out, put in the stock meat, about five pounds of knuckle of veal and as much beef; add to the stock all the trimmings and bones of the head, skim it well, and then cover it close, and let it boil for five hours; then strain it off and suffer it to stand till next morning, then take off the fat, set a large stewpan over the fire with half a pound of fresh butter, twelve ounces of onion sliced, and four ounces of green sage; let them fry for an hour, then rub in half a pound of flour, and by degrees add the broth until the mixture is the consistence of cream . . .

And so on and on. Eventually you season it by adding to each gallon of soup half a pint of white wine and two tablespoonfuls of lemon juice; let it simmer gently until the meat is tender, which will be in about three-quarters of an hour; take care that it is not overdone; stir it frequently, to prevent the meat sticking to the bottom of the stewpan. When the meat is quite tender, the soup is ready.

And about time too.

Dr Kitchiner gives a Mock Mock Turtle receipt, 'as made by Elisabeth Lister (late cook to Dr Kitchiner), Bread and Biscuit Maker, No. 6 Salcombe Place, York Terrace, Regent's Park – Goes out to dress Dinners on reasonable terms.' The main difference between it and the above seems to be that it uses Cow-Heel rather than Calf's Head and it cost 'only 3 shillings and a penny per two quarts'. In *Indian Domestic Economy and Cookery*, one Miss Robert described the manner in which the turtle was prepared on board East Indiamen. The mode is much the same as that given by Mrs Somerville, but the turtles would have been livelier and fatter: when they were brought home to England, barely conscious, lying on their backs, they grew miserable, thin and scraggy. Miss Robert also directed, 'If there should be any eggs in the turtle, let them stew in the soup for four hours.' Sir Francis, a century later, said tersely, 'For practical purposes this dish is made of turtle soup bought in a bottle, poured into an equal quantity of very good beef stock, simmered for half an hour and served very hot.'

Nor had Buckmaster despised the use of tinned things: for Gravy Soup he directed, 'Open a four pound tin' (he is referring to Australian Meat), then he stood it in hot water to melt the jelly and fat, turned the meat into a basin and poured more hot water over it, put it on a dish, diluted what remained of the jelly with sufficient hot water to make three pints of stock, and added salt and pepper. Labour saving was coming into vogue but it is salutary for the young to understand that soup making did not always consist of opening a tin or carton.

My mother-in-law used to write letters, not the short 'thank you' sort but real ones, full of things she'd been thinking about or had caught her attention. I found one the other day in which she revealed that when Mr Gladstone was late home, Mrs Gladstone kept his soup warm by taking it in to bed with her. First I wondered whether he was late because of the exigencies of life in the political arena or whether he had been indulging in his hobby of following fallen women in order to point out to them the error of their ways. Then I reflected on how this pastime would now be viewed. Not, I think, with the unquestioning credulity enjoyed by Mr Gladstone. I wondered next what receptacle Mrs Gladstone put the soup in without fear of leakage. Maybe a stoneware foot-warmer. I have heard of people who made their morning tea with the contents of their hot-water bottle, but it can't have been exactly piping hot unless they woke up very early and must have tasted nasty. The Prime Minister's wife would have been better advised to employ a haybox – unless by using the bed she was seeking to convey some subliminal reproach.

A late edition of Mrs Beeton's *All About Cookery* gives the following:

> The box is easy to devise. It should be about thirty inches by twenty-four inches in width and depth respectively and fitted with a hinged lid which can be closely and securely fitted. The interior surfaces of the box should be lined with several thicknesses of newspaper, ordinary house flannel being used as an outer covering. The hay is packed tightly into the box, and a nest prepared for the reception of the vessel containing the partially cooked dish. An earthenware vessel is the most suitable for the purpose. The vessel is covered with a cushion made of house flannel and stuffed with hay and cork shavings, the latter such as are used for packing grapes in barrels. The box is then closed and may be left for several hours. When it is opened the meat will be found warm and thoroughly cooked. It may have to be re-heated for serving . . . All foods must be actually boiling with the lid on the vessel, when they are quickly placed in the hay box to finish the cooking.

Then comes a list of dishes most suitable to this method of cooking. 'Bacon or ham, boiled. Chicken, stewed. Hare, jugged. Irish stew. Rabbit. Steak, stewed. Vegetable soups. Beetroots. Porridge. Barley water. Apple rings. Pears. Figs. Prunes.' One wonders why there is no initial recommendation as to the cooking of the rabbit. Joint and stew him, I suppose, rather than just popping him in there – which reminds one of the horror stories about people drying off the Pekinese by putting him in the microwave. However, the haybox is an economical and foolproof method of slow cooking, if anyone can be bothered, and would make for a more interesting subject of conversation at the dinner table than the vagaries of the microwave, which, it has been revealed, destroys the useful nutrients in broccoli and other vegetables.

A Lady, under the heading 'Cookery For The Poor', writes:

> I promised a few hints to enable every family to assist the poor
> of their neighbourhood at a very trivial expense; and these may
> be varied or amended at the discretion of the mistress. Where
> cows are kept, a jug of skimmed milk is a valuable present, and
> a very common one . . . A very good meal may be bestowed in
> a thing called brewis which is thus made: Cut a very thick upper
> crust of bread, and put it into the pot where salt beef is boiling
> and nearly ready; it will attract some of the fat, and when
> swelled out, will be no unpalatable dish to those who rarely taste
> meat.

In olden times the lowly were the recipients of the manchet,
bread into which had dripped the juices of the meat eaten at
table by the upper classes. Jack Ty Coch and his brother Hywel
who brings our wood still speak of 'brewis' – and eat it. They
sometimes soak bread in Oxo, but Hywel says it is better made
with ham stock. He tells of a time when he was small and the
farmer's family ate the ham while the labourer, in another room,
had bread and stock. Which rather ruins my nostalgic image of
the yeoman and workers eating together. *A Lady* goes on to give
further directions:

> The cook should be charged to save the boiling of every piece of
> meat, ham, tongue, &c. however salt; and it is easy to use only
> a part of that, and the rest of fresh water, and by the addition of
> more vegetables, the bones of the beef used in the family, the
> pieces of meat that come from table on the plates [ingredients

scraped off the family's plates were known as 'broken victuals'], and rice, Scotch barley, or oatmeal . . . ten or fifteen gallons of soup could be dealt out weekly at an expense not worth mentioning, though the vegetables were bought. If in the villages about London, abounding with opulent families, the quantity of ten gallons were made in ten gentlemen's houses, there would be a hundred gallons of wholesome, agreeable food given weekly for the supply of forty poor families, at the rate of two gallons and a half each . . . The fat should not be taken off the broth or soup, as the poor like it, and are nourished by it.

The soup kitchen, an institution that we had thought gone, along with child chimney sweeps and picking oakum, has made a reappearance in our inner cities with the new proliferation of the homeless. The Temporary Relief Destitute Persons (Ireland) Act, popularly known as the Soup Kitchens Act, was passed in 1847 in the hope of relieving the population during the Great Famine. The recommended ingredients for soup were about as costly as broken victuals, and the Commissariat Officer in West Cork said of the starving that the 'soup runs through them without affording any nourishment'.

Our local church serves soup and sandwiches daily, while a few hundred yards down the road the Hare Krishna van offers rice and lentils to their clientele, many of whom are not strictly homeless but young backpackers, though I daresay they get hungry too, and the pigeons eat up the bits left over on the pavement.

A man called, according to a pencilled note on the title page, W. Blanchard Fitzgerald, but styling himself *Fin Bec*, in his book *The Dinner Bell*, gives Venetian Quenelles Soup: 'Let two ounces of butter and an equal quantity of flour brown in a saucepan, add a little more than an ounce of grated Parmesan or Gruyère cheese and half a glass of strong stock; mix all together into a paste, take the saucepan from the fire, and add to the paste six yolks of egg; mix well again, and arrange the *quenelles* in it, with a little stock and serve.'

I cannot imagine what has gone wrong here. These senseless lines must have baffled many an aspiring Venetian Quenelles Soup maker. After three more receipts we find Venetian Soup and wonder whether it is the printer who has got in a muddle and somehow parted soup and quenelles in a moment of absent-mindedness. But no – Venetian Soup reads, 'Break into a saucepan six whites of eggs, add a few drops of lemon juice, salt and pepper. Pour into the saucepan, gradually, while stirring, some cold stock; then put the whole on the fire, and let it warm to the necessary thickness, stirring all the time, and taking care that it shall not burn.' Perhaps, you think, the quenelles should go into this concoction, but no again, for it concludes, 'Then pour it over fried bread and serve.'

I have come to believe that perhaps, rather than lacking an editor, *Fin Bec* was mad, drunk or malevolent. Take, in a manner of speaking, his Cauliflower Soup: 'Put a pinch of parsley in the water in which some cauliflowers have been boiled, and some very fresh butter; season according to taste, boil for some moments and pour onto bread. Onions burnt with flour can be added to the water, if preferred. In both cases, a few branches of cauliflower should be left in the water.' It is possible, of course, that he had never set foot in a kitchen or seen water boil, but in that case, why did he embark on his enterprise? He claims on the title page to be 'teaching the mistress how to rule a dainty and thrifty cuisine, and the cook how to prepare a great variety of dishes with economy,' and it may be that he was one of those men who cannot believe that there is any area of expertise in which he would not excel if he only troubled to exert himself. I have known several such. Loftily amused by the harassed frown of the Mistress or the frenzied visage of Cook he might have thrown his book together in an idle moment just to prove how simple it all was. See his misleading words on sauces, or his '*Calf's Head en Tortue*' which is disgusting and his '*Calf's Head en Papillotes*' which is actually treats of liver and is even more senseless than his Venetian Quenelles, and don't neglect to study his salad suggestions.

Janet has now looked over *Fin Bec* and is quite certain that he never made so much as a piece of toast and had not the remotest idea of what he was talking about. Astonished, she read out a piece on polenta cakes, remarking that whoever had given him the recipe had neglected to mention that polenta must be cooked before being put in the pastry cases. His ignorance of the very basics of cookery is again revealed when he deals with '*Bloaters, Breaded*: Split and coat them with egg and breadcrumbs,' he says and then *boil* them. No, no, no. His book might better have been called 'The Knell of Doom'.

Many other people considered themselves qualified to advise the inexperienced and therefore vulnerable: some of their suggestions are not to be acted upon but are too fascinatingly frightful to be ignored. *The Universal Cook Book* offers its version of *Bouillabaisse*, a perfect example of the reason why the French hold our culinary endeavours in such contempt. It consists of the trimmings of fish, a pint of milk, mixed herbs, salt and pepper, parsley, an onion and one egg. There are dozens of versions of the real thing but it is more of a stew than a soup: the reflections of Countess Morphy will be found in the section on fish.

Carême, obviously impressed by the charming Lady Morgan,

composed an 'English Fish Soup' in her honour. So: fillet an average-sized brill, a sole (size unspecified) and a small eel. Chop up the bones and trimmings and put them in a medium-sized pan with the pulp of a lemon, the peelings of a pound of truffles, two onions, two leeks, a stalk of celery, a carrot and a bottle of champagne; the vegetables all having been finely chopped. Add half a bay leaf, a small pinch of nutmeg and cayenne, two cloves, two well-rinsed anchovies and a little salt. (Why not just leave the anchovies unrinsed, one asks oneself?) Simmer all that for an hour and then sieve it through silk and pour it into a good veal stock. Now comes the complicated part. Sauté the fillets of fish and shape them into little scallops. Make a quenelle forcemeat with a large whiting and crayfish butter and form it into balls using coffee spoons. Poach them in consommé. Cut up the truffles – previously cooked in consommé, too – with a root slicer measuring an inch in diameter and then cut scallops 'two lines thick'. When the moment comes, drain the quenelles and put them in the tureen with the scallops of fish (drained on a napkin), together with the truffles and twenty mushrooms blanched pure white; twenty-four oysters, a like number of shrimp tails, and the tails of the crayfish that went into the butter for the quenelles. There are further directions involving the clarification of the broth, but the very word 'clarification' seems out of place here. This was considered one of Carême's simpler efforts.

Janet calls this next 'Salmon and Custard Soup': it is taken from the *Bird's Cookery Book* which has 'A Message to the Modern-Minded Housewife' from Sir Robert Bird, Bart., MP, telling how the 'brilliant inventive genius, Alfred Bird, F.C.S.' invented Bird's Custard, 'with the purpose of discovering a food, which, by reason of its purity, nourishment and easiness of digestion, would bring health to his delicate wife'. Sir Francis

Colchester-Wemyss is very dismissive of 'the stuff made from so-called custard powder, which appears to consist of cornflour mixed with some yellowish substance'. When Bird made white sauce into yellow custard, it was poured over British puddings with the same profligate enthusiasm as was gravy over meat.

The soup contains a quart of milk, an ounce of butter, small tin of salmon, two pint-packets of Bird's Custard Powder, one and a half teaspoons salt, and pepper to taste. You mix the custard powder with three tablespoons of the milk, boil the remainder and pour onto the paste, then stir in the melted butter and season. Remove the skin and bones from the salmon, mash well and mix with the sauce. Reheat and serve at once. Another concoction that Janet refers to simply as 'Disgusting Soup' requires mashed potato, Daddies or HP sauce, Worcestershire Sauce, an Oxo cube and water. You don't want to know the details.

Caroline and I included in *Darling, You Shouldn't Have Gone to So Much Trouble* an ersatz *Bonne Femme* soup. It consisted of dried onion, tinned carrots and instant potato. It was of course inedible, but none of the reviewers seemed to realise that we were aware of this. A furious correspondence raged for some time in the literary journals.

Nine

SAUCE

ꭍauce making is not what it was. The TV chefs seldom devote their programmes to demonstrating the basic rules of this once essential skill, despite the fact that, as Sir Francis said, '. . . with a knowledge, even elementary, of sauce-making, good living is within the reach of anyone – and [that] without it our feeding is only a step or two removed from that of savages who eat without discernment, or discrimination, or any enjoyment beyond that of satisfying hunger'.

Escoffier said, 'The preparation of sauces requires a great deal of care. One must not forget, in fact, that it is through the subtlety by which our sauces are constructed that the French cuisine enjoys such a world-wide supremacy.' He lists the three fundamental sauces: the *espagnole*, 'which is in fact just a brown roux bound with brown stock,' then comes the *velouté* 'which only differs from the *espagnole* by being made with white stock, bound with a roux kept as white as possible'. These were used in the various preparations of fish, meat, poultry and game, their purpose being to heighten the flavour, while *béchamel*, 'from the economic point of view may be considered the queen of sauces . . . since it lends itself to many delicious preparations, and harmonizes with eggs, fish and meat as well as with poultry and many different kinds of game and vegetables'. The Marquis de Béchamel was *maître d'hôtel* to Louis XIV and his sauce was made by boiling three-quarters of a pint or so of white stock with peppercorns, onion, carrot, parsley, bay leaf, salt and pepper, reducing it to half a pint, then melting two ounces of butter, adding one ounce of flour and half a pint of milk, and gradually mixing everything together.

'Following this,' Escoffier adds, 'we have tomato sauce, which also plays an important part in modern cookery.' He is not, of course, speaking of the kind that comes in bottles. Mrs Marshall put tomatoes in her Brown Sauce, which was made with flour, butter, the aforesaid tomatoes, and two quarts of 'good-flavoured stock made from cooked meat bones'. She says this sauce can be kept ready for use by being boiled up once or twice a week, which is dangerous advice. Not that these old cookery writers didn't consider themselves inordinately careful: Pierce insists that:

One of the first points essential to the observance of the cook is the critical severity regarding floating fat. In level glance directed, he easily detects the 'eye of fat' with its varnished, oily surface, as it floats on all gravies, sauces, and the like fluids, when they are not thickened . . . In pastry and ragouts, such as haricot of mutton, Irish stews and the like, where the above is concealed by the absorption of the vegetables, it is most noxious, and can be detected by the taste alone. In the made dishes, the cook must severely criticize this fat, as he can easily separate it before the juices have been mingled therewith, and before the flour or *liaison* takes it up in the thickening.

Grand chefs spent hours and hours fussing over their stocks and sauces and gravies, skimming and sieving and clarifying, and they put meat glaze in their mayonnaise since, according to Escoffier, it was 'specially used to finish off certain sauces, by giving them lightness, flavour and refinement'. We can now buy canned bouillon if we feel the need of additional stock, but I don't because we have no idea of the state of the cows who went into its formulation. There are also jars of numerous types of sauces to brighten up the chicken, but when I feel the need of a short cut I use a tin of condensed mushroom or celery soup. This is cheaper and not as instantly recognisable as commercial sauce, and it certainly saves the time we would once have been expected to lavish on our 'made' dishes.

As Kinsey Millhone, Sue Grafton's private-eye heroine, says in *I For Innocence*, 'I've been told novice cooks are chronically engaged in this hoary ruse. Cream of celery soup over pork chops . . . Cream of mushroom soup over meat loaf . . . Cream of chicken soup over a chicken breast with half a cup of rice thrown in . . .' She adds that the 'best part is you have company once, you never see them again', but she is too optimistic. The company probably relishes the dish. Most of my American recipes rely heavily on cans; it must be something to do with the rigours of pioneering days, when fresh food was not easily available and you had to travel hundreds of miles to the store through hostile territory, but using tinned foodstuff required care: 'Tinned foods should be kept as cold as possible. Never open the tin until required for use at once. To test the quality of the food within, press the bottom of the tin. If it makes a noise like the rattle of a sewing-machine when pressed it is not air-tight, and must not be used.' (A recent investigation into the numerous deaths on an early polar expedition showed that food poisoning from improperly canned food was one of the major causes, and one is still advised never to buy tins that are dented.)

The EU has now devised a 'lump test'. A tinned sauce with more than twenty per cent lumps is considered by Eurocrats to be a vegetable and therefore liable to import and export tariffs more than fourteen times as high as those imposed on sauces. They sieve the sauce and count the lumps, and if it turns out to be a 'vegetable', the export tariff can amount to nearly three times the price of the product.

Carême was contemptuous of Roman cookery because they put herbs and spices in all their dishes, usually all the same ones, and had *garum* with everything. His contempt was shared by 'the aesthetician' Von Rohr, who considered Apicius' approach to be the height of 'destructive cuisine' since everything was minced, mangled, chopped, squashed and drowned in sauce. This is an instance of the pot calling the kettle black, for Carême's 'Champagne Sauce' took two scalloped 'average-sized' soles, two baskets of mushrooms, two onions, some diced carrots, two shallots, a small garlic clove, a seasoned bouquet, a little pepper and mace and half a bottle of champagne. This was slowly reduced, sieved, mixed with two spoonfuls of sauce *allemande* and four baskets of mushrooms and their stock and, at the last moment, were added more champagne, a little glaze and some Isigny butter. His 'Montpellier Butter' comprised chervil, tarragon, salad burnet, chives, anchovies, capers, pickles, hard-boiled egg yolks and a little bit of garlic. You blended some of these and ground the rest and mixed them with butter and olive oil and some tarragon vinegar, and to make it greener you put in spinach juice. It sounds nearly as time-consuming as – though more palatable than – Apicius' rose dish for which you had to gather a lot of roses and snip out the white parts, then you crushed them and put some *garum* in and sieved them. Then you took the sinews out of four brains and crushed them with eight souples of pepper and poured the rose mixture over them. Then you broke eight eggs over all this, poured on a cup of raisin wine and some oil and cooked it over hot ashes, finally sprinkling it with ground pepper. It is impossible to imagine what *garum* did to the scent of roses. An enterprising manufacturer in the nineteenth century attempted to market a version of *garum* but it never caught on. Worcestershire Sauce and the various Asian fish sauces are probably similar.

The Victorians were as mad about gravy as the Romans were about *garum* (which, though it consisted basically of fish guts left to rot in an earthenware jar in the sun, was conceivably not as potentially toxic as Liebig's *pièce de résistance*, beef tea). One might get the impression from the cookery books that gravy came, in the scheme of things, just after God, death and the social order: it was used with everything from meat to fish to spinach and poached eggs: and 'to improve the flavour of scrambled eggs, add a dessertspoonful of rich brown gravy just before they are served,' while Mrs Somerville says, speaking of sauces for fish, 'good brown gravy is suitable'. Sir Henry Thompson enthuses, 'The Englishman . . . cares not how little "sauce" is supplied – he demands only gravy.' As Mrs Todgers put it in *Martin Chuzzlewit*, 'There is no passion in human nature, as the passion for gravy among commercial gentlemen. It's nothing to say a joint won't yield – a whole animal wouldn't yield – the amount of gravy they expect each day at dinner.'

In an 1811 copy of her book, *A Lady* begins, 'As the following directions were intended for the conduct of the families of the author's own daughters . . . she has avoided all excessive luxury, such as essences of ham, and that wasteful expenditure of large quantities of meat for gravy, which so greatly contributes to keep up the price, and is no less injurious to those who eat it, than to those whose penury obliges them to abstain.' My earliest copy of *A Lady*'s work once fell into the gravy, for some of the pages are stuck together by an ancient brown goo and the adjacent pages heavily discoloured. I am sure there is an admixture of tears.

She says, 'Gravy may be made quite as good of the skirts of beef, and the kidney, as of any other meat, prepared in the same way. An ox-kidney, or milt, makes good gravy, cut all to pieces, and prepared as other meat; and so will the shank end of mutton that has been dressed, if much be not wanted.' She adds that shank bones of mutton are 'a great improvement to the richness of gravy; but first soak them well, and scour them clean . . . tarragon gives the flavour of French cookery, and in high gravies is a great improvement . . .' Then she describes how 'To draw Gravy that will keep a week' and says 'Don't take off the fat till going to be used' – a measure one of my Syrian friends insists on. (Judging by Mouna, Syrian cookery is among the best in the world.)

After this come *Clear Gravy*, *Cullis or Brown Gravy* and *A Gravy without Meat*, which consists of small beer, water, pepper, salt, lemon peel, cloves, walnut-pickle or mushroom ketchup and fried onion: '. . . turn all the above into a small tosser with the onion and simmer it covered twenty minutes'. There is *A Rich Gravy* and *Gravy for a Fowl when there is no meat to make it of* – this requires the feet, gizzards, neck, liver, parsley, thyme, flour, butter, mushroom ketchup and 'it will be very good'. *Veal Gravy*, *Gravy to make Mutton eat like Venison* and *Strong Fish Gravy* – eels, flounders, 'a little crust of bread toasted brown', mace, pepper, anchovies, lemon peel and horse-radish, simmered in water.

It must have been this insatiable demand that gave rise to the production of artificial gravy: gravy browning, gravy powders, gravy cubes, gravy granules, even cartons of gravy are now available, and judging by the advertising campaigns gravy must be as popular as ever. Manufacturers appear only to advertise products for which there is already great demand – gas, electricity, telephones, chocolate, gravy. Ah, Bisto! The Tikka Masala, which a politician once claimed was now the National British Dish, is not your traditional Indian recipe but has been adapted and altered to suit British tastes: that is, liquid has been added in order to make a sauce with all the comforting connotations of gravy.

My daughter has rung me up from far-flung corners of the world to ask how to make gravy. I tell her the following: Pour off most of the fat from the tin in which you roasted the meat; then, if you must, add a little flour and mix it up scratching the bits off the bottom of the pan, then pour in the delicious water in which you have cooked the vegetables (you will of course have used the minimum quantity and be left with only a mugful, or possibly two), boil it, pour in a glass of wine or port or whatever and boil again, stirring all the while. This is not what Victorians meant by gravy but is greatly preferable to the slurry that is sometimes found inundating the meat and two veg. The child of my daughter, when asked one day whether he would like, as a treat for lunch, fish fingers and baked beans, replied that he would prefer 'a proper dinner like Drandma makes [he has trouble with his g's], with dravy'.

Middle Europeans are also fond of it: we once had Czech visitors who insisted on cooking a meal for us, which took them all day and consisted largely of gravy and potatoes. The friend who had introduced them explained morosely that they liked gravy and put it in their vodka and weaned their babies on it and cleaned their teeth with it.

'The wars of the French Revolution, by cutting off all communication with the continent caused the memory to fade, even of the material elements of gusto in the land, where, though there were twenty religions there was only one sauce, and that one melted butter.' Pierce commented crossly, 'The saucy Neapolitan who made this last remark of our own, our native land, would have shown more philosophy had he been shocked at the characteristic of his own country, which though it could boast of twenty sauces had but one religion.' (This Neapolitan was his country's ambassador at the time.) Talleyrand and other of his countrymen said it too, which was only to be expected. The despised substance of which they speak and which was known as 'melted butter' was not.

It was a flour-based sauce with butter in it: much the same as what was called, by the time I was subjected to it, white sauce. (The Victorians also had 'white sauce' but it was based on veal gravy or the 'neck and feet of a fowl'.) It was served, seasoned with salt and pepper on fish and vegetables, or with sugar on boiled puddings and was, admittedly, horrible. It was usually either too thick or too thin and frequently full of lumps. 'Paper 'anger's paste' was the coarse term used to describe it. Our Victorian ancestors were in two minds about melted butter sauce. National pride forbade them from accepting the French or Neapolitan view, but common sense and the taste buds precluded them from boasting about, or even eating, it if it could be avoided. This ambivalence was best decided by an obstinate insistence that, *properly prepared*, there was nothing to match it.

A Lady directs, '*To melt Butter; which is rarely well done, though a very essential article.* Mix, in the proportion of a tea-spoonful of flour to four ounces of the best butter, on a trencher. Put it into a small saucepan, and two or three tablespoons-ful of hot water; boil quick a minute, shaking it one way all the time. Milk used instead of water requires rather less butter, and looks whiter.' She mentions it on the introductory page of the 1811 edition of her book: 'we rarely meet with butter properly melted . . .' and includes it with 'good toast and water and well-made coffee' among the items that would, when properly prepared, distinguish the excellent from the indifferent housewife.

Buckmaster wrote, 'Making melted butter is one of those simple things which every servant of all-work is expected to know by instinct, but is one of those things rarely ever properly done . . . The great point in preparing melted butter is this: – as soon as it has come to the boil to take it off the fire, and then add cold butter, which gives it the flavour of butter . . . The essential condition of success is that the flour and butter should be of the very best, or good melted butter is impossible, no matter what recipe is followed.' He mentions the late Lord Darnley who spoke of one of the Barons of the Exchequer as 'a good man, a most religious man: he had the best melted butter I ever tasted'.

Catherine Ives remarked in *When the Cook is Away*, 'The ordinary white sauce which we all know far too well takes about a quarter of an hour to make. Some people call it "Melted Butter Sauce" which is misleading and inaccurate; some people call it "Hot Office Paste", for which they only too often have adequate justification.' The 1930s' scornful attitude to all things Victorian finds further expression here – in this case, perhaps, justly. I have made it, to *A Lady*'s directions, and it certainly lacks the element of thrill. *A Lady* also suggests

'*A very good Sauce, especially to hide the bad colour of Fowls*. Cut the livers, slices of lemon in dice, scalded parsley and hard eggs; add salt, and mix them with melted butter, boil them up, and pour over the fowls. This will do for roast rabbit.' One cannot believe that the sauce produced would be any more agreeable than the discoloured fowl it was supposed to disguise.

When the ancestors meant to imply what we would call melted butter they called it Dissolved or Oiled Butter. *A Lady* had prescribed, 'Put two ounces of fresh Butter into a sauce-pan; set it at distance from the fire, so that it may melt gradually, till it comes to an Oil – and pour it quietly from the dregs. *Obs.* – This will supply the place of Olive Oil; and by some is preferred to it either for Salads or Frying.'

It is an old idea and may have arisen from the patriotic suspicion of olive oil, which was regarded by the English as suitable mainly for medicinal purposes and applied, warmed, to children suffering from earache. 'It is astonishing to what extent in England the prejudice exists against oil as an article of food. How common it is to hear someone say, "I cannot digest oil in a salad, I am obliged to mix it with cream instead." We are not prepared to say which of the two, cream or oil, is, according to chemical analysis, the more digestible, but we can testify, both from hearsay and experience, that good oil, even in cases of weak digestion, has been found to be both nourishing and beneficial.' Sir Francis, not entirely liberated from ancient and xenophobic prejudice, suggests for lettuce, 'A very delicate dressing is melted butter. This is melted till quite liquid, seasoned with salt and pepper and perhaps a little sugar, and then poured over the leaves, turning them all the time, so that each piece has a thin coating of butter.'

The terrifying *Fin Bec* gives his Hollandaise Sauce: 'Melt some butter over a very slow fire, or better still in a *bain marie*' (so called 'after the woman alchemist, the "Jewish witch Marie" who lived sixteen hundred years ago . . . a glorified type of double saucepan in which she brewed her potions and love-charms' – Moira Meighn), 'let it settle, add a few drops of lemon juice as you beat it, and a little salt; pass through a fine sieve, put a little more salt, and serve up in a sauce bowl.' Now *that*'s what I'd call melted butter. He says of his hollandaise, 'This is the most simple sauce' which, done his way, I suppose it is, but what we call hollandaise is composed of egg yolks, lemon juice and butter and isn't simple at all. If you're in a hurry or a bad mood you curdle it. A blender is a help but you still have to be careful. *Fin Bec* confuses matters further with his 'Sauce without Butter: take the yolks of three eggs, six spoonsful of oil, pepper and salt; warm in a *bain marie*, stirring the while.' Now if that had been a sauce with *butter* rather than oil, it *would* have been hollandaise, and if he was trying to make mayonnaise he was surely going the wrong way about it.

The Dictionary of Daily Wants says Robert Sauce, or *Sauce Robert* (it is said that the Normans introduced it) is one of the oldest known to the English. 'Put an ounce of butter into a saucepan; set it over the fire, and when browning, throw in a handful of onions cut in small dice; fry them brown, but do not let them burn; add half a spoonful of flour, shake the onions in it and give it another fry; then put four spoonsful of gravy, and some pepper and salt, and boil it gently ten minutes; skim it. When ready to serve, add a teaspoonful of made mustard, a spoonful of vinegar, and the juice of half a lemon, and pour it round the steak or chops. They should be of a fine yellow brown, and garnished with fried parsley and lemon. The sauce must not boil after the mustard is put in, otherwise it will curdle.'

The *Lemco Cookery Book* has its own version: 'One ounce butter, half a pint of water, half an ounce of flour, one dstp. vinegar, half a teasp. *Liebig Company's Extract of Meat*, half a small onion, one dstp. *Mushroom Ketchup*, salt and pepper, one dstp. minced parsley. Heat the butter till brown, fry in it the onion, also the flour, until browned; now add water, *Liebig Company's Extract of Meat*, salt and pepper, boil five minutes, pass through fine strainer, add parsley, ketchup and vinegar, and serve in tureen with *fish* [my itals].'

There were in fact numerous sauces (although mostly based on melted butter) even in the English kitchen (Miss Acton lists a hundred, one charmingly called 'very good egg'), but I think the only ones that deserve to be remembered on a daily – or at least weekly or possibly seasonal – basis are onion, cheese, bread, horseradish, mayonnaise, hollandaise, Cumberland and . . . I suspect there are other useful ones that have momentarily slipped my mind . . . parsley, cranberry, apple . . . Anyway, few of them are what the Old Masters meant by sauce and none of them takes days to prepare. The Victorians used these with the appropriate fish or meat, but nothing except melted butter was permitted to overshadow or rival the sacred Gravy (oddly enough, across the USA in diners you will find on offer biscuits – what we'd call scones – and 'gravy' which is what we would call white sauce); and on the whole, Britons turned up their noses at the sight of the sauceboat, muttering, 'messed-about foreign muck' or similar expressions of insularity and contempt. They did however esteem many bottled sauces, some of which persist to the present and are quite handy if used with discretion: just a hint of Worcestershire Sauce in the Shepherd's Pie for instance.

Heinz Salad Cream, which the manufacturers once declared was to be withdrawn from the market, has been reprieved, much to the relief of many people of all conditions including at least one famous chef. It is rather like those jokes that can be told to individuals but not in company: everyone quite enjoys them but they wouldn't like it to be widely known. Salad cream is useful to serve with fish cakes – mix it with chopped capers, parsley and chives and it is scarcely recognisable. During the War my mother used to make salad cream with a cup of evaporated milk, a teaspoon of mustard, the same of sugar, a pinch of salt and a splash of vinegar: you could grate horseradish into it, or if you had no horseradish you could increase the quantity of mustard and mix it with grated carrot.

Boiled dressings were once widely used, being 'more popular than mayonnaise in England'. According to a book called *What Every Cook Should Know*, 'Cornflour is good to use because of its smooth texture when cooked. It is boiled with water and a raw yolk of egg and seasonings are added. Butter or oil is mixed in during the final process, and vinegar is added to flavour.' The authors suggested that this uninviting substance should be poured into jars and thinned down with water or vinegar before use. And according to *The Household Manager*, 'There are various ways for compounding the mixture for salad, as, with cream, yolk of egg boiled hard and passed through a sieve, a portion of beetroot passed through a sieve, and other things of the kind, so as to make up a rich sauce for the salad.' The book modestly asserts that 'No guide for the compounding is equal to experience,' and adds the helpful information that, 'Sauces also may be bought, ready-prepared for salads, the epicure preferring the plainest and simplest.'

There are still people who won't touch a mouthful of anything without splashing on brown sauce, although these are fewer than they used to be. Couples with differing attitudes to food once regularly fell out if she had cooked a delicately flavoured lemon sole or chicken breast with a freshly tossed salad and he reached automatically for the HP ('Shake, oh shake the ketchup bottle, first none'll come, then a lot'll.' – Ogden Nash). And chefs who fly into a tantrum if they see a customer looking round for the salt, get beside themselves if one is so ill-advised as to request the ketchup.

Sir Francis notes, 'As a final word on sauces, do not forget the sugar in mint sauce. Many a lamb has been spoiled by having a bitter mess of vinegar poured over its remains.' Which might explain the French contempt for this flavoursome enhancement of the *gigot*. Someone writing in *The Girl's Own Indoor Book* of her travels in France, 'was much amused a few weeks ago to see written on a menu (bill of fare) "English mint sauce"; but my amusement was turned to disgust when I had taken some, and discovered that it was warm gravy with chopped mint in it – no vinegar! It would be difficult to imagine anything more flat.'

Sir Francis also wrote:

The late Sir James Agg-Gardner, who knew more about eating and drinking and good living generally than most people, was dining some years ago in a restaurant in Paris, where the chef was one of the super cooks of his time. Sir James, who had ordered his dinner beforehand, reached the fish course – a sole with a very special sauce – and, perhaps absent-mindedly, took the pepper pot in his hand and was about to dust some of its contents on to his plate, when he felt his arm seized from behind and heard an agitated voice saying, *C'est assez saisonné, Monsieur, c'est assez saisonné.*

This was the chef, who was watching to see how his chef-d'oeuvre was received, and could not bear to see it massacred. Sir James admitted for the first time in many years he blushed, and had quite a business to pacify the outraged artist, with whom he entirely sympathised.

And once when Grey Gowrie and his brother were children, dining with an aunt and her rich and grand German Jewish husband, Grey's brother asked for the salt. The uncle demanded, in his heavily accented tones, to know what things were coming to when, in his own house, it was suggested that cooking should be performed at the table. Some people hurl salt all over their dinner before they have begun to sample it, which is both reckless and improper. The polite mode is to put a little heap on the side of the plate.

Tegetmeier writes, 'Condiments are substances employed to season food, to render it more digestible, and stimulate the stomach to increased action. Those most in use in this country are Salt, Vinegar, Mustard, Pepper, and the various Spices . . .' He continues in the then customary fashion to tell us that they 'act by increasing the relish for food and stimulating the digestive process, beginning with the mouth, where the flow of saliva is increased by them . . . Hence their use is very great with defective appetite and repulsive food . . .' By 'repulsive' I imagine he means to imply food that the diner does not greatly care for rather than downright rotten.

Pickles were popular and might have helped people to force down their plates of rehashed mutton, etc. Mrs Raffald has about thirty-five receipts for pickles (it was a way of preserving vegetables, fruit, meat and fish as well as a relish) and gives instructions: 'Pickling is a very uſeful thing in a family, but it is often ill managed, or at leaſt made to pleaſe the eye by pernicious things, which is the only thing to be avoided, for nothing is more common to green pickles in a braſs pan for the ſake of having them a good green . . . it is poiſon to a great degree, and nothing ought to be avoided more than uſing braſs or copper that is not well tinned . . .' *A Lady* (whose receipts are sometimes suspiciously similar) says, 'Keep them closely covered; and have a wooden spoon, with holes, tied to each jar; all mettle [*sic*] being improper.' (Spelling had still not quite settled down. Dipt and dipped, flour and flower, peal and peel, ketchup and catsup, etc. often appeared in the same pages. A later edition of *A Lady* has 'metal'.)

Mrs Raffald says to make *Indian Pickle or Picadillo* you must 'Get a white cabbage, one cauliflower, a few ſmall cucumbers, radiſ h pods, kidney beans, and a little beet-root, or any other thing you commonly pickle . . .' and you salt them and dry them for three days 'in the ſun-ſ hine or before the fire' and put them in a large earthen pot in layers and add mustard seed, ale-alegar and turmeric, 'boil them together, and pour it hot upon your pickle, and let it ſtand twelve days upon the hearth, or till the pickles are all of a bright yellow colour, and most of the alegar ſucked up; then take two quarts of ſtrong ale-alegar . . .' and so it goes on, with the addition of mace, pepper, cloves, nutmeg and garlic. *A Lady* has this too but says it will 'not be ready for a year'.

From *The Dictionary of Daily Wants*: 'Although pickles are very agreeable to the palate, and impart a relish to food, especially cold meats, they are very indigestible, and should be carefully shunned by dyspeptic subjects. The greater part of pickles purchased in shops is especially deleterious, as it is customary to mix copper with the preparation, in order to give the vegetables a bright green appearance; and this addition amounts to poison.' And according to Pierce, 'Among vegetables the cucumber, as pickled by the Hebrews in this country, is rendered not only a palatable, but certainly one of the least injurious of the common pickles of England, and so cheap as to be within the reach of the poorest Hebrew. In Russia, people have a similar mode of pickling them, so as to render them a delicacy.'

Curry was also appreciated and far more popular than we now suppose. The Raj had brought it home to people and Indian food was demanded by many retired administrators. Cecil Woodham Smith records that the Duke of Norfolk suggested during the potato famine that 'The Irish should learn to consume curry powder, on which, mixed with water, he appeared to believe the population of India was nourished.' Mrs Johnstone says:

> Instead, however, of using currie-powder as obtained in shops, we would advise every cook to keep the several ingredients, each good of its kind, in well-stopped vials, and to mix them when they are wanted, suiting the quantities of the various ingredients to the nature of the dish. Fish, for example, requires more acid than fowl. Some people like a great deal of cayenne, others detest the taste and smell of turmeric, and some are all for ginger. To use currie-powder mixed in the same proportions for every sort of viand and of taste, may do very well for those who entertain a mysterious veneration for the Oriental characters inscribed on the packages, but will not suit a *gourmand* of any knowledge or experience.

And Buckmaster informs us, 'So far as I have been able to inquire, I find there is no universal curry powder in India. The native cook suits the seasoning according to the dish. He has one kind of curry for fowl, another for fish, and another for meat. Curry powders were first compounded to suit long voyages at sea, when it was impossible to obtain the ingredients in a fresh condition.' While *Anon*, he of the evil temper, wrote, 'Indian Curry Powder is mostly compounded by Jews, and of the worst materials, and when brought to England has lost its flavour and not worth using, and if much eaten will cause paralysis.' A further note about curry powder in *The Gentle Art of Cookery* advises, 'Vencatachellem is the best, but there is difficulty in obtaining it owing to a family quarrel.' It is back on the shelves so there must have been a reconciliation.

As for something to pour on the pudding, Wine Sauce was favoured. The most usual consisted of Melted Butter with added sugar and a slosh of wine. Eliza Acton has, amongst others, a Punch Sauce with white wine, rum, brandy, sugar, butter, a little flour and the rind and juices of oranges and lemons. She also has fruit sauces – raspberry, redcurrant, pineapple, cherry – and says, 'Clear rich fruit syrups . . . make the finest possible sauces for sweet puddings.' Melted jam is easier and what could be better than cream? It does not get much of a mention in the old books since, admittedly, it would not go well with a hot, fat-rich suet pudding. If thick, the cream, with flavourings added, usually *was* the pudding.

Ten

FISH

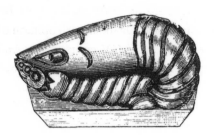

'*F*ish,' says an authority, 'is unpleasant to South and East African Negroes, many Mongol tribes and the Navaho in New Mexico,' which may be so, although I know a number of young Anglo-Saxon individuals who will only eat fish if it is tuna, canned; while my youngest grandson, who is of African descent, is the only child I know who relishes mackerel. Countess Morphy wrote in the 1930s:

> Racial and climatic factors are responsible for the wide divergencies in national cookery and food, and the study of the comparative cookery shows the unbridgeable gulf which exists between people. North, South, East, West – learn what they eat, and you will realize why they have always clashed. In Europe itself, the abyss between the palates of one nation and another explains the enmity and hostility which exists between human beings whose conception of feeding is completely antithetic.

So that's why we have wars. Still, once you put aside the arresting image of the eaters of *bouillabaisse* descending breathing fire and slaughter on those who prefer their fish in batter, with chips, the proposition is not as improbable as it seems at first glance. The focus is not quite that perceived by the Countess, but food *can* lead to trouble between nations. Look at the French and Germans and our beef. Or the Belgians with their sewage-fed livestock. Or the British opinion of those who eat dog or horsemeat. Or the GM controversy. And it is not so long since everyone else utterly despised the English cuisine, and the English returned the compliment – though mutual distaste did not extend to marshalling the troops. The Englishman was wont to gag at the scent of olive oil, while everyone else thought that we couldn't cook at all.

But it was the Reformation that biased the English against fish. 'Before the Reformation,' said Buckmaster, 'the people of England were celebrated for good living, hospitality, and abundance of food . . . Long before France attained any distinction English cooking was the best in the world. With the Reformation a great change took place. Vegetables and fish were regarded as popish food; and the making of soup and the cooking of fish gradually fell into disuse.' The *Encyclopaedia of Domestic Economy* declared, 'It is much less the custom to keep fish in ponds at present than it was in former times when the Roman Catholic was the established religion of this country: in consequence of which fish was almost an essential item of food two days in the week.' And someone else mourned the fact that 'we have had no National fish cookery since the Reformation'. As Kent said in *King Lear*: 'I do profess to be no less than I seem: to serve him truly that will put me in trust, to love him that is honest, to converse with him that is wise and says little, to fear judgement, to fight when I cannot choose, and to eat no fish.' To eat beef or mutton on fish days was the test of a true believer, a sort of badge of good Protestantism, and eating fish on Fridays a 'Popish mummery'.

Lord Cecil tried to encourage the fishing industry in the reign of Elizabeth I by reinstating a fast day, but he was unsuccessful and 'the recovery of the fisheries had to wait till the natural inclination of human stomachs for fresh whiting and salt cod should revive itself'. Meanwhile the fishermen took to piracy to make a living: this not only kept the skills of seamanship fresh and vital, but probably increased them as the ruthlessness and cunning of the brigand were added to the courage and patience of the fisherman. (A 1940s book thought people might have forgotten *au maigre* as a term. 'Any dish made without meat. Literally a thin dish, served during Lent and on Fridays and days of abstinence.' The writer then adds, on a note of evident astonishment, 'Some of the maigre dishes made with eggs and fish are far more appetising than meat dishes.')

All advisers on the subject wrote on the same lines about the fitness of fish for food. 'If the gills are red, the eyes bright and prominent and the whole fish stiff, it is fresh,' whereas if it exhibits the signs that in *Homo sapiens* indicate the hangover, 'the gills pale, the eyes sunk and the body flabby, it is stale . . .'

As time went by, fish came back into favour and eventually took its place as a course at all formal dinners as well as forming the main dish on humbler occasions, although it was not considered anything like as useful as meat. 'Fish as a nutritive article of food comes between meat and vegetables, being not so good, however, in this respect as the former. High authorities upon the subject say that where a fish diet is the rule and not the exception, the human frame loses much of its natural power.' Jockeys at Newmarket who needed to 'waste' were never allowed to eat meat if fish could be obtained. One of those high authorities wrote of fish that, 'Being less nutritive than meat, a greater quantity is necessary for sustenance.' On the other hand, 'Being less stimulating than butcher's meat, it occasions less febrile excitement, and being extremely tender and soluble it is more easy of digestion; and though not sufficient in all cases to restore power to habits debilitated by disease, it is well-suited for invalids, for inhabitants of towns, and for sedentary or studious persons.' This writer, too, notes sadly, 'Since England became a Protestant country the cultivation of fresh-water fish has been neglected.'

I have a work called *Sylvia's Book of Family Management*. My copy was awarded as a prize to Herbert S. Thomas by the Farnworth Pleasant Sunday Afternoon Brotherhood. It does not appear that Mr Thomas referred to it much since it has an unused look despite being more than one hundred years old. Perhaps he felt his manhood would be compromised, bearing in mind the feminine connotations of the title, but he cannot have known what he was missing. The illustrations for a start: those brightly coloured Victorian representations of extraordinary dishes – Calf's Head, garnished, *Paté à la Financière*, Chartreuse of Partridges, etc. The last are strangely reminiscent of certain aspects of Westminster Cathedral, at once stolidly reassuring, marbled and fanciful. *Sylvia* wrote, 'A noted medical man who has devoted much attention to the good of people in humble life, expresses the opinion that working men eat too much meat, and therefore that it would be a good thing if Catholicism was generally prevalent, so as to limit more of the population to fish at least one day a week.'

On the Continent the old monastic habit of keeping fish

ponds and tanks had survived. 'In Austria,' wrote Sir Humphrey Davy, 'every inn has a box containing grayling, trout, carp, or char, into which water from a spring runs, and no one thinks of carrying or sending *dead* fish for a dinner. A fish barrel full of cool water, which is replenished at every fresh source among these mountains, is carried on the shoulders of the fisherman: and the fish when confined in wells are fed with bullocks' liver cut into fine pieces, so that they are often in better season in the tank or stew than when they are taken.'

We now have 'fish farms' again, but the pessimistic hold that the fish get fat through lack of exercise and fall prey to the diseases that proliferate through close confinement with their fellows; while the pollutants that befoul the seas concentrate in a smaller compass and the unfortunate creatures swim round aimlessly, squinting blindly through the fog of their own waste.

Dr Kitchiner suggested that, 'The very indifferent manner in which the frying of fish is usually performed, we suppose, produced the following *jeu d'esprit* . . . "The King's Bench Reports have cooked an odd dish, An action for damages, *Fry* versus *Fish*. But sure, if for damages action could lie, It certainly must have been *Fish* against *Fry*."' It has been suggested that people are still a little nervous about the skill called for in cooking fish: I can't think why but it seems that those concerned with promoting it have long considered it necessary to offer encouragement to potential consumers. *The ABC of Fish Cooking* which, judging by the inset picture on the cover of a lady in a cloche hat gazing fondly at a herring, dates from the 1920s, begins, '"Ye gentlemen of England who live at home at ease, Ah! little do you think upon the dangers of the seas." So runs the famous old song most of us have known from child-hood . . .' Then it launches into poetic enthusiasm:

> If you love romance, and in your leisure moments are not above being stirred when you read a 'thriller', just pause and ask your-self what adventure can be surpassed by the fisherman's life which he is leading every day a few miles from your doorstep . . . The fisherman is the last of the adventurers. Your meat grazes placidly in a meadow until it is led to the slaughter-house – the butcher has replaced the hunter – but the fisherman must still take his life in his hands and face the perils of the seas, to bring you his catch. The fisherman loves his life. Not for worlds would he exchange the freedom of the great ocean, the thrill that comes after fighting through a storm, the triumph of bringing home a catch snatched from the icy jaws of the wintry seas, for a life within four walls.

The introduction concludes by advising the reader to hang up the little book in her kitchen and, when cooking fish, to glance at the cover. (Apart from the lady in the hat it shows the sea and storm-tossed fishing vessels.) 'Then perhaps one night, when the wind is howling round your chimneys, sitting cosily round the fire, you will remember the fishing fleet afloat on the dark stormy seas . . .'

At about the same time as *The ABC of Fish Cooking* made its appearance, E. G. Boulenger wrote of the fisherman's lot:

> The stakes are often high, the risks are great, and the crew must work hard to get back to port with a cargo calculated to find favour with the owners. Once the fish begin to fill the nets, washing, sleeping, and in fact all creature comforts go by the board. The fish must be gutted, washed, and stowed below upon the ice – a layer of fish and a layer of ice alternately. All such work has to be done on a pitching, rolling deck awash with

slime and blood, and continually drenched by spray that is deluged at intervals with a cataract of lively fish, some dangerous to handle, and all most unwilling to be 'cleaned'. Sometimes this Herculean task goes on by artificial light. In winter-time the conditions are often terrible. The Iceland trawler is frosted over like some monster wedding-cake, and the fish as soon as they are aboard become frozen hard, rattling upon the deck like so many stage properties.

Around 1788, the first mention of deliberately frozen fish appeared – specifically salmon, which 'enables the proprietors of the fisheries at a distance to send it to London . . . this has amazingly altered the price of the fish and increased the value of the fisheries, although a great deal of fish is often spoilt by this mode and the flavour materially injured by freezing.' Now it is said that frozen fish may be superior to fresh, since when it was frozen it was fresher. The first frozen fishfinger appeared in Britain in 1955. The Chinese, as so frequently happened, were ahead of the rest of us and were freezing boat-loads of fish in the fifteenth century, and Francis Bacon caught his fatal cold in 1626 while stuffing a chicken with snow; but it was Clarence Birdseye in the early twentieth century who truly realised the potential of the technique.

Now our fishermen, evilly served by the machinations of Europe, are much reduced in numbers and in a bad humour. They were among the first to be betrayed by Edward Heath in his eagerness to get his feet under the table in Brussels at whatever cost. Sir Con O'Neill, the chief British negotiator at the EEC deliberations (whose given name, it was said at the time, occasioned some surprise among his French colleagues), dismissed the destruction of the industry with the words, 'The question of fisheries was economic peanuts, but political dynamite,' which neatly encapsulates the politician's sense of priorities.

After the hyperbole of *The ABC of Fish Cooking*, the recipes come as something of an anti-climax. Kedgeree: One pound cooked fish (dried or fresh), two ounces rice, one ounce margarine or butter, one hard-boiled egg (if liked), salt and pepper. Flake the fish, boil and dry rice. Put all except the egg into a saucepan and stir till hot. Pile on hot dish and decorate with the egg. This dish can be conveniently prepared overnight and heated up. 'You can make this into a party dish by adding more sliced hard-boiled egg, chopped chillies or almost anything your fancy dictates. Delicious, too, with just an added spoonful of curry powder. Use more butter in this case and serve for supper or lunch with a sprinkling of powdered coconut.'

This is a dispiritingly limited kedgeree, typical of the new, cautious approach to cookery in the 'servantless household'. My mother-in-law sometimes mixed tinned sardines (oil and all) and chopped hard-boiled eggs with rice and, while it was quite edible, it was not company fare. She had been brought up with servants to do the cooking and spent her brief married life in India with the usual complement of domestic staff and never quite got the hang of preparing meals herself, not even kedgeree. Elizabeth Craig, magnificently helpful as ever, wrote: 'I always have in my cupboard three tins of sardines. Should I require one for sandwiches or toast before next shopping day there will still be two left to draw upon should emergency arise. Should emergency arise, and one tin, or the two tins be required in the kitchen, then I order three more.'

Mrs Johnstone, writing before the grand approach to food was smothered by gentility, has an observation on curried fish. 'Currie has become a favourite way of dressing fish, though till of late it found no place in any book of cookery. It is cheap, convenient, and even elegant . . . Lobsters, prawns, oysters, or muscles [*sic*] may be added to fish-currie, and are *curried* by themselves. Dressed fish make good currie. The currie may be any shade of colour, from pale gold to deep rich brown, by browning the fish and onions more or less, or adding browning.'

Indian Domestic Cookery gives a fish curry which reads like exotic poetry:

Take your fish, and cut it up into small pieces; wash it all with oil and basun (i.e. pounded raw gram); wash it in water to remove the basun; fry it in ghee with a sufficiency of salt; then for each seer of fish take six chittacks of ghee; put the ghee with eight or ten dried chillies, a pinch of fenugreek seed and kalah gerah; then mix with the fish a few dry chillies pounded, some turmeric also, with roasted coriander seeds, fenugreek, and kalah gerah, also some sliced onions, and a clove of garlic, pounded; rub this well over the fish, and put it into the ghee with the fried chillies, and put the whole into sufficient water to boil. An acidity may be given with tamarind juice, green mangoes, vinegar or lemon; vegetables may be added in the same way as directed for vegetable curries, putting in a layer of vegetables and then a layer of fish, shaking the saucepan to prevent the fish from breaking and burning.

Obs. – The vegetables usually added to fish curries are cabbage, cauliflower, fennel, mathee, moringa pods and leaves.

Countess Morphy describes Thackeray's enthusiasm for *bouillabaisse*. He wrote a verse about it:

> This bouillabaise [*sic*] a noble dish is,
> A sort of soup or broth or brew,
> A hotch-potch of all sorts of fishes,
> That Greenwich never could out-do;
> Green herbs, red peppers, mussels, saffron,
> Soles, onions, garlic, roach and dace . . .

The Countess says it can never taste the same on a foggy day in London, Birmingham or Manchester. 'You want the hot sun of Provence, the exuberant and voluble waiter, the Marseillais, bubbling with enthusiasm over his famous local dish; and even if his black beard occasionally gets imbibed with it – well it is all part of the fun . . .' It was probably remarks like this that led to the ill-feeling between nations. However, all are now agreed that the constituents of *bouillabaisse* differ from district to district (there is also a freshwater variety called *pochouse*), rely on the skill of the cook to get a well-flavoured stock together without boiling the fish to rags, and should be eaten in close proximity to the place where the fish was landed.

The *Encyclopaedia of Domestic Economy* states, 'In the ocean there appears to be an inexhaustible store of food in the finny tribes of animals,' and cod was once so plentiful that it was said, albeit fancifully, that a mariner could step out of his ship and go for a stroll on their backs. 'Lewenhoek counted several millions of eggs in the roe of one cod fish of middling size, a degree of increase that must render them inexhaustible by human means.' (When Kipling's *Captains Courageous* was being made into a film, the studio bosses suggested that he add some sex appeal, whereupon he delivered the information that 'A happily married lady cod fish lays about three million eggs at one confinement.') Now, a mere hundred or so years later, due to overfishing, cod is an endangered species and more expensive than salmon. Nevertheless, those that manage to stay out of the public eye can grow large: one weighing ninety-seven pounds was cut open at a fish factory in Australia and found to contain a human head. It would not have come by this by its own exertions – cod are idle creatures and float around with their mouths open swallowing anything that drifts their way. Boulenger considered that since cod was fifty per cent water and lacking in muscle tone because of its laziness, it had very little food value and possessed the sole merit of being easily digested.

Before people grew to prefer fillets and cutlets, the head of the cod was the favourite part. 'This was a great affair in its day. It is still a formidable, nay, even a respectable-looking dish, with a kind of bulky magnificence, which at Christmas-tide, appears imposing at the head of a long board.' Thus Mrs Johnstone. When she comes to describe a stage in its preparation which involves sliding it on to a deep dish, glazing it with 'beat' eggs and strewing it with fine breadcrumbs, Peregrine Touchwood adds a note: 'Modern cooks at this stage *skin* cod and haddocks. All true *gourmands* detest *flayed* fish. Where not nicely *crumbed* and *browned* they are absolutely horrific and spectral.' Other writers said you had to remove the skin carefully in order to prevent the fish from tasting too fishy.

Mrs Rundell, who gives directions – complete with a diagram – for carving a cod's head and shoulders with a fish trowel, tells us that 'the parts about the back-bone on the shoulders are the most firm and the best. About the head are many delicate parts, and a great deal of the jelly kind. The jelly part lies about the jaw-bones, and the firm parts within the head. Some are fond of the palate, and others the tongue; which likewise may be got by putting a spoon into the mouth.' She says, 'Some people boil the cod whole; but a large head and shoulders contain all the fish that is proper to help, the thinner parts being overdone and tasteless before the thick are ready.' (Picture the scene if anyone now should place a cod's head on the table.) 'Dr Paris states that the pulpy, gelatinous skin of the turbot and the glutinous parts about the head of the cod, though highly prized by gastronomes are very apt to disagree with invalids.'

Smoked cod's roe is increasingly hard to find and the tara-masalata that you buy ready prepared, smooth as face cream, is not the same as that you made yourself, chopping and mashing in the crumbs of Greek bread and lemon juice and olive oil. There were many recipes and variations but ours was the best. Ask Alfred. Salt cod, which mainly came from Newfoundland (now fished out), became the national dish of Portugal and was treasured by many other nationalities since it kept for a good time in the days before freezing. In France now you can buy it in tins and find it ready-prepared in delicatessens, and as far as I'm concerned it can stay there, having lost something in the translation. The main thing to remember is that salt cod needs long soaking to get rid of the saltiness. In country districts here it was sometimes pegged down in a running brook, and I can only imagine that someone must have been delegated to keep an eye on it for fear of herons, pike, foxes, etc. or the neighbours. Eliza Acton suggests serving it in the old English way with egg sauce and boiled 'parsneps', which reminds me that at Christmas time someone in my father's family never failed to observe that *his* father's favourite feast dish was salt cod with mashed carrots and swede. (He was a Finn.) The sweetness of the vegetables offset the saltiness and it was probably delicious, but the English seem to prefer their fish preserved by smoke rather than brine.

Apart from the head, cod was not as popular in the eighteenth century as pike and carp, which goes to show how fashion dithers back and forth. An English gentleman in the 1930s, having given a list of the fish considered suitable for English gentlemen, adds 'with such a selection the English housekeeper is never driven to fish such as carp and pike, the cooking of which occupies whole pages in continental cookery books . . .'

A French friend holds that potatoes alone are the correct accompaniment to fish while my mother tended to favour brown bread and butter. In a Cleikum Club note, Sir John Sinclair says 'Fish do not agree with vegetables except the potato.' Somebody then (probably Mrs Johnstone since you can more or less find your way through the passage without a compass) writes, 'Here he is wrong: the people in Orkney and Shetland, who live a great deal both on fresh and salt fish, consume cabbage in large quantities with it, and are entirely free from the scurvy, and the cutaneous diseases which overrun the people of the Hebrides, who raise no vegetables' – which is interesting but rather beside the point if Sir John was recommending the modest potato simply because it does not overpower the flavour of the fish. There is nothing to stop them eating their cabbage separately.

A 'high authority' also states, 'Few species of vegetable appear to be eaten with fish. Potatoes and parsneps are the principal of those which are found by experience to agree well.' He is cautious about sauces, considering that the various kinds eaten with fish are 'probably the cause of most of the faults laid to the charge of this useful aliment; these sauces are to be suspected, when purchased, as we cannot at all times be certain of their composition; and it is well known that they are sometimes deleterious'.

Certainly, fish only needs the simplest of sauces or the point is lost. Having said that, one perfect dish prepared by the aforesaid French friend consists of poached halibut, boiled new potatoes and *aioli*. Fish seems able to cope with garlic. The delicate scallop is best with only breadcrumbs and minced garlic fried in butter: more acid things – lemon, tomato – disguise the taste (Atheneaeus said much the same thing about a dish of female tuna tail – if you put vinegar on it you take away all its merits), and you might as well throw them away as put them in soup. The same goes for lobster unless you're going to the trouble of making a *bisque* with it. The Greeks of antiquity ate a lot of fish, fussing in what seems an exaggerated manner about the precise locations where they were to be caught and the nationality of those who cooked them – not a Sicilian or an Italian because they were too liberal with the cheese and vinegar. The cheese which they applied was probably the soft, white sort. I cannot immediately think of a similar present mode, but we do put grated cheese on fish pies and some mix it with breadcrumbs for their *Coquilles St. Jacques*.

When the Albertine rose is just coming into bud I tend to think, poetically, Poached Salmon. This has something to do with the appearance of the rose – shades of pink, petals/flakes – and something to do with the time of year. When summer starts you feel you can serve cold food with a clear conscience. There are many advantages to this, the main one being the avoidance of the round-up to get everyone seated before lunch goes cold. While on the subject of summer food, it is noteworthy that people in some cultures prefer their food lukewarm, rather than the English 'piping hot' – the taste can be negated if the buds are burned – but this is feasible only where olive oil is used. Dairy and meat fat congeal, as does gravy, and are not nice if kept waiting.

Once, when I cooked a salmon, I wrestled it into the fish kettle, covered it with cold water and brought it just to the boil, whereupon I removed it from the heat and left it, covered, to cool. Simple and cooked to perfection. So it was doubly annoying after this efficiency to find the salmon leaping from the kettle tray on to the kitchen table – not by itself in some supernatural, posthumous act of autonomy – but because I dropped it. Its head came off, the flakes slid from their state of seeming perfection, and the fish lay there, disordered and a reproach. I was alone at the time, so I manhandled it on to a plate and pushed it all back together again. Then I tastefully arranged slices of lemon and cucumber along its length and you'd hardly have known it had died. The secret is never to panic.

We sometimes roast, or to be more correct bake, salmon: this does much to dispel any muddy aspect. We put slices of lemon inside it and a lot of butter all over it and subject it to high heat until the skin crisps. A more detailed and elaborate method, from John Nott's *Cook's Dictionary*, goes as follows:

> To *Roaſt* a Whole ſalmon – Draw your ſalmon at the Gillſ, and ſtuff in his Belly ſome whole ſweet herbſ, as Thyme, Roſemary, Winter ſavoury, ſweet Marjoram, a ſmall Onion, and Garlick; ſcale the ſalmon, wipe off the ſ lime and Lard him with pickled Herringſ, or a ſalt Eel; then ſeason large Oyſterſ with Nutmeg, and fill up hiſ Belly with them; baſte him with Butter, lay him upon ſtickſ in a Tin Dripping-pan, ſet it into the Oven; draw it out, turn the other ſide upwardſ, then put ſome Claret in the Dripping-pan under it, with Wine, Anchovieſ, Pepper and Nutmeg; let the Gravy drip into it; baſte it out of the Pan with Roſemary and Bayſ; when the Fiſh is done enough, take all the Fat off the Gravy, boil it up, and beat it thick with Butter; then diſh your ſalmon, pour the ſauce over it; rip up hiſ Belly, take out ſome of the Oyſters, put them into the ſauce, take away the Herbſ, and ſerve it up hot.

This is only one of John Nott's twenty-six receipts for salmon. (He had twenty-seven for pike, fifteen for carp, eleven for tench and five for cod.) He compiled his dictionary mostly from published books dating from approximately 1650 to 1715, and his intended readers would have been those with the charge of running the newly built country mansions of the noblemen, magnates and rich merchants of the time; people with access to the parks, fish ponds, ice-houses, kitchen gardens, orchards and orangeries, vast kitchens, still-rooms – and of course, servants – that characterised the Country House.

Another of his receipts: 'To Dreſſ a ſalmon with ſweet ſauce – Cut your ſalmon into ſlices, flour them, and fry them in refined Butter. Then ſoak them a little while in ſweet ſauce made of red Wine, ſalt, Pepper, Cinnamon, Cloveſ, ſugar, and green Lemon, and ſerve them up with what Garniture you think proper.'

To make fish cakes Mrs Somerville thriftily uses the 'Remains of Salmon . . . in the following manner: mince it, mix with a few bread-crumbs, a little flour, a little chopped parsley, pepper, and salt (those who choose it may add a little curry). Bind all together with an egg, and make them up into round balls, or flat cakes, and fry them.' We use mashed potato. 'Or a pretty dish may be made by filling a mould with the best pieces, and filling in a savoury jelly. To be turned out when cold.' We do that too.

Dr Kitchiner said, 'All river Fish should be eaten fresh except Salmon, which, unless crimped, eats better the second or third day; but all Thames fish, particularly, should be eaten very fresh; no fish eats so bad kept . . . Crimp him by cutting to the bone on each side, so as almost to divide him into slices; and now hold him by the tail that he may bleed.' People no longer do this. Cooks in favour of the practice would have been puzzled to read 'a fresh fish not crimped is generally trout' followed shortly by 'Trout – they are much improved by crimping.' This contrary advice led me to further investigation, and thus to the *Encyclopaedia of Domestic Economy*:

Crimping is a process adopted for the purpose of improving fish. Sir Anthony Carlisle has investigated the change thus produced; and we are indebted to him for some curious observations upon the subject. Whenever the rigid contraction has not taken place, the process may be practised with success. The sea fish destined for crimping are usually struck on the head, when caught, which, it is said, protracts the term of its irritability [the amusement caused by the image of a cross cod evoked by this term may be countered by the definition, 'the peculiar susceptibility to stimuli possessed by living matter']; and the muscles which retain this property longest are those about the head. Many transverse sections of the muscles being made, and the fish immersed in cold water, the contractions caused by this crimping take place in about five minutes; but if the mass be large, it often requires thirty minutes to complete the process, which is for the purpose of giving firmness to the fish.

It sounds to me like yet another waste of time, occasioned by that slavish adherence to theory which so often distinguishes the Thinking Man, yet even in the 1930s we find, 'A fresh salmon unless he is crimped, is inclined to be tough, and should be hung, so to speak, for a couple of days . . . It must be admitted that a crimped salmon is a horrible sight, but the process is well worth while, as the flesh becomes tender, and is improved in every way . . . under no circumstances [for cold salmon] should the skin be removed.' The fish-skin debate rumbles on.

Soyer considered turbot the finest of flat fish, 'and so it was, no doubt, considered by the Romans: hence the proverb, *Nihil ad rhombum*, although Linneaus, from his classification would make us believe it was the brill or brett . . .' Soyer preferred them of 'a middling size . . . and if bled when caught, so much the better'. And, 'Should you be at the sea-side and buy one rather cheap because it has red spots on its belly, remove them by rubbing salt and lemon on the spot.'

I once simmered a turbot in a grill pan, but bits of enamel came off and stuck to it. The Victorians had recipes for boiling most sorts of fish, but I think God intended the flat kind to be fried or grilled (unless steamed between two plates for children or invalids). Whiting were generally fried with their tails in their mouths, which made it difficult to cook them evenly in shallow fat, but it was the *mode*. One directive for pike reads, 'Tie the head and tail together by means of string passed through the eye-holes so as to bend the fish in the form of a circle.' Then it was boiled. *The Cook's Oracle* says of smelts, gudgeon, or other small fish that they should be egged and put in very fine bread-crumbs, but 'Biscuit Powder is better.' Better still is pinhead oatmeal or bran. 'Fry them in plenty of clean lard or drippings. When they are delicately browned they are done. This will hardly take two minutes.'

'The centre bone of a fried sole is removed with a pair of forks. It is not considered correct to fillet a fried sole, as the flesh adheres to the forks, but in the case of a grilled sole, by all means, yes,' said *The Concise Household Encyclopaedia*. Sir Francis says:

> Soles are cooked whole or filleted: some recipes, such as Colbert, are always for whole fish, some may be for one or the other, and some for fillets only.
>
> For filleted sole there are a vast number of recipes, ranging from the simple fried fillet to such complicated dishes as *Timbale de Sole Carême* or *Grimaldi* or *Villaret*, and sauces which include almost every possible thing that can be put into a sauce. One cannot help thinking that with a fish of such charming delicacy

as a sole, strong concomitants are out of place, and especially does this apply to onion, which is the dominating note in dishes such as *Sole Bourguignonne*, *Duglère*, and *l'Amiral*.

Quite. And I still think it perverse to put grapes in them.

Mackerel has a special reference in *The Dictionary of Daily Wants*. 'When the Sabbath was observed far more strictly than it is to-day, there was a special law allowing fishmongers to sell mackerel on Sundays because, once caught, it spoils more quickly than any other fish. Once it was called "scavenger of the sea" because it was said to feed on drowned sailors, but this is now discounted.' More sea creatures than is generally acknowledged feed on drowned people when given the chance; it is best not to speculate on the eating habits of what you're eating. A while ago we were told to eat plenty of fish such as mackerel because they contained this valuable, beneficial type of oil and then, as is so sadly usual, we were told *not* to eat too much of them because the oil caused them to retain quantities of the pollutants that are dumped in the ocean.

Herrings – *The Dictionary of Daily Wants* again – are 'a well known small sea-fish. As an article of food, fresh herrings, although somewhat oily, are wholesome and agreeable if partaken of moderately; but if kept long they are apt to offend the stomach, and are only fit to be eaten by persons of strong digestion.' It goes on earnestly to advise a 'large admixture of potatoes or other vegetable food' in order 'to counteract, to a certain extent, the unwholesome properties of this fish when dried'.

I have long nurtured a nostalgic image of a worker, plodding home from the counting house through the fogbound streets of a maritime city, to a small terraced dwelling with the window (there seems to be only one) gleaming redly through the dark: inside there waits a welcoming grilled kipper. Net curtains come into it too, and a hint of polished brass, and maybe just a touch of aspidistra. And there it ends. 'Kippers and curtains' were considered by the rising classes to be oxymoronic but I find something reassuring in the conjunction. Anyway, when Catherine of France decided she would marry Owen Tudor, a deputation of English Lords was sent to Anglesey to check out his circumstances. They found his mother sitting in a field, surrounded by her goats, and eating a dried herring. They amended their account of this episode as follows for, after all, the family was of 'high blood': 'The lady was seated in state, surrounded by her javelin men, in a spacious palace, eating her repast from a table whose value was so great, that she would not take hundreds of pounds for it.' An early example of spin.

A few years ago, Janet's Beloved took her to the seaside at Orford in Suffolk and they brought back for me a newly smoked kipper. Like most of us I was accustomed to the usual yellow/brown, tanned article which varies in quality, is sometimes merely dyed, and often resembles a small, well-used saddle even when bought from reputable establishments. This kipper was a revelation; freshly smoked, plump and juicy, it reminded me of the mantra of the old agony-column writers before they dealt exclusively with sexual practices. They would say regularly that infatuation was not to be confused with true love and when the real thing came along, you could not fail to recognise it. Dr Harte wrote in 1633, 'A Red Herring doth nourish little, and is hard of concoction, but very good to make a cup of good drink relish well, and may well be called *The Drunkard's Delight*.' I was once on an island in Russia where, in the summer, someone sets up a small outdoor café with slatted wooden tables and benches. Laid out on a board were dozens of lake fish, salted, smoked and dried: a friend explained regretfully that many of the lay persons living on the island drank a lot and indiscriminately broke off and ate bits of this fish (on which flies were walking) in order to sustain a thirst.

Here is a recipe for red herring: '*Red Herrings. Great Yarmouth 1823*. Choose those that are large and moist. Cut them open and pour over some boiling small beer. Let them soak ½ an hour. Drain and dry them. Heat through before the fire and rub them over with cold butter. Serve with egg sauce or buttered eggs. Mashed potatoes should also be sent up with them.'

Or draw a red herring across the fox's path to destroy the scent and 'set the dogs at fault'. There were not, if we except Mary Webb, many animal rights protestors in days gone by so I don't know who would have been so naughty as to upset the Hunt in this manner.

There is a notable difference between kippers and bloaters, namely: 'Herrings caught near enough to the shore to be taken in and cured without being salted. The best bloaters come from Yarmouth' and retain their innards. 'Bloaters should always be split open like a haddock, and cooked on a gridiron kept for the purpose . . . After the bloater is cooked, rub a little piece of butter over the inside, which makes it look rich and moist, and improves the flavour. The great advantage of cooking bloaters in this way is, you avoid the dreadful gush of offensive steam that issues forth on opening them when they are cooked whole without first being opened. Indeed, the great drawback to bloaters is the unpleasant odour . . .' as *Cassell's Cookery* candidly stated.

The Romans, it is said, fattened their lampreys on human flesh. Mrs Raffald, describing them as 'curious fish with no scales, no paired fins and a cartilaginous backbone', gives a method of potting them which commences with the brutal instruction to take the creatures alive 'and run a ∫tick through their heads . . .' I don't know why a 'surfeit' of these creatures should have killed Henry I: it seems likelier that they were past their best. Francatelli says there are two sorts, 'The sea or marine lamprey, which is abundant at Gloucester and Worcester, where it is dressed and preserved for the purpose of being given as presents,' and the other sort which is smaller and found in the Thames.

In 1847 someone wrote, 'It is a curious fact in natural history that the manner in which eels breed is yet a problem not completely solved.' At one time it was believed they developed from horsehair, then they were thought to be viviparous until Sir Humphrey Davy observed that no facts were produced in proof of the assertion and in his opinion they laid eggs. All I know, off hand, is that the Sargasso Sea comes into it somewhere. Conger eels were 'found chiefly around the Channel Isles and off the Brittany coast. In some cases they reach the girth of a man's thigh and are extremely difficult to catch.' We saw Moray eels at SeaWorld in San Diego: they lived in what resembled an underwater block of high-rise flats, and were leaning out of their windows waving their heads about like idly gossiping neighbours mulling over some event happening in the place below. Many sea creatures are perceived as alarming by those accustomed to living on land but these were indescribably frightening.

Buckmaster says, 'In preparing fish there is no occasion for cruelty. I once spoke to a cook who was brutal enough to justify his cruelty by saying that the more eels suffered the better they were; and I am sorry to say that this absurd and utterly false impression exists in the minds of many cooks.'

The famous chef Monsieur Ude directed, 'Take live eels, throw them into the fire, and as they are twisting about on all sides, lay hold of them with a towel in your hand and skin them.' 'The cruelty inflicted on eels is proverbial,' observed Mrs Johnstone. In reference to this practice, she says, 'M. Ude belongs, we presume, to the revolution of 1789, not to that of 1830,' and repeats Dr Kitchiner's advice, which is to pierce the spinal marrow through the back part of the skull, 'when life will instantly cease'. Later cookery books assumed that the raw materials of dinner would already be dead by the time the cook got hold of them. In the summer of 2001 there was a move to ban angling on the grounds of cruelty since fish have feelings too.

Janet's parents had friends, Mon and Bob, who went regularly on fishing trips and would bring back live eels as a present: passing the house very early in the morning, they would slide them, wrapped in a plastic bag, through the letter box, and the eels, as often as not, would slither out and along the passageway gathering, according to Janet, fluff as they went. Being thus accustomed to eels she accepted, at a *Marai* in New Zealand, a dish of eels that had been prepared to a local method, smoked and then buried – or buried and then smoked. Either way, they were notable for that *haut goût* which, when associated with fish, does not recommend itself to the cautious British diner, the bloater being as high as most will go.

Eel, Pie and Mash shops are fewer now than they were but still survive in odd spots in London. They were always tiled, with bare, scrubbed tables and galvanised tanks full of live eels in the window. You could have eels stewed or jellied, sprinkled liberally with malt or chilli vinegar; or a meat pie with mashed potato (no butter or milk was used, only the water in which they were boiled) and 'liquor' which was parsley sauce (made with water) and again sprinkled with vinegar. The hungry would order, 'Double, double, double,' which speaks for itself, and you ate with a spoon and fork for there were no knives provided. Beloved was brought up in the East End of London and is a connoisseur. We all believe that it was Jewish immigrants who first provided fried fish for sale. And while we all think we once knew when chips were first married to fish, now none of us can remember. (I do know now – see Chapter Sixteen.)

Those who interest themselves in these matters are still talking about the continuing existence of the coelacanth: it seems a lady was in a fish market in Africa when she saw one being carried by on somebody's shoulder and recognised it instantly, which deserves the fullest credit for keen observation. I have passed friends in Marks & Spencer whom I last saw at Christmas and have failed to recognise them, and the coelacanth had not been seen around for millions of years. A prehistoric fish – the gwyniad – survives in the lake just over the mountains from us – 'it dies the moment it is taken out of the water . . . is nearly a foot in length, but is considered as an insipid fish. The poorer classes salt them.' I would certainly not be able to distinguish it from its fellows in a fish market. I've never cooked one and am told it is rather unrewarding, having more than the usual complement of bones. Anyway, it would feel oddly impious to cook a prehistoric fish. For the benefit of the curious, two are preserved in formaldehyde in a jar at the White Lion in Bala.

I am, however, in favour of cooking pike, the 'water-wolf' who preys on ducklings. There are few things more calculated to upset the tender-hearted than the sight of a small, feathered creature being dragged below the surface to its death by a cold-blooded fish. (Though the human race cannot afford to be too critical. I recently read an account of an early nineteenth-century jape: some tricksters caught an owl and strapped it to the back of a duck, which they then returned to the pond. The man writing of this episode admitted that it might be considered rather cruel, but could hardly suppress his titters: '. . . it *was* so droll to watch.') Janet's brother-in-law once brought back a pike he had caught just so that they could see what it was like close to; it was terrifying, said Janet, about three feet long but could turn in the bath with ease and great speed. It also survived, wrapped in sacking, the trip from Buckinghamshire to London and then back again to be released.

Pike are unusually bony – Sir Walter Scott's Dr Redgill warns us that, 'The bones of pike which are sharp and pronged, and so very hard that they will not dissolve in the stomach, ought to be watchfully avoided.' So should you have one to hand and be wondering what to do with it, your best course is to poach it, pick off the flesh, pound it to a pulp with butter and mace and pot it. (There used to be two sisters living on the shores of Windermere who potted a neat pike, but what mostly keeps them in my memory was their habit of smoking clay pipes.)

Once, speeding back from Paris by Eurostar, I found pike on the menu – Pike flan with curried *beurre blanc* – and ordered it to refresh my memory. It wasn't actually a flan but more of what would have once been known as a 'shape', turned out in a puddle of curried butter. The stewed peppers and tinned tomatoes were a touch misconceived as an accompaniment but the pike was fine. In French it was *gateau de brochet* and in Flemish it was called *Taartje van snoek met blankertbotersaus*, which was confusing, since I remember the British public being exhorted to eat something called snoek during the War and everybody hated it, and I'll swear it wasn't pike. Janet found a reference to snoek, 'A fish very common in Australia and New Zealand, where it is known as the barracouta. Rarely heard of in this country until the post-war period of World War Two,' which makes the matter only *more* confusing, particularly as war-torn Britain's snoek came from South Africa. The Ministry of Food distributed a poem:

> When fisher-folk are brave enough,
> To face mines and the foe for you,
> You surely can be bold enough,
> To try fish of a kind that's new.

'Receipt for Dressing a Pike', by Isaak Walton:

First open your pike at the gills, and, if need be, cut also a little slit towards the belly. Out of these take his guts, and keep his liver, which you are to shred very small with thyme, sweet marjoram, and a little winter savory; to these put some pickled oysters, and some anchovies, two or three, both these last whole, for the anchovies will melt, and the oysters should not; to these you must add also a pound of sweet butter, which you are to mix with the herbs that are shred, and let them all be well salted. These, being thus mixed, with a blade or two of mace, must be put into the pike's belly; and then his belly so sewed up as to keep all the butter in his belly if it be possible . . . But take not off the scales. Then you are to thrust the spit through his mouth, out at his tail. And then take four, or five, or six split sticks, or very thin laths, and a convenient quantity of tape or filleting; these laths are to be tied round about the pike's body from his head to his tail, and the tape tied somewhat thick, to prevent his breaking or falling off from the spit. Let him be roasted very leisurely, and often basted with claret wine, and anchovies and butter mixed together, and also with what moisture falls from him into the pan. Then, to the sauce which was within, and also that sauce in the pan, you are to add a fit quantity of the best butter, and to squeeze the juice of three or four oranges. Lastly, you may either put into the pike, with the oysters, two cloves of garlic, and take it out whole when the pike is cut off the spit . . . This dish of meat is too good for any but anglers or very honest men; and I trust you will prove both, and therefore I have trusted you with this secret.

Also in Walton's time there was a dish called minnow tansy, 'now out of use'. They were gutted, well washed in salt and water, and after their heads and tails were cut off they were put with yolks of eggs, 'well beat with cowslips and primrose flowers, and a little tansy shred small, and fried in butter: the sauce being butter, vinegar, or verjuice and sugar'. *The Dictionary of Daily Wants* says that in certain seasons they are 'taken in such numbers as to be made into a cake with eggs and flour', and observes approvingly, 'The minnow is an elegantly shaped fish, very active and sportive, a kind of dappled or waved colour, like to a panther . . .' When Alfred was small he lived near the canal in Kentish Town where little boys used to fish – amongst the supermarket trolleys, discarded condoms and dismembered bodies – for minnows. Please God they didn't eat them.

Carp, kept as they were in monastic fish ponds, grew large and tame until they fell out of favour in the United Kingdom. Some of the smarter grew so large and tame that they were preserved as a curiosity, hand fed, admired and petted. In the 1920s there was still one in the pond at Versailles who was said to remember the French Revolution and only surfaced when there was trouble afoot in Paris. He was never subjected to the following: '*To boil a Carp.* ſcale it, gut it and ſave the Blood in Claret, then boil it in a good reliſh'd Liquor half an Hour, make ſauce with the

Blood, Claret, and good ſtrong Gravy, three or four Anchovieſ, a whole Onion, ſ halotſ ſ hred, a little whole Pepper, a Blade of Mace, a Nutmeg quartered, let all theſe ſtew together; then melt the Butter, thicken it, let your Fiſh be well drain'd, put to the ſauce and add ſome Juice of Lemon.'

Sturgeon is yet another endangered species once quite commonly served. At one time it was considered a royal fish, 'for every one caught in England belongs to the Queen, with the exception of the river Thames, which belong to the Lord Mayor'. Soyer suggested that you should, 'Take a piece of sturgeon about two pounds weight, and on sending a piece of meat to the baker's to be baked on a stand in a dish, put the sturgeon under it, with a little water, salt, pepper, etc., and a little chopped eschalot may be used; you can also put potatoes round it. Peas, if in season, are a good accompaniment with melted butter.'

Somebody somewhere wrote what we all know:

Caviare is the favourite food of the Russians, prepared from the hard roes of the sturgeon chiefly; the roe is cleaned from the strings and fibres, steeped in strong brine, or salt pickle. It is then dried, and pressed, into casks or tubs, and formed into small cakes about an inch thick, and three or four inches in breadth. The red caviare is salted and smoked. The fishery of the sturgeon, for this purpose, is extremely profitable to those engaged in it, and likewise to the government of Russia . . . To be good, caviare should be of a reddish-brown colour, and very dry. It is to be eaten alone, or with oil and lemon, or vinegar, or with a sauce and pickle like anchovies.

That does not sound like caviar as we serve it and true connoisseurs eat it with no accompaniment except vodka.

A certain Mr Beale, in the nineteenth century, was collecting shells on the shores of the Bonin Islands when he encountered a 'most extraordinary animal' creeping on its eight legs towards the water. 'It seemed alarmed and made great efforts to escape, but the naturalist had no idea of consenting to the termination of so unexpected an interview with the odd-looking stranger,' so he trod on one of its legs and then grabbed hold of another one and then 'gave it a sudden jerk to disengage it' (the poor thing was clinging to the rock). 'This seemed to excite it into fury' which by now was hardly to be wondered at and, 'it suddenly let go its hold of the rock and sprang on its assailant's arm, which was bare, and fixing itself by its suckers endeavoured to attack him with its powerful beak. The sensation of horror caused by this unexpected assault may be readily imagined. Mr Beale states that the cold and slimy grasp of the ferocious animal induced a sensation extremely sickening, and he found it requisite to call to the captain, who was occupied in gathering shells at a little distance.'

I don't know what Mr Beale had expected, but they proceeded to jump on the wretched creature and hack it with the boat knife: 'It did not surrender, till the limbs by which it so tenaciously adhered were successively cut off.' The Victorians were notoriously wasteful of wildlife and we may be sure that Mr Beale and the captain did not cook and eat this octopus. We are told that cephalopods are unusually intelligent, which strikes us, prejudiced as we are against things with tiny heads and eight legs, as strange but caused me to feel some sympathy with Mr Beale's antagonist. It must have experienced its own sensation of horror on being confronted with a heavily bewhiskered Victorian naturalist.

The Maltese make octopus stew and do not expect the visitor to shrink from the sight even of tentacles and suckers once they are lying in helpless disarray on a plate. However I have seen people removing their spectacles before addressing themselves to this dish, which is called *Stuffat Tal-Qarnit*. Squid and octopus, like mince and liver, need very slow or very quick cooking. In a tiny restaurant in Fatima I once had squid stewed with beans, each as tender as the other. It was put on the table in the casserole it had been cooked in so everyone could help themselves, and brought smiles of contentment to the faces of several Irish priests sitting next to us. In Ancient Greece, when a baby was ten days old its father took all his clothes off and ran round in a circle with it while friends brought it presents of octopus and cuttlefish. I don't know why. In 1895 someone suggested that 'the well-known symbol called the *swastika*' might have been derived from conventionalised representations of the octopus, and the widespread use of this symbol as a lucky charm for children might have originated in the Amphidromia ceremonies (the running round in circles). Most people agree that it comes from the Sanskrit *svasti*, good fortune, and some also hold that it is a formalised image of the joyful, somersaulting child, which seems more plausible. Now it only signifies evil.

'The oyster . . . is a topic ever open to discussion among those who can appreciate the pleasures of the table.' In the early nineteenth century the oyster fishery was so important in Britain that it was regulated by the Admiralty Court. 'During the season, the consumption of oysters is so immense, and no article of diet is more generally used by every class.' So said Mrs Johnstone. She continues:

> Oysters are conceitedly said to be in season in every month of the year that has an *r* in its name, beginning with September

and ending with April; but the season in many places extends from August to May . . . Oysters, when just dredged, may be so packed in small barrels as to keep good for a week or ten days, and in this state they are sent to distant places. Oysters may be dropped out of the shell into a bottle, and kept in their juice for a little time by pouring in a little olive-oil, and corking the bottle closely. They may also be preserved good for some time by *feeding*; and custom, which brings *gourmands* to admire game when in a state of putridity, has taught some epicures to relish the flavour of stale oysters better than those recently taken from the beds. The fresher oysters are, they are the better, but when to be kept, lay them bottom downwards in a tub, or any vessel suited to the quantity to be preserved, and cover them with water in which a good deal of salt is dissolved. In this manner Apicius sent oysters to Tiberius when he was in Parthia. Change the water every twelve hours. Most cooks direct that this delicate animal should be fed with oatmeal or flour sprinkled in the water; and others, on the principle which leads a mother of the parish of St. Giles to give her new-born darling a drop of gin, are for feeding them with white wine and breadcrumbs!

Anon wrote that oysters 'should be obtained direct from their bed. Nothing can be worse than stale oysters; and it is a strange fact that there is not a shop between Cheapside and Hyde Park where you can depend on getting an oyster fresh from Billingsgate . . . A penny-post letter the previous evening to Pym of the Poultry, will ensure your having on the following morning, per Parcel Delivery Company, as many as you may order.' In some ways, those were the days. The English used to put them in steak and kidney pudding and Americans still put them in stuffing for the turkey.

Things Not Generally Known gives a 'culinary folly' originally taken from *A Lady* (1748): 'How to Roast a Pound of Butter – Lay it in salt and water two or three hours; then spit it, and rub it all over with crumbs of bread, with a little grated nutmeg; lay it to the fire, and as it roasts, baste it with the yolks of two eggs, and then with crumbs of bread, all the time it is roasting: but have ready a pint of oysters stewed in their own liquor, and lay it in the dish under the butter; when the bread has soaked up all the butter, brown the outside, and lay it on your oysters. Your fire must be very slow.' It is so untrue that the old jokes are the best.

It seems that shrimps used to be classed with winkles and whelks as suitable only for the lower orders. 'The Periwinkle and Whelk – are well known univalved molluscae, of little importance as general food, though eaten by the poorer classes, and sufficiently wholesome,' said *A Naturalist at the Dinner Table*, while commenting that, 'The excellent shrimp, a victim to our racial snobbishness, is not as often served as an *hors d'oeuvre* as it should be. The reason is that no "really nice person" likes to be seen peeling and eating one at table. And yet we need have no fear of losing caste if observed behaving in a precisely similar manner towards its larger and more aristocratic relation – the prawn.'

A Mere Shrimp appears in a newspaper cutting from the 1920s, which someone had cut out and pasted in the back of a cookery book:

> I'm proud of being a shrimp. There may not be much of me, but what there is is jolly good. Only most of you do not know it, and turn up your noses at me, and think I'm just a sort of relish with cheap tea. Come off it! Epicures know better.
>
> I can be a devil of a fellow sometimes, when I'm made to be. Here's a way to make me devilish. Put two tablespoonfuls of butter, a little chopped parsley, a dash of cayenne pepper – don't

be too dashing! – a teaspoonful of made mustard, a tablespoonful of lemon juice, and a dessertspoonful of Worcestershire sauce into a stewpan; hot up, mixing thoroughly. Then stir in a quart of me, shelled, beheaded, and betailed; cook for five minutes or so. Then serve me on hot buttered toast. Oh, but you'll find me a tasty little thing!

There is a lot more of this drollery, concluding with: 'Don't you forget that I've been honoured by the notice of Master William Shakespeare, whom I often used to meet at supper at the Mermaid. Did he not speak of "Pretty, little tiny kickshaws"? Them's me.'

Originating from the French *quelque chose*, meaning *something*, 'kickshaws' apparently referred to little delicate luxury dishes. A similar conceit occurs in *The Restaurant at the End of the Universe*: 'I am the main Dish of the Day,' says 'a large fat meaty quadruped of the bovine type'. After this surge of winsome sadism it comes as a welcome contrast to read elsewhere the robust simplicity of, 'In certain parts of the Chinese Empire shrimps are eaten alive. They are served up for the table in a vessel which contains wine and strong vinegar, a mixture which is intended to cause the creatures to leap about, rendering them specially acceptable to the epicure.'

Miss Acton gives instructions on how to shell shrimps and prawns quickly and easily. 'This though a most simple process, would appear, from the manner in which it is performed by many people to be a very difficult one; indeed it is not unusual for persons of the lower classes, who, from lack of a little skill, find it slow and irksome, to have recourse to the dangerous plan of eating the fish entire.' You must hold the head firmly in the right hand and the tail in the other and straighten the fish 'entirely', then press your hands quickly towards each other and break the shell of the tail with 'a slight vibrating motion of the right hand, when it will be drawn off with the head adhering to it . . .'

Lobsters, says *The Cook's Oracle*, should be bought alive. 'The lobster merchants sometimes keep them till they are starved, before they boil them; they are then watery, have not half their flavour, and like other *Persons that die of a consumption — have lost the Calf of their Legs* . . . They should be *Heavy and Lively*.' Mrs Johnstone writes that, 'Apicius, who ought to be the patron saint of epicures, made a voyage to the coast of Africa on hearing that lobsters of an unusually large size were to be found there; and after encountering much distress at sea, met with a disappointment,' which reminds one of the headline, 'Not Many Dead'. She goes on, more interestingly, to say that some naturalists affirm that 'in the Indian seas, and on the wild shores of Norway, lobsters have been found twelve feet in length and six in breadth, which seize mariners in their terrible embrace, and dragging them into their caverns, devour them! However this may be, the lobsters and crabs for being *devoured* are best when of the middle size.'

In Dorothy L. Sayers' novel *Have His Carcase*, Mrs Lefranc at the inquest of Paul Alexis wails:

'But as for his poor face . . . It's been nibbled right away by those horrible creatures, and if I ever eat a crab or lobster again, I hope Heaven will strike me dead! Many's the lobster mayonnaise I've ate in the old days, not knowing, and I'm sure it's no wonder if they give you nightmare, knowing where they come from, the brutes!'

The court shuddered, and the managers of the Resplendent and the Bellevue, who were present, despatched hasty notes to the respective chefs, commanding them on no account whatever to put crab or lobster on the menu for at least a fortnight.

I am not in favour of the habit, usual in some restaurants, of bringing your lobster, still living, to meet you, although I was doubly annoyed in one expensive establishment when, having suffered the poignant experience of being waved at by lunch, we were presented with an impostor, which had obviously been dead and frozen for some time. Someone in a French restaurant once paid five hundred pounds for all the lobsters there and released them into the sea. Indeed, this seemed for a time to be quite a fashionable custom.

When it comes to flavour, I think the humbler crab has the edge over lobster. I have also always considered the clam as a rather undistinguished object, its only purpose to appear in chowder with cubes of potato and salt pork, but in certain states in the USA the Clambake is one of the high points of the year. For a Clambake of twenty servings you will need two hundred soft-shell clams and fifty hard-shell clams; four dozen ears of corn, partially husked; five broiling chickens, quartered; ten sweet potatoes and twenty frankfurters; and twenty one-and-a-half-pound lobsters OR five pecks of soft-shelled crabs. *And* a sand pit about a foot deep and three and a half feet across, lined with smooth round rocks which have not been baked before, a wet tarpaulin, four bushels of wet rock seaweed, a pail of sea water and enough firewood to heat everything for at least four hours.

'When ready to serve have handy plenty of towels and Melted Butter and Beer.'

Eleven

FLESH

$\mathcal{T}$he importance of meat in the ancestral scheme of things cannot be over-estimated. For centuries the word was interchangeable with 'food': 'sitting down to meat' was taking your place at table, but no other food rivalled meat, as in flesh. Despite the studied scientific approach that the Victorians imagined they brought to the subject, there is an almost religious fervour apparent in their writings, which leads one to speculate on the possibility of unconscious reference to those ancient, widely held convictions that failure to make regular bloody offerings to the gods and spirits would cause the world to stop going round. There is a hint of sympathetic magic in their approach, an irrational passion for blood – what they saw as the basic element of life.

Many of those who believe in the innate goodness of mankind are loath to accept that people ever ate each other, or even killed each other much, until the rise of Western civilisation. They insist that the customs of the Savage made perfect sense in the context of his circumstances. In the 1930s an archaeologist held that the carved representations of carnage found in Mayan or Aztec ruins were of purely mythical events designed to placate the gods. Considering the nature of these representations, even this would not reflect well on the preoccupations of the artists, but further digging and research proved that these were records of actual happenings and thousands of victims had been sacrificed by having the hearts torn out of their living bodies.

There is something perversely comical in the attitude of anthropologists who ascribe unworthy motives not only to the conquistadors, which is fair enough, but also to the missionaries who sought to dissuade the conquered people from their pristine practices. One of these was eating the enemy. The choicest cuts were prepared with peppers, served on a bed of corn, and offered to the king and the highest officers of the court. This, explains the anthropologist, was a sort of tribute to he who formed the dish, for the king hoped to absorb his characteristics by ingesting his flesh.

Pierce, with fewer illusions about human nature or appetite wrote:

> And if the wild Indian dines on his conquered enemy, in preference to any more ignoble quarry, it is because his savage instinct teaches him to carry out the savage principle of warfare to its legitimate extreme. Besides which, to eat his enemy, is the highest compliment he can pay to his prowess, short of allowing himself to be the eaten party. More civilized warriors (those of the Dahra, for example) content themselves by merely roasting their enemies; in some sort making up for the shortcoming by roasting them alive.

Pierce might nevertheless have been disconcerted to learn that a later generation was to find evidence of cannibalistic practices amongst a group who could have been his ancestors – the bones of butchered humans in a hidden cave in the English countryside – a discovery that would have shocked and astonished the Victorians.

In his lengthy dissertation on the virtues of meat, Pierce wrote:

> It is evident that the constituents of the blood, which are so different from those of the juice of the flesh, must undergo a whole series of changes before they acquire the form and quality adapted to the production of the living muscle – before they become constituents of the juice of flesh. In flesh we eat these products, prepared, not in our organism, but in another; and it is extremely probable that they, or part of them, retain, when introduced into a sound organism, the power of causing the same changes, and producing the same effects, as in that organism in which they were formed.

The word 'osmazome' was the most significant and widely used among the food writers of the eighteenth and nineteenth centuries; it occurs again and again in the treatises of the time. It was, according to Brillat-Savarin, 'that highly sapid part of meat which is soluble in cold water, as distinct from the extractive parts which are only soluble in boiling water'. Whatever it was it is seldom mentioned now. Brillat-Savarin, having given it a page to itself, then lists the other elements of meat: Fibre (forms the tissue of flesh and is visible after cooking), Bones (composed of gelatine and phosphate of lime), Albumen (found in flesh and blood, congeals at a temperature of less than 122 degrees), then on to Gelatine, Fat and Blood.

Gravy, that substance on which you might think the entire British Empire was launched, was composed of 'osmazome and extractive matter' and since there was none to be found in fish it could be defined as distinguishing feasting from fasting. Which only goes to show the difficulty inherent in following the thought processes of those flourishing in an age other than our own: we so seldom start from the same premise.

Brillat-Savarin gives an account of a fishing village where daughters outnumbered sons (forty-nine to four) and suggests that the super-abundance of females has always been due to 'debilitating circumstances', i.e. no meat. (In the summer of the year 2000 he posthumously gained an ally: an expert found that carnivorous mothers had a hundred and six boys for every hundred girls, while vegetarians had eighty-five boys per hundred girls.) Soyer, wearing the hat of Hortense, wrote, 'Fish, of course, do not afford the same amount of nourishment as meat, as they contain but a slight quantity of osmazome; but its flesh is refreshing, and often exciting. A curious circumstance has been observed in respect to the animate parts of the creation which draw their nourishment from fish, as in birds and the human race, that they produce more females doing so than males.'

There have always been dissenting voices, people who could see no reason or excuse for meat eating. Plutarch wrote:

> You ask me upon what grounds Pythagoras abstained from feeding on the flesh of animals. I, for my part, wonder what sort of feeling mind, or reason, that possessed who was the first to pollute his mouth with gore, and to allow his lips to touch the flesh of a murdered being: who spread his table with the mangled forms of dead bodies, and claimed as daily food and dainty dishes what but now were beings endowed with movement, with perception, and with voice?

My cleaning lady in London refused to eat anything which once had a face.

And there were, through the ages, many others (famous and unknown) who revolted against 'kreophagy', often with good reason. Plutarch had described a method of 'slaughtering swine, for example, they thrust red-hot irons into their living bodies, so that, by sucking up, or diffusing the blood, they may render the flesh soft and tender. Some butchers jump upon or kick the udders of the pregnant sows, so that, by mingling the blood and the milk and the entrails of the embryos that have been murdered together in the very pangs of parturition, they may enjoy the pleasure of feeding upon unnaturally and highly inflamed food.'

But most of the Victorians who, I feel sure, never carried on like that, had no reservations about meat eating. In *Sylvia's Book of Family Management* we find, 'It is beyond all question that the greatest nutritive power of all food is possessed by meat – lean meat.' She calls on Dr Livingstone to bear witness. 'Being a Scotsman, and therefore naturally impressed with the efficiency of oatmeal,' he had thought about what he might most usefully eat in the course of his travels and concluded that, since many of the natives of Africa supported existence on such things as manioc, cassava and taro, he would try and do likewise, suspecting that 'animal food is unnecessary and injurious in hot climates'. However, on suffering some 'very peculiar derangements of health for which he could not account' and simultaneously being struck with a 'ravenous appetite for animal food', he abandoned his first opinion, ate some meat, and felt much better. Spending time with the Bakwains, he wrote that they often killed sixty and seventy head of large game in a single week; everyone 'partook of the prey and the meat counteracted the bad effects of an exclusively vegetable diet'. He noted approvingly that above all else they esteemed roast beef, and concluded that the English too, in their love of it, 'show both good taste and sound sense'. On the next page, Sylvia says that tough meat is best for the labouring man; meat from 'well-fed animals at full growth, and even a trifle old, some of whose flesh makes the jaws ache to masticate it'. Tender meat, she says, is not favourable to the production or maintenance of physical strength.

Sylvia, who, I am convinced, was a committee composed of a number of those Victorian gentlemen who prided themselves on their scientific knowledge, then addresses herself to the awful subject of gristle: 'There is an unaccountable impression in the minds of some people – perhaps most people' she writes patronisingly, 'that gristle is an element of strength; that it is, in fact muscle, and an instrument of power in the animal upon which it is found. From this it is inferred that the eating of gristle must be a good and strengthening habit.'

I remember when children were expected to swallow any bits of gristle that appeared on the plate. I always assumed that this was merely because you were not permitted to spit anything out – anything short of a fish bone or lead pellet, that is – but now I'm inclined to believe that those who ruled at the table had, at least, some subliminal feeling that it was good for you. Sylvia was eager to appear up-to-date even if it meant disagreeing with the popular wisdom; she stated robustly that the notion that gristle and the jelly deriving from it is strengthening is 'a complete delusion' and 'when gelatinous matter is completely separated from whatever it may be mixed with, it proves to be simply mucus, disgusting to take and tasteless'. She goes on, 'So far from increasing, it diminishes the nutritive value of the food it may be mixed with, though it does pall the stomach, and so satisfies or rather impairs the appetite, which is another of its delusive qualities. These remarks apply to: Gristle of all kinds. Tendons and cartilage of the feet, ears of calves, pigs and other animals.'

So the prized calf's-foot jelly recommended for children, invalids and young ladies wasting away from one of the numerous and mysterious afflictions to which young ladies were prone was, according to Sylvia, useless. As far as I can tell she was alone in this opinion. Everyone else was enthusiastically in favour of it. Not only was it valued for its medicinal properties but, said Mrs Johnstone, 'French cooks candidly allow that Calves' Feet Jelly is an English invention, and give us credit for it. It is indeed the great Chief of the whole tribe of moulded jellies and deserves both the pains and praise bestowed upon it . . .' Prepared gelatine had already been invented, but as a 'first rate female cook' remarked, 'I have a better jelly from my feet, and a nice little dish of the meat, for the price of the *dry stuff*.' In a book from 1834, I found two newspaper advertisements for 'Nelson's Patent Opaque Gelatine': 'Jelly is made with the greatest facility in a few minutes, possessing the whole of the nutriment without the impurities of the calves' feet' and is 'strongly recommended to Captains of Vessels and others going on voyages, it being . . . warranted to keep in any climate.'

In the year 2003 scientists turned their attention to Chicken Soup (long known in the vernacular as 'Jewish penicillin'), and gave it to some ageing rats, who promptly performed better in memory tests, while their blood became 'similar to that of three-month-old rats – fluid and with no risk of thrombi formation'. It seems that the soup contains a substance called proline, which is found in collagen, 'the connective tissue that dissolves when carcasses are boiled' (and is injected into the upper lips of film stars giving them the appearance of having sustained a smack in the chops). Boiling converts collagen into gelatine – 'a mixture of proteins called pep-tides, one of which is proline'. The soup, with its gelatine – and 'the thicker the broth, the higher the concentration' – is thought to prevent blood clots, boost memory, improve the symptoms of diabetes, ease sore throats and colds, protect the membranes of the stomach and prolong life. So much for Sylvia.

Soyer wrote that 'Theagenes, an athlete of Thasos, eat [*sic*] a whole bull; Milo of Crotona did the same thing – at least once.' Cattle were smaller in the olden days, so it's not as though they were tackling full-sized Aberdeen Anguses, but still . . . Milo's habit of showing off caused his downfall in the end. He is said to have carried his own statue to Altis; 'and it is further reported of him that he held a pomegranate so firmly in his hand, that it could neither be forced from him by any other person, nor could he himself dismiss it from his grasp' which must have been inconvenient. But then, on the borders of Crotona, he found a withered oak into which wedges were driven in order to separate the wood. In a fit of ill-considered confidence he tried to tear the oak asunder, but the wedges leapt out, the oak sprang back and Milo was trapped. After a while the wolves came and ate him. There is a gruesome coincidence here, for Guillaume le Breton tells us that the Welsh fighting man used only to squeeze his meat in the cleft of a tree before eating it, and the Vidame of Chartres reported that the Scots did much the same, compressing raw deer flesh between two batons of wood until it was hard and dry.

There is a theory that the method of making the South African dried beef, biltong (which sustained the early Afrikaner trekkers, as its American counterpart, jerky, did the pioneer frontiersmen), was taken to the Cape by Scottish settlers, and another theory that in the West Indies it was the Caribbee Indians who taught the colonists how to cure the flesh of the cattle to form what they called *boucan*: the French 'made therefrom *boucaner*, which the *Dictionaire de Treveux* explains as "to dry red without salt"; hence comes the noun *boucanier*'. And so we have a name for those bloodthirsty pirates and sea-robbers, chiefly natives of Great Britain and France, who first got together about 1524 and would have preferred to be known, if it was left to them, as The Brethren of the Coast.

Reading about something entirely different I discovered that a Vidame of Chartres had married the widow of Gilles de Rais. Gilles de Rais was thought by some to be the original Bluebeard who, when sentenced to death, made a statement in open court admitting to crimes so abominable 'that all who heard were chilled with horror'. Later, addressing the fathers of the families who were present, de Rais said, 'Beware, I beg you, of bringing up your children amidst the delights of life and the fatal pleasures of idleness; for the greatest evils arise from the pleasures of the table and the habit of doing nothing . . . Idleness, delicate meats, the frequent use of mulled wines, are the causes of my transgressions and my crimes.' It is usual now to blame an ill-considered diet for various forms of delinquent behaviour, but since he had murdered hundreds of children and made a pact with the Devil, this seems an insufficient rationale.

Brillat-Savarin quotes a Croat captain who dined with him in 1815. 'When we are in the field and feel hungry, we shoot down the first animal that comes our way, cut off a good hunk of flesh, salt it a little and put it under the saddles, next to the horse's back; then we gallop for a while after which (moving his jaws like a man tearing meat apart with his teeth) *gnian, gnian, gnian*, we feed like princes.' Brillat-Savarin mentions smoked Hamburg beef, and Arles and Bologna sausages among 'raw' meats, and Parma ham tastes all right, but on the whole, people with time at their disposal preferred their meat cooked. He considered that the one disadvantage of raw meat was its viscous quality: it stuck to the teeth; 'apart from that it is not unpleasant to taste'. I don't know about this. Those who relished steak tartare usually added a lot of Worcestershire Sauce and other accompaniments to it, and now it is seldom served.

Soyer: 'All ancient legislators have bestowed the most serious attention to the rearing and preservation of cattle. The Mosaic law, in this respect, enters into details that reveal the most profound wisdom, a delicate and minute research which cannot be too much admired.' He makes no mention of the apparently ineradicable human urge to tease cows. I went to a rodeo in Texas where the bull was brought to a pitch of irritation by having a strap strategically laced about its hind-quarters and a cowboy would attempt to sit on it for more than eight seconds; the English used to bait bulls, the Spanish and Portuguese fight them (there is a saying to the effect that the Spanish, who endeavour to kill the bull, need long arms, while the Portuguese, who merely annoy it, need long legs), and in olden times youths and maidens used to dance on them. The Romans, however, prized their cattle, and although a white bull was sacrificed in the Mithraic worship, 'Mention is made of a certain citizen accused before the people and condemned, because he had killed one of his oxen to satisfy the fancy of a young libertine, who told him he had never eaten any tripe.' I think there is more to this story than meets the eye. It seems that Asiatics, Greeks and Romans were particularly fond of offal, or what the Americans call 'organ meats'; Athenaeus, describing a 'feast of the most exquisite elegance', names double tripe among the dishes, while at a dinner at which Philoxenus, one of the generals of Alexander, was a guest, there were first served large basins containing the intestines of animals, 'disposed with art around their heads'.

There are numerous ancient recipes using brains, heads and offal – 'the parts of animals that are not joints. Once despised and very cheap, now in great demand and expensive.' This description is from the 1940s. However, the insides and extremities of animals are neither as highly nor as widely esteemed today, particularly since the brains and spinal cords were identified as harbouring the BSE prion, but our English ancestors were fond of umble pie which consisted of the stones, sweetbreads, liver and lights of the deer. Pepys was eating this medieval dish in the seventeenth century, although rather begrudgingly, saying of his host 'He did give us the meanest dinner of beef shoulders and umbles of venison,' but the estimable Mrs Raffald in the eighteenth century makes no mention of it. (I had assumed that everyone knew the origins of the phrase 'to eat humble pie' but recently read a piece by a distinguished gentleman of mature years who had only just heard of it. Umble pie was for hoi polloi.)

'Dear Hortense,' writes Eloise. 'Indeed you are a great woman and a profound philosopher. I am charmed with the spirit and the soundness of your judgement, after so many reverses of fortune, caused by the too bold speculation of your unfortunate but devoted husband.' (Here I find myself muttering 'Snap'.) This had caused Hortense to leave the 'beautiful but troublesome elegance' of her villa to live in a cottage. 'You think I miss my semi-sumptuous table of St. John's Wood. It will astonish you when I say, Not at all! . . . The little we have on our table is culinary perfection; no dish is ever spoiled by being

either under or over done – or too lazily or too little seasoned.'
Once a week there was a market at Coventry, a mere seven miles
from Hortense's rural residence. 'It is my hobby to go there
regularly, and with my scientific knowledge of Cookery, I purchase most excellent provisions at a very low price – do you
know why? Because I choose articles that are not in demand.'
She goes on to point out that everyone, 'even poor men', insists
on a good joint of meat for dinner, leaving what they consider
the inferior pieces on the hands of the butcher. Hortense was far
too smart not to utilise the despised bits.

Mrs Rundell explains how to prepare cow-heels. 'Boil them;
and serve in a napkin with melted butter, mustard and a large
spoonful of vinegar.' She also gives a recipe for 'Calf's Haggis
in the Monmouthshire Way':

> Use the small gut only (discarding the belly, lung, caul &c.). Cut
> the intestines open with a small knife, and cleanse them by hand
> washing through half a dozen buckets of water, so as to get
> them thoroughly sweet; then place them in cold water in a pot,
> and put the pot on the fire until the water boils. Then the haggis
> will begin to curl, and it will be time to take it up. If left to boil
> too long it will get a bad colour. It is now fit for use. Before it is
> fit for the table it must have a second boiling. It is served up with
> onion-sauce the same as tripe.

This is not haggis as the Scots know it, seeming to consist only
of the casing. I do not understand what Mrs Rundell was doing
here.

So popular was the stomach lining of the cow that, until quite
recently, there were special tripe shops where it was pre-cooked,
needing only to be taken home and served, sprinkled with salt,
pepper and vinegar, or stewed until tender – or roasted or fried:
opinions varied, one author advising, 'Do not fry tripe on any

consideration. It is detestable.' He said it should be boiled in the traditional way with milk and onions and served with English mustard. Janet notes that the smell of this dish, which she cooked for her parents, is also detestable. Honeycomb tripe was held to be the best kind and of all meat dishes the most digestible. The French, despite their changing attitudes to cookery (they are beginning to opt for fast food and sliced bread), still treasure it, or at least they did when I last enquired. The country would seem diminished without *Tripes à la mode de Caen*.

There is a general idea that tripe is despised in England because it is associated with the austerities of the Second World War, but once upon a time when the British were more adventurous they ate the face, the tails, the kidney, the liver and lights, the heart and the testicles, as well as the tongue, palates, feet, stomach, sweetbreads and brains. I only once ate tripe and that was in hospital when the other choice was something worse. I think it an acquired taste. I associate sweetbreads with childish resentment since the name leads one to expect something on the lines of pudding and I remember an early disappointment. 'Clean the tongue well,' writes *A Lady*, 'and salt it with common salt and saltpetre, then boil it; add likewise a fine young udder with some fat to it till both are tolerably tender; then tie the thick part of one to the thin part of the other and roast them together. Serve with good gravy and currant-jelly sauce.' She ends on a minatory note, 'This is an excellent dish.'

In *Warne's Everyday Cookery – Economical, Practical and Up-to-Date Recipes* (1929), Mrs Mabel Wijey (First-class Diploma of the National Training School of Cookery) suggests Roasted Ox Heart (*Coeur du Boeuf*), accompanied by a picture that does nothing to recommend it – indeed, it looks more suited to a medical textbook. Janet remembers a time when she was supposed to cook a heart and her parents refused to eat it as she insisted on demonstrating, whilst cleaning it, how a heart beats, squirting water in and out of the various chambers and openings.

You now have to travel far to find unashamed displays of viscera offered for sale, or indeed, any parts of the animal that are over-evocative of the living beast: no longer do haunches hang from hooks or pigs' heads stare from the butchers' windows of Britain. Small cuts of meat identifiable only by the label, ready for cooking and wrapped in plastic, line the supermarket shelves, but our present pusillanimity in the matter of meat and its provenance, our reluctance to associate it with the animal it comes from, are not universal. I have bought beef from a whole carcass hanging under a palm tree by the road from Port Said and not been unduly disconcerted, since I remember when the butcher flourished in Britain and meat was exhibited openly – although, admittedly, there were fewer flies.

I was once in Munich, staying just short of Maximilianstrasse, the Rodeo Drive of the city, which was lined with shops offering the then 'fashionable' shapeless and undistinguished garments at fashionable prices. Fleeing this depressing spot, we soon discovered the market area where, in a stretch of about a hundred yards, there were seven small butcher's shops with whole baby pigs hanging upside down from hooks and the heads of their larger relations beaming up from among the trays of sausages, which were many and various – white, black, pink and freckled. There were skinned hares too, but for some reason their heads were stuffed shyly into paper bags. There were plates of tripe and dishes of calves' feet, huge joints of beef and whole hams jostling for space in the windows. Bavarians do not share our timid attitude to flesh.

Nor did Josep Pla, the Catalan author, who could not be doing with pretentious dishes to please ignorant tourists but preferred basic peasant fare. The Catalan dish *Amonida de carn de perol* requires the stomach, kidneys and head of a pig – cheek, tongue and ear. I would very much like to know if anyone still makes it with all those elements. Whether they do or not, the fact remains that in Germany, Spain and France, and for all I know, every other country in the world with the possible exception of the USA, slaughtered animals are presented in all their unashamed nudity.

Is it that only the British abide by the regulations imposed by Brussels or have we misunderstood the directives?

It is interesting to note, bearing in mind the shuddering apprehension of the desert traveller that he might be offered the sheep's eye in the Bedouin tent as a mark of high favour, that 'Many like the eye; which you must cut out with the point of your knife, and divide in two.' So says *A Lady* in her description of how to carve a calf's head in the 1833 edition of her book.

There was once something called the Calves' Head Club, 'erected by an independent set of people, in derision of the day and defiance of monarchy', whose members met in a blind alley near Moorfields on 30 January to gloat over the death of Charles I. They ate calves' heads, dressed several ways: a large pike with a small one in its mouth (this was intended as an emblem of tyranny); a large cod's head to 'represent the person of the king singly, as by the calves' heads before they had done him together with all of them that suffered in his cause', and a boar's head with an apple in its mouth to 'represent the king as bestial, as by the others they had done foolish and tyrannical'. Then they burnt the Eikon Basilike, swore an oath on Milton's *Defensio Populi Anglicani*, and swigged liquor out of a calf's skull. The company consisted of Independents and Anabaptists, and Jerry White, formerly chaplain to Oliver Cromwell said grace and led them all in the *Anniversary Anthem* 'as they impiously called it'. It is this sort of behaviour that has done much to define the English character, in the eyes of others, as lacking in refinement or the most basic elements of taste: bone-headed in fact.

My husband was a member of something less coarse called the Beefsteak Club which, I think, had once sunk into oblivion but has been revived and dusted down. In 1863 Pierce wrote:

> The Beefsteak Club, one of the oldest clubs existing in London, consists at present of very few members. Its rules are singular, reminding us of those periods when Birthday Clubs, Long-nose Clubs, Anti-connubial Clubs, &c. &c. were in existence. It has amongst its archives a few memorials of the celebrities of the bygone age; amongst others, the pewter hot-water plate used by George IV, with his name scratched thereon with a fork, by himself, when prince, and from which he used to partake of the succulent steak, reeking hot from the gridiron.

The Sublime Society of Beefsteaks was founded by John Rich in 1732 after the success of *The Beggar's Opera* had made 'Gay rich and Rich gay', and the story is that one night the Earl of Peterborough was visiting Rich when his carriage was late in arriving. Instead of pouring himself a glass of something, as is usual when the guest's cab is stuck in traffic just round the corner, Rich grilled him a steak as he waited. The old Lord, for some reason, was thrilled by this and suggested a weekly renewal of the experience at the same time and place. The story of its origins is apocryphal (someone else says it was founded by the actor Estcourt in 1700), but the Society flourished, with membership limited to twenty-four and a lot of mightily droll rules and penalties for breaking them. Any infringement and the culprit had to stand in a corner in a white sheet, and many were the side-splitting japes that the members practised on each other. It had calmed down somewhat by the time my husband attended. You just had to sit wherever you were put at a long table and call the waiters Charles – or it might have been Fred – whatever it was it struck me as a touch discourteous. This is part of their anthem:

> Then Hogarth was a steaker devoted and true,
> For in France, when the gate of proud Calais he drew,
> A good English sirloin he placed in full view,
> Singing, Oh! the roast beef of old England!

Once upon a time, roast rib of beef with all the tracklements was our foremost celebratory family dinner (although we never ran to a sirloin). According to another dubious historical 'fact', 'This joint is said to owe its *name* to King Charles the Second, who, dining, upon a Loin of Beef, and being particularly pleased with it, asked the name of the Joint; and said for its merit it should be *knighted*, and henceforth called *Sir-Loin*.'

All that knighthood business was of course piffle. The proper spelling is surloin from the French *surlonge* – above the loin.

Once, when I was staying on a dude ranch in Texas, we were presented each evening with a slab of steak – the quantity of which would have sufficed for a family – served by disgruntled cowboys who would clearly have preferred to be out riding the range and resented having been seconded to waiter's duty, their spurs clacking on the lino. It was accompanied by a potato of pumpkin-sized dimensions and sour cream. With horseradish sauce one might have managed a fraction of it, but as it was it went away largely untouched. I also heard tales of cattle that no longer roamed the range but were confined in pens and over-fed until their insides fell out and had to be forcibly re-inserted by those self-same cowboys. When the BSE scare was at its height it was rumoured that it was also occurring in America and on the Continent and not only in Britain – which always seemed improbable. A talk-show hostess got herself into trouble with the ranchers of Texas when she said she would eat no more beef: she had to apologise and retract, for if Americans were to min-imise their intake of ribs, steak and hamburgers the economy would collapse. The sight of Old Glory brings immediately to mind thoughts of Coca-Cola, jeans and beef – rather than rev-erential musings on democracy and the Constitution. Back across the Atlantic, beef no longer holds the position in the national affection that once it did (it was indeed closely associ-ated in the public perception with the Union Jack), but here are some old receipts for nostalgia's sake, including a sirloin of beef, roasted from the *Encyclopaedia of Domestic Economy*:

Fifteen or twenty pounds in weight will require from three and a half to four hours roasting. As the upper, or *outside* as it is called, has seldom the same depth of meat as the under, or *inside*, it should be papered over for a couple of hours, and the fat also on the inside. Garnish it with hillocks of horseradish.

To Roast a Fillet of Beef: Raise the fillet from the inside of the sirloin, or from part of it, with a sharp knife; leave the fat on, trim off the skin, lard it through, or all over, or roast it quite plain; baste it with butter, and send it very hot to table, with tomata [*sic*] sauce, or *sauce piquante*, or eschalot sauce, in a tureen. It is sometimes served with brown gravy and currant jelly; it should then be garnished with forcemeat-balls, made as for hare. If not very large, an hour and a quarter will roast it well with a brisk fire.

Obs. The remainder of the joint may be boned, rolled, and roasted, or braised; or made into meat cakes; or served as a miniature round of beef.

I've been wondering about the feasibility of attempting to roast meat as opposed to baking it, which is what we do when we put it in the oven. This particular mode, at which Ulysses excelled, was the norm for thousands of years. You need a clear, hot fire and a spit – which is where the difficulty arises. Failing a Homeric hero, unless you were prepared to turn it yourself, you'd need a small boy (according to Aubrey, 'they licked the dripping pan and grew to be huge, lusty knaves'), some sort of clockwork device, or a dog on a wheel:

> Was ever cur so cursed? (he cried)
> What star did at my birth preside?
> Am I for life by compact bound,
> To tread the wheel's eternal round?

I feel sorrier for the dog than for the developing knaves. (In passing, *When the Cook is Away* has another idea for the deployment of a 'small boy' when preparing *Manderines de Faisan* – 'Pound the meat in a mortar. If a small boy happens to be near he will do this for you with vigour and delight. Pestles and mortars are generally proof against breakage, and unnecessary labour is so uneconomical.') For roasting you'd also need a fire-screen to shield the spit-turner from what Soyer would doubtless call the calorific influence of the flames, and you'd have to baste the meat constantly with the drippings, which would be falling into a receptacle conveniently placed for the purpose. Towards the end of the cooking time you would dredge the joint with flour and dry mustard or herbs to make a crisp outer coating. The dripping from a spitted roast is different from (and superior to) the fat of baked meat since it has been – for want of a better term – dripping throughout the cooking process rather than boiling away round the meat in the oven. I wouldn't want to make a habit of spending Sundays in this fashion, but I would like to try it once in the country, where there is no central heating but a good log fire. It is obviously simpler just to push the beef in the oven, but those who tried their meat both ways at the time when the closed range was coming into fashion, swore that the old method was incomparably better. I found an old clockwork roasting jack, complete with lengthy spike and the bit to hold up its end, in a market in Cahors but left it there when someone pointed out that since they confiscate your eyebrow tweezers, I would have trouble persuading the airline personnel that it was not a weapon of mass destruction.

In the preface to the new edition of *Mrs Beeton* (1890 and Isabella had been gone some time), baking 'is one of the most convenient and economical modes of cooking. There is a great prejudice against it, as far as regards meat, by comparing it with roasting,' but done properly it wasn't too bad. 'It is more trouble to open the door, draw the baking-tin to the edge and baste than to take up the ladle and use it in passing to and fro' – which leaves out of consideration the amount of splattered fat that must have posed a challenge to the scullion charged with cleaning the hearth. The designation 'Master Cook' was applied to men of the Ulysses stamp in so far as their roasting skills went. These heroes survive in only three establishments: Simpson's in the Strand, the Mansion House and the Worshipful Company of Cooks. They are unique in being permitted to wear a black –

rather than white – chef's hat, a pragmatic concession to the inevitable consequences of supervising the spit with your head up the chimney. (Barbecueing – which is a crude form of grilling – is one of the few culinary tasks which the average man likes to reserve to himself. On countless patios on long summer evenings, the women of the house will nod sagely and remind the company that this is an atavistic relic from the days of hunting and gathering and I see no unassailable reason to suppose them incorrect.)

It was common practice for those without ovens to take their joints, pies and puddings to be cooked, for a small fee, in the residual heat at the local baker's, when he had finished baking his bread. There had been a statute of Charles II against labour on Sunday containing 'an exemption in favour of cooks' shops, which had been extended to the baking of meat, puddings, and pies on a Sunday . . . it was "as reasonable that the baker should bake for the poor, as that the cook should roast or broil for them" . . . the laborious part of the community were entitled to indulgence, many of them not having the means of dressing their dinners at home.' Soyer, speaking as Hortense, refers to 'this semi-barbarian method of spoiling food' and to 'small folk . . . running to the baker's on Sunday with either their legs or their shoulders under their arms'. He demands to know how the baker can be held responsible for 'the proper cooking of this awkward squad . . . How can he prevent the potatoes from galavanting [*sic*] from one dish to another . . . Is he to be answerable if an eel crawls out of Mrs Armstrong's pie' to be found 'reposing under one of Mrs Smith's ribs?' I wondered about this myself. There must have been some arguments.

During the Second World War, people used still to try and 'roast' the tiny little joints of meat which were all the ration permitted: this was a waste of time and resources since only larger cuts are amenable to this treatment and those pitiful fist-sized bits of beef ended up tough and dry and inedible. The wiser stewed or pot-roasted them, enduring the loss of face that this entailed since the Roast Dinner was not merely an institution but a sign of probity and patriotism. Dougie Byng, a star of revue and cabaret, once somehow acquired a steak during the War when he was on tour and asked his landlady if she'd boil it for him. She answered in the affirmative and he said, 'I thought you would, you daft old bat.' I think he was too well mannered for this story to be true but it serves to illustrate the lack of *savoir faire* in the later English attitude to meat.

As for the rest of the cow, most nineteenth-century books give something like thirty recipes for preparing it. Braised steak with onions is the simplest and once ranked with Shepherd's Pie and macaroni cheese as the thing to eat when imagination failed, which was often.

There is surprisingly little mention of the stew as we know it: in earlier cookery books, entrées, hashes and other made and *réchauffé* dishes are far more common. In 1932, Florence White in *Good Things in England* tells us that, 'Mr P. Morton Shand [he wrote *A Book of Food* in 1929] objects to the word "stew" but it is quite as good a word as "ragout" and means exactly the same thing.' It doesn't quite. '"Casserole" cooking,' insists Florence White, 'is only a fashionable word for our own hot-pots,' continuing revealingly, 'It is never really necessary to add wine to English hot-pots, "jugged" dishes or stews.' This is why beef stew is not the same as *Boeuf Bourguignon* and stewed chicken is different from *Coq au Vin*.

It was held by many experts that, 'to dress vegetables with meat is wrong, except Boiled Beef and Carrots'. (There seem once to have been almost as many songs about food as there are now about love. 'Boiled beef and carrots, boiled beef and carrots, dah dah de dah dah de dah dah dah dah . . .') But the landlord of the Jolly Sandboys in *The Old Curiosity Shop* presided over a stew of tripe, cow-heel, bacon, steak, peas, cauliflowers, new potatoes and sparrow-grass, all bubbling away in a large iron cauldron – which, when you come to consider it, would have destroyed the point of all the individual ingredients.

Miss Acton's 'German' stew consists of equal quantities of beef and cabbage with some onion and salt and pepper. Her 'Welsh' stew is probably perfectly harmless but unlikely to rouse excitement, and there is nothing Welsh about it if you except the leeks. She also includes an English stew, flavoured with lemon rind and juice, mushroom catsup, soy and port or white wine. She says the intelligent cook will find it easy to vary this 'class of dishes' in numberless ways. How true. Another recipe (not Miss Acton's) for 'English' stew ran: 'Cut cold meat of any description into slices; pepper, salt, and flour them, and lay them in a dish; take pickles of any or of every kind at discretion, sprinkle them over the meat; then add half a teacupful of water to a small quantity of the vinegar belonging to the pickles, a little mushroom katsup, and any gravy that may be set by for use; stir all together, and pour it over the meat. Set it before the fire in the Dutch oven, or in the oven of the kitchen range, for about half an hour before dinner time.' This particularly ghastly concoction goes some way towards explaining the incidence of indigestion.

'Mrs Phillips' Irish Stew', as given to Dr Kitchiner, was composed of five thick mutton chops, two pounds of potatoes, six onions, salt and pepper, three gills of broth or gravy and two teaspoonfuls of mushroom catsup. 'A small slice of ham is a great addition to the dish.' The writers of nineteenth-century cookery books were always saying this and the small slice of ham constantly recurs. Perhaps it was a vague gesture towards France, for small cubes of fat ham or bacon do help to cheer up the blander meat dishes, and certainly ham must have had a more distinctive character in 1817. Someone known only as L. S. R. wrote in 1674 that he considered bacon the 'soul of all the best stews' and he put it in everything, but one of those flaccid, flat, pink squares that appear in plastic boxes in supermarkets would add nothing to this or any other dish.

We now tend to think of beef stew in French terms – *casserole*, *daube*, *marmite*, etc. – but Miss Acton mentions only *French Beef à la Mode* (seven or eight pounds of rump simmered for four or five hours) and *Beef Steaks à la Francaise* which roughly translates into steak and chips. She was untouched by the increasingly hysterical reverence accorded to French cuisine by the fashionable and showed little sign of the giddy passion for the social climbing that went with it. Another commendably measured opinion reads:

The English imagine that the more genuine flavours and greater nourishment are to be found in their dishes than in those of the French; the latter, on the other hand, assert that in English cooking too much is left for the digestive organs to perform. The state of intineration into which solid food is reduced by French cooking is that into which the digestion must bring it before it can complete its operation; and as in English cooking this is not, according to French notions, sufficiently brought about, it is regarded as the cause of the frequent derangement of the digestive organs, and consequent hypochondriacal affections, common to the English.

But the French, we must remember, were always fussing about their *mal à foie*, which made them universally *grincheux*.

Miss Acton, who was writing more in the eighteenth-century tradition of English country-house cookery (largely home-grown produce) rather than in the later, more elaborate and somewhat messier mode, felt no need to apologise. She speaks calmly as one on equal terms, giving praise where praise is due: 'A French cook of some celebrity orders the palates to be laid on the gridiron until the skin can be easily peeled or scraped off; the plan seems a good one, but we have not tried it.' This is evident in '*Beef Palates* (*Neapolitan Mode*): Boil the palates until the skin can be easily removed, then stew them very tender in good veal broth, lay them on a drainer and let them cool; cut them across obliquely into strips of about a quarter-inch in width, and finish them by dressing with any of the receipts for dressing macaroni.'

One author wrote frankly, 'With regard to *made dishes* as the horrible imitations of French cookery prevalent in England are termed, we must admit that they are very unwholesome. All the juices are boiled out of the meat which is swimming in a greasy heterogeneous compound, disgusting to the sight, and seasoned so strongly with spices and cayenne pepper, that it would inflame the stomach of an ostrich.' (My husband cut out of a newspaper a reference to the introduction of ostrich meat into our super-markets and pasted it into a notebook beside a long passage about these creatures from Pliny. This serves to illustrate, more or less, the extent and nature of his interest in food.)

This is what *The Dictionary of Daily Wants* calls a 'casserole':

Having cleaned and drained half a pound of rice, moisten it in a stewpan, with some fat; that which gathers on the top of liquor in which meat has been boiled will do. Strain some broth or soup, add to it a large quantity of grease, some pieces of fat bacon and a little salt; mix it with the rice to make it swell as much as possible; stir it frequently over a slow fire to keep it from sticking; when it is soft strain it through a cullender and press it well with a wooden spoon. The mould being selected for the casserole, raise it with the fat drained from the rice, taking care that every part of the inside of the mould be well greased; then cover it with rice, and place a piece of the crumb of the bread in the middle, and cover it with rice also; press it in equally with a spoon, and let it cool. When the rice has become firm, dip the outside of the mould into boiling water; add a covering of paste made with flour and water; flatten it all round with a spoon, and make an opening in the top with a knife, then put it into a very hot oven, baste it with the grease, and when it has become a fine colour, take it out of the oven, remove the crust, and the bread; next displace some of the rice from the inside, leaving sufficient to resist the weight of whatever may be put inside it. Fill it with minced meat, ragout, fricassee of chickens, macaroni, or scallops of fish that have already been served at the table; return it to the oven, and when thoroughly browned, serve.

This awful thing is regurgitated in *The Gentle Art of Cookery* in slightly modified form; finally steamed rather than baked and served with tomato sauce round it. It is followed in the book by a receipt for Oatmeal Pie, which was made of slices of a cold joint coated in oatmeal, layered with raw potato and onion and covered with a crust made of oatmeal and dripping.

Miss Acton's 'Saunders', especially if you stay with the sausage meat, is by way of contrast, edible:

Spread on the dish in which the Saunders are to be served, a layer of smoothly mashed potatoes, which have been seasoned with salt and mixed with about an ounce of butter to the pound. On these spread equally and thickly some underdressed beef or mutton minced and mixed with a little of the gravy that has run from the joint, or with a few spoonsful of any other; and season it with salt and pepper, and a small quantity of nutmeg. Place evenly over this another layer of potatoes, and send the dish to a moderate oven for half an hour. A very superior kind of Saunders is made by substituting fresh meat for roasted; but this requires to be baked an hour or something more. Sausage-meat highly seasoned may be served in this way, instead of beef or mutton.

Caroline Blackwood and I included this recipe in *Darling, You Shouldn't Have Gone to So Much Trouble* and I was once on a live radio programme in New Zealand when the interviewer, who obviously thought I wouldn't remember and would therefore be entertainingly humiliated, asked me to recite it. As it happened I had worked on the book to the point of madness, categorising, editing, querying, etc. and on hearing the name Lucien Freud would utter automatically 'Tomato Soup', or at the mention of Sue Lawley, trill 'Spicy Chicken' (they had kindly contributed these recipes). So I told the listeners how to make 'Saunders' and then the interviewer asked why I was such a fervent royalist. I'm not. I don't much care one way or the other, so the programme sank into mutual incomprehension with a baffled subject and a disconcerted interviewer. Serves her right.

Miss Acton also has a recipe for what would now be known as meat loaf or, possibly by those concerned with tone, as *pâté*. She calls it 'Beef Cake' and in future I believe I shall do the same.

Sir Francis notes, 'In Europe meat is beef, mutton, lamb, pork, and veal – on the Continent there is an enormous preponderance of veal, and it always seems a mystery where it comes from. There appear to be very few cows, and some at least of their progeny must be kept to grow into more cows. No veal is imported, but in spite of this the prevailing dish is veal. In England, where cattle of all kinds seems vastly more numerous than abroad, veal is comparatively scarce.' However, *The Dictionary of Daily Wants*, a hundred years earlier, had fifty-six receipts for cooking veal – more than for any other type of meat – as well as information on its dietetic qualities, the choice of joints, how to carve the various parts and how to choose it:

> The flesh of a bull-calf is firmer than that of a cow, but is seldom so white; the fillet of a cow-calf is generally preferred, on account of the udder. If the head is fresh, the eyes are plump, but if stale, they are sunk and wrinkled. If a shoulder is stale, the vein is not of a bright red; if there are any green or yellow spots in it, it is very bad. The breast and neck, to be good, should be white and dry; if they are clammy, and look green or yellow at the upper end, they are stale. The loin is apt to taint under the kidney; if it is stale, it will be soft and slimy. A leg should be firm and white; if it is limp and flabby, with green or yellow spots, it is not good.

If, after that, anyone still fancied veal, *A Lady*, who remarks that 'the whitest is not the most juicy, having been made so by frequent bleeding, and having had whiting to lick,' gives a method:

> To roll a Breast of Veal – Bone it, take off the thick skin and gristle, and beat the meat with a rolling pin. Season it with herbs chopped very fine, mixed with salt, pepper and mace. Lay some

thick slices of fine ham; or roll into it two or three calves' tongues of a fine red, boiled first an hour or two and skinned. Bind it up tight in a cloth, and tape it. Set it over the fire to simmer in a small quantity of water till it is quite tender; this will take some hours. Lay it on the dresser, with a board and weight on it till quite cold.

Pigs' or calves' feet, boiled and taken from the bones, may be put in it or round it. The different colours laid in layers look well when cut; and you may put in yolks of eggs boiled, beet-root, grated ham, and chopped parsley, in different parts.

No one I know will now eat veal since learning of the ghastly conditions in which calves spend their brief lives. We are aware that hens, for instance, also have a lousy time, but there is something about the look in calf eyes . . .

In the previous century, Macaulay had said of Croker, a fellow MP and writer, 'I detest him more than cold veal.' I now give, as promised, *Fin Bec*'s '*Calf's Head en Tortue*':

The remains of a boiled calf's head may be treated in the following manner. Put into a large saucepan a quarter of a pound of butter, a pound of bacon, three spoonfuls of flour, pepper, salt, a little water, and a bottle of good white wine. Add two onions, a bouquet, and some cloves. Prepare the things which are necessary for a *tortue* viz. quenelles of veal, cockscombs and kidneys, pieces of calf's tongue and brains, sweetbread cut up, mushrooms, etc. Put these into the sauce, and when they are cooked, take out the onions and the bouquet and the cloves, and put the calf's head in, and let it just boil. Then put it into a dish, and the sauce over it, also some gherkins, crayfish, and nasturtium seeds preserved in vinegar.

But perhaps *Fin Bec*'s most baffling offering is '*Calf's Head en papillotes*': 'Put some slices of liver in pickle, and throw in a well-oiled piece of paper between two thin slices of bacon, with herbs. Put the liver on the gridiron, and serve up when it is of a good colour.' It is always being said now that there is hardly a decent editor left on the planet – the implication being that once upon a time you fell over them in the street – but on the evidence of the above, certain essentials slipped past them. Or maybe *Fin Bec* was too vain to admit the need of any eye other than his own.

In 1878 he wrote, 'Madame de Genlis boasted that she had taught a German lady how to prepare seven delectable dishes. Mme de Genlis had reason to be proud of her present to her friend, more especially as that friend belonged to a country the *cuisine* of which is, even now, contemptible.' This – from *Fin Bec*. However, I've never felt much inspired by Teutonic cookery although it must certainly be filling and comforting in a hard winter. Sausage, cabbage, potatoes and gravy, especially with dumplings, are probably just what is needed after a long day in the cold: a book of German cookery gives twenty-three recipes for dumplings to be served with soup, meat or fruit – which reminds me of an experience I had in Belgium many years ago. Staying with friends my father had made during the War, we were served a bowl of cherries with meatballs swimming in the juice. If you suspend disbelief this is no odder, really, than pork with apple sauce, but it came as a surprise. (Another astonishment awaiting us in Villard de Lans, deprived as we were not only by wartime scarcity but by the English mode of butchering the pig, was a tranche of pork such as we had never previously seen; white and tender and grilled to perfection.)

In the USA, where fat has usurped the place of the devil as the prime enemy of mankind, I read a suggestion for rinsed mince. You fry it with garlic and onions and then you run it all, in a sieve, under the hot tap, thus ridding it of fat and, I should think, all of the taste and much of the nutrient value. Meatballs are usually good but it's best to make them yourself. The same goes for sausages, which are not 'contemptible' at all so long as they're not composed of the detritus from the abattoir floor. One agrees with *Cassell's Cookery* that:

Sausages are always best home-made, for the best of reasons viz., that you then, and only then, know what is in them. Every house should have a small sausage machine, which, in addition to simply making sausages, will make rissoles, forcemeats of all kinds, as well as croquettes. Indeed, a small hand sausage machine repays itself quicker than almost any other kind of kitchen utensil. Sausages are best served up on toast, then the fat that runs from them can be poured over them and soaked up and eaten, and not emptied to help swell that household disgrace – the cook's grease-box.

Sausages must have been particularly useful in the days before dentistry reached its present peak. Teeth were always a source of pain and annoyance and frequently extracted. (*The Dictionary of Daily Wants* says of the dentist, 'the operator has most power and control, and can see best what he is about, if he set the patient on the floor, throw his head far back, and fix it between his knees'.) Here is an old recipe that could be mumbled by the gums:

To Make The Best Sawsidges That Ever Were Eat – Proceed as follows: Take a leg of pork, and cut off all the lean, and shred it very small, but leave none of the strings or skin among it; then take two pounds of beef suet and shred it very small, then take two handfulls of red sage, a little pepper and salt and nutmeg and a small piece of onion, chop them altogether with the flesh and salt; if it is small enough put the yolkes of two or three egges and mix all together, and make it up in a paste if you will use it, roule out as many pieces as you please in the form of an ordinary sawsidge, and so fry them; this paste will serve a fort-night upon occasion.

We make this in much the same way as the long-dead cook who was so rightly pleased with his 'sawsidges, only I use the food processor, add toasted breadcrumbs (not too fine), a glass of port, and a lot more onion (previously lightly fried), and I leave out the egg yolks because they make the end result too compacted and dry. This sort of 'paste' is not for those frightened of fat (we use the fat of the pork rather than beef suet) and those who are must simply decline to accept it, for a 'fat-free' version would be inedible. Nevertheless, the advice given by *Cassell's Cookery* to serve sausages on toast in order to soak up the fat and eat it is going *too* far.

My friend, the late Jennifer Paterson, came in for considerable criticism when she mixed food with her bare hands in her cook-ery series, which is irrational in any moaner who unthinkingly eats *chorizo*, for I have seen Spanish butchers mixing sausage meat with their brawny arms naked up to their streaming armpits. My editor Jill once told me, haltingly, of an establishment famed for its delicious meatballs where the cook rolled them under her armpits, infusing them with her own sweat. Oh God.

Twelve

ONE MAN'S MEAT

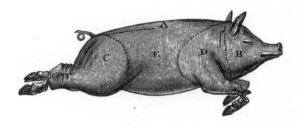

$\mathcal{A}$s someone asked in 1882, 'If the system of flesh eating is defensible, why must the method of supply be concealed from all thought and reference? Why is the slaughter house unmentionable?' It seems that even then the English urban dweller was succumbing to hypocrisy and an excess of fastidiousness, though few yet shrank from the sight of the sucking pig laid out on the charger with an apple in its mouth or, according to *Indian Domestic Economy and Cookery*, a lime.

When I was a child, no one would eat pork in the summer any more than they would eat oysters in a month without an 'r' or expect strawberries in December, but modern methods of refrigeration have made it less risky. Soyer is rude about the pig – 'its vile and stupid ugliness, its depraved habits, and its waddling obesity' – but it is now held that in many physiological respects we resemble the pig more closely than we do the ape; scientists are cloning them and hope to eventually succeed in breeding them in order to supply spare parts for humans. (The Canadians have just produced a genetically modified pig which has only twenty-five per cent of the usual phosphorous in its urine – making it 'less harmful' in its use as manure. Fancy that.) Moreover, human flesh is said to taste like pork and certain cannibals refer to the former as 'long pig', cooking it in the same way.

Pigs would not, given the option, choose to live in sties in the vicinity of people: their admirers claim that they are, by nature, cleanly and highly intelligent beasts corrupted by their proximity to humankind, and even Soyer was shocked by that Roman 'culinary atrocity': stifling the young before they were littered. This 'disgusting dish' led him to deplore the 'refinement of incredible gluttony', the 'frightful depravity and atrocious cruelty which, together, prepared the downfall of the Roman colossus'. There is a rhyme about a pig and a drunk finding themselves in the same gutter; it ends, 'You can tell a man who boozes by the company he chooses, and at that the pig got up and walked away.' It was always said of this animal that you could use every part of it except for the squeak and after that the bones were boiled for soup – or to make jelly or in the final analysis, glue.

Francatelli tells, 'How to Make the Most of a Pig, After it is Killed. Cottagers sometimes feed a pig for their own consumption, and therefore it is that, in the hope that many, if not all, of you may have it in your power to do so, I will give you proper instructions showing the best way to make the most of it . . .' Francatelli's directions conclude, 'When a pig is killed, the blood should be caught in a pan, and a little salt must be stirred in with it while yet warm, to prevent its coagulation or thickening. This will serve to make you some hog's puddings, an excellent thing in its way . . .' I rather prefer Mrs Raffald on this subject and will let her speak later.

Many families used to keep pigs, which were slaughtered by the local butcher. Janet remembers her mum's description of a pig, kept by neighbours when she was young, being killed and the blood collected as described above – the neighbour beating the blood with her bare hands to keep it liquid for use in black pudding.

'The young are seldom fit to roast under a month and there will generally be found in a litter one larger than the rest. This is not, as is supposed by some, the mother's favourite, but is the strongest and manages, by thrusting the others aside, to get the largest share of milk. Of course he is the first for roasting.' There is clearly a lesson in there somewhere.

Dr Kitchiner writes that a sucking pig requires very careful roasting and 'like a young Child must not be left for an instant . . . Lay your Pig back to back in the dish, with one half of the head on each side, and the EARS one at each end, which you must take care to make nice and *crisp*, or you will get scolded, and deservedly, as the silly fellow who bought his wife a pig with only one ear.' (This is another of those once ubiquitous jokes that lose their point with the passage of time.) I baked a pig's head for the Roman dinner; its ears swelled up with hot air like balloons. One of Apicius' recipes for sucking pig might have been called 'In A Pig's Ear' rather than '*Porcellum Farsilem Duobus Generibus*'; it requires the cook to put stuffing in an ox-bladder with a bird-keeper's reed pipe attached to the opening: you squeeze it into the pig's ears and then close them with paper.

I find over-detailed recipes counter-productive and have increasing sympathy with the cookery writers of old, who assumed that the cook will have some awareness of what goes on in the kitchen and how to proceed. I am not claiming that those recipes which specify nothing but the ingredients are easy to follow, but I find just as annoying the modern method of supplying endless columns of weights and measures in imperial and metric right down to the last quarter of a teaspoon of salt. A certain Professor Alden in 1932 made an attack upon the vagueness of the English cook. He said that she takes from a pound to a pound and a half of flour, as many eggs as ought to be enough, seasoning to taste, puts it into an oven of unspecified warmth and then sits down to see whether it will turn into an Irish stew or a pancake. Then there was the Irish cook who said, 'You must take more than you'd think of flour, Ma'am, just what you know of butter, the slightest taste in life of baking powder and the fill of the small jug of milk.' Until about the middle of the nineteenth century and the advent of the meticulous Dr Kitchiner, all the writers of cookery books were majestically inexplicit, seemingly taking it for granted that they were addressing professionals who would be fully cognisant of the basic rules of cookery and were looking only for a few extra suggestions and novelties.

From *The Forme of Cury*, compiled in about 1390 (it is said, by Richard II), to Mrs Raffald in 1791, the experts said things like, 'Take as much meat as is needed' and 'as many currants as you may require', which is of no help to the beginner, but Apicius is the vaguest of all. For instance there is '*Porcellum Lacte Pastum Elixum Calidum Iure Frigido Crudo Apiciano*' (his own receipt): 'In a mortar put pepper, lovage, coriander-seed, mint, rue. Pound, moisten with *liquamen*, add honey and wine and blend with *liquamen*. Dry the hot boiled pig with a clean cloth and pour the dressing over.' The only clue here as to what to do with the pig comes with the final assumption that you've boiled it. It is not a dish for the tyro but is addressed to his peers by an experienced, hardened chef. Deep calleth unto deep. Thus might Rowley Leigh converse with Anton Mosiman. The medieval cook must have been a person of energy and muscle tone and not of a nervous disposition, for to prepare a 'pigge in sauge' you must 'Take a pigge, draw him, smyte off his hede, kut him in iiij quarters, boyle him til he be ynow, take him uppe and lete cole, smyte him in peces,' then season him with 'sauge' and 'cowche thi pigge in disshes and caste the sirippe theruppon.' The result, considering the 'sirippe', must have been something like sweet and sour pork.

I have always been glad that wild boar no longer roam the countryside having once read an account of how they attacked wanderers and gored them to death. I never could forget it. (My third son now lives in France in *sanglier* country and I will not walk in the woods.) It was in the winter of 1947 when snow filled the lanes to the top of the hedgerows and I couldn't go to school. I sat by the kitchen range with a bag of mint imperials and a book about Robin Hood and there was a picture of this horrible little striped pig with boot-button eyes and a short snout and long tusks standing with his family over a corpse. There was once a scholar of Queen's (my husband's college, so he liked this story) who foiled a wild boar which charged him as he was strolling along reading Aristotle. With remarkable presence of mind, he stuffed the volume down the creature's throat and made his escape. On reflection there is some sort of rude pattern here, for whenever anyone picked up one of my husband's books he would remind them not to keep the place with a bacon sandwich. (I have just heard that wild boar are again at large in the English countryside.)

It is said that the Druids who never wrote anything down and so left themselves open to wild surmise, would, at the Winter Solstice, offer a boar's head to Freya, goddess of Peace and Plenty, and as time went by, it seems brawn, served with mustard, was the invariable *hors d'oeuvre* with which banquets opened; while, on special occasions, the complete boar's head would be carried in shoulder high, grinning, gilded and ornamented. 'The boar's head, I onderstonde, Is first service in the londe.' One of my books has a picture, dating from Edwardian times, of this scene being enacted at Queen's where, I suppose, they had special reason to gloat. We still serve pâté as a first course but few of us have made brawn ourselves by boiling the boar's head and picking all the meat off. I did it once but never again. I seem to remember ending up with surprisingly little brawn compared to the size of the pig's head and, anyway, there was something altogether too personal in contemplating its features. Nor did I go to the lengths advised by *A Lady*: to split and nicely clean a hog's head, take off the hair and snout and take out the eyes and the brains, cut off the ears and rub a 'good deal' of salt into it: then you let it drain for twenty-four hours and laid more salt and saltpetre on it. Wait three days, then put it with some more salt in a pan and cover it with water. Wait another two days. Wash it, then boil it till the bones come out. Skin it (and the tongue) and chop it up and then put it on one half of the skin and put the other half on top. 'The ears are to be boiled longer than the head, cut in thin strips, and divided about it, the hair being nicely removed.' Then you pickle it. It is 'a very convenient thing to have in the house.' 'If you approve' you can put the boned pig's feet round the outside and if it looks like going off, you can slice it and fry it. An ancient moralist deplored the new-fangled approach to 'cury' and would have preferred his dinner plain and simple. (The word 'cury', by the way, is not Olde Englishe for curry, as I once heard a TV chef explaining, but means 'cookery'.)

'Cookes with theire newe conceytes, choppynge, stampynge and gryndynge, Mony newe curies all day they are contryvynge and fyndynge.' Looking on the bright side, all that choppynge, stampynge and gryndynge is now unnecessary with the invention of the food processor and home-made pâté is within the capabilities of all. Here's a medieval sort: 'Take Porke and hakke it smal and Eyrown y-mellyd togederys and a lytel Milke, and melle hem togederys with Hony and Pepir and bake hem in a cofyn and serve forth.' Eyrown: eggs and cofyn: pie crust, but hold the hony, honey.

Another indication that many householders kept a pig and were expected to despatch it themselves is provided by Mrs Raffald's directions for roasting a pig:

ſtick your pig juſt above the breaſt-bone, run your knife to the heart, when it is dead put it in cold water for a few minutes, then rub it over with a little roſin beat exceeding fine, or its own blood, put your pig into a pail of ſcalding water half a minute, take it out, lay it on a clean table, pull off the hair as quick as poſſible, if it does not come clean off put it in again, when you have got it all clean off, waſh it in warm water, then in two or three cold waters, for fear the roſin ſhould taſte; take off the four feet at the firſt joint, make ſlit down the belly, take out all the entrailſ, put the liver, heart, and lightſ to the pettitoeſ, waſh it well out of cold water, dry it exceeding well with a cloth, hang it up, and when you roaſt it put in a little ſhred ſage, a tea-ſpoonful of black pepper, two of ſalt, and a cruſt of brown bread, ſpit your pig, and ſew it up; lay down a briſk, clear fire; with a pig-plate hung in the middle of the fire; when your pig is warm put in a lump of butter in a cloth, rub your pig often with it while it is roaſting; a large one will take an hour and a half; when your pig is a fine brown, and the ſteam drawſ near the fire, take a clean cloth, rub your pig quite dry, then rub it well with a little cold butter, it will help to criſp it; then take a ſharp knife, cut off the head, and take off the collar, then take off the earſ and jaw-bone, ſplit the jaw in two, when you have cut the pig down the back, which muſt be done before you draw the ſpit out, then lay your pig back to back on your diſh, and the jaw on each ſide, the earſ on each ſhoulder, and put in your ſauce, and ſerve it up. Garniſh with a cruſt of brown bread, grated.

Well never mind all that: just remember when you roast pork to put it on a grid and do not let the skin dip into the boiling fat or it will turn not into crackling but leather.

Bacon is 'The flesh of the pig salted, dried and usually smoked. If salted and dried and not smoked, it is known as green bacon,' while ham is 'The hind legs of a pig salted, cured and smoked, the hams are frequently cured with the whole side of bacon. Shoulders, cushions, collars, and other parts thus cured are also called ham, although they are really bacon.' The packeted bacon we now buy in supermarkets has something odd about it: it exudes not fat, but a milky-looking substance – the result I am told of plumping up the meat with water – and it sticks to the pan. ('Bacon should be soaked in cold water for three to four minutes before frying. This will prevent the fat from running, and will make the bacon go much further' runs an early suggestion for economy.) When I go to the States I come back with several packets of Canadian Streaky which gives up as much grease as the most ardent bacon-sandwich addict could wish. I do not know how Americans reconcile this with their terror of fat. Janet misses the days when you could lean in a relaxed fashion on the counter and instruct the grocer to cut 'half a pound of lean green back, number five' – the last indicating the dimension of the cut.

Bacon was often the only meat the poor could afford: the extravagance in poverty-stricken households usually consisted in the housewife throwing away the water it had boiled in. The wise and thrifty added dried peas to the cauldron, and if it was still too salt they put in potatoes and extra water. While on the subject of bacon, let us briefly consider eggs. '*Well-cleansed Dripping or Lard*, or Fresh Butter, are the best fats for frying Eggs,' says Dr Kitchiner.

> Be sure the frying-pan is quite clean; when the fat is hot, break two or three Eggs into it; do not turn them over, but, while they are frying, keep pouring some of the fat over them with a spoon: – when the Yolk just begins to look white, which it will in about a couple of minutes, they are done enough: – *the white must not loose* [sic] *its transparency, but the Yolk must be seen blushing through it.* – If they are done nicely, they will look as white and delicate as if they had been poached; take them up with a tin slice, drain the Fat from them, trim them neatly, and send them up with the Bacon round them.

The egg 'as a whole', we are told puzzlingly by J. F. W. Johnston in *Things Not Generally Known*, 'is richer in fat than beef. It is equalled in this respect, among common kinds of food, only by pork and by eels. The white of the egg is, however, entirely free from fat; and it is a very constipating variety of animal food, so that it requires much fat to be eaten along with it when consumed in any quantity, in order that this quality may be counteracted. It is, no doubt, because experience had long ago proved this in the stomachs of the people, that "eggs and bacon" have been a popular dish among Gentile nations from time immemorial.' Another book advises, 'Always use a silver fork for beating an egg instead of a steel one, as the phosphorous of the yolk attacks the steel and forms a disagreeable salt.' It happens to spoons too: we always had to have special ones for boiled eggs – plastic spoons came in useful if you'd lost the proper ones.

'Ham – Though of the Bacon kind, has been so altered and hardened in the curing, that it requires still more care,' says Dr Kitchiner, and advises that, 'In a very small Family, where a Ham will last a week or ten days, it is best Economy not to cut it till it is cold – it will be infinitely more juicy.

'Pull off the *Skin* carefully, and preserve it as whole as possible; it will form an excellent covering to keep the Ham moist . . .' Since the good doctor recommends 'a middling-sized ham of fifteen pounds' it is hard not to feel sorry for the 'very small Family' steadily chomping its way through fifteen pounds of ham in a week or ten days; but the sensible suggestion in regard to the skin gives me the same sense of fellowship that I have felt in foreign countries when I have found the cook adhering to familiar culinary practices, even when the finished dish is out of my experience. It must be admitted that while bacon is not as good as it once was, hams generally are no longer as difficult to render edible.

Spam came to our tables from the USA in 1941, and very welcome it was. No one could go out and buy an unlimited amount since it was subject to the points system (each person was allowed sixteen points a month to buy various tinned or dried things), so it was regarded as a treat. Its name, according to some, is the compacted version of Spiced Ham, just as the contents of the tin are the compacted version of the ham itself; others say it comes from 'shoulder of pork and ham' – but whatever its origins, the name fits it perfectly, fat and solid. Spam Salad no longer has the power to excite now that numerous hams, salamis, pastramis, and so on, are readily available, and Spam Fritters are no longer desirable now that fat is not in short supply but so universally frowned upon. Spam Curry however is still a favoured family dish. Both Alfred and my youngest son prefer it to anything that, say, The Ivy might offer.

My agent, when practising Kung Fu, used to dine on fried Spam and pak choi at the home of his instructor. I am told that Spam Appreciation Societies have now sprung up, while in the East – Japan and Korea – a whole new strand of cuisine has developed around this undoubtedly convenient substance: it has a fan club and a website of its own, both well-deserved, and I sent my youngest son one of their recipe books last Christmas.

Venison was once the favourite and exclusive meat of the upper classes (poaching the King's deer was a capital offence), but I think it over-rated, even if low in cholesterol: I once heard (possibly on *The Archers*) that it can carry BSE. *The Dictionary of Daily Wants* gives advice on choosing venison: 'When good, the fat is clear, bright, and of considerable thickness. To know when it is necessary to cook it, a knife must be plunged into the haunch, and from the smell, the cook must determine of dressing or keeping it.' Several old methods recommend boiling it before roasting, which leads one to suspect it might have been unacceptably tough. But then all meat was tougher in the olden days. Another method was to enclose it in a flour and water paste.

The author of *Domestic Management* (1813) wrote in terms

which would appeal to those who prefer their meat organic:

> Game, and other wild animals proper for food, are of very supe-
> rior qualities to the tame – from the total contrast of the
> circumstances attending them. They have a free range of exer-
> cise in the open air, and choose their own food, the good effects
> of which are very evident in a short delicate texture of flesh,
> found only in them. Their juices and flavour are more pure, and
> their *Fat*, when it is present in any degree, as in Venison, and
> some other instances, differs as much from that of our fatted
> animals, as Silver and Gold from the grosser metals. The supe-
> riority of Scotch Beef and Welsh Mutton is owing to a similar
> cause.

Thomas Love Peacock observed, before anyone worried about
cholesterol:

> The mountain sheep are sweeter,
> But the valley sheep are fatter;
> We therefore deemed it meeter
> To carry off the latter.

How circumstances alter attitude: there is nothing so enchant-
ing as a lamb and few things more exasperating than a sheep.
Nor are the features of the sheep capable of expressing apology
or shame, unlike the dog and sometimes even the cat. Cows
can look reproachful and vaguely threatening, rather like
one's mother; horses can look mad in both senses of the
word; pigs look as though they can see a joke not immediately
apparent to the rest of us, but once a sheep is grown up and
out of the playful stage it only looks sheeplike. Some shep-
herds are able to recognise individuals and deny that they

are stupid, but if they are not, one has to suspect them of malevolence (one author excuses the apparent idiocy of the domestic sheep on the grounds that it has 'in the course of a long and intensive breeding lost most of its initiative'). They used to come down from the lush hillside to eat the dahlias in my mother's garden and only a summer since one spitefully ate the hydrangea while another consumed the fuchsia. It is difficult, when one is annoyed with a creature of another species, not to attribute human qualities to it. When people do something appalling it is usual to say that they are behaving like animals, but the saying works better the other way round. Lambs and babies have a lot in common too: it is hard to grasp that the small, amusing, delightful things will mature into, on the one hand, sheep, and on the other, the people next door.

Despite the doubts now expressed in some quarters about the wholesomeness of lamb – the fear that scrapie might be passed on to human beings and the possibility that some may be radioactive – it is still thought of as a staple of English diet. Many of us would feel bereft without roast lamb and mint sauce and the ever-comforting Shepherd's Pie. Ernest Joyce Mills in 1929 describes how, on an Antarctic expedition, 'All the sheep were killed today and hung in the rigging, the temperature being about refrigerating point.' It is a picturesque vision – a ship setting sail with the homely carcasses wafting in the Antarctic breeze. The expedition sounds like hell, but the author's tone is invariably cheerful and undaunted. 'At first it is difficult to persuade one unaccustomed that seal and penguin meat can be made appetizing; but seal to the palate is similar to beef and penguin breast compares favourably with wild duck.' I doubt it. It is likely that they taste more like that ancient Welsh delicacy, Pickled Puffin. Being still conservative in our food habits we cannot eat anything new unless we can relate the flavour to something old to which we are used.

Mrs Beeton says sternly that the fat of lambs is never distasteful. Many a nurse and mother will have recited this to a chair-bound child as he sat staring, revolted, at a congealing cut off the joint, forbidden to leave the table until he'd eaten up every scrap. She holds that the most delicious sorts of lamb are the South Down breed, known by their black feet, and of these, those that 'have been exclusively suckled on the milk of the parent ewe are considered the finest'.

When purchasing your lamb you should look for certain signs:

> by which the experienced judgement is able to form an accurate opinion of whether the animal has been lately slaughtered, and whether the joints possess that condition of fibre indicative of good and wholesome meat. The first of these doubts may be solved satisfactorily by the bright and dilated appearance of the eye; the quality of the fore-quarter can always be guaranteed by the blue or healthy ruddiness of the jugular, or vein of the neck; while the rigidity of the knuckle, and the firm, compact feel of the kidney, will answer in an equally positive manner for the integrity of the hind-quarter.

All of which is a further indication of a more intimate association between consumer and consumed than is now usual. Mrs Beeton then tackles (with diagram), the intricacies of carving the forequarter of lamb. When the carver has divided the shoulder from the breast, the ribs from the brisket, and then carved each constituent part ready for his guests, he 'should ask those at the table what parts they prefer – ribs, brisket, or a piece of the shoulder'.

This scene is seldom enacted now in the domestic circle, certainly not with the same meticulous attention to the co-ordinates of the joint and the details of its composition. For centuries, when meat was held in high regard, he who cut it up and served it out was a person of some importance: carving, when people ate heroic quantities, was also hung about with ritual; a skilled carver, so it was said, could impale a joint on a fork, hold it high in the air and cut off perfect slices which would fall, neatly in order, on the plate beneath. Rather like those bartenders who juggle bottles: very clever, you concede, but why bother?

In Elizabethan times the lady of the house took over the task. As Mr Cordy Jeaffreson says:

> Having been thus called to the head of the table for her lord's convenience instead of her own dignity, the mistress of the house soon made it a point of honour to occupy the place, which had in the first instance been conceded to her as a servant, rather than as principal lady. Ere long, with her characteristic cleverness in making the best of things, and stating her own case in the way most agreeable to her self-love, she regarded her carver's stool as a throne of state and affected to preside over the company, though the terms of her commission only authorized her to help them to food.

'Carving is not to be considered alone as an accomplishment to be displayed at the tables of others; it is in fact a very requisite branch of domestic management, and highly important in an economical point of view; for it is notorious that a joint of meat ill-carved will not serve nearly so many persons as it would if it were properly carved,' said *The Dictionary of Daily Wants*; and 'One of the most important acquisitions in the routine of daily life, is to know how to carve well. Every person who mixes with society at all, is likely to be called upon at any moment to perform this office; to refuse to undertake it savours of ill-nature and selfishness; and to perform it in an awkward and bungling manner, is painful and unpleasant for lookers-on and exceedingly humilitating to the operator.' ('Would you pass me that chicken?' asked a young lady cheerfully when she had inadvertently propelled it on to the lap of a diner.)

Many authors warned of the embarrassments incurred when the meat was tough. *Anon* writes, 'It was nine o'clock, if not past, when the haunch was brought in. I shall never forget its appearance; at first I thought that they had placed on the dish, by way of joke, the saddle belonging to some post-boy, who had rode on it as many years as the lady of the mansion was old. The poor host tried to carve it, but to cut it was impossible. It was done, it was overdone, and was like cutting old cable.'

Another adviser says, 'The carver must carefully avoid all clumsiness of attitude and deportment; squaring the elbows, tucking up the coat-sleeves, dropping the knife and fork, splashing the gravy, and over-turning the glasses, are evidences of awkwardness and ungracefulness on the part of the carver.' *A Lady* tells us, 'the carving knife for a lady should be light, and of a middling size and fine edge. Strength is less required than address in the manner of using it.' Some ladies were still attending 'carving schools' in the nineteenth century, and according to *Home Queries* 'if the carving be not done with the skill of an artist the meal is but a poor affair and dishonoures [*sic*] both guest and host. To carve ill is to show that one's learning in polite affairs is lacking . . . [It is] a noble art that should be carried out with artistry, as a painter would transfer a beautiful scene to canvas, not slapping colour from a brush.'

In passing, the oldest carving fork in existence belonged to Henri IV and 'is of sufficient length and strength to secure a baron of beef', or so they say. In 1847 it was still preserved in the castle at Pau.

The Boke of Kervynge, printed by Wynkyn de Worde, contains a list of the terms used in carving. You must break a deer, lesche brawn, rear a goose, lift a swan, sauce a capon, frusshe chicken, spoyle a hen, unbrace a mallard, dismember a heron, display a crane, disfigure a peacock, unjoint a bittern, untach a curlew, allay a pheasant, wing a partridge or quail, mince a plover, thigh a pigeon, woodcock or any other small birds, border a pasty, tyer an egg, chine a salmon, string a lamprey, splatt a pike, sauce a tench, splay a bream, side a haddock, tusk a barbel, culpon a trout, fynne a chevon, traunsense an eel, traunche a sturgeon, undertraunche a porpoise, tame a crab, and barbe a lobster.

But back, as they say, to our *moutons*. I have discovered that this saying originates in the old French play of *Patelin*. A woollen draper went to court to complain that his shepherd had stolen some sheep from him, but kept wandering from the point to reiterate that his antagonist's attorney had likewise robbed him of a piece of cloth. It sounds like an early version of those interestingly convoluted courtroom dramas where nothing is quite as it seems. The judge, whenever the attorney was mentioned in connection with the theft of this cloth, would call out, '*Revenons à nos moutons.*' An example of how the legal profession looks after its own.

I don't know where mutton went. Every now and then it is said to have returned and people write articles about it in the Sunday supplements, but the word seldom crosses the lips of a butcher, while improbably large pieces of sheep are still described as lamb. 'Mutton is considered in its prime at five years old; but as this is rather difficult to find, the nearer it approaches that age the primer it will be.' Tinned mutton was once known to the Royal Navy as Fanny Adams. One dictionary says, 'From a girl murdered and cut up c. 1812', which goes to show how the unregenerate members of society disregarded the well-intentioned efforts to improve their minds. (She was actually killed in 1867.)

John Nott describes how '*To dreſſ a ſhoulder of Mutton in Blood. ſave the Blood of a ſheep, take all the ſtringſ and Knotſ out of a ſhoulder of Mutton, lay it in the Blood five or ſix Hourſ to ſoak; then ſtuff it with ſweet Herbſ, then put it into a Caul, ſprinkle it with Blood, and roaſt it. ſerve it up with Veniſon or Anchovy ſauce.*' *A Lady* gives thirty receipts for mutton, treating it as belonging to quite a different category from the younger version. Roasted leg of mutton should be served with currant jelly or onion sauce, salad and potatoes. If boiled, it should appear on the table with caper sauce, mashed turnips, greens and carrots. Mutton chops and boiled potatoes were standard fare in the appropriately named Chop Houses patronised by men working in the City. There was a long running argument as to whether steaks and chops should be turned frequently or only once. It was finally concluded by the gourmet that once was best, an opinion which holds to this day.

The author of *Dinners at Home* suggests Saddle of Mutton: 'This is a less expensive dish for a small party than is imagined. The Alderman's Walk being cut out, makes one dish, a roast joint the second, and the following day it can be heated up by placing a piece of buttered paper over it, and roasting it again carefully; and after that the remains can be made into rissole cutlets, the bones being put into the stock pot.'

Sir Francis on rissoles:

The final fate of fifty per cent of cold mutton and cold beef . . . the meat, including all the gristle is put through the mincer, mixed with a very small amount of cornflour and milk, or of some vague gravy to make the mass stick together, made into balls about the size of a fives ball, patted slightly to flatten them, coated with egg and breadcrumb, and then frizzled in an eighth of an inch of fat in a frying-pan, first on one side and then on the other. The result is a hard top and bottom, with a soft middle, and the whole thing greasy. Each one, though not very large, is a quite considerable helping of solid meat in its most indigestible form, and entirely devoid of attraction.

A certain anecdote recurs in varying forms in several of my books. Soyer, in the guise of his heroine, Hortense, puts it this way:

> *Cutlets A La Victime* or Victimized Cutlets: Here *ma belle amie*, is a terrific title for a receipt . . . which I must tell you was done by a culinary artist of Louis XVIII of France, at the palace of the Tuileries, and first partaken of by that intellectual monarch and gourmet, who, at the end of his stormy reign, through a serious illness, was completely paralyzed, and at the same time, the functioning organs of his digestion were much out of order; being a man of great corpulence . . . much food was required to satisfy his royal appetite.

His physicians racked their brains for ways of supplying this food in 'the smallest compass', while the head cook took a few hours off for reflection. 'After profound study by the chief and his satellites a voice was heard from the larder . . . crying "I have found it, I have found it."' Enter a young man called Alphonse Pattier bearing three mutton cutlets tied together. He put them on a spit until the two outer ones turned brown then black and then threw them away, merely serving the middle one 'which seems to have received all the nutriment of the other two'. Hortense describes this as the tip-top of extravagance but felt compelled to acknowledge its therapeutic value.

Charles Pierce's version involved beef and another apprentice, or as Pierce calls him, an *élève* of the highest schools of the cuisines of Paris, employed by the Vicomte de Vaudreil. One day he got permission to visit the kitchens of Prince Esterhazy to watch the Prince's cook, Monsieur Mingay, going about his business. On his return:

> the Vicomte hearing that his cook was in a state of astonishment from something he had witnessed . . . summoned him to his presence and asked the nature of the culinary miracle which 'casts into the shade all other triumphs of the art.' The young man explained that he had arrived at lunchtime and his Excellency had ordered something simple and easily digestible as he was 'suffering from langour' [which probably translates as a hangover], so *le chef* Mingay had cut three fillets of beef, broiled them, placed the choicest-looking on a hot plate and . . . 'pressing the juice completely out from the other two, he poured it on the first! Oh, Monsieur, how great the prince! How great the cook.'

How easily impressed the apprentice, one might think.

The ancient Britons did not eat that 'skippish creature' the hare, nor do the Jews – not, according to Plutarch, because it was unclean but because it resembled the ass 'which they revered'. The general consensus was that this was yet another joke, which serves to illustrate further the often elusive nature of ancient humour. The Romans thought that a person who ate hare for seven consecutive days would grow more beautiful and the Chinese thought that a hare lived on the moon. We used to think that hares went mad in March but naturalists have concluded that their odd behaviour is part of their courting ritual – in the course of which most species make fools of themselves. The pagan goddess Eostre had a hare's head and must therefore, one imagines, have looked like an early denizen of DisneyWorld and, as a consequence, we still have the Easter Bunny.

In my case, jugging a hare also falls into the category of things that you only do once. To be correct you should conserve the blood in order to thicken the sauce. I did not do that but I felt uneasy jointing it into its constituent parts, having been affected by that 'effeminacy' despised by Soyer, which characterises the over-civilised – an ancient receipt directs that you must 'hacke hem into gobbetys'. Now, since the hare is under the protection of our autochthonous saint, Melangell – a seventh-century maiden who rescued one from Brochwel, Prince of Powys when he was out hunting – hare is off the menu. Mrs Glasse, whose recommendation 'First catch your hare' caused hilarity in the dining room for many years, not only never said it but, it seems, did not exist. The book attributed to her was, according to Edward Dilly, a friend of Dr Johnson, written by Dr Hill, a literary swashbuckler who died of gout, a disease for which he claimed to have an infallible cure.

'Some cooks,' says Dr Kitchiner, 'cut off the head and divide it, and lay one half on each side of the Hare.' Others, to go by numerous illustrations, left the head in place. One writer says you know the hare is cooked when the eyes start out. Kitchiner is oddly inconsistent in the matter of heads; when he comes to the rabbit he advises, in an unexpected fit of delicacy, 'at all events cut off the head before you send it to table – we hardly remember that the thing ever lived if we don't see the Head, while it may excite ugly ideas to see it cut up in an attitude imitative of Life.' *The Dictionary of Daily Wants* suggests that while carving a hare you should hold it firmly and 'stick the fork into one of the eyes, which will render the operation more easy of accomplishment'.

When the Cook is Away notes, 'If you live in the country and someone brings you a hare straight from the fields into your kitchen and asks you to deal with it, my best advice is don't. If the car is out of order and the nearest fishmonger is not within walking distance it would be even better to buy a bicycle than cope with skinning and cleaning of the hare yourself.'

The Normans brought rabbits to Britain and kept them in Coney warrens, whether or not because they realised that, left to themselves and released into the wild, rabbits breed like rabbits and become a pest, I do not know. Their motives might have been ascribed either to careful husbandry or selfishness. Poaching them was a crime so the latter is more likely. In Victorian times rabbits were 'frequently found to be mischievous animals by the farmer, costing him much trouble and expense'. To deal with this problem he could find 'a fair opportunity for the amusement of ferreting' or, 'When a number are come upon suddenly at the edge of the wood frequented by them, it often happens that the old ones will immediately take the covert, but not so the young ones, who prick up their ears, and perhaps raise themselves up to examine you: now take your shot.'

Here again one is ambivalent: if not the sheep then the rabbits wreak havoc among the flowers and Mr McGregor hates them; but as the little ones sit trustfully in the grass outside the kitchen window, washing their wee whiskers, only a psychopath could 'take his shot'. And it is perfectly true that the older, uglier ones, perhaps aware of their lack of sentimental appeal, take to the hills at the sight of a human – I see them doing it every day.

One of the interesting aspects of old cookery books is the newspaper clippings they harbour. In an edition of Mrs Beeton's *Family Cookery* I found several dating from a time when Lloyd George was seventy-four and had just handed to his publishers the sixth and last volume of his war memoirs. He now planned to relax and grow fruit and potatoes and raise chickens. On the same page was an article about Mr Leo Chertok, 'America's playboy of finance . . . a dapper, cigar-smoking money-man'. He had planned to seek the blessing of Mussolini for a scheme to develop a 15,000 square-mile mineral concession in Walaga Province, Western Abyssinia, until his child caused him to change his mind. 'In my business you've got to be tough. And I am tough. But when my little son said, "Daddy, are you going to start another war?!" – that was quits. I decided to step clean out.' What a splendid fellow you think, until you read that the US Government had put pressure on him and he'd had to admit that his company had paid for the concession by supplying Abyssinia with munitions from South America left over from the Chaco war.

Back to our rabbits – 'How many different ways there are of cooking them!' says 'Housewife' with an exclamatory flourish, proceeding to list four. 'You can even curry them,' she adds joyfully, 'and they make the most delicious forcemeat.' The strange thing is that she offers no recipes but ends on a pleading note: 'Hunt me out your favourite rabbit recipe. It may be one that mother used to use and handed down to you; or one that you have discovered for yourself. Whatever it is, do write it on a postcard and post it in time to arrive not later than next Wednesday.'

I believe 'Housewife' was no such thing. I think she was the beer-swilling, chain-smoking racing correspondent who had been instructed to do something useful while the 4.30 at Epsom was rained off. He offers a bribe – 'Five shillings will be paid for every recipe published' – and the note of desperation is unmistakable. Mrs Beeton has twenty-seven rabbit recipes and a real housewife would have had the *nous* to read a few and alter them slightly for the purposes of her column – the way everyone else does. Take 'Rabbit Fried, With Tartare Sauce'. Mrs Beeton recommends marinading the cut-up joints, which is a good idea if you give the ingredients some thought. She directs that the rabbit should be immersed in a quarter of a pint of salad oil, a tablespoon of chilli vinegar, the same of malt vinegar, one chopped shallot, a bay leaf and a blade of mace, which I don't believe would do anything for the rabbit unless it was completely tasteless to begin with. The best rabbit has not come from some battery hutch in China, but from the thyme-clad hills around wherever you're about to eat it (above Lake Como is good) and needs only to be soaked in olive oil, lemon juice, more thyme and a touch of garlic. Then flour the pieces, fry them, and serve them up with your freshly made tartare sauce. Mrs Beeton says you should chop pickled gherkins into mayonnaise but you can do better than that with a bit of imagination.

Janet's Beloved has revealed that rabbit and pickled belly of pork was a dish popular with the working classes and gave rise to the rhyming slang for chattering: 'rabbit and pork' equals 'talk'.

Thirteen

ANOTHER MAN'S POISON

I recently heard a suggestion, which reminds me of Swift's 'modest proposal'. There is a plan to kill baboons and sell their meat. There will be baboon ribs and steak and canned baboon to be marketed, so they say, in Africa and Eastern Europe, and the teeth, hands and various other parts of the creatures' anatomy will be transported as aphrodisiacs to those countries where there is a demand for such things. Baboons are so closely related to man that eating them must surely seem akin to cannibalism, and since people have contracted kuru, a form of CJD, from eating the brains of their dead relations and there is a theory that AIDS passed to humanity from the apes, then, certainly from a health point of view, this does not seem a good idea. (An American book advises, 'Never handle rabbit or *any* wild meat without using gloves, because of the danger of tularaemia infection.') We have enough trouble already with genetic modification, factory farming, and the rest, without branching out into near anthropophagy. One rather hopes the whole thing is indeed a

Swiftian joke, although there are frequent reports of people carrying contraband bush meat into this country in suitcases.

Somewhere they eat fox for Christmas dinner. I don't suppose this would placate the anti-blood sports faction, and when foxes can't get anything else they eat mice and earthworms or, when practicable, the contents of urban dustbins – which cannot be wholesome. The vicar's wife once found herself standing at the wych gate watching helplessly as a vixen carried one of her fat hens into the far woods; this tested her liberal principles, for there were plenty of rabbits and pheasants available and the fox had no need to raid the hen house. She has bad luck with hens: she lived for a time on Tristan da Cunha and says there are few things more dispiriting than seeing your poultry being blown by the wind out over the Atlantic.

Nor would I want to eat bear: people have contracted trichinosis from eating bear's paws, which were once considered a delicacy in Russia. My fourth son has some land near Yosemite and when we visit I find myself reflecting that it is more in the natural order of things for bears to eat people. An early martyr, one of the companions of St Perpetua, shared my reservations about them: he said he could contemplate, if not with equanimity at least with resignation, the prospect of being mauled by lions or wild cows but he drew the line at bears. Should you chance to see one before he sees you, proceed as following:

> Use about an eight-pound roast off the rump of a young bear. Cover with cold water, add three or four medium-sized onions (sliced), and let soak about four hours. Remove from water and wipe dry. Cut one small clove garlic into small pieces and, using a sharp knife to make holes, force garlic deep into meat. Get garlic as near bones as possible. Season with salt and pepper. Brown in hot bacon drippings. Bake in open pan for three hours at 350 degrees F, turning the meat several times while cooking.

This is a worrying recipe. Young bears ('cubs will need about two and a half hours cooking') might well still be attended by their mothers, who are notoriously irritable when anything threatens their offspring. Choose, rather, an old friendless bear and double the cooking time. 'If marinated at least twenty-four hours in an oil-based marinade, all bear, except black bear, is edible. The polar bear is stated by Sir John Ross to be particularly unwholesome, although the Esquimaux feed upon it, and apparently without inconvenience.'

In Texas they'll tell you that rattlesnake tastes like chicken (this claim is made on behalf of innumerable creatures from rabbit to crocodile), but it doesn't and never will take the place of *coq au vin*. I ate fried rattlesnake and chips at a sort of rattlesnake fair in Sweetwater, Texas, where there were hundreds of the things lying around, dead and alive: even the living ones seemed somewhat listless and it was whispered that the daring cowboys who had captured them had actually first lightly anaesthetised them with gas. There were rattlesnake handbags and belts on sale, rattlesnake fangs dangling from keyrings and necklaces, pickled rattlesnakes in jars, and even rattlesnakes in bottles of alcohol. I detest snakes but I did get the feeling that their rights had been violated.

If the words 'rabbit stew' outrage no one but the committed animal lover, the word 'pie' prefaced by the word 'squirrel' causes even the non-vegetarian to look sceptical. Red squirrels may be considered too sweet to eat but as there are hardly any left this is immaterial. Perhaps the grey sort is considered too similar in appearance to rats, but even rats have sometimes been considered a delicacy, during the Siege of Paris for example ('pickled poodle and scrambled rat'). Somebody said they weren't bad at all, but that might just have been whistling in the wind. It is probable that they were said to taste like chicken. (It has been hinted that during the siege of Kashgar the defenders, having finished off the rats – and cats – started on their wives and children, but I daresay the story was put about by their enemies.)

Anyway, the prejudice against cooked squirrel seems to be unique to these islands, although according to the *Encyclopaedia of Domestic Economy*, 'the squirrel is tender meat, and a favourite dish in Sweden and Norway. It is sometimes eaten by the lower classes in England.' In 1946 the Ministry of Food recommended squirrel pie and issued instructions on how to make it. Few availed themselves of it. I did once discuss with a marquis methods of cooking squirrels. He seemed to know a surprising amount about it – but he is an accredited eccentric. Lady Salisbury says, 'Grey squirrels? Oh, if people only knew how perfectly delicious they are, they wouldn't be such a widespread problem. I have an excellent old receipt for cooking them in a cream and white wine sauce.' Lower classes? Fiddlesticks. Americans have no reservations: 'Gray squirrels are the preferred ones; red squirrels are small and quite gamey in flavour.' (They were supposed to be one of Elvis Presley's favourite dishes.) It is claimed that they are low in cholesterol and a nuisance in the nut trees. Here is one of the ways in which they prepare them, but it seems probable that the author of the recipe discovered a horde of squirrels ravaging his orchard, lost his temper, seized his shotgun and, when the smoke had cleared, found that he had acquired seventeen corpses. Not being a person of great imagination, he settled on this number for his dish:

Take seventeen squirrels, three cans tomato sauce, two pounds onions, chopped, two heads garlic, four stalks chopped celery, two bell peppers, chopped, cooking oil, four tablespoons flour, salt and pepper to taste. Cut up meat. Salt and pepper. Brown meat in pot with one-eighth-inch cooking oil. Add small amounts of water from time to time to prevent sticking. Remove meat when tender. Make small roux in large pot with oil and flour (4 tbsps). Add onions and small amount of water if they stick, cook until tender. Add bell peppers, garlic and celery. Add tomato sauce and extra water if it becomes too thick. Simmer until vegetables are tender. Add squirrels and simmer until oil comes to top. Salt and pepper to taste. Serve over rice.

There is something strangely irritating about this recipe. It tells us both too much and not enough. Why repeat the quantity of flour? Why does it say chopped celery but onions and bell peppers, chopped? And how do you prepare the garlic? These are minor matters but the cook does not need tiresome distractions. And why a small roux in a large pot? This has something of a poetic flourish about it and blurs our image of the author as a severely practical man. It is all vaguely unsatisfactory.

The *Encyclopaedia of Domestic Economy* assures us that, 'The guinea pig is not spoken favourably of as food.' Nonetheless, they have always been a popular dish in South America, and Mrs Meighn, in *The Adventure Book of Cookery*, tells the following tale:

> The story of Great-Aunt Jessica preventing war by cooking Aunt Moira's guinea pigs is so funny that you must hear it.
> It happened somewhere abroad, while Uncle Jasper was

being a diplomat. A diplomat is a man who argues men of other countries into or out of making wars and other things. It happened on a very hot thundery day, when a foreign diplomat, who thought a lot about good cooking and good food and was rather thinking about forcing his country to make war on England, was coming to lunch.

Uncle Jasper had told Aunt Jessica how glad he was she had ordered a specially good lunch, when the butler rushed in crying that the cook had small-pox, and the thunder had made the meat bad so there would be 'No lunch! No lunch!'

'No lunch', said Uncle Jasper, 'Nonsense! No lunch means war! See to it, Jessica!'

Now, the only way Aunt Jessica could 'see to it' was by seeing if her daughter, my Aunt Moira, who was then quite little, would sacrifice her guinea-pigs.

'I won't!' said Aunt Moira, and louder than thunder were her cries of sorrow and despair at the thought of letting her darling guinea-pigs get cooked, even to prevent a war. But at last Uncle Jasper persuaded her to say, 'Yes! for England's sake.' To try to comfort her, he wrote poetry to put on a tombstone over the little guinea-pigs' skins. Meanwhile, Aunt Jessica, who was crying too, because she hated more than anything having to cook animals she knew, conjured up a delicious dish described on the lunch menu as 'Poulet Prestidigitateur' . . . We laughed a lot the day Aunt Jessica showed us how to make 'Sauce Prestidigitateur', the sauce that turns dull odds and ends of meat or vegetables into something exciting, and makes guinea-pigs and rabbits seem like chicken.

Here again we have the euphemism 'chicken': I have found non-avian bones in a Chinese chicken takeaway and suspected the presence of cat. The *Encyclopaedia of Domestic Economy* corroborates this suspicion. 'The cat is not avowed as food in any European nation; but the occasional substitution of this animal for a rabbit is known to travellers.' When Janet's mum was in service, a favourite dish in the nursery was 'Chicken Snow' and on family occasions, Cook would receive a request for it to be sent to the dining room. No one upstairs knew that it was made from rabbit but at least Puss was not involved in this deception.

Other people eat dogs, but 'the faithful companion and friend of man, is not employed as food among the European nations'. Even the most liberal of those who don't, tend to find the practice repugnant though, on his successful South Pole expedition, the pragmatic Amundsen, after having to shoot one of his dogs, noted the other members of the team 'partook of it with relish. We ourselves tried some substantial steaks and found the meat excellent.' Hurley, a member of Shackleton's 1915 Trans-Polar expedition noted, 'Hunger brings us all to the level of other species, and our Saying "that sledge dogs are born for work & bred for food" is but the rationale of experience.' Some wag said in reference to the Koreans who eat dog the year round 'a puppy is not just for Christmas', but I see no reason to wax liberal and permissive about this habit: dogs and humans have lived too closely together for too long for it to be anything but an abuse of friendship. It has been said that rather than man domesticating dog it happened the other way round and the wild dog, as the hour of the wolf approached, drew closer to the camp fire where discarded bones were littered, saw he was on to a good thing, and elected man as his best friend and protector.

Horse worship was one of the earliest religious cults in the British Isles and may be one of the reasons why horsemeat has never been considered suitable for human consumption in this country. The *Encyclopaedia of Domestic Economy* says:

The horse cannot be enumerated among the animals which supply us with food, although its flesh is eaten and much relished in some countries. Among the inhabitants of Europe there is a great repugnance to the use of horse-flesh, except in cases of famine. In England it is never employed as human food, but only for cats' and dogs' meat; but it is confidently stated, that in a manufactory in Paris, where every part of the horse's carcass is converted to various uses, the workmen often eat the flesh, and that parts of it are not infrequently substituted for butcher's meat in some of the low eating-houses of that capital. Those who have tasted it speak of the flesh of the young horse as extremely palatable; and there can be no doubt that it is wholesome. It is well known that the Tartars have always been extremely fond of horse-flesh, which they eat nearly raw, and likewise smoke it for keeping.

Another book notes:

Among the most polished nations of the 15th and 16th centuries, the *powdered* (salted) *Horse* seems to have been a dish in some esteem. Don Anthony of Guevera, the Chronicler to Charles V, gives the following account of a Feast at which he was present. 'I will tell you no lye, I sawe such kindes of meates eaten, as are wont to be sene, but not eaten – *as a Horse roasted* – a *Cat in gely – Lyʒards* in hot brothe – *Frogges fried &c.*' Dr Johnson records in his dictionary a note from Bacon's *Natural History*, 'Horſ fleſh – The Chineſe eat horſefleſh at this day, and ſome gluttonſ have coltſ fleſh baked.'

There was a public outcry a few of years back when it was revealed that the soldiers' horses in France went for butcher's meat compared with the 'honourable retirement' of our police and cavalry horses, and when Janet and her Beloved (a keen racing man) were in France recently, he was appalled to find *burger du cheval* appearing as a choice on a home-cooked food menu at a restaurant. They made their excuses and left. Near where my third son lives in France there are two *Boucherie Chevaline*, one of the few things to remind us in this homogenised age, when McDonald's signs leer from every corner, that we are in a foreign country.

There are, however, some exceptions to the above declarations. You can always rely on *Anon*:

> There were two heavy thick soups, followed by a full-grown turbot, I should think measuring two feet across; at the other end of the table was half of a salmon, weighing at least twenty pounds, with lobster and anchovy sauces. There was also put on the table six silver side dishes, containing God and the cook only knew what. Then there came the eternal boiled fowls and bill-sticker's paste. I forget what was at the other end of the table, but in the middle was a horse's tongue. There is not a horse that dies in London, or within reach of it, that the tongue is not pickled and dried and sold as a Russian rarity.

This was quite possibly true.

Captain Scott, normally a traditionalist, deviates from the norm for once and records in his diary on the ill-fated Polar expedition, 'We have all taken to horse meat and are so well fed that hunger isn't thought of [and] the dogs are simply splendid, but came in wanting food, so we had to sacrifice poor Little Michael, who like the rest, had lots of fat on him. All the tents are consuming pony flesh and thoroughly enjoying it.'

Concern for keeping the British – at all costs – well fed on meat infiltrated the highest levels of decision making. It is recorded that, in 1847, 'The attention of the late Sir Robert Peel was directed to the gradual diminution of animal food . . . with a view of increasing the quantity and keeping down the price, he removed all restrictions on the importation of foreign cattle, which had been prohibited in the interest of the British farmer.'

The first kangaroos we saw, on a visit to my son in Australia, were gathered in a grassy graveyard in Perth; they are the most improbable of creatures – the sort that cause you to question all of your previous assumptions about the nature of things – part human, part rabbit. The *Encyclopaedia of Domestic Economy* says, 'The kangaroo when young resembles venison, some say mutton; when old it is tough. It is much sought after as food, but from the scarcity of quadrupeds there, is becoming rare where formerly it was abundant.' (Now that Australia has millions of ovine quadrupeds, rather than leaving them alone, people are killing kangaroos to make more grass for the sheep.)

Surprisingly, a 1930s edition of Mrs Beeton contains recipes for Kangaroo, Wallaby and Parrot, while a specifically Australian book of the same era does not. It is more concerned with cocktail, tennis, after-theatre and children's parties than with the culinary possibilities of the indigenous wildlife. Instead of witchity grubs and bold, back-to-the-earth, barbecue-type things there are dishes such as *filet mignon*, with a picture of the chef putting the finishing touches to it. Food photography was in its infancy, so what we see is not a glistening, coloured close-up (I have been told that substances such as boot polish are now often applied to give the joint or gateau that succulent appearance), but a dim black and white (grey) image of what looks like a bit of a muddle. Described as the chef's 'masterpiece', its exaggeratedly ornate presentation doesn't march at all with the brusque, no-nonsense attitude we associate with Australia.

An American book published at the same time does have ideas

for indigenous meat, birds and fish. Opossum: 'If possible, trap 'possum and feed it on milk and cereals for 10 days before killing . . . Serve with Turnip greens.' Raccoon: 'Skin, clean and soak overnight . . . Simmer . . . Stuff with Bread Dressing and bake.' Muskrat: 'Sauté until golden . . . Serve with Creamed Celery.' Woodchuck, beaver, peccary, moose, elk . . . The last two, like pork, go well with 'sweet and sweet-and-sour garnishes and sauces'.

Earlier, the *Encyclopaedia of Domestic Economy* had referred to the zebra, 'considered in Africa an excellent food'; the hippopotamus, 'a huge unwieldly creature . . . when old is coarse, fat and strong being inferior to beef'; the tapir, 'a large and hungry quadruped much addicted to the water. The American Indian compares its flesh to beef . . .'; the elephant, 'is eaten in Abyssinia also in Sumatra and said to be well tasted'. Some steaks that were cut off the elephant that was shot at the Exeter Change, on being cooked, were declared to be a 'pleasant' meat. And so on, through rhinoceros '. . . like musty pork' and the walrus, whose 'flesh was dark red and coarse'.

Captain Grey, writing of the Australian Aborigines, had observed, 'There is no sight in the world more revolting than to see a young and gracefully formed native girl stepping out of the carcase of a putrid whale.' The whale, says the *Encyclopaedia of Domestic Economy*:

being the largest of all animals, we might suppose that its flesh is too coarse for food: that, however, is not the case. This animal, being one of the *mammalia*, suckling its young with milk, and breathing air without separating it from the water by means of gills, is not properly a fish, and its flesh is much like beef. Parts of the animal, particularly about the tail, are said not to be contemptible as food even by those who are not pressed by hunger; and some species, as the spermaceti whale, are very generally consumed by the Greenlanders, and other inhabitants of the arctic regions.

And Dr Kitchiner reproduces information about Sea Beef – 'Flesh of the whale, a mammal, is usually bought in frozen condition, in which it should be kept until required for cooking. When thawed out, it develops a fishy taste. This can be counteracted to some extent by steeping in a solution of bi-carbonate of soda. If casseroled, the flavour resembles beef.' Most references stressed that whale did *not* taste fishy. During the Second World War a strip cartoon in the *Daily Mirror* featured 'Patsy' and her recipes for coping with rationing. 'Whale meat – this *is* a discovery – unrationed and no points either – fried and stewed. You'll find it jolly good we promise you. Whale meat will make a good curry too. And you can make hamburgers out of it, if you put it through the mincer. And a rattling good whale meat and onion pie or pudding with kidney if you can get it. But don't try roasting it – it doesn't work.' The British never took to eating whale.

'That unwieldy marine animal the Porpus was dressed in a variety of modes, salted, roasted, stewed &c. Our ancestors were not singular in their partiality to it; I find, from an ingenious friend of mine, that it is even now, A.D. 1796, sold in the markets of most towns in Portugal; the flesh of it is intolerably hard and rancid.' And, 'A mammal, eaten in some countries. It was once a favourite dish at the feasts of Henry VIII. The flesh of young porpoises has been compared to that of veal. To cook, it is sometimes thinly sliced, egg-and-breadcrumbed, then fried. No longer brought to market.'

Otters, expediently considered as fish – after all, they lived in the water – were 'permitted by the church of Rome to be eaten on maigre days, and Pennant states that the Carthusians, an order never allowed to taste flesh during their whole lives, made no scruple about serving up a roasted otter in their refectory'. Beavers, 'fat and delicious', also qualified, presumably because their tails have no fur. To cook beaver tail, you toast it over a fire until the skin burns and can be peeled off. It may then be roasted or boiled. You have to feel sympathy with the wistful greed which engendered this debate.

Charles Darwin writes in *The Voyage of the Beagle*: 'In the morning we had caught an armadillo, which, although a most excellent dish when roasted in its shell, did not make a very substantial breakfast and dinner for two hungry men.'

'While we are thus considering the curious dishes of olden times,' said Dr Kitchiner:

> we will cursorily mention the *singular diet* of two or three nations of antiquity; noticed by *Herodotus* – The *Androphagi* (the cannibals of the ancient world) greedily devoured the carcasses of their fellow-creatures: while the inoffensive *Cabri* (a Scythian tribe) found both food and drink in the agreeable nut of the Pontic Tree. The *Lotophagi* lived entirely on the fruit of the *Lotos Tree*. The savage *Troglodyte* esteemed the *living serpent* the most delicate of all morsels; while the capricious palate of the *Zyguntini* preferred the *Ape* to every thing.

As Kitchiner expressed it, 'What at one time or place is considered as beautiful, fragrant and savoury, at another is regarded as deformed and disgustful.' And who would disagree?

Fourteen

FOWL

'Take chykens and scald them, take parsel and sawge, without any other erbes, take garlec and grapes, and stoppe the chykens ful, and seeth them in good broth, so that they may esely be boiled thereinne. Messe them and cast thereto powder-douce.'

Henri IV of France remarked expansively that he wished every peasant to have a chicken in his pot on Sundays, but until intensive breeding and factory farming came along, chicken in this country was regarded as a treat and offered with a flourish only on festive occasions. There were tender ones for roasting and tough old boilers that needed long, slow stewing. Chickens now are usually tender but tasteless, unless you have a truly unconfined one, and are easy to cook: roast, fry or stew them. You can hardly go wrong unless you undercook them, thus running the risk of salmonella poisoning.

Powder-douce, in the above recipe, was probably a bit of ground cinnamon or ginger, nutmeg, pepper and a little sugar. It is interesting to note, in passing, that medieval persons like the

French — and like our American cousins — did not aspirate their 'erbs.

We are now advised against putting stuffing in fowl in case it prevents them from cooking properly throughout, but they nearly always did in the olden days. Make a forcemeat of four ounces of veal, says *A Lady*, and two of scraped ham, two of fat bacon, two of suet, two hard yolks of eggs, sweet herbs, lemon peel, anchovy, salt, pepper, cayenne, and beat it all in a mortar with a teacupful of crumbs and the yolks and whites of three eggs. Stuff the inside of the fowl. Then she says, '*To force fowl etc.*: Is to stuff any part with a forcemeat, and it is usually put between the skin and flesh.' I expect she means as well as inside, but I can see the inexperienced cook bursting into sobs having followed the first instructions before reading the second.

The Dictionary of Daily Wants notes that:

> The male bird is preferable to the female. The age also greatly influences its tenderness and flavour, the flesh after a certain time becoming tough and coarse . . . if upon lifting the dead bird by the beak it will bear the weight, the fowl may be considered an old one, but if the beak breaks off, the bird is a young one . . . A person purchasing a fowl should not judge of its weight by appearance, as various arts are practiced to impart a plump appearance which they do not possess . . . Above all, dealing with itinerant vendors should be carefully avoided; in most cases, men clad in smock frocks and otherwise 'got up' to represent the country dealers, are in reality artful denizens of London, who purchase the refuse stock at the large markets at nominal prices, and thus palm them off to the public at enormous profits.

It is extraordinary how some things never change. The labels reading 'free range' and 'farm fresh' are the modern equivalent of the impostor Farmer Giles in his smock, while a huge conspiracy to pass off chickens judged fit only for cat food on to the public was only recently uncovered.

In the index to *Modern Cookery* by Eliza Acton is a passage entitled '*Goose: to deprive of its strong odour.*' *What* strong odour you wonder? Does she mean to imply that the goose has gone off? Do geese putrefy faster than other creatures? Actually, I think they may, for one Christmas I bought a huge frozen one and left it to thaw out in the bath. It was beginning to smell high before it was free of ice, so I had to put the plug in and bathe it in vinegar – as recommended by all olden-day cooks for meat moving too swiftly towards that condition to which we all must come. I suppose it is a kind of precautionary embalming.

Miss Acton writes:

> We extract, for the benefit of our readers, from a work in our possession, the following passage of which we have had no opportunity of testing the correctness:
>
> 'Geese with sage and onions, may be deprived of power to breathe forth any incense, thus: Pare from a lemon all the yellow rind, taking care not to bruise the fruit nor to cut so deeply as to let out the juice. Place the lemon in the centre of the seasoning within the bird. When or before it is brought to table, let the flap be gently opened, remove the lemon with a tablespoon; avoid breaking, and let it instantly be thrown away, as its white pithy skin will have absorbed all the gross particles which else would have escaped.'

'Green geese,' says Miss Acton, 'are never stuffed' but served only with 'good brown gravy. To this sorrel-sauce is sometimes added at not very modern English tables.' Now we've gone post-modern, sorrel sauce without the gravy would probably make a highly favourable impression. Conserve the fat jealously to make the best roast potatoes ever – it is now sold in super-markets in tins. A green goose is simply 'a young goose, so called until six months old. It is the country name for a gosling.'

Having thought about cooking a goose, I kept finding refer-ences to these unfortunate birds. Once upon a time they were shod with tar and made to march from Wales to London where they were slaughtered. We all know about the French and *pâté de foie gras*, force-feeding them until their livers become diseased – a practice inherited from the Romans – and now I learn that the Swedes had their own methods of being unkind to the creatures. In *The Girl's Own Indoor Book*, I read, 'I have a recipe for what is called "swart" or black soup; it commences with what seem to me directions for torturing a goose. One is told to take a goose and pluck out some feathers from the neck, then to make a cut in the neck with a penknife, so as to bleed the goose into a decanter, the blood to be saved to use in the soup. But, as I am sure none of you will wish to make *swartsoppa*, I will not give the remain-der of the directions!' A merciful lacuna.

Dr Kitchiner wrote,

'But the most extraordinary of all the Culinary Receipts that have been under my eye, is the following diabolically cruel directions of Mizald, *How to roast and eat a Goose alive*. Take a Goose or a Duck, or some such 'lively creature' (but a goose is the best of all for this purpose), pull off all her feathers, only the head and the neck must be spared; then make a fire round about her, not too close to her, that the smoke do not choke her, and that the fire may not burn her too soon: nor too far off, that she may not escape free; within the circle of the fire let there be set small cups and pots full of water, wherein salt and honey are mingled: and let there be set also chargers full of sodden Apples, cut into small pieces in the dish. The Goose must be all larded, and basted over with butter, to make her the more fit to be eaten, and may roast the better: put then fire about her, but do not make too much haste, when as you see her begin to roast; for by walking about, and flying here and there, being cooped in by the fire that stops her way out, the unwearied Goose is kept in; she will fall to drink the water to quench her thirst and cool her heart, and all her body, and the Apple Sauce will make her dung, and cleanse and empty her. And when she roasteth, and consumes inwardly, always wet her head and heart with a wet sponge; and when you see her giddy with running, and begin to stumble, her heart wants moisture, and she is roasted enough. Take her up, set her before your guests, and she will cry as you cut off any part from her, and will be almost eaten up before she be dead; it is mighty pleasant to behold.

I suppose this must be another joke. Dear me.

A friend of a friend kept two geese in her Hampstead garden. One Christmas they killed one for dinner. Its mate stood beneath the window honking in grief, dissipating the festive atmosphere.

The turkey, which as we all think we know, was introduced to the first settlers in America by kindly disposed Red Indians/Native Americans, was brought to Europe at the beginning of the sixteenth century. By the eighteenth century there were thousands of them in the Royal Park at Richmond, but 'in consequence of the frequent fights between poachers and keepers, it was thought proper to destroy them'. This seems defeatist but turkey meat is over-rated. I know a man in New Mexico who deep-fries his turkey for Thanksgiving in a cauldron of boiling oil. I haven't sampled it but those who have say it prevents the bird from drying out and makes for the best possible end result. Otherwise, the only time a turkey is useful is when you have to cater for a great many people: there is no point in offering a twenty-pound bird to a party of six as they listen to the Queen's Speech. They all know it will be back.

A piece of rustic advice on husbandry from the Roswell Register of 1902. 'A duck does not "dump around" like a hen or turkey when sick. It is to all outward appearances well, or it is dead, there is small opportunity for doctoring.' There is something grimly practical about American cookery books, while at times they contain wildly imaginative flights of fancy. I cannot forget a cheese and onion ring with strawberry jam in the middle.

Sir Francis says:

> In French cooking a distinction is made between ducks which have been bled and those killed by stunning or stifling – without bleeding. The latter are practically always roasted, the former being generally braised in a casserole. A duckling is one of the many good things we have to thank Providence for, which responds to the simplest treatment. Roasted with a mild stuffing inside him, and presented with young potatoes and young green peas and finished with butter, he is at his beautiful best, so much so that one is sometimes almost inclined to regard any other method as painting the lily.

He goes on to discuss Salmi of Duck, which 'can be made with the remains of cooked duck, but is not in the same street as a salmi made as such from the start, thus:

> Roast a duck in a very hot oven till cooked on the outside. Cut

from the breast and thighs long narrow slices, and lay them on to a fireproof dish. Crush the carcass (which is barely cooked) to extract all the juice, add to this a glass of port, the juice of an orange, a spoonful of red-currant jelly, pepper, salt, a gill or so of sauce Espagnole and stock mixed. *Caneton à la Presse*, as served in a good restaurant, is excellent, and is always impressive, especially to young guests to whom such *tours de force* are a novelty. It is as simple as it is delicious, but it is not suitable to a private house.

It seems that the Duck Press was a necessary item of equipment in all the better restaurants.

Duck is no longer regarded as a Lenten dish but there was a lot of speculation about its suitability in the Middle Ages: since it was a water-borne creature, could the duck, like the otter, be counted as a fish?

Our house used to fidget up and down with the result that cracks appeared in the walls: this problem was caused by a lime tree next door absorbing all the moisture from the earth and it had to be cut down. Two pigeons used to live in it: they were not expert parents and their chicks used to fall out of the nest, but they seemed not to notice and kept coming back, wandering round the garden with the bemused air of householders who have mislaid, not the key, but the house itself. One of my London neighbours used to shoot pigeons and eat them. I think this inadvisable bearing in mind what London pigeons themselves eat, although I have eaten scrawny pigeon on the banks of the Nile . . .

I was once in a restaurant with Jeffrey Bernard and we ordered quail. Outside the window were London pigeons scavenging in the gutter and the thought occurred to us that, in the interests of economy, they might well be related to whatever it was on the plates in front of us. I have an American recipe where the birds are interchangeable. You take eight quail or twelve dove and brown them in oil. Then you pour over them a can of cream of mushroom soup, a can of cream of chicken soup, a half-pint of sour cream and a cup of vermouth. Cook at 325 degrees for one and a half hours. Perhaps this 'hoary ruse' makes up for the time you've spent plucking them.

From my windows in Wales I look out on flocks of pheasants, rootling round in the wet grass searching for things to eat, occasionally giving way to tantrums when one usurps the place of another, and generally resembling shoppers in a supermarket who are also keenly conscious of the pecking order. Nothing could be further from the pheasants' tiny minds than the sudden death which is being planned for them. They are hand-reared and perceive the gamekeeper as the Universal Provider rather than the Destroyer of Delight.

The Dictionary of Daily Wants advises: 'Pheasant, to choose – The cock bird is considered the choicest, except when the hen is with egg. If young its spurs are blunt and short, or round; if they are long and sharp, the bird is old. Examine the hen at the vent; if that is open and green, it is a sign she is stale; if she is with egg, it will be soft; if stale, the skin, when rubbed hard with the finger, will peel off.'

Anon quotes the French who say:

To the uninitiated this bird is as a sealed book; eaten after it has been killed but three days it is insipid and bad, neither so delicate as a pullet, nor so odiferous as quail. Cooked at the right moment, the flesh is tender and the flavour sublime, partaking equally the qualities of poultry and game. The moment so necessary to be known and seized on, is when decomposition is about to take place. A trifling odour and a change in the colour of the breast are manifested, and great care must be taken not to pluck the bird till it is to be larded and cooked, as the contact of the air will completely neutralize the aroma, consisting of a subtle oil, to which hydrogen is fatal.

For roast pheasant Mrs Beeton suggests that, as it is a dry bird, you should put a quarter pound of beefsteak inside it which is 'intended to improve the flavour and keep it moist, and not to be eaten with it, but it may afterwards be used in preparation of some cold meat dish'. I can't quite think what, unless you pounded it up and potted it but it doesn't seem worth the bother. Better to smother the pheasant in bacon and butter and put an onion or a lemon or an apple inside to help gently steam it. Mrs Beeton also says you should leave the head on, but I wouldn't. Mrs Raffald, calling from the previous century, says you should keep the tail feathers and 'When a pheaſant is roaſted, ſtick the featherſ on the tail before you ſend it to table,' but I wouldn't do that either. (Sometimes in the olden days, before anyone had hit on the germ theory of disease, when they'd cooked their bustard, swan or peacock, they dressed it again not only in its tail feathers but its whole skin – which would have made a hospitable tent for bacteria.)

When eating pheasant, watch out for lead pellets. Few hunters now achieve a clean kill. Opinions vary, some people insisting that the shot-up flesh has a better flavour, but the majority prefer to remove the mangled bits together with the shot since hair or feathers – whatever the outer coating of the victim – will have been forced inside it together with clotted blood. *Joy of Cooking*, an American book, notes, 'Game shot in an unsuspecting moment is more tender than game that is chased and will also deteriorate less quickly.'

Treat other little game birds in the same way. They can all be casseroled if they seem intransigently tough or you have so many you feel the need of a change. The custom of roasting woodcocks, snipes and quails with their insides intact is one that has never appealed to me. 'Roast them without drawing,' run the instructions, 'and serve on toast.' I have known people to salivate at the thought of this toast soaked in 'the trail, that is the excrements of the intestines . . . In helping, the lady must be careful to remove first a small bitter bag from the trail.' In India, Sir Francis sometimes 'indulged in trail toast – the trails of eight or ten snipe served on a fried croûton. It sounds nearly as extravagant as Nero's peacock tongues, but it may happen that there are more snipe on hand than can be used in the ordinary way.'

It was held that small birds should be underdone – a little pink – and there was an old saying that the well-cooked snipe was one that has flown only once through the kitchen. *Cassell's Cookery* said they should be served instantly because they so quickly lost heat, adding rather interestingly, while on the subject, that roast loin of mutton 'seems to possess the power of getting cold quicker than any joint I know'. Sir Francis said that small birds such as quail and snipe should always be served on hot water plates: these are useful if only one or perhaps two people are dining, otherwise they are a nuisance, needing to be first filled and then emptied, and carrying the risk of scalding.

The Girl's Own Indoor Book says: 'Many small birds are eaten, but I sincerely hope we shall not take to eating thrushes and blackbirds! I only regret that larks are eaten, and fear that if our other little songsters were brought to market as ruthlessly as larks are, our woods and gardens would soon be as void of song as are many parts of France.' The hunters on the Continent still insist on their right to blast them out of the air as they set off on their seasonal migration and some still set snares and nets to catch them and you can buy them preserved in bottles. In Violet Hunt's *Corsican Sisters*, written round about the end of the nineteenth century, one of the sisters rhapsodises about the blackbirds of her native country. 'Magnifique,' she says. Her English hosts enquire whether she speaks of their song or their plumage and she responds blankly that she meant their flesh.

But here in England in the late nineteenth century there were listed as edible, amongst others, ruffes and reeves, fieldfares and redwings, water rails and bitterns, stints and curlews, starlings *and* blackbirds. Francatelli had addressed himself to 'Industrious and intelligent boys' who live in the country and are 'well up in the cunning art of catching small birds'. When they'd caught a dozen or so, they were to pluck them, 'cut off their heads and claws and prick out their gizzards from their sides with the point of a small knife' and 'hand them over to your mother' who, he declared, would 'prepare a famous pudding for your dinner or supper'. We no longer eat small birds and any child now found catching them would be regarded as having behavioural difficulties (it has been noted that children who are cruel to animals develop into serial killers), as well as incurring the wrath of the RSPB, although a book published in England in the 1940s still notes that ortolan, knot, ptarmigan and rail can all be eaten and are 'much relished by epicures'.

Mrs Marshall could scarcely set eyes on a lark without thinking of new ways of preparing it. Her book has numerous illustrations of their beaked heads sticking out of pies or darioles or *vol-aux-vents*. The cook had to pluck and draw them and take out their eyes with a pin and to get enough ready for a dish must have taken all day – a lark weighs an ounce or two.

For *Larks à la Sotterville*:

Take some singed and cleansed larks, bone them, but leave the feet and bottom part of the leg bone on, then by means of a forcing bag and plain pipe farce each bird with a puree . . . [The puree as given is, in fact, an extraordinarily elaborate mix.] Form them into neat shapes, wrap each bird in a band of buttered foolscap paper, tie them up with thin string, put them in a tin with a little warm butter and bake for about fifteen minutes, during which time keep them well basted; set them aside till cold, then mask them with fawn-coloured *Chaudfroid* sauce and when this is set mask all over with aspic jelly. When quite cold trim them and dish them up on a border of aspic cream, standing them against a croûton of fried bread; then by means of a forcing bag and pipe garnish between the larks with finely chopped aspic cream; arrange here and there some *Financière* garnish that has been masked with aspic jelly and also some finely shredded cut truffles. Arrange just above the top of the larks the heads of the birds prepared as follows: Cleanse the heads and roll them up in buttered paper, then cook them in a moderate oven for five minutes; set aside till cold and brush over each with a warm glaze or cool aspic jelly; cut out with a pea-cutter some little rounds of hard-boiled white of egg to fit the birds' eyes; place these in the spaces and in the centre of this place a smaller round of red chilli, then mask over with aspic jelly.

The combination of careless savagery and the almost oriental attention to detail is particularly remarkable.

'The Swan was also a dish of state, and in high fashion when the elegance of the Feast was estimated by the magnitude of the articles of which it was composed; the number consumed at the Earl of Northumberland's table AD 1512, amounted to twenty,' Dr Kitchiner tells us and, quoting from *Culinary Curiosities*, 'The ancients considered the Swan as a high delicacy, and abstained from the flesh of the *Goose* as impure and indigestible.' And we learn, too, that 'The Crane was a darling dainty in *William the Conqueror's* time,' and the monarch himself extremely partial to it.

Seals, Curlews, Herons, Bitterns, and the Peacock – that noble bird, 'the food of Lovers, and the meat of Lords,' were also at this time in high fashion, when the Baronial entertainments were characterised by a grandeur and pompous ceremonial approaching nearly to the magnificence of Royalty: there was scarcely any Royal or Noble feast without Pecokkes which were stuffed with Spices, and Sweet herbs, roasted and served up whole, and covered after dressing with the skin and feathers; the beak and comb gilt, and the tail spread, and some, instead of the feathers, covered with leaf gold; it was a common dish on grand occasions, and continued to adorn the English table till the beginning of the seventeenth century.

In Massinger's play of 'the City Madam' Holdfast, exclaiming against city luxury, says, 'three fat wethers [castrated sheep] bruised, to make sauce for a single Peacock'.

This Bird is one of those luxuries which were often sought, because they were seldom found; its scarcity and external appearances are its only recommendation – the meat of it is tough and tasteless.

The Girl's Own Indoor Book notes, 'Cocks' combs are considered a great delicacy. I dare say my readers have often seen them preserved in bottles in French shops here. I do not myself think there is any taste in them, and class them with the dishes of peacocks' brains that were served long ago. Their merit was in their scarcity. The head of the peacock is singularly small compared to the body.'

Fifteen

PIES

The Dictionary of Daily Wants: 'Pastry, Dietetic Properties of – With most persons, and especially those who have weak digestion, pastry proves unwholesome; the richest kind of pastry is especially so, and lies in the stomach, a heavy indigestible mass, for hours. The plainer kind of pastry is the least injurious, and even of this small quantities should be eaten. Invalids should scrupulously avoid pastry of any kind.' Pies and pasties were nevertheless relished by the ancestors. Pies, or 'coffyns' as they were – perhaps advisedly – known, were made in a deep dish and left open to the air, while the pasty was closed with a lid. Just reading about mediaeval or Elizabethan pastry causes a sensation of impending crisis in the digestive tract. Pastry is one of those things that one feels has improved with the passage of time although now, as ever, everything depends on the cook's lightness of touch.

Mrs Raffald's eighteenth century 'Paſte for a Gooſe-Pie' was made in much the same way as it is now, only there was more of it than is presently usual. 'Take eighteen pounds of fine flour, put ſix pounds of freſh butter, and one pound of rendered beef-ſuet in a kettle of water, boil it two or three minutes, then pour it boiling hot upon your flour, work it well into a pretty ſtiff paſte, pull it in lumps to cool, and raiſe your pie, bake it in a hot oven; you may make any raiſed pie in the ſame way, only take a ſmaller quantity in proportion.' What astonishes the modern consumer is the quantity of butter used in this goose pie. Whenever I have cooked a goose it has almost swum out of the oven afloat in its own melted fat. I have wondered if geese were leaner then, but this cannot be since so many ointments and unguents depended on the grease – Old Wives rubbed it on people's chests when they noticed those 'mild flu-like symptoms that might develop into flu or the Black Death'.

To make the Goose Pye – Mrs Raffald instructs:

Bone your Gooſe, or only ſlit it down the Back; take out the Breaſt-bone, break the otherſ; take two Rabbetſ, cut them in Pieceſ, ſeaſon with four Ounceſ of ſalt, two Ounceſ of Pepper, and two Nutmegſ. If your Gooſe, &c. be large, ſtick the Breaſt of the Gooſe with Cloveſ, put half a Pound of Butter in the Belly, lay another half Pound over the Bottom of the Pye; lay in the Gooſe, the Breaſt downwardſ; fill up the void ſpaceſ with your Pieceſ of Rabbet, lay three Pound of Butter on the Top, bake it; and, when it comeſ out of the Oven, fill it up with clarified Butter.

Nowadays it is only as you venture north in Britain that you will find those robust, upstanding pies of pork or mutton at their cholesterol-laden best. On the shelf behind all the usual cuts of meat will be seen golden-brown pies, large and small, flanked by unashamed tubs of dripping. Therein lies the secret: you can't construct a proper pork pie with some effete substitute for animal fat. (Some fat is essential if food is to be palatable and the fat-free concoctions proudly advertising themselves on the supermarket shelves, are to be avoided since their contribution to weight loss is probably due to the fact that the purchaser will take one mouthful and throw the rest away.) Nor, of course, can you consume too many pork pies unless you mean to work off your energy. They are food for warriors. I once had a theory about this, but like most historical theories, it may not stand up to close examination. It had something to do with cooking methods and warfare, the timing of dishes and the frequent necessity to drop everything and flee.

The Celts, I seem to remember, never mastered the art of slow cooking because before the meat would have time to get tender, the Romans or Anglo-Saxons or the neighbours descended on them, ravaging and pillaging. Thus, everything was rapidly boiled in iron pots over an open fire or griddled on a hot stone, while the Scots – who eventually realised that the pie offered a useful means of conveying victuals to the high ground when time pressed – invented the stout crust which is made with boiling water and stands up to rough treatment. The very earliest fast food. Do not take my word for this. It is also now being suggested that the Celts never existed as a separate racial strand. Like the Cornish pasty, the southern answer to the problem of how to transport a meal to work without dropping bits, the pie was designed to succour people engaged in heavy manual labour. The Bedfordshire Clanger consisted of suet pastry, minced meat and onions, salt and pepper and jam: one end of the pastry was spread with the meat and onions, a strip of pastry was pressed down the middle and the other end held the jam. It was rolled up tightly and the ends were flattened and turned over to keep the contents of the roll inside, the whole tied in a floured cloth and boiled.

A Lady observes of Savoury Pies, 'There are few articles of cookery more generally liked than relishing pies, if properly made; and they may be made of a great variety of things.' An ancient one known as Pasty Royal, as prescribed by Sir Theodore de Mayerne, 'Must be at least twenty or four and twenty hours in the oven, which said oven must all the while keep shut, to the end that it may yield a sufficient heat whereby the said pasty may be thoroughly baked.' Clear enough, but hark, it goes on: 'Which said pasty you must often take out of the said oven to supply it with broth or gravie as often as it shall be wanting.' Poor cook. This dreadful pasty begins with a leg of mutton, skinned, boned, mortified and 'chopt. And as you chop it you must season it with salt spices.' You make your paste of rye-crust 'and give it at least two inches in thicknesse, proportionately according unto the bignesse of your pasty, and raise the paste thereof high enough.' You lined it, bottom and sides, with fat bacon 'in slices' and put in a good handful of ox suet, then your mutton, and, 'in case chestnuts be in season, you may add thereunto, a reasonable proportion after they shall have been first half roasted'. You covered it with rye-crust at least a finger's breadth thick, and you had to make a hole in the 'said lid'.

Then you 'boyled' the bones, skin and sinews for an hour and a half until you had a pint only of the 'said liquor and broth' and made use of it in the following manner, viz . . . No. The recipe for this pasty and its relationship with the oven is too exhausting to give verbatim. You put it in, you took it out, you poured in broth, you put it back, you took it out and looked inside, you put it back again 'till it hath continued in the oven for the space of fifteen or sixteen hours' then you 'again draw it forth of the oven and shall take off its lidd, for to embellish your pasty . . .' In short, you tossed in quartered hard-boiled eggs, 'muserons', cockscombs, sweetbreads, a 'small clove of garlic' and a drop or two of vinegar and some sweet spices, and put it back. After at least three more hours if the 'sauce or liquor thereof be perfectly consumed' it was done. Now, 'You shall take out of it the clove of garlic which you did put into it,' fasten the lid down again and 'if it so be that the said pye be not eaten up at one meal, you may cause it to be heated up again in the oven until such time as it is quite expended.' The grim warning 'Do Not Reheat' meant nothing to the Elizabethan cook.

A Pudding Pie, a piece of meat baked in a dish of batter, is mentioned by Taylor in 1630: how this dish came to be called 'Toad in the Hole' we are unable to divine. Somebody remarked that it does not lend itself to the French translation – *Crapaud en Trou* has an eerie ring. Lamb's Tail Pie was made at lambing time when the lambs' tails were docked. The tails were cleaned, scalded, cut into pieces and put into a pie dish with mint, salt and pepper. The crust was made with mutton fat. Pigeon Pie was a popular dish because there were a lot of pigeons. I once had cold pigeon pie at Longleat, sitting, rather pointedly I thought, under a deserted dovecote. *Pigeonniers* abound in parts of France and animal lovers think how picturesque – not realising they formed a kind of larder for the living, providing a constant source of fresh meat.

The London Pye took advantage of the sparrows of which there were also a lot. (This is no longer so. The 'spadger' has almost disappeared from the streets of London. No one knows quite why.) The pie required 'Eighteen cock sparrowes or larks, potato roots, eringo roots, luttice stalks, chestnuts, dates, oysters, citron rinds, hartichokes, yolks of hard eggs, lemmons, barberies, gross pepper, nutmeg, Cinnamon, cloves, mace and corrents.' The whole has to be liquored 'when it is baked, with white wine, butter and sugar'. This is little different from the original Mince Pie, except that mutton or beef rather than sparrows would have formed the meaty element. Many pies had hard-boiled eggs in them. I suspect that this was because people with many hens often had many eggs and it was a neat way of using them up.

People used to eat rooks, too. One author in 1893 found this unsettling. He heard the sound of shots and went out to discover a man shooting rooks and the boys of the village pulling their heads off to 'prevent them tasting bitter'. And then the author realised that 'the one significance of these poor dead things was "rook pie". Well, I know it is morbid sensibility. I know I ought to take a manly delight in slaying my feathered fellow-creatures. All the same, I could not get the thought out of my head that half a minute before that rook had been sailing and cawing in the evening sunlight and that before you could say "Caw!" it was a poor lifeless lump of feathers with its head pulled off . . .' The author was working up to a homily on life and death.

Sir Francis was always concerned with methods of adding comfort to his hunting and shooting expeditions and was considerate of 'People who have not a footman or a chauffeur.' They would be well advised, he says, to limit those dishes that would mean dirtying plates. Nevertheless, he was particularly fond of something he called 'Pedro Pie': 'Every household that ever takes lunch out-of-doors in the winter should possess a Pedro pie-dish – though probably it may have to be specially made.' It had a perforated lid, under the usual sort, upon which you spread mashed potato. Beneath that, in the dish proper, were little odds and ends of all kinds – mixed remains of cooked mutton, poultry, rabbit 'and especially game', and carrots and onions together with 'other available vegetables, such as cooked French beans, tomatoes, mushrooms, butter beans, potatoes (cooked); glass of port or sherry; red currant jelly; some good stock, and a little roux'. Devoted as I am to Sir Francis, I don't care for the sound of this at all. We are also reluctant to jettison leftovers but usually manage them more neatly. Pedro Pie sounds as though it might easily have slopped over in the rumble seat. Sir Francis' Turnovers are a better idea, being conveniently portable – he adds, making allowances for the widespread abhorrence of onion – that two types should be provided, some with and some without and different in shape.

The Dictionary of Daily Wants has 'Scrap Pie':

> Grease a flat dish, and make a common paste with dripping or the fat that has settled on the liquor of boiled meat; two pounds of flour and three-quarters of a pound of fat will make a large pie. The crust will be greatly improved by the addition of a teaspoonful of bread-powder or little carbonate of ammonia. Having rolled out the crust, spread a thinnish layer carefully over the dish. Fill it with bits of cold meat of any kind that have been collected from the plates or trimmed from a joint, or in any other way. [*What* other way?] Chop them all up together, with a little parsley and thyme and an onion. If there is not meat enough to fill the dish, cold potatoes may be laid at the bottom, either mashed or cut in thin slices, or slices of vegetable marrow. A little cold gravy will be an improvement. Moisten the edge crust, that the top when laid on may adhere firmly. Cover and bake. When the top crust looks well done it is enough. This will turn out whole, and is excellent eating, either hot or cold.

Janet makes a pie that utilises the leftover limbs of a roasted fowl when the fastidious have eaten only the white breast meat: the darker and actually more succulent bits are unrecognisable when combined with the other ingredients – softened mushrooms, leeks, white wine and béchamel – and there is no need to tell anyone where you got them from. Nor that you bought the puff pastry. Jennifer Paterson praised Janet's chicken pie.

Every now and then we used to make a steak and kidney (often known as Kate and Sidney) pudding, though without the kidney (another taste I never acquired since the first one I ever saw cut open exuded the aroma of a public lavatory), but the kitchen filled with steam which condensed and ran down the walls. In Ye Olde Cheshire Cheese in Fleet Street they used to make the pudding with two pounds of cubed steak, four quartered lamb kidneys, four quartered hard-boiled eggs, mushrooms, raw oysters and larks. A man writing in 1925 described the ceremonial attending the presentation of this dish. A visiting American, so he says, would be contriving to take the chair at the head of the table where, according to legend Dr Johnson once sat, and at one-o'clock precisely a fiddler playing 'The Roast Beef of Olde England' would lead a procession of three waiters, the cook bearing the pudding, and the host who was going to carve it, from the upstairs kitchen. It was served with boiled potatoes and crusty bread and everyone could have 'follows', i.e. seconds if the pudding held out, and then there was stewed cheese, 'a toothsome but most deadly indigestible morsel'.

Hortense details 'Labourer's Pie': 'For the following I pur-chased last market day at threepence a pound, four pounds of mixed pieces, or odds and ends of meat . . .' She put them in a dish with alternating layers of potatoes and onions and put a pie crust on top. She gives minute directions as to the making of pies and tarts:

> Everybody (you say, Eloise) knows how to make either. So they pretend. Well, I assure you, that among the artisans in this

neighbourhood, when I now and then visit their dwellings, for the purpose of teaching them a few profitable family dishes – I can tell you, without jesting, that I have seen as many as six county wives out of half-a-dozen who had literally spoiled both food and the appearance of their tarts and pies; they seemed to have been unfortunate to have all been favoured with the same receipt.

Lightness does not then seem to have been an important consideration. 'Mix your paste well, which requires to be very hard,' directs Hortense, going on to offer a piece of advice '*Useful to the Middle Classes* and a receipt for *Sweet Royal Paste*': 'Here is a little bit of extravagance from the Camelia Lady, as they call me here . . .' (The addition of conceit to the transference of sex puts Soyer in a strange light. He seems to take herself – as it were – more seriously than do our present-day female impersonators.)

I have a nostalgic longing for a complete set of truly elaborate fish knives – and forks – once considered indescribably common. At one time the polite were supposed to eat their fish with two forks, and after that it was felt that if you were the right sort of person, your general cutlery would be composed of the sort of metal that did not react unfavourably to the odour of fish. Our fish pie could be eaten with a spoon if you felt so inclined. Take some boneless fillet of cod (or whatever), mix in the food processor a cupful of parsley, a cupful of olive oil, salt, black pepper and several cloves of garlic, and pour the results over the fish. Boil and slice some potatoes, lay them on top and put bits of butter on them. Then put the whole thing in a hot oven for a short time, just long enough to cook the fish. If the potatoes haven't browned you can put it under the grill for a moment but I never bother. A comforting dish, pretty nearly foolproof and simpler than all the business with the mash and the prawns, which usually go hard anyway because of their inability to keep in time with the other fish.

Stargazey Pie is one of those famous dishes perhaps better honoured in the breach than the observance. You prepared herrings – or pilchards – and put them in a buttered dish with chopped onions and breadcrumbs. Then you put in bits of fat bacon and filled the dish with egg custard. When it was nearly done you put on a pastry lid and left the fishes' heads sticking out of it, gazing skywards. There is a Finnish dish called *Kalakukko*, which also consists of fish and bacon in a rye crust. I think it is one of those things to which you must be bred in order to accommodate it. It is said that no Finnish maiden could marry before she had perfected her *Kalakukko*. Perhaps that is why my grandfather married an Englishwoman.

I recently came across a recipe for Lord Woolton's Pie. Lord Woolton was Minister of Food from 1940 to 1943 when rationing was in force and his suggestion for a pie was greeted with stunned astonishment and derision. It wouldn't have been so bad if he had refrained from describing it as a pie. If he had only advised people to fill up on vegetables they would have grumbled, but they would not have been as resentful and contemptuous, for to the people of Britain, a pie was something with meat in it, unless it was the sort you put custard on – apple or plum or gooseberry. Lord Woolton's version was a mere travesty, a snare and a delusion and an insult to a people deprived of meat but not of their intelligence. It became the butt of endless jokes; the sour kind that spring from a deep wound to the feelings and was infamous for many years. The people suspected Lord Woolton of trying to put one over on them.

Here is the suggested recipe, which could be adjusted to accommodate vegetables in season. A pound of vegetables diced: say, potatoes, swedes, cauliflower, carrots. If you were so fortunate or corrupt as to possess an onion, which were in unbelievably short supply (remember to thread the one you had on a length of string to dip in the stew, remove and conserve for the next time), you could fling that in too, in truly profligate fashion. Then you cooked all this carefully in very little water with a spoonful of oatmeal and a teaspoon of vegetable extract, stirring often to prevent sticking, sprinkled chopped parsley over it, put mashed potato or a wholemeal crust over that and baked it. 'Eat it hot,' advised Lord Woolton sensibly, for cold, this pastry must have resembled damp cardboard. Here, I think, is the root of the problem. The pastry crust was made without fat and there was no butter to put on the mashed potato. Lord Woolton (except, of course, we all know that it wasn't really him but probably his wife or his secretary) suggested serving the pie with brown gravy which would, I imagine, have been composed of some type of industrial powder and it sounds a little unappetising.

The other day, before I had been reminded of Lord Woolton, I reinvented his dish, thinking of it as a meatless Shepherd's Pie – more a 'Gardener's Pie': Stir fry, in olive oil, chopped onion, carrot, swede, Jerusalem artichoke and celery with a pinch of herbs and, after a while, a vegetable stock cube dissolved in a wine glass of water. When the liquid has evaporated, put it all in a dish, cover with mashed potato and grated cheese and brown in the oven.

A Lady has some suggestions for meatless pies: '*Potato Pasty*.
Boil, peel, and mash potatoes as fine as possible; mix them with
salt, pepper, and a good bit of butter. Make a paste: roll it out
thin like a large puff, and put in the potato; fold over one-half,
pinching the edges. Bake in a moderate oven.' That would
be nice with the addition of some cubed cheese. '*An Herb Pie*.
Pick two handfuls of parsley from the stems, half the quantity of
spinach, two lettuces, some mustard and cresses, a few leaves of
borage, and white beet leaves; wash and boil them a little; then
drain and press out the water; cut them small; mix and lay them
in a dish, sprinkled with some salt. Mix a batter of flour, two eggs
well beaten, a pint of cream, and half a pint of milk, and pour it
on the herbs; cover with a good crust, and bake.' An upside-
down quiche, in fact. Marigold Pie, an ancient country pudding,
was made with savoury egg custard and marigold petals baked in
a pastry case until the custard set. It was served with cheese.

Miss Acton, in her section on pies and fruit tarts, writes rather
wearily that, 'The limits to which we are obliged to confine this
volume compel us to omit many receipts which we would gladly
insert.' She says they can be found in almost every English cookery book, but in the index to Dr Kitchiner the only notable entry
is 'Pie: Jeffrey Hudson, in a:' – then you look in the body of the
book and find the wretched things coyly lined up under the
heading 'Puddings and Pies', while under 'Tartlets' is the direction 'See Pies'. Mrs Raffald has no pies in her index, but there
they all are in Chapter V with observations: 'Raiſed pieſ
ſ hould have a quick oven, well cloſed up, or your pie will fall
in the ſides; it ſ hould have no water put in till the minute it
goeſ to the oven, it makeſ the cruſt ſad . . .' On the third page
in she has an apple tart, which, being uncovered, is not what we
mean by pie. Tarts do not appear in the index but they're in
there somewhere because she tells you how to make a crisp paste

for them – and icing – white of an egg, sugar, gum, 'beat it half an hour'. (It is this sort of thing that sends Cook to her room, there to pluck moodily at the counterpane.) She does have a sweet pie among the savoury ones, but it is made of marrow or beef suet, veal steaks and more marrow or suet – 'it makes them eat tenderer' – as well as the raisins, currants, cinnamon, candied citron and 'ſweet mountain or ſack'.

And all the old books have mince pies. *The Dictionary of Daily Wants* has a selection of types of mincemeat. One consists of two pounds of beef, four and a half pounds of suet, eight large apples, six pounds of currants, two rounds of bread, an ounce of nutmeg, half an ounce of cloves, pepper and salt to season, one and a half pounds of sugar, rind and juice of six oranges, rind and juice of two lemons, one pint port wine and a pint of brandy. Others contain calf's feet and pickled ox-tongue, and you had to leave it for a few weeks for the flavour to develop. It also has 'Egg Pie: Mince the yolks of twenty-four eggs, two pounds of suet, half a pound of bread-crumbs, an ounce of candied peel, two ounces of sugar, one tablespoonful of orange-flower water, half an ounce of allspice, a pound of minced raisins, half a pound of currants, and two dozen sweet almonds; cover, bake, and serve with wine sauce.'

Another book has kidneys in its mincemeat. I am lost for words.

A Lady, God bless her, is frank, open and simple on the subject of tartlets: 'Currant and Raspberry – for a tart, line the dish, put the sugar, and fruit, lay bars across, and bake.' She candidly lists them in the index, 'iceing' [*sic*] for them, pippin, prune, orange, codlin, rhubarb, raspberry with cream. She does leave out the currant and raspberry but nobody's perfect.

In the old Celtic calendar, 31 October was the last day of the old year, its night the occasion for witches and warlocks to roam abroad holding their wicked revels. This custom of playing 'all sorts of games' went to America with emigrants from Scotland and the North of England, and has now unfortunately returned, heavily embellished – although, so far, without quite the same extravagance. Christianity transformed it into the Eve of All Hallows, but the ancient ways lingered on. We've been in Los Angeles at this time, where one would be hard put to it to escape the impression that the most significant festivals are Hallowe'en and Thanksgiving, Christmas being the feast of Rudolph the Red-Nosed Reindeer, and Easter, of the Bunny – lit up and rhinestone encrusted. In the end these junketings have a remarkably similar flavour. You buy lots of things and clog up the municipal garbage disposal system with glamorous cardboard boxes and wrapping paper and then you eat too much. Hallowe'en offers the added annoyance of bands of children (carefully supervised now, of course, by whichever parent has custody at the moment), going from house to house lisping, 'Trick or Treat?' You hand out buckets of candy, hoping the Tooth Fairy will wreak a vicarious, carious revenge.

If your young insist on following 'tradition' you will need a pumpkin. In the old days it would have been a turnip and it must be admitted that hollowing out a pumpkin and giving it an expression, although not easy, is simpler than tackling a turnip, solid and intractably compacted as they are. Having performed this feat you are left with a lot of pumpkin pulp. The profligate will fling it into the bin but using it up gives a certain satisfaction. Since pumpkin doesn't taste of anything except, very slightly, pumpkin, it can only act as a vehicle for other flavours. For soup, you stew it and add almost anything you like. With the rest, and there does tend to be a lot of it, make Pumpkin Pie.

Searching for a recipe for Pumpkin Pie I looked in *The Practical Cook Book and Housekeeper's Guide*, published by the Life Insurance Company of Virginia organised 1871, and found at the top of the page 'Don't Spend All Your Earnings. Money Paid for Life Insurance Is Not Spent But Saved,' and at the bottom, 'Mrs Mary Davis, Concord, N.C. (insurance of son Luther F. Davis): "My son had only paid one premium, however, the claim was paid just as prompt as if he had been paying several years . . ."' and on the opposite page, Alexander Munford of Petersburg, Va. is thankful and appreciative for 'the prompt satisfactory settlement on claim paid me on my son, David Munford, who was drowned at Wilcox Lake on July 6th.' Pumpkin Pie seems out of place amidst all this tragedy but this is how to do it:

> 'Cut pumpkin into pieces, remove soft part and seeds. Cover and cook slowly in its own steam until tender. Remove cover and let it get almost dry. Press through a sieve. To two and a half cups of pulp add two cups of milk, a teaspoon each of salt, butter, cinnamon, and ginger, two teaspoons of molasses, two eggs, and sugar to taste. The beaten eggs are to be added last, after the mixture is cold. Pour into open crust, and bake slowly, 40 minutes.'

The book continues: 'The great preacher, Talmage, said once in his sermon, "A dead family man uninsured is a dead defaulter." The great Baptist preacher, Rev. Dr Anderson, of Boston, said, 'I believe it is a Christian duty to carry a reasonable life insurance."' Then back to the recipes, 'Peanut cookies will prove a delight to most members of the family . . .' That should cheer up the relict.

In the past, the wealthy ordered elaborate pies for their banquets, dreaming up novel ways of making them more interesting, for example putting live birds inside and then raising the lid with whoops of merriment. Walpole gives some details:

> Another favourite dish at the tables of our forefathers, was a Pie of stupendous magnitude, out of which, on its being opened, a flock of living birds flew forth, to the no small surprise and amusement of the guests.
>
> > Four-and-twenty Blackbirds baked in a Pie;
> > When the Pie was open'd, the birds began to sing –
> > Oh! what a dainty dish – 'tis fit for any King.
>
> This was a common Joke at an old English Feast. These animated Pies were often introduced 'to set on' as Hamlet says, 'a quantity of barren spectators to laugh; there is an instance of a Dwarf undergoing such an *incrustation*. About the year 1630, King Charles and his Queen were entertained by the Duke and Duchess of Buckingham at Burleigh on the Hill, on which occasion the previously mentioned [and indexed] Jeffrey Hudson, *the Dwarf*, was served up in a cold Pie.'

They sometimes put frogs in, too, to frighten the ladies, and all in all one feels these celebratory occasions, then as now, were best avoided by the fastidious. In Tudor times they made pastry stags, filled them with claret and poked them with a dagger to see the 'blood' flow. This, apparently, rendered the ladies helpless with mirth. At Trimalchio's Feast there was a boar in a bonnet with baby pastry pigs hanging from its teats. In came a hunter who made a hole in the boar, thus releasing a flock of thrushes. The tradition has survived amongst the vulgar in the form of the 'cake' which opens to reveal scantily clad girls leaping out, intoning 'Happy Birthday' or anything appropriate to the occasion.

My own feeling is that when you get a blonde hopping out of a cake, the Four Horsemen cannot be far behind. As *The Household Manager* put it, 'As soon as they are on all sides attacked, [they] tottle, fall, and crumble, and no longer present anything but glorious and ephemeral ruins, like every other work of man – all pass away, whether they be temples, columns, pyramids or pies, "like the baseless fabric of a vision, and leave not a wrack behind".'

Sixteen

ONE VEG.

$\mathcal{I}$ have a book dating from the 1930s wherein it states, disarmingly, that the expert writing on the subject knew very little about vitamins but would keep us informed of developments. Vitamin C was among the first to be identified and is still the popular favourite. Oranges were at one time generally supposed to be the richest source of this life-enhancing element, but then it turned out that other fruit and vegetables, including potatoes, contained even more of it; and now they say that too much vitamin C could cause heart disease by thickening the lining of the arteries, while vitamin A might contribute to the development of lung cancer. One enthusiast, some years ago, turned yellow and died from overdosing on carrot juice. We were told to eat up all our potato skins until someone suggested they could be a contributory cause of bowel cancer and anyway, if there were pesticides present, that was where they would tend to congregate – in the skins. Spinach was once considered to be essential to vitality and longevity – remember Popeye? – but then it was found that someone had made a mistake in his calculations and any broad-leafed vegetable was in the same league. That was before they discovered Strontium 90 lodged in the aforesaid broad-leafed vegetable. Now tomatoes, which, like potatoes, belong to the family of Deadly Nightshade, are said to be the clue to, if not life everlasting, then robust health, so those who prefer cream on their pasta are headed for an early grave.

I was brought up in the belief that the Victorians boiled their vegetables for far too long. In the 1960s and 1970s I knew people who still boiled cabbage for hours with a lump of soda to keep it green, but more advanced thinkers had taken to steaming it briefly in order to 'conserve the goodness' and not drown the vitamins in gallons of water; then it was said only recently by some expert or another, that the latest view on vegetables is that they should be 'well cooked' in order to 'release the goodness'. Another fruitful subject for argument or, more probably, another source of confusion.

Brillat-Savarin lists Starch, Sugar, Sweet Oils, Gluten, Mucilage and Gum as the constituents of vegetables. He allows that vegetables offer variety and resources in the way of nourishment, but since the existence of vitamins was as yet unsuspected in the eighteenth century, vegetables on the dining table were in the position of maiden aunts at a wedding – they had a right to be there, and even contributed something to the festivities, but they were never the *raison d'être* of the occasion. In the nineteenth century they were indeed often the object of suspicion. According to the *Encyclopaedia of Domestic Economy*:

> Only a small part of the numerous tribe of plants are available for food in their natural state; unlike the animal kingdom in this respect, the greater number of vegetables are useless as food, and many are extremely deleterious . . . The fibrous and membranous parts of vegetables are not easily digestible, or not at all.

The skins of fruits, in general, pass through the stomach unchanged . . . The green leaves of vegetables, though in general acting somewhat on the bowels, are apt to produce acidity and flatulence with dyspeptic persons, and are therefore less fit for them than farinaceous food.

Taking the opposing view, Richard Phillips, an early nineteenth-century philanthropist, prison reformer and passionate advocate of vegetarianism, wrote, '*Because* the human stomach appears to be naturally so averse from receiving the remains of animals, that few people could partake of them if they were not disguised and flavoured by culinary preparation; yet rational beings ought to feel that the prepared substances are not the less what they truly are, and *that no disguise of food, in itself loathsome*, ought to delude the unsophisticated perceptions of a considerate mind.'

Mrs Pender Cudlip was more in agreement with the carnivorous faction:

Has it ever been the lot of one of my readers to cater for that most unpleasant person, a total abstainer and vegetarian? The cheapest and most disagreeable guest who ever gloomed my hearth or entered my portals was a being of this order, and she was infinitely more difficult to deal with than the most fastidious *gourmand* I ever knew. She would not drink milk or eat eggs, and when, in despair, I put a *plat* of five new potatoes before her, she raged round upon me, asking was she a pig that I should offer her roots.

The mention of roots (potatoes are actually tubers) reminds me of something I read in which the writer was discussing a group of dispossessed wayfarers – I forget where. He said that when they complained of having been forced to subsist on roots they meant, at the worst, mangel wurzels; they were probably speaking of potatoes or carrots or beetroots and not, as I had assumed, the tough old roots of something in the way of trees or shrubs, deemed, under normal circumstances, to be inedible. In old cookery books, roots are often differentiated from vegetables and herbs, while it is taken for granted that a diet without meat is a form of starvation.

The vegetarian of whom Mrs Pender Cudlip was writing sounds like an early slimmer. Mrs Pender Cudlip was herself accustomed to dine on, for example, soup, flounder *souchet*, curried salmon, scalloped oysters, Russian salad with prawns, capon with scraped smoked ham, crown artichokes (stuffed with chicken), saddle of Welsh mutton with redcurrant jelly, spinach, stewed peas, new potatoes, roast ptarmigan, a French salad, Camembert cheese, one jelly and a tart. By contrast her vegetarian friend had dry toast and cold tea for breakfast, toast and water for lunch, and for dinner, bread fried in salad oil with 'some kind of vegetable' and a cup of strong black coffee. Clearly not a weak-willed woman, for this was her invariable diet. She stayed for six weeks with Mrs Pender Cudlip who wails, in italics, that she herself grew *thin on it*, and this 'though I ate and drank as usual'. A novel occurrence in the saga of slimming. In passing, the dinner enjoyed by Mrs Pender Cudlip cost one pound, nine shillings and two pence and served eight people.

The vegetarian, despite her abstemious habits, had not allowed standards to slip. In her own home everything was perfect of its kind:

. . . showy napery, gleaming silver, glittering glass! In the centre

317

of the table, in a vase that has a mirror for its base, white flowers always in bloom. Arranged round the edge of the mirror, in a clever contrivance that holds water, is a border of blue or violet flowers; tall, graceful jugs and goblets of Bohemian and Venetian glass hold iced and plain water, lemonade, soda-water &c. Some oranges are in an old blue and white delft dish to her right; on the left a glass dish holds some olives. A silver toast-rack stands well filled before her. A tiny fountain plays over some carefully picked watercresses, keeping them fresh. Raw and cooked fruits are arranged with an eye to colour in various old china dishes about the table.

Sounds delightful. But the prospect of no meat gave Mrs Pender Cudlip a fit of the megrims (migraine).

Usually when we have vegetarians in our midst and the time comes for Sunday lunch, I give them everything except the meat and they are content. Few people enjoy nut cutlets and most vegetarians are now past the stage of trying to persuade themselves they've got meat on the plate when they haven't: vegetarian sausages, burgers and roasts are seldom palatable. Scientists are engaged in attempting to construct an artificial fillet steak but I was once persuaded to bite into a bit of ersatz 'lamb' and it was foully disgusting. Disguising food is, however, an ancient habit. Somebody somewhere suggested, 'This favourite way of making one thing out of another for diversion, originated probably from the expedient relative to Nicomedes, King of Bithnyia. When three hundred miles from the sea, the monarch longed for fish, on which his cook contrived to produce something which satisfied both his eye and palate.' I cannot imagine how, but the cook of Louis XV could 'on a very strict fast-day [only one meal being allowed and that without flesh meat] place on the table the *semblances à s'y méprendre* of all kinds of poultry, game, and butcher's meat, made out of vegetables, *accommodés au maigre*, as

318

our neighbours coaxingly term it'. A slice of aubergine cut thinly from top to bottom and fried in tempura batter looks very like a fillet of fish but tastes stubbornly of aubergine. According to Mungo Park in his *Travels in Africa*, 'People who live on vegetable food have an unconquerable desire for salt,' but I have seen no evidence of this.

Soyer, as Hortense, writes on the subject of vegetables:

In describing to you, dearest, the different ways these may be dressed, I beg of you to make a constant use of them at your own table, as you will find that they will be much better than partaking of half-raw greens, cabbage, turnip tops, spinach &c. which are so often served up at tables in this country, and are less inviting in flavour, and consequently, do not get consumed as much as they ought, which causes more meat to be eaten, and, instead of refreshing the blood, as all vegetables will do in their season, only irritate it. Do not misunderstand me respecting our English way of partaking of plain boiled vegetables: I do not wish you to give them up entirely, but by adopting both plans, you will find it a great advantage in your domestic cookery. For my part I never object to our plain boiled vegetables, but merely to the neglectful way they are cooked and served up, often swimming in water. In France, no family in the middle station of life ever dine without their dish of dressed vegetables, upon which as much care has been bestowed in cooking as upon the principal dish of the dinner, and is often eaten alone.

Mrs Marshall noted sternly:

It is time that a lesson were taken from continental housewives and that we in this country should look upon vegetables as separate and distinct food, and make them into independent and palatable dishes, and not serve them as mere adjuncts to meat. The Vegetarian Society is doing great good in this respect, and through its efforts we may look for some improvement in vegetable cookery. When this comes to pass, this class of food will fulfill its intended functions, and a diminution of indigestion and dyspepsia will be the result.

She stated, as the nineteenth century drew to its close, that the joint at dinner is 'not complete unless accompanied by vegetables and maybe other additions . . . in fact it has been observed that whenever the vegetables are distinguished for their excellence, the dinner is always enjoyed.' She considered that two vegetables were generally sufficient for an ordinary dinner party and urged the hostess to widen her mind on the matter, quoting from an 'authority': 'There are many English houses, hotels, and even clubs, where the boiled potato makes its daily appearance with a regularity which drives a diner to despair and a gastronome to the verge of suicide. Old and new, hard or soft, white or black, the potato is still boiled and boiled only . . .' She points out that there are lots of things you can do with a potato and says the other vegetables should be 'chosen to accord with the joint' since:

some of the homely kinds such as turnips, parsnips, carrots, etc. are heartily enjoyed by persons who would loathe them when merely boiled. In Roman Catholic countries where Lent and other fasts are rigorously observed, the preparation of vegetables has secured greater attention than in this country . . . Green peas, French beans, cabbage, or something similar, with spinach, occasionally seem to be the sole repertoire of English cooks. Cardoons, egg plants, salsify, celery roots and other delicacies are almost ignored. Asparagus, artichokes, tomatoes, sea kale, sorrel, endive, lettuce, and others, though used to some extent, deserve far more attention than they receive at present . . .

When she comes to the chapter on 'Entremets of Vegetables', Mrs Marshall pursues her theme. In France:

> The dish of some vegetable at the end of dinner is as eagerly looked for and anticipated as the pudding or tart is by children at an English table. At continental hotels a course of vegetables alone is invariably served, but in almost all English hotels one gets only those which accompany the meat and go to make a confused pile on the plate . . . It is certainly an English habit [she continues, getting worked up] to take vegetables only with the meat, and to look upon a 'dish of herbs' as food only fit for peasants . . . An artichoke is about the only vegetable which is taken separately in England, and this is because it cannot be eaten with a knife and fork; asparagus occasionally falls under the same arrangement.

Despite the apparent common sense displayed here, Mrs Marshall was prone to doing things like puréeing carrots and putting them in little pastry cases with little pastry rings round, while, for instance, Francatelli (in common with other experts) tortured his vegetables into shapes called *Chartreuse* – 'a mixed preparation, consisting of vegetables symmetrically and tastefully arranged in a plain mould, the interior of which is garnished with either game, quails, pigeons, larks, fillets, scollops, tendons, etc.' – into macedoines and timbales, and squashed utterly for soups and garnishes. In progressive volumes of Mrs Beeton the illustrations show a gradual decline in this custom until, by 1915, the vegetables may be recognised by their form for what they are.

'How curious it is, dearest,' wrote Hortense:

that two of the most simple productions of Nature – a plant and a root, which were introduced by that *preux chevalier* of Queen Elizabeth, Sir Walter Raleigh – should have produced such wonderful effects as they have upon society; and how singular it is that the one, which might naturally be supposed to be baneful, should be advantageous, and that which was beneficial should be a curse. Such has proved to be the case within these three years; for whilst the first – tobacco – has produced a large revenue to the country to aid in supporting its administration, the latter – the potato – has tended to pauperize a large portion of the kingdom, and drained it of its wealth.

Passing over this interesting viewpoint, here is another example of the unreliable nature of history, an aspect that troubled Sir Walter Raleigh himself; it was not, after all, he who introduced the potato to Europe. Some say the Dutch had been growing it before he brought it home in 1586, while Clusius, 'the botanist of Leyden' writing in the same year, says it had been cultivated in Italy prior to that date. 'Cuvier denied that Europe derived the potato from Virginia and Banks agreed with him, stating that Coccius, in his *Chronicle*, printed in 1553, mentions potatoes under the term *papas*. Herriott, who accompanied Raleigh's expedition to Virginia, called them *openawk*, and Sir Robert Southwell, President of the Royal Society, announced in 1693 that potatoes had been introduced into Ireland by his grandfather who 'first had them of Sir Walter Raleigh'.

'But at what time the potato became a staple article of the food of the Irish people is neither clear,' writes the name-scattering author from whom I gleaned the above confusing information. He says it was first grown in gardens as a rarity, used at table as a delicacy, and described by herbalists as an introduced exotic. Gerard mentions it in 1597 but it is not believed to have been cultivated by the people as a general article of food until the end of the seventeenth or the beginning of the eighteenth century. Mr Boyle, into the hands of whose family the Youghal estates – 'the cradle of the potato' – of Sir Walter Raleigh passed in 1602, had a letter from his gardener describing 'this esculent . . . as very good to pickle for winter salads and also to preserve'. This shows, says the author, that the potato had not then become an article of common food among the Irish, even around the location where it was first cultivated. Sir W. Petty was speaking of it as their food in 1672, d'Urfey in 1689, and someone said that after the arrival of William III, the 'natives had been prevented enjoying their beloved beniclabber (thick milk) and pottados'.

We can only be sure that Sir Walter did not introduce the potato into Ireland in order to benefit the natives since his ambition was to eradicate them. (Potatoes were called 'Raleigh's fatal gift to Ireland' because of the alcohol the Irish distilled from them.) But nor could he have been so prescient as to foresee the potato famine, which began in 1844, and the catastrophe which would result from the Irish dependence on one main source of food. As Cecil Woodham-Smith wrote in her biography of Queen Victoria: 'The magnificent wheat harvest of 1847 was useless to the starving Irish. They had been allowed to become so dependent on potatoes that if grain had been given to them they had no means of milling or using it.'

'The sweet potato,' according to the *Encyclopaedia of Domestic Economy*, 'is a tuberose root common in tropical countries, but of quite a different species from the common potato. It forms a sweet nourishing food used as potatoes. This plant had been introduced into England by Sir Francis Drake and Sir John Hawkins before the common potato; but, though it is cultivated in other parts of Europe, our climate was found to be too cold for its growth in the open air.' So it all depends, as Professor

Joad the philosopher would have said, on what you mean by 'potato'. In the time of Queen Elizabeth I it was known as 'a meate for pleasure' being 'either roasted in the embers, or boyled and eaten with oile, vinegar and pepper', and was restricted to the court and the aristocracy.

'Potatoes can take the place of oatmeal, porridge, and the puddings of Scotland, the *kasha* of Russia, the *mamaliga* of Roumania, and the *polenta* of Italy; but being new in a long history of human food, they are looked at askance.' That was written by a food theorist in 1944, but when potatoes as we know them were introduced into the diet it wasn't long before people fell upon them with enthusiasm; and in many countries they eventually took the place of bread at main meals (although parts of France were resistant), serving to sop up the gravy as readily as the ancient manchet. During the Second World War they were heavily recommended by the Ministry of Food as a source of calories but, since butter was in extremely short supply, the potato boiled or baked was a sorry article, though fried or roasted it was quite acceptable. One winter the crop was frosted and the resulting potatoes were disgusting, but on the whole they were regarded as much with favour as with resignation.

The food theorist writes, of the competition between man and animals for feeding stuffs: 'In wartime we ourselves experience this competition which occurs in nearly every country, meat production having to be cut down because starchy food produces only one fifth of its weight when consumed by pigs.' In other words, leave the pigs in peace and eat the potatoes yourself. He quotes one Arthur Young in relation to potato consumption in Ireland:

Mark the Irishman's potato bowl placed on the floor, the whole family upon their hams around it, devouring a quantity almost incredible, the beggar seating himself to it with a hearty welcome, the pig taking his share as readily as the wife, the cocks, hens, turkeys, geese, the cur, the cat and perhaps the cow – and all partaking of the same dish. No man can often have been witness of it without being convinced of the plenty, and I will add the cheerfulness, that attends it.

The 'almost incredible' quantity averaged out at about six or eight pounds of potatoes per person per day: with buttermilk and eggs, states the theorist, this would be enough to keep the person nourished. He takes the view that potatoes were the staple diet only of the poor and that the better off would invariably choose something more *recherché* from the menu; but whenever my dearest friend, who had spent many of her early years shivering in vast, draughty, Irish dining rooms, was with us, I made her potato dishes, for she esteemed them above everything else with the possible exception of oysters. She remembered without enthusiasm the dinners of her youth, which varied, she said, between dry pheasant and drier ham, enlivened by discussions with her neighbour at table on the state of the crops, and she used to much prefer eating potato cakes in the kitchen. At one point the government, seemingly with time on its hands, exerted itself to instruct us all to eat five egg-sized potatoes a day.

Hortense wrote on the 'Irish Way of Boiling':

In Ireland . . . it is cooked so that it may have, as they call it, a bone in it; that is, that the middle of it should not be quite cooked. They are done thus:- Put a gallon of water with two ounces of salt, in a large iron pot, boil for about ten minutes, or until the skin is loose, pour the water out of the pot, put a dry cloth on top of the potatoes, and place it on the side of the fire without water for about twenty minutes, and serve . . . by this plan the potato is both boiled and baked.

The Gentle Art of Cookery mentions the beautiful Irish silver potato rings which were used to hold them, remarking that 'when the Irish have exterminated one another' some future archaeologist will deduce from them 'that the potato had some occult significance'.

I long looked in vain for early evidence of the chip as we know it. Miss Acton's 'Fried Potatoes', 'Crisped Potatoes', or 'Potato Ribbons' are what we would call crisps. The American term, 'french fries', is again truer to tradition than we credit. (It has been rumoured that the secret of perfect french fries lies in the use of horse fat.) The French were eating chips in the 1700s and Thomas Jefferson, ambassador to France at the time, had returned to America with the method. 'Potatoes fried in the French manner.' In 1853, the American Indian chef George Crum (from chief to chef – how unexpected are the ways of fate) who presided at Moon Lake Lodge, Saratoga Springs, was asked by a guest – some say it was Cornelius Vanderbilt – for thinner and yet thinner fried French potatoes. The crisp, or – as Mrs Marshall (and others) gracefully acknowledged, the Saratoga potato – was born.

I know this because one day as I grumbled about the lack of recorded history in regard to the British chip, my eldest grand-daughter turned to her computer, and that was what she found. A little while later, by the purest chance (the way you hear an unusual word and then it crops up everywhere), I read in *The Times* an article by Jonathan Meades entitled 'Out of the frying pan into the deep fat fryer . . . the long journey of fish and chips from Spain to Spitalfields', in which he confirmed my impression that deep fat frying had been considered by the British until recently to be not quite nice. He says the earliest fish and chip shop had been instituted in the East End in the 1860s by Sephardim, the descendants of Iberian Jews. I knew I knew it – it was merely that the details had escaped me.

I also used to know how the puffy chip (crisp on the outside, plump and airy on the inner) came about, but have forgotten the details again. Something to do with the chef in the galley on a train ascending an Alp, whereupon the pressure altered and caused the fat in which he was cooking his potatoes to cease boiling. When it started again (I imagine the train was by now descending), his potatoes swelled into the most perfect chips. It is said that the process should be precisely observed, but I find if I cook chips for a few minutes, remove them from the heat, and after a while return them, the result is satisfactory. My earliest Mrs Beeton does have 'Potatoes, Fried (French Fashion)', but again insists on thin slices and the use of a frying pan (not deep fat). However, she does recommend the double dip: 'The immersion of the vegetable in the grease a second time after it is partially cooked, causes it to puff or "gonfler", as the French say, which is the desired appearance for properly-dressed fried potatoes to possess.'

Janet found another version of the origin of the puffy chip which attributes it to the chef of Louis XIV, who was preparing the royal supper whilst on a military campaign. The King was late owing to bad weather and muddy roads and the food had to be heated up. Beloved has a culinary masterpiece – egg and chips – the chips are precision cut, washed, towelled, and dried with a hairdryer. The kitchen is out of bounds during the various procedures – which can take all afternoon in preparation and execution – and the remainder of the evening he spends in clearing it all up. My fifth son took a four-page list of instructions detailing all this when he left for Australia – I doubt that he has ever used them. (No sooner had I placed the historical chip to my own satisfaction than the Swedish Food Administration announced that the carcinogen acrylamide came into being when food was fried at high temperature.)

A final use for potatoes. 'To restore oil-paintings, peel a potato and halve it. Rub over the painting with the flat side, cutting a new surface when the moisture becomes exhausted. Sponge afterwards very gently with clean, tepid water, and allow to dry.' I once tried this. It didn't work but, mercifully, did no further damage to the painting.

Jerusalem Artichokes, according to the *Encyclopaedia of Domestic Economy* were, 'natives of Brazil, having been brought to England in 1617, and before potatoes were so generally adopted, were much in use' and 'at first greatly preferred'. As *The Dictionary of Daily Wants* put it, 'When cooked it is agreeable to the taste, but not very nourishing; it is, however, easy of digestion, and less productive of flatulence than many other vegetables,' while Hortense remarked that it was:

> anything but appreciated as it deserves to be . . . I choose about twelve of the same size, peel them, and shape them like a pear, but flat at the bottom, wash them well, boil gently in three pints of water, one ounce of salt, one of butter, and a few sliced onions; when tender, I make a border of mashed potatoes on a dish, fix them on it point upwards, sauce over with either cream sauce, white sauce, melted butter, and place a fine Brussels sprout between each, which is exceedingly inviting, simple, and pretty.

This switch from 'girasole' to 'Jerusalem' is explained

whenever the vegetable is mentioned in modern recipes. The soup made from it was once called Palestine Soup.

Carrots were introduced by Flemish settlers in the reign of Elizabeth I and there does not seem to be as much argument about this as there was about the potato. 'This plant was so esteemed that the ladies wore the leaves as ornaments in their head dresses.' The leaves are undeniably pretty: children used to grow them from carrot tops in saucers of water before they were encouraged to make things from egg boxes, loo rolls and plastic bottles. We were told as children that carrots are good for the eyesight. 'How often do you see a rabbit wearing spectacles?' some waggish uncle would enquire. Apparently it's true.

Pierce wrote:

> Carrots, for instance, are, of all vegetables, perhaps the most congenial to men as well as animals, since they contain an immense proportion of saccharine matter, and juices not only fragrant and highly nutritive, but purifying to the blood. The nourishing qualities of this vegetable stand in their relative division, per cent, as – starch 3, gluten 3, and sugar 94. Yet with this vast amount of saccharine matter, the carrot when whole, or cut only into pieces, if eaten without thorough mastication, afterwards defeats the trituration of muscular action when in the alimentary canal; therefore, to most persons who, either in the hurry of business or in the excitement of conversation, eat quickly, the carrot may be considered as very indigestible food.

It would seem that vegetables as well as meat used to be markedly tougher than those we are accustomed to. *The Dictionary of Daily Wants* reads, '*Carrots Boiled*. Scrape, wash, and clean them; if large, cut them into two or four pieces. Set them over a fire in boiling water with some salt in it, and boil them for two or three hours. Very young carrots will only require one hour,' but the ever reliable Miss Acton gives 'a simple but excellent receipt' for 'Carrots in Their Own Juice', which my household would recognise as Vichy carrots.

Mrs Johnstone says, 'Yellow turnips, mashed and eaten with milk, are recommended in scurvy and consumption. Physicians recommend turnips and carrots to be boiled separately in three successive waters, drained well and mashed together with new milk and salt. Dr Anthony Todd Thomson recommends this dish strenuously to convalescents restricted to a vegetable diet, and prefers it himself to any other kind of vegetable food. So do I. It is the dish my grandfather ate with his salt cod – if swedes are 'yellow turnips'. I boil them together, just the once, and add a lot of butter.

Parsnips, like carrots, were much appreciated for their sweetness before sugar became available. It is said that the French despise parsnips and keep them only for animal fodder, which seems inexplicable since they well outstrip the *navet* in taste and texture and make a subject for discussion as the diners argue about precisely which spice the flavour evokes. Mrs Somerville's advice for parsnips: 'Wash them well and boil them in plenty of water; when done, which you can tell by trying with a fork, scrape off the outer coat, and either mash them and serve them like mashed turnips, or scrape them into shavings and serve with melted butter over them.'

Some of the latest news is that onions are good for you, not just in the way all vegetables are good for you but specifically, as a guard against osteoporosis. So far the scientific investigators have experimented only on rats, giving them dried onion every day for four weeks, whereupon their bones (those of the rats) become thicker and stronger. We are said to have a lot in common with rats, so we could also benefit. Soyer quotes, without attribution, 'Whoever wishes to preserve his health must eat every morning, before breakfast, young onions, with honey.' He goes on, 'Such a treat is assuredly not very tempting: besides, this rather strong vegetable leaves after it a most unpleasant perfume, which long reminds us of its presence: wherefore this recipe has not met with favour, and indeed, it is much to be doubted whether it will ever become fashionable.' I was once told, probably by the Classical Scholar, that the Ancient Greeks broke their fast on a raw onion, and old-wife wisdom has long held that onions, raw, roasted, boiled, or taken in the form of soup are a cure for the common cold. An old cure for a bad cold is braised onions in their skins with just the root end chopped off.

Miss Shepherd, *The Lady In the Van*, used to dine on a raw onion. We went to see Alan Bennett's play at the Queen's Theatre and it all came back to me, for the van used to be parked next door to us in Alan's garden. As an elderly person with a less than conventional lifestyle (she lived in her van and a Reliant Robin as a second home for many years) who needed to take care of her bones, Miss Shepherd was wise in her choice of vegetable; also, considering her age, somewhat unusual, for her mother would probably have considered onions vulgar and possibly unwholesome. I had an uncle who refused onions even in stew and he was not alone. Less fastidious people used to include the skins in their stews and broths to add a golden colour.

Pierce wrote 'dishes in which onion, eschalots, and garlic are perceptible to the taste are fit only for those who brave

indigestion, and for a time refrain from mingling in society.'
Swift's advice went:

> There is, in every Cook's opinion,
> No savoury dish, without an onion . . .
> . . . But lest your kissing should be spoil'd,
> The onion must be thoroughly boil'd.

The answer to the social problem is to make sure that when you consume a cheese and raw onion sandwich, those in your vicinity have one too, while the chewing of parsley to obviate the effects has been recommended for centuries. Another of the disadvantages of onions, apart from the effect on the breath and on the fingers of the cook, is the way they make you weep: some advise a piece of bread held between the teeth as you slice them up, or likewise a teaspoon; peeling them under water (which is no use when it comes to chopping), or leaving the root end on until you've sliced up the rest. Nothing works, except leaving them in the freezer for half an hour before attacking them. This helps.

To restore hair when removed by ill-health or age – Onions rubbed frequently on the part requiring it. The stimulating powers of this vegetable are of service in restoring the tone of the skin, and assisting the capillary vessels in sending forth new hair; but it is not infallible. Should it succeed, however, the growth of these new hairs may be assisted by the oil of myrtle-berries, the repute of which, perhaps, is greater than its real efficacy. These applications are cheap and harmless, even when they do no good.

It was also believed that a peeled or cut onion left around would attract noxious elements and be unfit to eat, and if left in a freshly painted room would absorb the paint fumes.

Mrs Johnstone notes:

The Leek is one of the most honourable and ancient of pot-herbs. It is called *par excellence* 'the herb'; and learned critics assert that our word porridge or pottage is derived from the Latin *porrus*, a *leek*. 'From Indus to Peru' the adoration of the *garlic*, *onion*, and *leek* is universal. The *leek* is besides the badge of a high-spirited, honourable, and fiery nation – the Ancient Britons. In old poetry of the Northern nations, where a young man would now be styled the *flower*, he was called the *leek* of his family or tribe – an epithet of most savoury meaning.

She continues, '*Cock-a-leekie*, a soup which Scotland probably owed to France long before the Union of the crowns . . . must be very thick of leeks, and the first part of them must be boiled down into the soup till it becomes a lubricious compound.' Worlidge observes of Wales, 'I have seen the greater part of the garden there stored with leeks, and part of the remainder with onions and garlic.'

In Llanfyllin only the other day, Janet bought a pound of leeks – she handed them to the salesgirl, who turned to her colleague enquiring, 'Are these spring onions?'

'Of all plants,' says Sir William Temple, 'garlic affords the most nourishment, and supplies the best spirits to those who eat little flesh. It clears phlegm, dissipates cold slimy humours &c.' It still stands in high esteem as anti-carcinogenic and purifying to the system. I think it was Norman Douglas who claimed that if you regularly ate enough of it after a while you would no longer stink.

At one time the English were advised – if they were so bold as to touch it at all – merely to rub a garlic clove once round the salad bowl and then discard it. Now the fussy yet health-conscious can ingest it, deodorised, in capsule form. Which is no fun at all.

Seventeen

TWO VEG.

$\mathcal{P}$eas were cultivated in the East 'from time immemorial' and introduced into Europe in the Middle Ages. In the eighteenth century the English ate their peas off a knife with a rounded blade end. ('I eat my peas with honey, I've done it all my life. It makes the peas taste funny, but it keeps them on the knife.') My grandfather had a set of 'pea forks', which are mostly spoon with four short tines and practical for the purpose, but they never seem to have generally caught on: people still apparently consider it unseemly to scoop up peas with any implement, preferring to pursue them, individually if necessary, round the plate with the fork pointing downwards.

Mrs Gaskell wrote in *Cranford*:

> When the ducks and green peas came, we looked at each other in dismay; we had only two-pronged, black-handled forks. It is true the steel was as bright as silver; but what were we to do? Miss Matty picked up her peas, one by one, on the point of the

prongs . . . Miss Pole sighed over the delicate young peas as she left them on one side of her plate untasted, for they *would* drop between the prongs. I looked at my host; the peas were going wholesale into his capacious mouth, shovelled up by his large, round-ended knife. I saw, I imitated, I survived! My friends, in spite of my precedent, could not muster up courage enough to do an ungenteel thing; and if Mr. Holbrook had not been so heartily hungry, he would probably have seen that the good peas went away almost untouched.

Hortense exclaims lyrically:

Young Green Peas! Do not those words sound pleasant to the ear, dearest? I fancy that, merely by raising my eyes from the paper on which I am now writing, I shall see all our garden in buds and blossom . . . But alas! . . . the serious and uncheerful Father Nature, by laying out his universal and snowy tablecloth over this for the present ephemeral vision which the inviting words green peas had produced upon my senses . . . I shall here content myself by giving you the receipt how they ought to be cooked when you can get them – plain boiled, because their original flavour is so fresh and delicate, that any addition except a little fresh butter would be certain to destroy their aroma.

Mrs Somerville said, 'A few mint leaves are boiled with green pease, meant to prevent flatulency from eating them.' Freezing has made the process simpler and since, as the jingle had it, they are as fresh as 'the moment when the pod went pop' there is no reason to scorn the frozen pea unless you like podding them. I used to, when I wasn't in a hurry. The ideal is to sit outside the kitchen door, under the shade of a tree, with a colander on your lap, slowly pop the pods, run the peas out with your thumb and eat quite a lot of them. It is maddening if there are too many flat pods with mere pea foetuses in them. (A young person at the till in Marks & Spencer was confounded by one of the purchases made by my friend Rebecca, which had to be identified in order to be weighed. 'Peas,' she explained, as the queue grew restive. He had never before encountered them in the pod.) Colonel Kenney Herbert advised cooking them in their own juice in something with a lid, adding butter, a bit of salt, a bit of sugar, a bit of mint, and boiling the jar in a saucepan of water for an hour. My fourth son surprised me by demonstrating a method of dealing with frozen peas: he puts them in a pan without water, adds a knob of butter and a pinch of salt and stirs them until they thaw, at which point they are perfectly cooked. (This son has further surprised me by acquiring a restaurant in Los Angeles. It is called Tangier and stands on Hillhurst Avenue near where Hollywood and Sunset Boulevards converge, should you happen to be passing.)

A Lady gives instructions for drying them '*as practised in the Emperor of Russia's kitchen*. Shell, and scald, and dry them: put them on tins, or earthen dishes, in a cool oven once or twice, to harden. Keep them in paper bags hung up in the kitchen. When they are to be used, let them lie an hour in water; then set them on with cold water and a bit of butter, and boil them until ready.' And have pease pudding with ham or mushy peas with fish and chips or pea soup . . .

> The cabbage tribe has ever been a first-rate favourite with writers on diet, whether ancient or modern. Volumes have been composed, not merely in praise of the demulcent cauliflower and brocoli [*sic*], but of the common white and red cabbage. Besides their use in soups, and in correcting the putrescent qualities of animal food, they are said to be correctives of the consequences of excess in wine. Arbuthnot says the juice of the red cabbage baked is, with the addition of honey, an excellent pectoral; and red cabbage stewed in veal-broth, with calf's lights and pistachios, is on the Continent esteemed a specific in

consumption – a malady, by the way, for which a remedy has been discovered in chickens, oysters, jellies, fruits, and every favourite aliment – in short, in whatever the discoverer fancies he himself could thrive on, and live for.

So said Charles Pierce, who considered that:

Vegetables are improved in digestibility and agreeableness by being reduced to a pulp. Even cabbages of every kind, which are but a coarse food, and not to be eaten excepting by persons of the strongest digestive powers, and then with great discrimination, at a time when either the cabbages are very young, or have had their tenacity overcome by frost; if reduced to a pulp, may be dished with cutlets of any kind, and much of the bad result is done away with; but they should be fresh. The pulping, or *purée*, which breaks down the fibre, overcoming that which resists digestion, and so sets free and mingles the imprisoned juices – that pulping is often in an incomplete stage at English tables.

Ignore that. Some vegetable purées are very acceptable, but not as a general rule.

I remember a cartoon of a mother and child gazing at a dinosaur skeleton. The caption read, 'They wouldn't eat up their greens. That's why they got extinct.' There is said to be some element in the genus *brassica* which does not appeal to the infant taste buds and there have always been scenes at the dinner table over cabbage and sprouts and spinach; broccoli was once banned from the White House because Mr President didn't like it. If no one makes a drama of the matter, most children will eventually change their minds. In the meantime, let them eat fruit.

All my books suggest ways of cooking greens. Mrs Raffald: '*To boil Cabbage*. Cut off the ſide leaves, and cut it in quarters, pick it well, and waſh it clean, boil it in a large quantity of water, with plenty of ſalt in it; when it is tender, and a fine light green, lay it on a ʃieve to drain, but do not ʃqueeze it, if you do you will take off the flavour; have ready ʃome very rich melted butter, or chop it with cold butter. Greenʃ muʃt be boiled in the ʃame way.'

When I was a child, people would insist on putting soda in their greens: it made them taste like the smell of boiled bed-sheets. The Romans used nitre. *A Lady* suggests wormwood.

Two helpful notes are, 'Cabbage water must not be poured down sinks, as it causes an offensive smell. When cool pour it on the ground: it is an excellent fertilizer,' and 'Waste leaves of veg-etables and potato-peelings should be burned; if thrown into the dustbin they will decay, and help to create bad smells and fever.'

There was once, in France, a Canon Chevrier, who always caused his spinach to be cooked on Sunday and reheated every day with more butter until he ate it on the following Friday. I have not tested this mode because something tells me that even for the butter lover this is excessive. Miss Acton gives a French receipt for spinach as an *entremet*: you boil it, drain it, throw it into plenty of cold water and then, when it's cool enough, you form it into balls and squeeze out all the water with your hands. Then you:

> Chop it extremely fine upon a clean trencher, put two ozs of butter in a stewpan or bright, thick saucepan, lay the spinach upon it, and keep it stirred over a gentle fire for ten minutes, or until it appears dry: dredge in a spoonful of flour, and turn the spinach as it is added; pour to it gradually a few spoonsful of very rich veal gravy or, if preferred, of *good* boiling cream (with the last of these a dessertspoonful or more of pounded sugar may be added for a second course dish, when the true French mode of dressing the vegetable is liked). Stew the whole briskly

until the liquid is entirely absorbed; dish and serve the spinach very hot, with small, pale sippets round it, or with leaves of puff pastry fresh from the oven, or well dried after having been fried. For ornament, the sippets may be fancifully shaped with a tin cutter. A proper seasoning of salt must not be omitted in this, or any other preparation of the spinach.

Many authorities suggest adding a teaspoonful of sugar to spinach, but a dessertspoonful is surely too much and the end result sounds odder than the good Canon's sort. Miss Acton then gives an English version which leaves out the sugar but retains the 'thick rich gravy' and ends, 'When a perforated tin shape, ordinarily used for moulding spinach, is not at hand, one of earthenware, slightly buttered, will serve nearly as well.' Mrs Beeton has a picture of a dish of spinach, perfectly moulded and adorned with diamond-shaped cuts reposing in a lordly dish.

I think our present spinach, like all vegetables, is markedly tenderer than it used to be – we once bought some garden-grown in Welshpool market and had to steam it for longer than we were accustomed to with the supermarket variety, which needs only a few minutes of heat to surrender completely. In the end we threw it away. Before the retailers were so obliging as to wash it for us, it was a chilly and demanding ritual that befell the preparer of spinach. 'Take it leaf by leaf from the stalks, and be very careful to clear it from any weeds that may be amongst it, and to free it by copious and repeated washings from every particle of sand or earth.' I remember it well. Now you can get such young and tender spinach that you can eat it raw with oil and vinegar dressing.

Moira Meighn has a suggestion for spinach and beetroot leaves: 'The best way to cook spinach, or its first cousin, beet-root leaves, is in the top of a double saucepan over boiling water. Add a tablespoonful of Marmite and butter to every half pound

of leaves and cook them for twenty to thirty minutes.' Don't.
Actually, many people seem to go slightly mad when faced with
a basket of spinach. *The Gentle Art of Cookery* suggests boiling a
pound of it and seasoning it with salt, sugar, lemon rind and two
crushed macaroons, and garnishing it with ratafias. Or cooking
it the 'Italian way' with sultanas, raisins, anchovy butter and
fried bread. Later on it offers 'Cold Purée of Spinach Garnished
With Glacé Cherries': 'Hand it with slices of cold tongue served
on lettuce leaves on a long dish.'

A headline in a national daily paper one day announced that the
previously unsuspected Brussels sprout could cause symptoms
similar to those consequent on a hangover. Brussels has even
more to answer for than we thought. It has never been advisable
to get downwind of a field of sprouts in decline, but few can
have realised this humble *brassica* had other maleficent properties.

Miss Acton says:

These delicate little sprouts, or miniature cabbages, which at
their fullest growth scarcely exceed a large walnut in size, should
be freshly gathered. Free them from all discoloured leaves, cut
the stems even, and wash the sprouts thoroughly. Throw them
into a pan of water properly salted, and boil them quickly from
eight to ten minutes; drain them *well*, and serve them upon a
thick round of toasted bread buttered on both sides. Send good
melted butter to table with them. This is the Belgian mode of
dressing this excellent vegetable, which is served in France with
the sauce poured over it, or it is tossed in a stewpan with a slice
of butter and some pepper and salt; a spoonful or two of veal
gravy (and sometimes a little lemon-juice) is added when these
are perfectly mixed.

Many hours of time have been wasted by people who were told that it was necessary to cut a little cross in the stalk end of sprouts. It is not.

I used to be favourably inclined to a salad of raw sprouts, shredded, with a walnut oil and garlic dressing. No one else was enthusiastic about it and now they have the perfect excuse for refusing it and demanding the unseasonable lettuce instead. *Fin Bec* prepares 'a salad of cauliflower, French beans, Brussels sprouts, and potatoes' to go with cold turbot in 'uniform slices'. He would. He also gives a strange recipe for 'Stewed Olives':

> Brown in butter a few spring onions and some finely chopped parsley; moisten with gravy or good bouillon, a glass of white wine, some capers, and an anchovy pounded in a spoonful of olive oil. Put into the sauce some olives cut into spirals. Let it just boil, and thicken the sauce with some butter and flour, mixed and browned apart. The centre of the olives may be filled with a cooked stuffing.

How, for goodness sake, if they are cut into spirals?

All the books are most insistent on washing and checking vegetables, particularly cauliflowers, for insects before use. There used to be many more of them about. Nott gives a receipt for 'Colly-Flowers with Butter'. 'Boil them over a quick Fire, in Water, ſalt, with two or three Cloveſ. When they are boil'd let them drain dry, and lay them in little Diſ heſ, or Plateſ. Knead ſome Butter with Flour to thicken the ſauce; then melt it with ſalt, white Pepper, Nutmeg, Vinegar, and ſ lices of Lemon, and pour over the Colly-Flowerſ.'

'Choose those that are close and white,' said *A Lady*. 'Cut off the green leaves, and look carefully that there are no caterpillars about the stalk. Soak an hour in cold water: then boil them in milk and water; and take care to skim the saucepan, that not the least foulness may fall on the flower. It must be served very white, and rather crimp.' She was promptly contradicted by Mrs Johnstone: 'All vegetables should be enough boiled. The cook's rule of having cauliflowers *crisp*, is as inimical to health as offensive to the palate. NB If cooks and ladies will have their cauliflowers *crisp*, as they call it, why not serve them *raw*, and then eaters will be aware of them.' One wonders what her reaction would have been if confronted with a dish of crudités.

Mrs Somerville says that 'broccoli is cooked in every way the same as cauliflower, and sometimes it is served on a slice of toast dipped in the water in which it was boiled, with melted butter over it.' Mrs Raffald boils broccoli 'In Imitation of A∫paragus'. For asparagus itself, *A Lady* describes 'Asparagus forced':

> Cut a piece out of the top of three French rolls; take out all the crumb; do not enlarge the opening, or the crust will not fit exactly again. Fry the rolls brown, in fresh butter; have ready a pint of cream, the yolks of six eggs well beaten, a little salt and nutmeg. Stir this mixture over a slow fire until it thickens.
>
> Boil a hundred of small asparagus: save tops enough to stick the tops of the rolls with, cut the remainder of the green part of the grass small: put it into the cream, and fill the rolls with it hot. Before the rolls are fried, make a few holes in the pieces of the crust cut off, and stick the tops in. This is for a side dish in a second course.

The method is somewhat baffling but the result sounds nice.

'So well was the cultivation of vegetables understood by the Romans, that at Ravenna asparagus were raised for the tables of the great, of which three weighed a pound,' notes Mrs Johnstone. I rather went off them in Munich when they were in season and the market stalls groaned under vast heaps of them, most of them white from having been kept in the dark and disconcertingly corpse-like. I prefer the English early sprue, thin and leggy and tender, and sold mainly in street markets. Perhaps *A Lady* had sprue in mind for her 'hundred asparagus'.

Celery now is more appreciated raw but Mrs Raffald has a receipt for stewing the outside and green ends by boiling till they are very tender, adding a slice of lemon and a little beaten mace, thickening with butter and flour, and 'put to your gravy' the beaten yolks of two eggs, half a grated nutmeg, and a teacupful of good cream. *The Dictionary of Daily Wants* offers the somewhat strange '*Celery fried*. Blanch the celery in some rather strongly salted water, and let it stew gently in a little strong stock. Take out the celery, draw it, and dip it into batter; then fry it in boiling dripping. When it is done it is to be powdered with sugar, and candied with a salamander.'

In the country the things that you want to pick in the hedgerows – gooseberries, blackberries, sloes, etc. – are frequently defended by cohorts of nettles and particularly vicious thistles. A cohort, by the way, is a tenth part of a Roman legion, (according to some experts containing three maniples or six centuries) and not a close acquaintance or colleague. Originally it meant an enclosure (*hortus* – garden), so allowing for a little poetic licence the word is applicable to these inimical weeds. In the early spring, if you're quite certain no one has sprayed them with chemicals, you can make nettles into soup (this was always held to purify the blood), which is more like converting than exterminating them and more satisfactory.

Mrs Pender Cudlip mentions 'a luxuriant growth of the ill-natured weeds . . . I remember hearing from a nurse of my mother's that, properly managed, they make a most excellent tea; if tea, why not a vegetable for the dinner-table. Properly served with good melted butter, I believe they would be delicious.' Her husband, however, disagrees: 'The day you have them, I'll dine out . . . I have a vivid recollection of having nettle-rash when I was a boy, and a servant who hated me told my mother that nettle-tea was a certain and speedy cure for it; it was the mostly ghastly potion I have ever swallowed.'

I fry young nettle tops in butter. If you persevere, they suddenly go crisp and I knew someone in the country whose mother used to fry dock leaves in bacon fat. She had never done it herself and nor have I, though I don't quite know why.

Broad beans are one of the few vegetables in all my books for which no exotic preparation seems to have been thought of, although *The Gentle Art of Cookery* gives Dumas' way of cooking them – all he does, in effect, is add parsley, butter, shallots and salt and pepper. The authors give a recipe containing a quart of broad beans, mixed herbs, chopped ham and stock: these were stewed and then you added two ounces of sugar and a quarter of a pint of white wine, which, on reflection, does sound strange.

An English woman travelling in Europe in the nineteenth century gave vent to her outraged feelings with an exclamation mark when a servant girl 'who came from a rather out-of-the-way village' brought some young broad beans to eat raw, sliced, and 'dressed as salad!' When we still had a Greek shop in Camden before the advent of the supermarkets, the proprietress, Mrs Haral, advised me to steam young broad beans, pod and all.

A Victorian said that, 'The great objection to the red kidney beans is their colour, which offends the English eye.' Odd. They are surely no more garish than red cabbage. A Mexican friend tells me that in order to allay the flatulence associated with beans you should bring them to a full boil, put the pan containing them into the sink and throw in a handful of bicarbonate of soda. When the resulting foam and froth have subsided you rinse them and return them to the stove with fresh water. Bring to the boil again and simmer until tender.

Francatelli, in his *Plain Cookery Book for the Working Classes* says:

> In France, haricot beans form a principal part in the staple articles of food for the working classes, and indeed for the entire population; it is much to be desired that some effectual means should be had recourse to for the purpose of introducing and encouraging the use of this most excellent vegetable among the people as a general article of their daily food, more especially in the winter season. If this desideratum could be accomplished, its beneficial result would go far to assist in rendering us in a measure independent of the potato crop, which, of late years, has proved so uncertain.

He also bewails the fact that both beans and lentils are 'at present imported and retailed as a mere luxury to such as possess cooks who know how to dress them.' He suggests the use of both green and Puy lentils as 'equally nutritious'. I am unfashionable and prefer the red ones, which I use in lentil soup – a staple when we had visitors in the country – using up the leftovers in the fridge to vary the taste. (Janet's Beloved never forgave me after finding the remains of a sausage roll in his, although I had removed the pastry first.)

Let us consider the mess of pottage, which was mostly composed of 'lentiles'. My nineteenth-century edition of the Bible, which has copious observations from various scholars added at the foot of the page throughout, notes condescendingly that they are 'now used chiefly as fodder for cattle' but were 'in early times held in great repute for food, after being ground into meal and boiled with a moderate amount of suet into a chocolate colour.' I don't know to what authority they referred for this description but it sounds somewhat repellent and hardly worth a birthright. One Dr Shaw wrote that 'Beans and lentiles, when boiled and stewed with oil and garlic, are the principle food of persons of all distinctions in the East.' Dr Robinson, alluding to his purchasing some says, 'We found them very palatable, and could well conceive that to a weary hunter, faint with hunger, they might be quite a dainty.'

Despite the patronising tone this is more like it. In Egypt this dish, made with beans, is called *ful medames*. We used to have it for breakfast before venturing, thus fortified, into the souks or desert. The friend we were staying with would lean over her balcony and screech down to the man who ran her errands and mended her cistern and he would go away and come back with a dish of beans wrapped in a copy of *Al Akram*.

Mrs Johnstone says, 'The Romans, who were delicate in their eating, prepared their mushrooms at table with an amber or silver knife.' (There was a long-held fallacy repeated in *The Gentle Art of Cookery* – that you could test mushrooms by putting a silver spoon in with them as they cooked. If it turned black you threw them away.) 'The following test of the qualities of mushrooms is given, though we do not vouch for its accuracy – Boil a peeled onion with the mushrooms; if it remains white, they are safe; if it becomes black or livid, there are bad ones among them. NB – No sort of mushroom will poison a Frenchman.'

'*Poisonous Mushrooms!* Within the last week grave cases of

poisoning by supposed "mushrooms" gathered in Hyde Park and Regent's Park have fallen under treatment at Middlesex Hospital. The symptoms were urgent and included violent delirium . . . it is by no means so easy as is generally supposed to distinguish from the poisonous fungus.' That was in the mid-nineteenth century but something similar happened not so long ago. It is undoubtedly gratifying to find wild free food, especially in London, but you have to be cautious. Another nineteenth-century work says, 'Cooks should be perfectly acquainted with the different sorts of things called by this name by ignorant people, as the death of many persons has been occasioned by carelessly using the poisonous kinds.' It goes on to describe the *eatable mushroom* in worryingly vague terms and seems unaware that there are other edible sorts besides those designated *field*. I was in Finland a while since and learned that there are two thousand different varieties, of which some five hundred are edible, about ninety palatable, and around ten popular. Fifty are poisonous and a dozen lethal. They say that mushrooms easily absorb dust and dirt and it's better not to pick them near roads, factories or city parks.

A few years ago a number of Russians were killed by eating previously safe mushrooms which had undergone some crucial change, possibly caused by radiation: the mushroom begins to sound like that fish, the fugu, so prized by Japanese gourmets but fatal if the chef fails to remove the toxic element. Take (very carefully) the false morel (*Gyromitra esculenta*), which is 'extremely poisonous when fresh'. You have to clean them and cook them twice, throwing away the water each time. After this you still have to rinse them thoroughly under running water and – what's more – during the time they're boiling, the kitchen door and windows should be open. You may wonder if it's worth the effort but the admirers of the false morel claim the result is a supremely aromatic and delicious ingredient for soups and sauces.

It was once considered that mushrooms had no nutritive value, but the Finns hold that *Scutigir ovinus* is as nourishing as veal, and that all mushrooms contain more fibre than carrots or wheat bran. Every autumn the Finns (three out of five) go mushroom and berry picking, and are permitted not only in the forests but also on private land, as long as they ask politely.

It is only recently – well, maybe seventy years or so ago – that the tomato found its way into the sandwich. The *Encyclopaedia of Domestic Economy* informs us as follows:

> *Tomato, or Love-Apple*. This is a native of South America, and tomato is the Portuguese name. The fruit is about the size of a small apple, contains a very agreeable acid, and is now much used in gravies, soups and sauces. It is also served at table boiled or roasted, and sometimes fried with eggs. When green, it makes good pickle and ketchup, and is found in our vegetable markets: even in its unripe state it makes an excellent sauce, like apples or gooseberries, for roast pork or goose; when fully ripe, it makes an excellent store sauce.

The *Encyclopaedia* also observed of tomato preserves and pickles that they were 'not employed in any other way' in England; while *The Dictionary of Daily Wants* says, 'In Italy whole fields are covered with it [tomatoes], and scarcely a dish is served up into which it does not enter as an ingredient.' Most people are mildly surprised to learn that the tomato is not native to the Mediterranean, but a comparatively recent introduction.

Mrs Johnstone noted, 'These have rather gone down in France, but are like some other fashions when ebbing there, coming into vogue amongst us,' and suggests, '*Tomatas roasted –*

Prepare them by cutting off the stalks and roast in a Dutch oven turning them occasionally for ten or twelve minutes.' This is, or it was a short while ago (fashion changes so suddenly), the very latest mode in tomato preparation, superseding the sun-dried sort which, for a time, were found everywhere and in everything. *The Domestic World: A Practical Guide In All The Difficulties Of The Higher Branches Of Domestic And Social Economy* states that, 'this delicious wholesome vegetable is spoiled by the manner it is served up to the table. It is not one time in a hundred more than half-cooked; it is simply scalded and served as sour porridge. It should be cooked three hours – it cannot be cooked in one.' It goes on, remarking in passing that tomatoes are even better if boiled rapidly for one hour and then simmered three hours more, may be canned, are improved by the addition of some butter, which 'makes the dish actual food instead of mere relish', can be dried in pulp form or cooked with eggs stirred in. It concludes, 'We beg of those who use this excellent food to try what cooking will do for it. It has been eaten half-cooked long enough.' You can laugh, but we are now told that cooked tomatoes, purée and sauce are better for you than raw and help, for example, to stave off prostate troubles.

Pasta is as essential to the vegetarian diet as are the pulses. Buckmaster had observed earlier that macaroni was to the South of Europe what bread is to us, generously conceding that as an article of food it was rather more valuable since it contained more gluten. He went on to add, 'In this country it is usually introduced as a sort of luxury among the middle and upper classes' and concluded that there was no good reason why it should not enter more largely into the food of 'the people'.

It is suggested that the Italians got the idea from the Chinese, but the English were making macaroni cheese in the fourteenth century: 'Take and make a thynne foyle of dowh and kerve it on peces and cast hem on boillyng wat and seeth it wele. Take chese grate it and butt caste bysethen and above as losyns and sūe forth.'

In America you can buy it in a packet, but it is not macaroni cheese as we know it. (Beloved refers to macaroni cheese as 'prison food' – I do not like to ask him why.) It was once suggested that some macaroni needed two or three boilings, which seems excessive, although I admit I have an unsophisticated tendency to prefer pasta well-cooked rather than *al dente* which, being chewy, reminds me of gristle and sinew.

One evening, some summers ago when staying on an Aeolian island, we dined in the house of an old gentleman who had bought a piece of the island many years before. He did so, he explained, because it had cost him the same amount that he lost at the gaming tables of Monte Carlo every night, and it had seemed like a better investment. We were sitting on the terrace as the sun went down when a number of princes arrived for dinner. They were all sensibly clad in shorts and one was barefoot, but they bowed over our hands and kissed the air with courtly foreign grace. I have a soft spot for the foreign aristocracy: now that they no longer barge round oppressing the peasantry, there is something charmingly comic about them.

After the melon and prosciutto came macaroni in tomato sauce. This, our host announced with modest pride, was a dish typical of the region. Naturally I didn't say that it was a dish we often prepared in Camden Town on Fridays and that, if I'd been responsible for it, I'd have been more prodigal with the garlic and less heavy on the basil – I do not greatly care for it. Pesto reminds me faintly of silage. Nor did I offer our recipe for chilled tomato soup, since this might also have seemed presumptuous coming from a visiting foreigner. After the macaroni came a very small fish like whitebait. For some reason our host chose to feed us with these from his fingers. The evening was further enlivened by the presence of a small rat, which scampered over the split-cane awning. A *principessa* showed signs of leaping on to her chair in the classic fashion of a woman confronted by a rat and the friend I was travelling with, into whom a devil seemed to have entered, laughed scornfully and attempted to seduce the creature with offerings of cashew nuts. Anglo-Saxons, she announced, were fond of all animals and afraid of none. With attitudes as various as this I don't think full European unity will ever be achieved.

When we returned the next day I was pleased to find that yesterday's leftover macaroni had been fried and was being served for lunch. I am always looking for ways of using things up. It made me feel quite at home and the macaroni was less *al dente* than the first time round. A truly local dish consisted of pasta with wild fennel, olive oil, and capers, which grow wild on the island: this cannot be reproduced in Camden Town for too much depends on the fresh, savage flavours.

On the subject of foreign travel, *The Girl's Own Indoor Book* tells us of an English woman travelling in Italy towards the end of the nineteenth century, who acknowledged that 'people live to a great age there' but failed to make any connection between this fact and their eating habits: she was quietly dismissive of what is now known as the Mediterranean diet and recommended to us all by the experts. 'Many of the Italian dishes are quite appreciated by us foreigners, but there is nevertheless much in their cookery, besides the use of olive oil, which does not seem to suit the English taste. For instance sauces are too plentifully used and *almost take the place of gravy* [my italics: the Victorians' reverence for this substance never ceases to astonish me].' Describing a dish of macaroni, she amends it to avoid the 'monotonous sameness' of a sauce made with tomatoes. 'Sprinkle each layer with grated cheese, pour in some very strong meat gravy . . .' As for funghi, 'The Italians are very fond of them, but as a rule, the English find them too rich.' She concludes with a mention of Christmas, taking the tone so typical of the Victorians: superiority modified by pity. 'Their festivities are not marked as ours are, by roast beef, turkey, and plum pudding. In some parts they have during the week a dish of stewed wild boar, with a sweet and sour sauce mixed with dried currants and *pignelli*, the fruit of the pine.'

There were undoubtedly unfamiliarities and inconveniences to be encountered when travelling abroad, but England could still be tricky, as our friend Mrs Pender Cudlip discovered while holidaying on the borders of the Black Country. Finding that the nearest shops were miles away, she went with her children in 'vain search for vegetables of even the humblest description'. They passed several groups of young men and boys occupied in 'loafing about' or resting, as young men will. 'Their furtive, sullen glances, and the ferocious tones in which they responded when I ventured to inquire my way, made me feel that there was more reality than romance in that picture in *Punch* some years ago in which a noble savage of this country is suggesting to a companion the propriety of "'eaving 'arf a brick" at a passer-by because the latter happens to be a stranger.' The lads saw off Mrs Pender Cudlip and family with peashooters.

Eighteen

SALAD

$\mathcal{A}$ ccording to John Evelyn, who helped found the Royal Society (and also sublet his house to Peter the Great – who wrecked it), salad is a 'Particular Composition of certain crude and fresh Herbs, such as usually are or may be eaten with some Acetous Juice, Oyl, Salt etc., to give them a grateful gust and vehicle . . . In the composure of a Sallet, every plant should come in to bear it's [*sic*] part, without being overpowered by some herb of a Stronger Taste, so as to endanger the native SAPON and vertue of the rest . . .'

There is a persistent idea that salads are un-English and came to us from the more culinarily perspicacious French. During their Revolution, a certain enterprising Chevalier d'Albingiac made a living by racing round London in his carriage mixing salads for the nobility and gentry, rather as White Russians later found employment as head waiters or cab drivers, but past English writers reject the notion of our indebtedness to the French. The salad is an 'English institution of great antiquity; a survival from the tables of the Middle Ages' asserts one commentator indignantly. It is true that the Vitamin C intake of Henry VIII, who subsisted on meat and pies, must have been virtually nil and his health suffered in consequence, as he grew obese and ulcer-ridden. He, however, had brought it on himself by dissolving the monasteries, where the monks grew herbs and vegetables, and propagating the notion that their cultivation and consumption were unpatriotic and popish.

Lady Morgan, who was not an admirer of Henry, wrote that, 'The French cookery displayed in the Field of the Cloth of Gold made an obvious impression on Cardinal Wolsey, the greatest man and the most liberal Amphitryon of the age, to whom his brute king was not worthy to be a scullion.' He introduced 'the elegancies of the French table' but died of dysentery after eating pears. Lady Morgan also regretted the consequences of the French Revolution: '*Fines herbes* were no longer known in the English garden; gravies were made with water; *entrées* were dressed with cream and hard eggs; and soups [reserved for great occasions] were flavoured with catsup and seasoned with cayenne and Mrs Glass's volume of *Hashes and Hodgepodges* became the church-and-state manual of orthodox cookery . . .'

In the time of Elizabeth I, however, Gerard had given a list of salad herbs which eclipses anything to be found on our supermarket shelves:

> . . . the Spanish nut, a kinde of floare de luce, onions, leeks, chives, garlic, turnip-tops, winter cresses, rocket, tarragon, other cresses, garden succorie, dandelion leaves, endive, lettuces of the garden, wild lettuces, beets, leaves and roots, spinach, orach, dock leaves, sorrel, roots of rampions, lesser house leeks, purslane, sampier leaves, water cresses, brook lime or water pimpernal, borage, bugloss leaves, hops, the buds or first sprouts, garden burnet, leaves of musk roses, rosemary.

The old ways had persisted for a time, as old ways will.

Mrs Johnstone wrote, 'As this is quite a delicate, *jaunty* branch of the culinary art, we would recommend that young ladies residing in the country should gather their own salad herbs, and dress salads for their families, which will give a better chance of a duty being well done, which in the hurry of the stew-pan, the spit, and the stove, the distracted cook must often perform with haste and slovenliness.' Buckmaster (I wonder who said it first) also suggested, 'Young ladies in the country . . . might render a national service if they would turn a little attention to mixing salads as well as to croquet and skating rinks.' He wrote, 'In this country we are perfect savages in the making of salads. The sauce is often served up in a bottle, and flabby wet vegetables are heaped up on a dish.' They are 'a very simple and harmless luxury, and in summer they make an agreeable addition to our ordinary food; if the vegetables are fresh . . . salads are rarely unwholesome'.

It must be acknowledged that in many a British household in living memory, salad consisted of a bowl of lettuce with sliced cucumber, tomato, pickled beetroot and hard-boiled egg, and was served only for tea on Sunday with salad cream or a spitefully vinegary dressing. (At the wedding reception of the undeniably affluent Apsley Cherry-Garrard and his wife Angela, in the early days of the Second World War before rationing was in place, there was served cold chicken and a salad of lettuce, tomato, hard-boiled eggs and Heinz Salad Cream, followed by a trifle made with Bird's custard.) Then, for a while, it became fashionable to present a green salad after the main course, but the custom is no longer as widespread in the dining rooms of

Islington as once it was. Now that green things are considered health-inducing with the same degree of conviction as they were once considered harmful, and slimming has become a kind of cult, it is common for people to regard various types of salad as a main course and no one is astonished. This is a notable departure from tradition.

People in the past had noticed that salad stuffs sometimes made them ill and occasionally killed them, but had not yet grasped the connection between this and the habit of fertilising things with raw sewage. The doctors of the time opined that it was their uncooked state that made them 'indigestible' and suggested 'boyling them'; a terrible heresy, according to some commentators, but Dr Kitchiner's version sounds acceptable. His 'Boiled Salad' consisted of boiled or baked Onions (if from Portugal all the better), baked Beet-root, Cauliflower or Broccoli, and boiled Celery and French Beans: 'added to this to give it an enticing appearance, and to give some of the crispness and freshness so pleasant in salad, a small quantity of raw Endive, or Lettuce and Chervil and Burnet is strewed on the top: this is by far more wholesome than the Raw Salad, and is much eaten when put on the table.'

Sir Francis said, when eventually the connection had been made:

Several most lethal diseases are contractible from eating imperfectly washed lettuce, and here perhaps is the moment to offer the advice not to eat lettuce salad in England or on the Continent unless in some way one knows for certain it is really clean: and never, never, never to venture on it in the East. It seems very hard to refrain from delicious-looking salad served in a French restaurant or an hotel in Bombay or Colombo, but wisdom enforces it, when one knows that much of the beautiful crisp lettuce produced abroad is grown in almost crude night-soil.

Mrs Johnstone took an impartial stance: 'Vegetable salads are at any rate a harmless luxury; and though they afford little nourishment of themselves, they make a pleasant addition to other aliments, and a graceful appearance on the dinner-table.' Another note of warning, though, comes with Miss Acton's 'Sorrel Salad', which 'though very refreshing and agreeable is not to be recommended when there is the slightest tendency to disorder of the system; for the powerful acid of the uncooked sorrel might, in that case, produce serious consequences'. Many books suggested that a lettuce supper was considered very conducive to repose. *The Dictionary of Daily Wants* says 'Lettuce, extract of – is reputed to possess, though in an inferior degree, the virtues of opium, without producing the deleterious effects,' and goes on to give full details of how it may be obtained and used.

Dr Kitchiner says of the salad herbs that you should endeavour to have them as fresh as possible: if you suspect they are 'not *morning gathered* [he means this literally and is not indulging in poetic menu-speak], they will be much refreshed by lying an hour or two in spring-water'; then carefully wash and pick them and trim off all the 'worm-eaten, slimy, cankered, dry leaves', which used to be a tiresome – or possibly pleasantly relaxing, depending on your point of view – task, now often denied to us since the flawless leaves may be enclosed in cellophane bags. (Even so, a doctor tells me, they should be well rinsed when you get them home.) However, Buckmaster gives the opposite advice: 'To soak green vegetables in water to keep them fresh, or to keep up their appearance of freshness is a mistake . . . If you must wash the vegetables do it quickly, and thoroughly dry them in a clean cloth before putting in the salad bowl.' In an article of 1942 on 'Teaching Your Daughter How To Cook', comes the command, 'Wipe the tomatoes, darling, you never know where they've been before they got here.' A phrase once on every mother's lips but sometimes now forgotten when everything seems to be immaculate.

According to Pierce, 'Some writers on salads have stated that it is in its richest flavour when it has not undergone washing. But others, remarking on the mould of the garden being dashed up by the wind and the rain upon the salad, and the worm in its feeding time passing over it, and often to be found lurking within it, contend for the necessity of its being cleansed, previously to being brought into use for the table.'

Delia Smith says she doesn't wash her salad, only wiping any bits that appear to need it. It used to be common to find a comatose slug, an earwig, or a small green caterpillar rearing up to greet you from the lettuce, and while I would not claim to miss seeing these creatures on the plate, it did make you feel a little closer to nature. It is now suggested that the preference for perfectly formed and unblemished vegetables may increase the risk of developing cancer: lettuce and other broad-leaf vegetables contain compounds called salycitate which fight plant viruses and are thought to be natural anti-cancer agents. Vegetables grown under controlled conditions are protected from the infections that initiate the release of these compounds and the best-looking cabbages are not the most desirable, black spotted ones are more beneficial. Handsome is as handsome does.

Eliza Acton says of French Salad, 'In winter this is made principally of beautifully-blanched endive, washed delicately clean and broken into small branches with the fingers, then taken from the water and shaken dry in a basket of peculiar form, appropriated to the purpose, or in a fine cloth.' She has a footnote: 'Salad baskets are also to be found in many good English kitchens but they are not in such general use here as on the continent.' I remember when we got our plastic spinner: no more standing in the yard waving wet lettuce round in a tea cloth. It was uniquely galling when you let go of an end and the salad flew out into the bushes.

I'm not so sure about Miss Acton's 'Yorkshire Ploughman's Salad'. 'Mix treacle and vinegar, in the proportion of one table-spoon of the first to two of the latter; add a little black pepper, and eat the sauce with lettuces shred small (with an intermixture of young onions when they are liked).' I was told emphatically never to cut lettuce, so it is interesting to read 'In England it is customary to cut the lettuce extremely fine; the French who object to the *flavour of the knife*, which they fancy this mode imparts, break them small instead.'

After giving 'The Poet's Receipt for Salad' Miss Acton writes: 'this salad is the result of great experience and reflection, it is hoped young salad makers will not attempt to make any improvements upon it.' The poet in question, who was so famous that she felt no need to name him, was the Rev. Sidney Smith (1771–1845): he who said that his lifelong ambition was to roast a Quaker, and of bishops, 'How can a Bishop marry? How can he flirt? The most he can say is, "I will see you in the vestry after the service."' His recipe goes as follows:

> Two large potatoes, passed through kitchen sieve
> Unwonted softness to the salad give;
> Of mordant mustard, add a single spoon,
> Distrust the condiment which bites so soon;
> But deem it not, thou man of herbs, a fault,
> To add a double quantity of salt;
> Three times the spoon with oil of Lucca crown,
> And once with vinegar, procured from town,
> True flavour needs it, and your poet begs
> The pounded yellow of two well-boiled eggs;
> Let onion atoms lurk within the bowl,

And, scarce suspected, animate the whole;
And lastly, in the flavoured compound toss
A magic teaspoon of anchovy sauce:
Then, though green turtle fail, though venison's tough,
And ham and turkey are not boiled enough,
Serenely full, the epicure may say –
Fate cannot harm me, – I have dined today.

Miss Acton translates the receipt thus: 'Two well-boiled pota-toes, passed through a sieve, a teaspoonful of mustard; two teaspoonsful of salt; one of essence of anchovy; about a quarter of a teaspoonful of very finely-chopped onions, well bruised into the mixture, three tablespoonsful of oil; one of vinegar; the yolks of two eggs, hard boiled. Stir up the salad immediately before dinner, and stir it up thoroughly.' My father used to make a potato salad rather like this – I always assumed it was a Russo-Finnish aberration and prefer the kind with new potatoes and mayonnaise.

Sir Francis wrote, 'Salads other than green can be made from many vegetables and fruits – tomatoes, cooked potatoes, car-rots, peas, beans of all kinds, beetroot, apples and bananas alone, or in judicious mixtures. For most of these a cream dressing such as Heinz Salad Cream or a mayonnaise dressing is suit-able,' and recommended as a 'party salad . . . Some heart of lettuce, a little mustard and cress with short stalks, two or three lengthwise slices of banana arranged on a half-moon salad plate with a dab of salad cream in the centre.' I don't think it would be welcome today: it has that tentative, faintly winsome feeling about it that characterised a certain strand of 1930s cookery –

innovative but not aggressive, a little unsure of itself and its own daring. He praises the avocado pear, describing it in some detail for those who had never come across one – which was useful, since an earlier description had noted, 'There are several varieties, the fruits varying in size and from about six ounces to four pounds in weight.' He says they could now often be bought in London but 'are not as perfect as those actually obtained in the tropics, as they have to be gathered before they are really ready, but they are very good all the same'. (A friend of my fourth son once brought us a morning-picked avocado in Los Angeles – oddly it didn't seem to taste any different.) Sir Francis recommends that they should be served with cold partridge or cold saddle of mutton, but 'perhaps the ideal is a slice of really successful pressed beef'. He was in the habit of detaching all the flesh with a teaspoon, mixing it with French dressing and serving it in the skin. 'There is something extraordinarily attractive about this exotic salad,' he says decisively, and one wouldn't argue with him about that.

Francatelli in his *Plain Cookery Book for the Working Classes* has a surprisingly modern 'warm' salad:

Having prepared any kind of salad you may happen to have, such as endive, corn salad, lettuce, celery, mustard and cress, seasoned with beet-root, onions, or shallot; let the salad be cut up into a bowl or basin ready for seasoning in the following manner: Cut eight ounces of fat bacon into small square pieces the size of a cob-nut, fry these in a frying-pan, and as soon as they are done, pour the whole upon the salad; add two tablespoonfuls of vinegar, pepper and salt to taste. Mix thoroughly.

From *The Dictionary of Daily Wants* comes 'Egg Salad': 'Boil six cloves of garlic for six minutes, and pound them with a few capers and two anchovies; mix them thoroughly with oil, salt, pepper, and vinegar, and serve with hard-boiled eggs, whole or cut in two.' Such profligate use of garlic is unusual.

Marjorie Hillis held that among those who must be shunned, the woman who puts marshmallows in her salad is pre-eminent. You might ask yourself, who would do such a thing? I believe that Marjorie Hillis had lunched at an American table and never recovered from the experience. Misunderstandings cloud our relationship with Americans: they often seem more foreign than the French, even though we are supposed to share a common language. For instance, today, if a Frenchman offers you a *salade* you know, on the whole, what he's talking about even if you don't understand or agree with a word of the rest of his discourse, while with an American you should be prepared for anything. Most dictionaries on this side of the Atlantic now define a salad as something composed of raw vegetables with a dressing, but Americans see it differently.

In one American compilation, out of sixty-five salad recipes, there are three based principally on lettuce while twenty-five contain marshmallows. Confusion arises from their use of the term 'salad', by which they frequently mean something jellied in a mould and turned out onto lettuce. Mrs Johnstone had noted earlier, 'Foreigners call many things *salads* which we would merely reckon cold, little, dressed dishes.'

One twentieth-century lady mixes up a packet of orange Jello with apple butter, diced celery, diced apple, chopped pecans, marshmallows and a pinch of salt, pours it into a greased mould till it sets, then serves it on a bed of crisp lettuce. 'Mayonnaise makes a delightful topping.' Another lady goes further. Her 'Apricot Salad' is made of tinned apricots, tinned pineapple, two packets orange Jello and a cup of small marshmallows. She melts them all together and leaves them to congeal, then she makes the 'topping' with half a cup of sugar, one egg, two tablespoonfuls butter, two tablespoonfuls flour and a cup of juice. She cooks this and cools it and adds either a cup of whipped cream or a package of 'Dream Whip' and she puts it on the Jello mixture and sprinkles it all over with grated American cheese. A recipe which yet another lady has the effrontery to call 'French Dressing' consists of a half-can of Campbell's tomato soup, three-quarters of a cup of vinegar, half a cup Wesson oil, a quarter cup sugar, a tablespoon Worcestershire sauce, three tablespoons grated onion, one tablespoon each of salt, paprika and mustard. 'Shake well. Keeps in the refrigerator indefinitely.' I bet it does.

A fourth lady's 'Cherry Salad' contains, amongst other things, cherry-flavoured Jello, cream cheese and a cup of 'either Coca-Cola or port wine', which reminds me of one of my friends, Aisling, who once told me that a trifle in a sternly Protestant household might well be moistened with vinegar rather than sherry. And here it must be admitted that many American habits that seem curious to us are based on traditions that the ancestors took with them when they left us behind: Hallowe'en, for example, and rounders. The mixture of sweet and savoury goes back to the time when dried and preserved fruit first became available here and mince pies were filled with currants and raisins and chopped meat; and our ancestors were passionately fond of things that wobbled – junkets and syllabubs and flummeries and jellies – so maybe American cookery is, in a perverted kind of way, more authentically British than our own, which grows increasingly Continental.

One evening after a particularly trying day, I turned for relief to a murder story, Sue Grafton's *'N' is for Noose*, and found the following:

This was the menu: iced tea with *Sweet 'n' Low* already mixed in, a green *Jello* square with fruit cocktail and an internal ribbon of *Miracle Whip*, iceberg lettuce with bottled dressing the colour of a sunset. For the main course, instant mashed potatoes with margarine and a stout slice of meatloaf, swimming in diluted cream of mushroom soup.

Sue Grafton is my favourite contemporary writer of murder stories, often telling us what her heroine had to eat. Dorothy L. Sayers is also good in this respect but others, e.g. Agatha Christie and Patricia Wentworth, although making it clear that even if the library were filling up with bodies the survivors had to have their three meals a day, seldom gave details of the menu – unless of course the victim had been poisoned. Patricia Wentworth's heroines in particular were frequently pale and interesting and given to faintness since they had had nothing to eat since lunch.

I have sometimes spoken dismissively of certain aspects of American cuisine, but despite the horror of the above, I have a feeling that the mediaeval cook might have recognised the underlying ethos and possibly greeted with delight the various short cuts on offer. On leaving Ellis Island, people from wildly varying cultures were forced by circumstance to eat what they could, putting, whenever possible, their own traditional touches to it. In an American book comes 'Wilted Leaf Lettuce': 'Mix lettuce and onion together. Fry bacon until crisp. To the bacon drippings in the skillet add the vinegar, water, sugar and salt. Bring to a boil. Beat egg until light. Add evaporated milk. Pour boiling liquid over egg mixture, then pour back into skillet and cook over low heat until slightly thickened. Pour over lettuce and sliced onion. Toss lightly until thoroughly mixed.' This is worse than Yorkshire Ploughman's Salad.

Then there's 'Cucumbers, European Style': 'Wash half-grown

cucumbers and serve on a plate as you would apples. Shake a little salt on the cucumber when eating.' Was this advice aimed at those who had never seen a cucumber before? The wilted lettuce has a 'mittel-European' flavour and cucumbers abound in those parts, so the author must have had some other culture in mind.

I have thought long and hard about 'Overnight Layered Lamb Salad', the recipe for which I discovered in another American cookery book. You put shredded lettuce, bean sprouts, water chestnuts, onions, olives, cucumber, slivered lamb and frozen peas (most of the other ingredients come out of a can), in layers in a glass dish, then you mix two and a half cups of mayonnaise with curry powder, garlic salt and a bit of sugar and pour it over the whole thing, garnish it with a cup of shredded Cheddar cheese, and leave it overnight. The lettuce alone will be limp and discoloured after twenty-four hours in dressing in the fridge and the constituent parts would surely be more palatable taken individually.

I wondered if it was someone's dim memory of a Salmagundi, an eighteenth-century dish, so I looked it up in Mrs Raffald and she seemed, if anything, even stranger:

Take the white part of a roasted chicken, the yolks of four boiled eggs and the whites of the same, two pickled herrings and a handful of parsley, chop them separately exceedingly small, take the same quantity of lean boiled ham scraped fine, turn a China-bason upside down in the middle of a dish, make a quarter of a pound of butter in the shape of a pine-apple and set it on the bason bottom, lay round your bason a ring of shred parsley, then a ring of yolks of eggs, then whites, then ham, then chicken, then herring, till you have covered your bason, and used all the ingredients; lay the bones of the pickled herrings upon it, with the tails up to the butter, and the heads lying on the edge of the dish; lay a few capers, and three or four pickled oysters round your dish, and send it up.'

This is a difficult dish to visualise since it isn't constructed *in* the basin but *on* it. I can't see why it doesn't fall off. Another was even more elaborate:

To make a grand ſallad for the ſpring. Take Cowſ lip Budſ, Violet-flowerſ and Leaveſ, young Lettuce, ſpinage, *Alexander* Budſ, ſtrawberry-leaveſ, Water-creſſeſ, Brook-lime &c, each apart by themſelveſ: Then take alſo Caperſ, Oliveſ, ſamphire, Cucumberſ, Broom-budſ, Raiſinſ and Curranſ parboil'd, Almondſ blanch'd, Barberrieſ, and other pickleſ; then lay a Turnip, or ſome other hard thing for a ſtandard in the middle of the ſallad, let it be formed like a Caſtle made of Paſte, waſ h'd over with the Yolkſ of Eggſ, and within it a Tree made in like manner, and coloured with green Herbſ, and ſtuck with Flowerſ; you must alſo have annexed to it twelve ſupporterſ round it, ſloping to it, and faſtened to the Caſtle; then having made four Ringſ of Paſte, each bigger than the other, the Biggeſt muſt compaſſ the Caſtle, and reach within three Incheſ of the Feet of your ſupporterſ; the ſecond muſt be within two Incheſ of that, and ſo place as many as you think convenient, and according to the Size of your diſ h, that they may be like ſo many ſtepſ, one above another; then place one ſort of your ſallad round on the uppermoſt Ring, and ſo on till you come to the Diſ h, laying a ſeveral ſort on every one; then place all your Pickleſ from the ſallad to the Brim of the Diſ h, each by itſelf; then garniſ h your Diſ h with all things ſuitable to the ſeaſon. Theſe grand ſalladſ are only for great Feaſtſ.

Remember that in Autumn, your ſtandard ought to be the Reſemblance of a Caſtle, carv'd out of Carrotſ and Turnipſ; in winter a Tree hung with ſnow; in ſummer a green Tree.

Nineteen

AFTERS

*W*hen sugar became more affordable and available ('it was a costly luxury until the increasing use of tea and coffee in the eighteenth century brought it into the list of principal food staples'), one of the consequences was more work for cook. It first appeared in conical, loaf form and you had to knock it about.

If ſugar, brought to the Quality commonly call'd *crack'd*, were put between the Teeth, it would ſtick to them as it were Glue or Pitch; but when it is boil'd to its utmoſt *caramel* Height, it will break and crack without ſticking at all, therefore you muſt obſerve very diligently every Moment; when it haſ attain'd to this laſt Degree of Boiling . . . and afterwardſ biting the ſugar ſo ordered with your Teeth. When you perceive that it doeſ not ſtick to the Teeth, but on the contrary *crackſ* and breakſ clever, take it off the Fire immediately.

You muſt firſt clarify your ſugar, and then ſet it on the Fire again, and boil it to its ſ*mooth* Quality, and you may know when it iſ come to that, by dipping the Tip of your Fore-Finger into it, and applying it to your Thumb, and then opening them a little; for a ſmall Thread or ſtring will ſtick to both, which will immediately break, and remain in a Drop upon the Finger; when thiſ ſ tring is ſcarcely to be perceiv'd, the ſugar had only boil'd till it is ſmooth; but when it extendſ it ſelf further before it than the breakſ, then the ſugar is very ſmooth.

Do not try this finger and thumb business: boiling sugar is hotter than hell.

In the opinion of *Anon*, who would sit down each evening to 'provocatives' – soup, fish, meat, poultry, game, maybe a vegetable or two, and a copious amount of spirituous liquor: 'It is strange to think how many persons make themselves ill by the thoughtless way in which they eat. If they would only consider their stomach as sensitive as their palate, they never would put sweets on top of a good dinner. They ferment and that is the cause of the disagreeable sensation known to all who eat unwisely.' (A large opera singer once remarked that it felt as though he had two stomachs because, no matter how much dinner he ate, he always wanted something sweet to follow.)

With the passing of time, the more modest household settled for three or four courses, and pudding in the role of 'afters' became a matter of some importance: baked, boiled, milk or fruity, it appeared at lunch and dinner. Previously, people who could not afford large quantities of meat had expected to fill up with bread, Yorkshire pudding, dumplings, etc. at the start of the meal. A letter to *The Times* in 1946 read, 'Brought up in the eastern counties, as a boy I was warned that I could only have meat if I finished my pudding first. Duck and green peas would have been "heralded" by a steamed batter pudding; roast beef by Yorkshire pudding; roast mutton by suet pudding; and boiled meats by boiled dumplings. In each case the pudding would have been served with gravy.' No surprise there. When this custom declined, the solemn, stolid suet pudding and rice, sago, semolina and tapioca, together with bread and butter pudding and the various charlottes, were relied on to extinguish any residual pangs of hunger.

Boswell on his rambles wrote:

Let us seriously reflect on what a pudding is composed of. It is composed of flour, that once waved in the golden grain, and drank the dews of the morning; of milk pressed from the swelling udder by the gentle hand of the beautiful milk-maid, whose beauty and innocence might have recommended a worse draught; who while she stroked the udder, indulged in no ambitious thoughts of wandering in palaces, formed no plans for the destruction of her fellow-creatures – milk that is drawn from the cow, that useful animal, that eats the grass of the field, and supplies us with that which made the greatest part of the food of mankind in the age which the poets have agreed to call golden. It is made with an egg, that miracle of nature, which the theoretical Burnet has compared to Creation . . .

With self-confessed tactlessness Buckmaster, at a Christian Young Men's Tea Party, said 'Half the young ladies of the present day would wonder how the apple got into the dumpling.' The young ladies and their mothers thought this 'impertinent' but, says Buckmaster cheerfully, 'As all the parties are now dead, there can be no impropriety in my referring to this circumstance.'

May Byron, in her book on farmhouse cookery states:

The pudding, from time immemorial, has been an English dish *par excellence*; and our forefathers simply ran riot in puddings. I have declined the insertion of puddings which would make the boldest stand aghast from their daring novelty in the way of ill-matched ingredients, or their excursion far afield into indefensible costliness . . . As sheer curiosities, I have included two rice puddings – one boiled, one baked, dating from about the year 1820, in Dublin. These are, I fancy, quite unparalleled, and I am loth that the recipes should be lost.

Having said which, she includes, among the rest, straight-faced and without remark, the following from the seventeenth century: 'Cauliflower Pudding – Boil the cauliflowers in milk, then lay them (without leaves or stalks) in a pie dish. Take three gills of cream, the yolks of eight eggs, and the whites of two. Season with nutmeg, sugar, mace, cinnamon, sack [sherry], or orange-flower water. Put it in the oven, bake it as you do a custard, and grate sugar over it when it comes out of the oven. Serve with a sweet rich wine sauce.' Her rice puddings sound, by contrast, unremarkable.

The ancestors relied heavily – and this would seem to be the *mot juste exactement* – on boiled puddings. 'Bring clean cloths and plenty of boiling water,' a cry so familiar to us from scenes of childbirth in the movies must daily have gone up in the kitchen. A simple 'Suet Pudding': Shred a pound of suet; mix with a pound and a quarter of flour, two eggs beaten separately, a little salt and as much milk as will make it. Boil four hours. It eats well the next day, cut in slices and broiled.' *A Lady* says suet is 'far better for the purpose than butter, which causes the pudding to be black and close'. (Suet, for those familiar only with the packeted variety is, 'a solid, fatty tissue, accumulating about the kidneys and omentum of the ox, sheep etc.')

There are hundreds of versions: those that did not harbour

meat usually contained 'raisins of the sun' or other dried fruit. They were made with flour or grated bread, suet, sometimes eggs, and flavoured with wine or brandy or lemon, citron or orange peel and juice. Ratafias and orange-flower water were much used and *A Lady* sometimes added Jamaica peppers or pimentos 'in fine Powder'. 'The greatest mastership is required to make the Pudding palatable: – the Suet, which others gape and swallow by gobs, must, for puny stomachs be minced to atoms, the Plumbs [*sic*] must be picked with the utmost care . . .' Plum-duff (which never contained any plums) was, according to the *Oxford English Dictionary*, a plain flour pudding with currants or raisins in it, boiled in a cloth or bag.

Miss Acton tells us that, 'The perfect manner in which the nutriment and flavour of an infinite variety of viands may be preserved by enclosing and boiling them in paste, is a great recommendation of this *purely English* [my itals] class of dishes, the advantage of which foreign cooks are beginning to acknowledge.' She includes the (unarguably foreign) 'Herodotus' Pudding: A Genuine Classical Receipt': 'Prepare and mix in the usual manner one pound of fine raisins stoned, one pound of mixed beef-suet, half a pound of bread-crumbs, four figs chopped small, two tablespoonsful of honey, two wineglassesful of sherry and the rind of half a large lemon (grated). Boil the pudding for *fourteen hours*' – her italics – but saying that seven hours will suffice. She gives close on fifty receipts for boiled suet and batter puddings and observes, 'Modern taste is in favour of puddings boiled in moulds but . . . they are seldom or ever so light as those which are boiled in cloths only.' Most of them had names, even though many were much of a muchness: The Elegant Economist's, The Publisher's, Queen Mab's, Welcome Guest's Own etc., as well as The Castle, Cabinet, and other generic titles. In the end, most of the suet puddings with raisins became known merely as Spotted Dick, although another more or less identical was called, rather anthropophagously, Sir William Watkins Wynne. He used to live round here and probably owned our bit of land as well as a lot of the rest of Wales.

The English Royal Family's Christmas Pudding consisted of:

> One and a quarter pounds suet, one pound demerara sugar, a pound each raisins and sultanas, four ounces each citron peel and candied peel, a teaspoon of mixed spice, half a teaspoon of nutmeg, a pound of breadcrumbs, half a pound of sifted flour, a pound of eggs (weighed in their shells), one wineglassful brandy, a half-pint of milk. Prepare all ingredients, well whip the eggs, add to milk, and thoroughly mix. Let stand for twelve hours in a cool place, add brandy, and put into well-greased basins and boil eight hours or longer. Sufficient for twenty to twenty-eight people.

A few years ago the Queen ordered her Christmas puddings from Tesco's.

A Lady has '*Observations on making Puddings* – The outside of a boiled pudding often tastes disagreeable; which arises from the cloth not being nicely washed, and kept in a dry place. It should be dipped in boiling water, squeezed dry, and floured when to be used . . . A pan of cold water should be ready, and the pudding dipt in as soon as it comes out of the pot, and then it will not adhere to the cloth . . .'

In the twentieth century, Elizabeth Craig in her *Economical Cookery* notes, 'Nowadays few puddings are boiled, because not one person in a thousand prefers the wet outside crust you get on a boiled pudding to the light, barely damp crust which characterises a well-steamed pudding.' The 'bag pudding' frequently mentioned in fairy tales (it was probably the round object in the red spotted hanky on a stick) was food for the poor wanderer and might have consisted of flour and water, boiled, and nothing else.

Hasty Pudding was much the same but capable of improvement: one eighteenth-century version went, 'Take three Pint∫ of Cream, a Pint and a half of Milk, ∫ea∫on it with ∫alt, and ∫weeten it with a Pound and a half of Loaf-∫ugar, make them boil; then put in fine Flour, Keeping it continually ∫tirring while you ∫trew in the Flour, and till it is both thick enough, and boil'd enough; then pour it out, ∫tick the Top full of fre∫ h Butter; ∫et over it ∫ome ∫ugar and ∫erve it up. You may al∫o eat it with Canary, or with Cream, or with both mix'd together.'

It was popular for centuries and there was a seven-verse song about it beginning:

> I sing of food by British nurse designed
> To make the stripling brave and the maiden kind . . .

There were hundreds of versions of Hasty Pudding. One that is still around is called blancmange, but is nothing like earlier things that had also been called blancmange.

Nott tells us that 'Blanc-Manger∫ are u∫ 'd in Inter-Me∫∫e∫s, or for middling Di∫ hes, or Out-Work∫ ' and are made with sweet almonds, peeled and pounded, cow's-foot jelly and a great deal of trouble, straining, pressing, pouring back and forth '. . . Or el∫e, when it is cold, it will be apt to part, the Jelly falling to the Bottome, and the Almond∫ ∫wimming at the Top; then put it up in Jelly Gla∫∫e∫.' *A Lady* uses calf's-foot jelly, together with a teacup of *very strong* coffee, a pint of *very* good cream, and 'as much fine Lisbon sugar as is pleasant'.

Or there was Flummery: 'Put finely ground oatmeal to steep in water for three days. Pour off the thin of the first water, and add more water. Stir up, strain, and boil this with a little salt, till smooth and of the thickness required, adding water at first; if it be in danger of becoming too stiff, a piece of butter is an improvement and a little white sugar. Serve in a basin with milk, wine, cider, or cream.'

Mrs Raffald had a more elaborate version – very much more elaborate:

> *To make Cribbage Cardſ in Flummery* – Fill five ſquare tins the ſize of a card with very ſtiff flummery, when you turn them out have ready a little cochineal diſſolved in brandy, and ſtrain it through a muſ lin-rag, then take a camel'ſ-hair pencil, and make heartſ and diamondſ with your cochineal, then rub a little cochineal with a little eating-oil upon a marble ſ lab, till it iſ very fine and bright, then make clubſ and ſpadeſ; pour a little Liſ bon wine into the diſ h, and ſend it up.

She also gave directions for jellied Moonshine, Moon and Stars, Eggs and Bacon, Solomon's Temple, Rocky Island, Fish-Pond, Hen's Nest, Green Melon, Gilded Fish, Hens and Chicken, Desert Island and several Floating Islands, recommending for the latter that you 'ſetſ heep or ſwanſ upon your jelly . . . there are ſ heep and ſwanſ made for that purpoſe; you may put in ſnakeſ, or any wild animalſ of the ſame ſort'.

Junkets were made of milk 'turned' with rennet. Seldom served these days, but if rennet (from a calf's stomach) frightens you, there are vegetable substitutes. It is too good to be forgotten.

And then there were syllabubs – dozens of them. Nott gives a nice simple one: 'A Worceſterſhire ſyllabub': 'Fill your ſyllabub-pot with cyder, put in a good Quantity of ſugar, and a little Nutmeg; ſtir theſe well together; then put in as much thick Cream by two or three ſpoonfulſ at a time, as if you were milking it; then ſtir it round very gently, and let it ſtand two

Hourſ, then eat it. If it be in the Field, only milk the Cow into the Cyder, &c. and alſo drink it.'

A Lady has, amongst others, an 'Everlasting or Solid Syllabub': 'Mix a quart of thick raw cream, one pound of refined sugar, a pint and a half of fine raisin wine, in a deep pan; put to it the grated peel and the juice of three lemons. Beat, or whisk it one way half an hour; then put it on a sieve with a bit of thin muslin laid smooth in the shallow end till next day. Put it in glasses. It will keep good in a cool place ten days.'

By the nineteenth century many sorts of compote were offered to privileged diners. The custards, creams, ices and soufflés are also more to modern taste though some sound extravagantly rich. 'Lemon Pudding à la Lyonnaise' took the yolks of nine eggs, half a pound of butter, a quarter of a pound of finely sifted sugar and the juice of a large lemon. You stirred it over a gentle fire until it became 'a thickness' then you put it in a bowl, mixed in the rind of one lemon 'upon which some sugar has been rubbed' and stirred it until cold and 'very light'. Then you added the whites of ten eggs beaten to snow and put it in a buttered mould, whereupon you baked it in the oven in a *bain marie* for about an hour and a half. It was served with wine sauce.

A Lady has 'Orange Fool': 'Mix the juice of three Seville oranges, three eggs well beaten, a pint of cream, a little nutmeg, and cinnamon, and sweeten to your taste. Set the whole over a slow fire, and stir it till it becomes as thick as good melted butter, but it must not be boiled; then pour it into a dish for eating cold.' Sounds alright. 'Spinach Cream' was made with eggs, custard, Naples bis-cuits or 'preserved orange, in long slices' and a quarter-pint of spinach juice. Further evidence of the different view of spinach that was taken in those days. She also has what she calls an 'Excellent Trifle', and one has to agree:

Lay macaroons and ratafia-drops over the bottom of your dish, and pour in as much raisin-wine as they will suck up; which when they have done, pour on them cold rich custard made with *more eggs* [her italics, but not much help since one custard has two yolks, one has five and one has eight] than directed in the foregoing pages, and some rice-flour. It must stand two or three inches thick; on that put a layer of raspberry jam, and cover the whole with a very high whip made the day before, of rich cream, the whites of two well-beaten eggs, sugar, lemon peel, and raisin-wine, well beaten with a whisk kept only to whip syllabubs and cream. If made the day before used, it has quite a different taste, and is solid and far better.

I make my trifle in much the same way, except for using fresh raspberries instead of jam, and it came as a revelation to Janet, who had awful childhood memories of stale sponge cake fermenting beneath festering fruit, topped with floury custard and no cream.

Stepping none too nimbly from the eighteenth to the nineteenth century, *A Lady* gets into a muddle with her puddings: some are clearly very old and a bit odd, e.g. 'Veal-suet Pudding' takes the crumb of a threepenny loaf, two quarts of new milk sweetened, six eggs, half a nutmeg, and a pound each of currants and 'veal-suet shred' in layers – bake. 'Or you may boil it in a basin if you prefer it,' while 'a very fine Amber Pudding' consists of a pound of butter, three-quarters of a pound of loaf-sugar finely powdered, the yolks of fifteen eggs well beaten and as much fresh candied orange as 'will add colour and flavour to it'; the same dish turns up a few pages later, though with half the quantities and is now called 'A Welsh Pudding'. But what is most disconcerting is the way she hops without warning from sweet to savoury and back: 'A George Pudding' (rice, apples, eggs and 'make it pretty sweet'), 'An Excellent Plain Potato Pudding' (boiled potatoes, butter, eggs, cream, white wine, lemon, sugar and 'if wanted richer, put three ounces more butter, sweetmeats and almonds, and another egg'), five meat puddings, and then back to the sugary sort.

At the end of her chapter on Sweet Dishes, *A Lady* again appears to lose the thread and reverts without explanation to savoury dishes, beginning with 'Savoury Rice'. It may be that she was led astray by the previous receipt for 'A Pretty Supper Dish', which consisted of sweetened rice boiled in milk and arranged in little heaps, but then she goes on to 'Salmagundy' ('a beautiful small dish if in nice shape . . .'), *Macaroni as usualy* [*sic*] *served*' (with cheese), 'Omlet', 'Ramakins', and various cheese and anchovy things – which might be explained as 'savouries' to follow the sweet dish, if she had not ended up with 'A Pepper-pot', which is a sort of stew made with vegetables in season, mutton, pickled pork and 'Half an hour before serving clear a lobster or crab from the shell and put it into the stew.'

Then she gives 'The Staffordshire dish of frying Herbs and Liver' and concludes with a note on how 'To Preserve Suet a twelvemonth'. I know too well how this sort of thing can happen and can only sympathise. I was looking up Exeter Pudding in *The Domestic World* when I was diverted by the words on the opposite page: *Eye, The Last Image on the* –. I knew that there had (when photography began) been an idea that the retina of a murdered person would retain the image of the murderer but that this had been proved a vain hope . . . So, after stating that,

'The last image on the retina of the eye of a dying person remains impressed upon it as on a daguerrean plate,' and adding a number of horrid details, the author quotes from the published account of the examination. 'We now applied a powerful lens, and discovered in the pupil the rude, worn-away figure of a man, with a light coat, beside whom was a round stone, standing or suspended in the air, with a small handle stuck as it were in the earth.' What is one to make of that?

Fruit pies, searching for which I wasted so much time, cursing quietly among my bookshelves, are still found more often on American tables than on British. *The Girl's Own Indoor Book* explains:

> Cakes and pies are commonly supposed to be the chief features of American cookery, but, like most sweeping assertions, this is only true to a certain extent. They are very fond of both, but it is only the country folk and the lower middle classes who indulge in these concoctions at almost every meal; the upper classes live very much as the upper middle classes in England, only better, for the Americans are fond of good living. In the country the chances are you will meet the inevitable pie at breakfast, dinner, tea, and supper; and you are certain to find an abundance of cakes of all kinds, hot and cold, for breakfast and tea.

'As American as apple-pie' goes the saying. With ice-cream it is *à la mode* and can be nice or nasty, depending largely on who made the pastry. Eliza Acton in 1855 offered a recipe for a baked apple pudding, which she says is 'appropriate to the Jewish table'. You need six ounces of breadcrumbs, three and a half ounces of pounded sugar and a pinch of salt all mixed together.

Take a pound of Russet or other good baking apples, 'pare them and then take them off the core in quarters without cutting the fruit asunder as they will then, from the form given them, lie more compactly in the dish.' What? Anyway, you put them in a deep tart dish with four ounces of sugar and the juice and grated rind of a lemon. 'Cover with breadcrumbs and bake in a somewhat quick oven for rather more than three quarters of an hour. An ounce or more of ratifias [*sic*] crushed to powder may be added to the crust or strewed over the pudding before it is served when they are considered an improvement.' This sounds like an early form of Crumble – for which there are no old recipes.

Carême's version of the famous Victorian 'Nesselrode Pudding' consists of forty chestnuts, a pound of sugar, flavouring of vanilla, one pint of cream, the yolks of twelve eggs, a glass of Maraschino, an ounce of candied citron, two ounces of currants, two of stoned raisins, half a pint of whipped cream and three eggs, and suggests that it takes only half an hour to make – but this is the second freezing time and does not take account of soaking the dried fruit, boiling, peeling and pounding the chestnuts, making a syrup and then a custard, combining the various ingredients, and the initial freezing – down in the ice house. *The Gentle Art of Cookery* says this pudding was invented by Count Nesselrode's chef, Mony, and 'the famous cook Carême was so jealous of its success that there was a fierce quarrel over it. It is a pudding worth quarrelling about.' I don't think it is. I think sweetened, vanilla-flavoured chestnut purée mixed with thick whipped cream is simpler and preferable.

Janet once made a medieval parsnip pudding with a garnish of primroses for her Beloved. It was expensive in ingredients and took her hours. I made her write out the recipe; but she concluded 'throw in bin'. And speaking of primroses, *The*

Dictionary of Daily Wants has 'Primrose Pudding': 'Take of petals of primroses, chopped fine, a quart; flour, half a pound, and a little salt. Mix these with water into a paste; form into a pudding; boil, and serve with melted butter and sugar.' By contrast, the book includes the following two thrifty recipes: 'Crumb Pudding' – 'Save all the crumbs left upon the table during the week, and add to these any waste pieces of bread. Put them into a basin with two ounces of treacle mixed up with them. Soak them in enough water to make them swell. Then tie them in a cloth and boil for half an hour.' 'Crumb Cakes' – 'Keep a bowl or pitcher with some milk in it, and from time to time throw in the crumbs of bread which break off when it is sliced, and also the dry pieces left on the table . . .'

Daily Wants also offers 'Potato Jelly':

> Take two or three large potatoes, wash, peel, and grate them: stir the pulp, thence procured, in a jug of water. Pass the mixture of pulp and water through a sieve, and collect the water which passes through into a basin. Let this stand for a few minutes, and a sufficient quantity of starch will have fallen for the purpose required. Pour off the water, and continue stirring up the starch at the bottom of the basin, while boiling water is being poured upon it; and it will soon and suddenly pass into a state of jelly. The only nicety required is to be careful that the water is absolutely boiling, otherwise the change will not take place. It does not require more than eight minutes to transform a raw potato into a basinful of most excellent jelly, which may be seasoned with sugar, spice, and wine to taste.

I have not tried this. I think someone should.

Mrs Somerville too has a 'Potato Pudding': 'Take six table-spoonfuls of nice mashed potatoes, a table-spoonful of sugar, ditto of orange marmalade, two ounces of butter, and four eggs;

pour it into a buttered mould, and bake for half an hour; turn it out, and sift sugar over it, or bake in a pie-dish.' Mrs Marshall's 'Saratoga Potatoes': Cut potatoes into thin slices with Marshall's Vegetable Slicer, fry until they are 'crisp and a light golden colour' and serve with salt and chopped parsley, 'they may also be sprinkled with a little caster sugar and finely chopped lemon peel and served as a sweet'. I think not.

Charles Pierce was suspicious of rice, although allowing that it was 'a food of immense culinary resource'. He said that it was binding and 'to some persons exceedingly unwholesome. And few others than the analytical cook, the *cordon bleus* or the Oriental cooks know how to dress a pilau, or boil rice to the point, simple as the process is, and should the rice be mixed with fatty matter, it becomes a compound unsuitable to taste and to health.' He went on to remark that the mixture of milk and rice was, 'not only of the same description as the preceding, but far more questionable'. On the other hand, if you combined rice with 'a marmalade of apples, or some other wholesome fruit or curries, you produce an agreeable dish'. Indeed, in the eighteenth century they seemed only to use rice for sweet dishes, with lashings of milk and cream – rice-tarts, frumenties, cheese cakes etc. – and very delicious they sound.

Sir Francis confided, 'Rice pudding . . . was my first love in the matter of sweets . . . On our birthdays it was our privilege to choose any pudding we liked . . . I always came in for the most bitter abuse from the ladies of the party because I always chose rice pudding – though a special one, in that added cream was specified.' From *The Girl's Own Indoor Book*:

Oriental Rice Milk – This dish, which is only a resource for invalids when forbidden better fare in England, is really a very nice one, prepared the Oriental way . . . It should be the consistency of thick cream when done, and the grains hardly to be recognised. If well done, it is a really tempting invalid dish, and not to be despised by healthy people. The English way is to put far too much rice, and boil far too quickly, and serve when half cooked, in fact. This way takes more time and trouble, but few good things are to be had without. If you will try it, my dear readers, some invalid will one day thank you, I feel sure.

A final thought on milk puddings, 'These cannot be cooked too slowly. If the milk boils the pudding spoils.' The book omits mention of tapioca and sago puddings – the latter dubbed 'frog spawn' by children, and a common curse of my own childhood.

Here is one of Mrs Meighn's extravaganzas: 'For every two tablespoonsful of *All-Bran* allow one dessertspoonful of milk and one tablespoonful of soft chocolate fudge . . . Mush it all up together and serve as it is, or if your family have a refrigerator, put it to freeze like real ice in the ice-cube box. Simple though this recipe is, it tastes so grand that I once gave it for the chief pudding at a big dinner party. The only addition I made was a cherry brandy sauce, with the cherries left in the brandy.' I keep thinking about this. It sounds horrible, but then brown bread ice-cream sounds a bit odd until you try it and then it turns out to be perfectly alright.

My family, living in Liverpool, grew to prefer Chinese dishes, as did the rest of the population: there are no Finnish takeaways in Britain. It was a tradition in the northern countries to add a handful of snow to the usual batter when making pancakes. It is said to make the pancakes lighter. I don't know whether it does or not, but it's gratifying to think of a use for snow. Finland has plenty and my father swore by it. One recipe says cook it before it melts – it makes holes in the pancakes – and an 'Observation' from *A Lady*:

> Snow is an excellent substitute for eggs either in puddings or pancakes. Two large spoonsful will supply the place of one egg, and the article it is used in will be equally good. This is a useful piece of information, especially as snow often falls at the season when eggs are dearest. Fresh small beer, or bottled malt liquors likewise serve instead of eggs. The snow may be taken up from any clean spot before it is wanted, and it will not lose its virtue, though the sooner it is used the better. Be especially cautious if there is any around that is stained yellow.

Oh, definitely.

Americans persist in referring to what we call pudding as dessert, the course once briefly known as The Sweet. We now shrink in refined distaste from this term, but the announcement, 'Spotted Dick and custard for dessert' still falls strangely on the ears of those who expect their dessert to consist mainly of fruit, while the word 'pudding' seems misplaced when applied to a frill of meringue in a froth of cream and a squirt of fruit juice. However, words do change meaning (it has just been suggested that Spotted Dick should be known as Spotted Richard to save embarrassment to ladies serving gentlemen with this popular dish): 'The Banquet of old was not, as now, a dinner but the Dessert, and was usually placed in a separate room, to which the guests removed when they had dined.' According to one

Gifford, 'The common place of banqueting, or eating the dessert was the garden house, or arbour, with which almost every dwelling was furnished.'

My husband used often to dine in Oxford colleges where the custom survived: after dinner, the dons and their guests would retire to another room to peel grapes. He was averse to fruit, especially oranges, due, we could only imagine, to some early traumatic experience – the mere scent of an orange would throw him into transports of rage. In fact few men eat fruit with the same enthusiasm as do women: perhaps this disparity originated in the time of hunting and gathering: the men replete with meat would refuse the nuts and berries while the women – who, according to the theory, were handed only the bones – were glad to fill up on dessert.

Pierce describes the conclusion of a Victorian dinner party: 'Whilst the dessert is being placed on the table, the appropriate plates at hand are laid before each guest, and if ice is to be served, the ice-plate is put on the dessert one, having at the time a d'oyley between them, accompanied by a dessert knife, fork, and spoon . . . each guest should have at least two or three glasses, for Claret, Port, and Sherry.' And there had to be jugs of iced water with tumblers 'here and there'. Then there had to be crystal dishes containing broken Wenham Lake ice (I heard somewhere that there was a company importing this from America by boat), spoons, grape-scissors, sugar vases with their ladles, 'and if there are walnuts and nuts in the dessert, then put on also nut-crackers and salt-cellars'. If there were indeed 'ices to serve, commence by offering them to the ladies' and if there were several sorts, 'although partaken of in very small quantities' each guest was invited to try them all at the same time, with ice wafers. 'Any of the following wines may be offered, viz. Malmsey, Frontignac, Sebutal, Constantia,

Alicante, Lunel, Pacaret, Cyprus, Imperial Tokay, or other sweet wines.'

Now the compôtes were handed, two by two; next the fruit, such as nectarines, peaches, pines or grapes. Melons should be cut in quarters, 'from pole to pole'. Pines (these were grown in hot-houses and were much admired. Becky Sharp 'longed above everything to taste one') should be taken off the table and cut at the side table in slices about double the thickness of a crown piece, commencing at the stalk end. This was so the pineapple could be made to stand up and, adds Pierce with a sudden and unexpected concession to economy, the confectioner could turn it into compôte 'if it be not eaten'. (I once knew a man whose cook used to scrape all the inside out of a pineapple, mix it with rum, cream and sugar and then put it back in the rind. This is hard work but he was a rich man: his dining room was hung with rather nasty Cézannes and he probably paid his cook well.) Some epicures tore up the portions with a silver or gold fork – the gold is preferred – avoiding the core, which 'we are instructed contains a principle acting chemically on the steel of the knife . . . the core and rind if eaten when cut with a knife, often produce painful results.'

Mrs Marshall, writing a little later, was still in agreement with the overall arrangement. 'Ices, sweetmeats of all kinds, fruit of all sorts, fresh and crystallized, biscuits both sweet and plain, and last, but not least, olives, all form part of the modern dessert, and nothing but want of attention and care can explain a failure in this part of the dinner. Fruit, flowers and foliage must be the best of their kind.' She had smartly cashed in on the passion for ice and her own brand of 'ice-caves' and freezers are advertised in her book, while her refrigerators were painted brown and white with brass and Japanned fittings – much fancier than ours. She writes that ices, once a luxury reserved for the wealthy, who kept ice insulated in straw in underground ice houses, were 'now in most towns the delight of street Arabs [this was the then non-PC term for scruffy little boys] who can by any means raise the "copper" requisite for their purchase'.

Immigrant Italians brought ice-cream making to a fine art. In Camden Town you need only send a runner down to Marine Ices at the bottom of the hill, which reminds me of Caroline Skynaston, she of *The Greatest Plague*, who sent down to Camden for her 'Trifles'.

A Mr Hudson Turner, researching something or other and described reassuringly as that 'sound antiquary', found mention in records of the thirteenth century in England only of apples and pears. 'Three hundred of the latter were purchased at Canterbury, probably from the gardens of the monks,' though Matthew Paris, describing the bad season of 1257, observed that apples were scarce and pears scarcer, while quinces, vegetables, cherries, plums and all shell-fruits were entirely destroyed. 'This apparent scarcity of indigenous fruits naturally leads to the inquiry, What foreign kinds besides those included in the term spicery – such as almonds, dates, figs and raisins – were imported into England in the following century?' (How sooth-ing to read, 'leads to the inquiry' rather than the now common 'begs the question', a term which actually means assuming the truth of the matter in the form of the query. My late husband was sensitive about such things.)

In the time of Edward I, a large Spanish ship came to Portsmouth and out of its cargo the Queen bought 'one frail of Seville figs, one frail of raisins or grapes, one bale of dates, and two hundred and thirty pomegranates, fifteen citrons and seven oranges'. The writer upon whom I am here relying seizes on this mention of oranges and concludes that since Le Grand d'Aussy couldn't trace them in France to an earlier date than 1333 and they were known here in 1290, then it must have been the Arab conquerors of Spain who introduced them and not the Portuguese, who were said to have brought them from China. He concludes with comparative (and untypical) brevity, 'An English dessert in the thirteenth century must, it is clear, have been composed chiefly of dried and preserved fruits – dates, figs, apples, pears, nuts, and the still common dish of almonds and raisins.' More than seven hundred years later you can still buy them, paired in packets.

Considering Sir Walter Raleigh's doubts about the reliability of history, it is unfortunate that he should himself have been the centre of confusion in the matter of fruit and vegetables. It was a Carew family tradition that their Sir Francis was first in the field and had raised three trees from pips given him by Sir Walter; whereas Sir William Cecil already possessed an 'orrange tree' when Sir Walter was only nine years old. The first orange to be introduced was the Seville sort: people stuck cloves in them and many grandees of the time had themselves portrayed clutching a pomander. They were bitter, and best used for syrup and sauces or on fish. Now, of course, in January, conscientious housewives make them into marmalade.

Someone wrote in the olden days, 'No English fruit is dearer than cherries at first, cheaper at last, pleasanter at all times; nor is it less wholesome than delicious. And it is much that, of so many feeding so freely on them, so few are found to surfeit.' According to the Venetian ambassador to England in the reign of

James I, however, cherry-eating competitions were a popular diversion in Kentish gardens and one young woman managed twenty pounds, beating her opponent by two and a half pounds before succumbing, as my source says gravely, 'to a severe illness'. According to *The Dictionary of Daily Wants*, cherries 'are a wholesome and nutritious food when partaken of in moderation . . . care should be taken to avoid swallowing the stones'. Many children were told that if they swallowed the stones, a cherry tree would grow in their insides. One of my aunts incurred the wrath of her daughters by telephoning an Important Person at the vaguely military place where they both worked, demanding that he go immediately to warn them that she had put cherry pies in their lunch boxes and the cherries contained stones. This was at the height of the Second World War.

Sir Francis Carew, who was clearly a keen gardener, on hearing that Elizabeth I was planning to come and stay with him, cleverly kept his cherries from ripening by covering the tree with canvas until 'when he was assured of her Majesty's coming, he removed the tent, and a few sunny days brought the cherries to their full maturity'. Not everyone was overjoyed to be honoured by a visit from the Queen since she brought her court with her, and often left bankruptcy in her wake. (People had similar reservations about Queen Mary: it was said that when she had paid a call they were constrained to count the spoons, and only recently it was revealed that a certain aristocrat was loth to entertain the Prince of Wales because of the expense.)

They were nervous about fruit as well as vegetables in the nineteenth century: 'That fruits are naturally healthy in their season, if rightly taken, no one, who believes that the Creator is a kind and beneficent Being can doubt. And yet the use of summer fruits is often found to cause most fatal diseases, especially in children. Why is this?' We might conclude that the

answer is that fruit not pampered in greenhouses probably flourished, like everything else, in close proximity to the cesspit.

I have always meant to settle down and grow more fruit and
plant some vegetables, but I lack the requisite patience and cannot
imagine why the term 'weedy' came to describe people of a weak
and feeble constitution: weeds are remarkable for their vigour
and determination and far superior to cultivated plants in their
ability to survive. However, we did plant four apple trees and a
plum tree. The plum tree is barren, but an old damson bears fruit
and has flung about itself a small wood of young trees – damson
daughters – damsels. This means that I shall feel compelled to
make damson jam: there is little else you can do with a damson,
for they are so sour that even if you wish merely to stew them,
you have to add so much sugar that you end up with jam anyway.
Damson wine, of course, is another possibility.

Tiny pearl-like gooseberries grow along the lane, more water-
proof than the equally tiny wild strawberries and thus likelier to
reach maturity in a healthy condition. They are uncomfortable to
pick since they have darning needle-like thorns along their
branches and lurk amongst banks of nettles and thistles.
'Gooseberry-picker' was an old term for a person doing an
unpleasant job that nobody else would take on, but the end result
is worth the struggle. Gooseberries are not nearly as common in
our supermarkets as the ubiquitous, year-round strawberry. I
keep meaning to make Gooseberry Tansy but have so far never
got round to it. This dish began in olden times and, at first, was
flavoured with the herb of that name and coloured green with
spinach juice. It went through various stages and changes until,
by the seventeenth century, it had nothing at all in common with

its origins except its name. You had to top and tail the goose-berries (the gooseberry-picker was probably made to do this as well, for no one in her right mind would volunteer to tackle a quart of gooseberries), then you took the aforesaid quart and cooked them with – as the instructions of the time so helpfully put it – 'enough sugar' – then you beat four eggs and grated a couple of handfuls of white bread into crumbs, then you mixed it up all together and stirred it over a low heat until it became a firm mass. If I ever do make this dish I shall put it into the oven to set rather than stand around stirring it at the risk of the whole thing turning into scrambled egg with added gooseberry. Some recipes include cream in the mix, but I'd rather just pour cream over the finished product.

A Lady tells us how 'To Keep Gooseberries'. You had to gather them before they became too large and put them in wide-mouthed bottles which were then put up to the neck in water in a boiler:

> When the fruit looks scalded, take them out; and when perfectly cold close and rosin the top. Dig a trench in a part of the garden least used, sufficiently deep for all the bottles to stand, and let the earth be thrown over, to cover them a foot and a half. When a frost comes on, a little fresh litter from the stable will prevent the ground from hardening so that the fruit cannot be dug up. Or, scald as above; when cold, fill the bottles with cold water, cork them and keep them in a damp or dry place; they will not be spoiled.

Or you could put the bottles in the oven 'when the bread is drawn' and then 'beat in new velvet corks' and 'if well secured from damp they will keep the year round'. The word 'botulism' comes to mind and one begins not to wonder why the nineteenth century was so suspicious of fruit.

Still, *A Lady* gives a sensible tip 'To Prepare Fruit For Children': 'A far more wholesome way than in pies or puddings, is to put apples sliced, or plums, currants, gooseberries, &c., into a stone jar; and sprinkle among them as much Lisbon sugar as necessary. Set the jar in an oven or on a hearth, with a teacupful of water to prevent the fruit from burning; or put the jar into a saucepan of water till its contents be perfectly done. Slices of bread or some rice may be put into the jar, to eat with the fruit.'

When it isn't too wet we gather wild raspberries that grow in the ditches along the edge of the woods. They have maggots in them but I find it soothing to sit in the evenings quietly picking them off: when the raspberries are sprinkled with sugar the maggots come up for air. Bilberry picking is another restful activity once you've climbed halfway up the mountain: you find a promising spot, sit in the low bushes and stare down until you see some bilberries. You lay claim to your territory and forbid anyone to come within a hundred yards or to speak unless some emergency has arisen: such as a bite from a horse-fly or a threatening cloud which might descend as mist and preclude anyone from returning home.

'It is a well-known fact that bananas can be eaten without fear or misgiving of any kind by all classes from children to old people . . . there are few people who do not fall in love with them at first bite,' says a 1930s booklet called *101 Ways of Cooking Bananas*. Still, you can have too many. I have an old letter from my aunt to my father, who was shooting in Shropshire with my grandfather while the females of the family stayed at home in Liverpool. A banana boat had docked and for some reason my grandmother had been presented with what sounds like crates of them. My aunt wrote that they had been eating nothing but bananas in every imaginable form from banana custards to banana fritters, and between meals, too, they ate bananas. Properly brought-up people scrape the sides free of those fragile strips before slicing. The first one I remember eating was dried. This was just after the Second World War: in 'the Duration' there had been none. (There may soon be none again – I read that a disease is ravaging some of the banana plantations.)

My booklet announces that, 'Their flavour is not impaired, nor is the nutritive value lessened to any degree in the process of cooking.' It adds hastily, lest there be any misunderstanding, 'Some people say that it is impossible to improve upon the banana by cooking it, for, in its raw state, this popular fruit is actually a kind of bread and is frequently regarded as complete in itself.' I don't know when they were introduced into this country – there is no mention of them in my earlier nineteenth-century cookery books although they were occasionally grown in hot houses – but they were so immensely fashionable in the 1930s that it seems unnecessary for Mr Hermann-Senn OBE (who compiled the booklet) to tell his readers, 'In the case of that popular breakfast dish – bacon – the value of it is increased if bananas are fried with it.' I have been told by Mexicans and West Indians that it is usually plantains and not bananas that are cooked, but we don't have as many plantains as we do bananas, so will have to make do with what we can. Perhaps not 'Bananas with Poached Eggs' or 'Banana Sauce' – which was made with added herbs, cayenne and half a teaspoon of redcurrant jelly, boiled and sieved, and must have been slimy. Nor should you on any account let banana fraternise with plaice, although in relation to savoury dishes the raw banana comes into its own in the case of extremely hot curries, having a similar calming effect to that of cucumber.

As if *101 Ways* were not enough, the original owner of my booklet has added eleven more, cut out or copied from the newspapers of the time. 'Banana Betty', a combination of the fruit baked in the oven with orange juice, brown sugar and biscuit crumbs, was apparently Shirley Temple's favourite. Another reads simply, 'I have recently come from America where a delicious dish, a combination of strawberries and bananas, is served. Cut strawberries in halves or quarters according to size, and mix with bananas cut not too thin. Sugar to taste and place in the refrigerator for about half an hour. This allows the strawberry flavour to permeate the banana.' Wow. (Cardinal Wolsey, it is said, was the first to pour cream on his strawberries. No one else had thought of it.)

My American book on thrift suggests that you should offer to relieve the greengrocer of those black bananas that are too far gone to sell. Freeze them. When you come to thaw them out, the inside will be deliquescent and you can squeeze them into a glass of reconstituted powdered milk and give it to your loved ones.

In the olden days when the company had polished off the roast beef, the boiled mutton, the venison patties, the boar's head, the carp, the turtle, the swan, the peacock and the dish of larks, together with various messes of pottage, the 'soteltie' would be ceremoniously carried in. A spell check would reveal this as 'subtlety' which, compared with the unembarrassed presentation of the previous quantity of viands, I suppose it was – in its way. One was described thus: 'Seint Andrew sitting on a hie Auter of a-state, with bemes of golde; afore him knelyng ye Bishoppe in pontificabilus; his Croser kneling behind him coped.' This was brought in at the close of the first course (consisting of eleven dishes) at the feast given at the installation of John Stafford, Archbishop of Canterbury, in 1443. These confections were composed of paste – what we would call marzipan (which name derives from Bread of St Mark which in Latin is *Marci Panis*; there are many other suggested derivations), an admirably tractable substance – and jelly; not the wobbly transparent sort we know but the ancestor sort, something more akin to glue, derived from boiled bones and flavoured with spices and flower water.

The 'soteltie' survives today in the form of the baby's birthday cake, though with rather different ingredients. Nor is it usually quite as elaborate as that offered for the delectation of the Archbishop. Nevertheless, its composition involves much thought and care: trains, boats, bears, cottages, castles, all manner of conceits are laboured over as the day approaches, while chunks of sponge cake, jam and icing are welded together to represent something of presumed significance to the infant. The unadmitted purpose is to draw astonished gasps from the adults present. Babies tend to rub it in their hair.

A droll suggestion from 1861:

> Buy a few chestnuts. Sit down and with a small knife keep on cutting slits in their skins till you cut your fingers. When you have finished them, put the chestnuts on the top bar of your grate and keep on till you have burned your hand. Take a seat opposite the fire and in a few minutes the fruit will pop out with great violence in the faces of the company and all over the room. They are now done, and if you can find them, which may perhaps be accomplished by groping about the floor, you will have an excellent dish of Roasted Chestnuts.

Twenty

CHEESE

$\mathcal{I}$t is said that cheese came about by chance when an Arab merchant filled a bag made from a sheep's stomach with milk to sustain him on his journey across the desert and found that the rennet had turned the milk into curds and whey. The problem with this tale is that it must have happened all the time, not just on one specific and significant occasion, but it's as good a story as any; and it is possible that others, seeing what had happened to their nice milk, left it under a ziggurat in disgust. Cheese is now remarkable for the numerous forms it takes, having started as milk. Stilton and Feta and Gouda and Caerphilly and Gorgonzola and Parmesan and Camembert, and the thousands of national and regional varieties, seem as implausibly related as the Great Dane and the Dachshund, the Chihuahua, the Husky, the Poodle, the Saluki, and the common mongrel who all, so we are led to believe, descended from the wolf. The French Cantal is said to be the oldest cheese extant.

The Ancient Greeks, the Romans, the people of the Bible, and anyone else with milk to spare and an animal's stomach, all mention cheese in their writings. Virgil wrote a poem about a peasant's dish of herbs, garlic and 'old cheeses, their surface pierced midway with rushes, suspended in baskets of close-woven fennel'. Job said to God, 'Thou hast poured me out as milk, and curdled me as cheese.' In the fifteenth century John Russell, who wrote a *Boke of Nurture*, seemed to think that cheese had a laxative effect: 'Hard chese wille a stomak kepe open,' which is not now the general view. A century later Andrew Borde listed the types of cheese then available, 'There is iiii sorts of chese. Grene chese, softe chese, hard chese and Spermyse.' 'Grene' cheese was so-called for 'the newnes of it, for the whey is not halfe pressed out of it,' and Spermyse was made with 'Curdes and the juice of herbes.'

'As an article of food,' says *The Dictionary of Daily Wants*:

> cheese is more wholesome when partaken of in small quantities, and accompanying other diet, than when eaten in large quantities or made a meal of. It is a generally received notion that cheese eaten at the conclusion of a dinner promotes digestion, its effects however are of a negative kind, that is, by acting as a temporary stimulant on the stomach; and even this is the case only with sound old cheese, which is neither too fat nor too far advanced in the process of putrefaction. Decayed cheese and new cheese are both very unwholesome.

Many people who have jettisoned all other old saws and sayings and wisps of ancient wisdom, persist in the belief that cheese at bedtime induces nightmares. Another thing they do at dinner is discuss whether it should come before or after the sweet course, which is an indication of how it has risen in the social scale: for centuries it was considered, on the whole, as peasant fare, although everyone found it handy when they travelled.

In Britain cheese was usually known as 'mousetrap', and Dorothy L. Sayers wrote of 'That impassive pale substance known to the English as "cheese" unqualified.' Sir Francis observed that, 'It is to France that anyone at all discriminating looks for small cheeses, of which there are multitudes, many of them excellent, which are never heard of outside their own locality.' General de Gaulle asked (I am certain in the tone of the proud parent of a difficult but precocious child, who says fondly, 'Did you ever *know* such a little rascal?') how it was possible to govern a country with two hundred and forty-six cheeses. Those found available on this side of the Channel were only Brie, Camembert, Reblechon, Port-de-Salut and Pont l'Evêque – 'It has something of a Camembert's flavour, without its extreme capriciousness.' Sir Francis, who made this remark, was dismissive of the cheeses of the Balkans, of Sweden and of Norway which 'can be had if anyone except their nationals can be found to eat them. A common Norwegian cheese smells like an over-ripe Camembert that has been steeped for a week in a horrible drain: which is possibly why it is plentifully be-sprinkled with caraway seeds.' He didn't care for Gorgonzola either, 'A strong, roughly flavoured cheese which, when at all over-ripe, smells like a cess-pit . . . those who like it are very fortunate, as there is scarcely a village whose grocer does not market this dreadful substance.' But he was not prejudiced against Roquefort, '. . . a strongish cheese, but not indelicately so, unless it has gone too far. It is a misfortune that the little creatures that it produces are as large as they are, and as active – a specially good mover will double up his back and flick himself a couple of feet across a mahogany table, which shows him up: on a white table-cloth he is scarcely visible.'

It is interesting that Sir Francis flinched from smells but didn't mind maggots. We sometimes prepare eggs with Roquefort as long as it is not wriggling. Make a thick white sauce, melt the cheese in it, pour it into ramekin dishes, break an egg into each and bake for about eight minutes. Or you could use the left-over Stilton as long as nobody has told you that the fungus which causes the blue veins is similar to that which causes Athlete's Foot.

An American cheese-lover, Clifton Fadiman, wrote in the 1940s or '50s:

> The blackest shadow, of course, is cast by processed 'cheese' . . . In preparation of this solidified floor wax – often the product of emulsification with sodium citrate, sodium phosphate or rochelle salts; of steaming and frequently blending odd lots of cheese; of paralysing whatever germs might result either in loss of profit or gain of flavour – every problem but one is solved: that of making cheese. Give our American children the processed corpse of milk and they will grow (I dare not say mature) into processed men, all package and no character. As for other processed plastics, remember only that the wrappings of foil are the cerements of death.

And while on the subject – just as there was once an English law designed to protect the wool trade, that shrouds should be made of wool – so there was once a statute in Wisconsin: 'Every person, firm or corporation duly licensed to operate a hotel or restaurant shall serve with each meal, for which a charge of twenty-five cents or more is made, at least two-thirds of an ounce of Wisconsin butter and two-thirds of an ounce of Wisconsin cheese.'

One day, not long ago, we bought a cheese in the supermarket in

Marylebone – it was small and round and wrapped in two oak leaves and it stank – it was French. A friend, taking note of all those factors, lost his temper. He has dairy-farming friends in Gloucester and if they, he said, had dared to present a cheese wrapped up in oak leaves, the entire weight of Brussels would have descended on their heads, and anyway they'd already been forced out of the cheese-making industry by the European regulations. We agreed that it was odd, and only the British appeared to be constrained by the rules. The scrap that was left of the cheese we had purchased went rapidly and reassuringly mouldy, thus indicating that it had not been treated with suspect preservatives. I distrust all foodstuffs that keep a youthful glow of health long past what could be considered a reasonable mortal span. Somebody has done something to them. We no longer make our own cream cheese by pouring sour milk into a muslin cloth and tying it to the tap so that it drips in the sink, since the last time we tried, it seemed that the milk had not gone sour but bad.

A Lebanese friend gave us a different sort of cheese. It is called *mujadalleh* and was made by her grandmama back home. She heats the milk long and slowly with some gelling agent, salt and herbs, and when it cools it forms into worm-like strands which she braids. What gelling agent and what herbs? I asked, but the language barrier foiled us. The texture is a bit like that of mozzarella, while the flavour is unlike anything else. It is best toasted. (My friend's grandmama, on being consulted, told us the specks in the cheese are called *Baraka*, which means 'blessing seed'; in Sufism, *Baraka* is a term which indicates holiness.)

The Dictionary of Daily Wants' 'Cheese Sandwiches' make the usual nineteenth-century concession to the notion that it is entirely pointless to eat anything without meat in it. 'Take two parts of grated Parmesan or Cheshire cheese, one of butter, and a small proportion of made mustard; pound them in a mortar; cover slices of bread with a little of this, and lay over it slices of ham or any cured meat; cover them with another slice of bread, press them together, and cut into mouthfuls that they may be lifted up with a fork.' The dear *Dictionary*'s 'Cheese Soup' tells us to:

> Have ready some good stock; then take half a pound of new Gruyère cheese; grate half, and cut the remainder in thin slices. In an earthen pipkin put a thin layer of grated cheese with some bits of butter; cover this with thin slices of bread; then a layer of the cheese in slices; then bread, next grated cheese; continue this alternately till all the cheese is used. On the last layer, which ought to be sliced cheese, put some pieces of butter; moisten it with some of the stock; stew it till it adheres to the bottom, and the stock is all dried up; then add the remains of the stock with salt and pepper, and serve very hot.

If, presumably, you can hack it out of the pipkin.

However, we do make Cheese Pudding in the way the *Dictionary* advises. Mix eight ounces of white breadcrumbs with six ounces of grated cheese. Heat a pint of milk gently with two ounces of butter until the butter melts. Pour over the bread-crumbs and cheese and stir. Beat four eggs with salt, pepper and dried mustard. Mix all together, pour into a buttered dish and leave to stand for at least an hour. Sprinkle with a little extra grated cheese just before baking in a hot oven for approximately forty minutes until golden and risen. It can also be eaten cold and the quantities are variable. The *Dictionary* suggests that it should be baked in puff pastry, which would require more time and effort but, one must admit, would make an impressive dish.

Toasted cheese was always said to be the Welshman's favourite treat. Lady Llanover wrote in 1867 that Welsh toasted cheese was quite different from English melted cheese: you held a slice to the fire 'but not so much as to drop' and toasted it on both sides, then put it on your crisply toasted bread. This would require skill and vigilance and I've never tried it. The correct term is Welsh Rabbit, not Rarebit.

A note from *Things Not Generally Known*: The 'Bread-And-Cheese-Ordeal. The most easy method of a criminal proving his innocence, amongst all the extraordinary modes of trial which prevailed anciently, seems to have been what Muratori styles the *judicium panis er casei* (the judgement of bread and cheese). If, after the priest had blessed this food, the prisoner was able to swallow it, he was acquitted.' Otherwise . . .

Don't have cheese for supper with this thought on your mind, and 'As a matter of course, young ladies do not eat cheese at dinner parties.'

And so to bed.

SELECT BIBLIOGRAPHY

Acton, Eliza, *Modern Cookery*, London: Longmans, Green, Reader &
Dyer, 1868

Arthur, Timothy Shay, *Trials and Confessions of a Housekeeper*,
Philadelphia, USA: J. W. Bradley, 1859

Beer, Gretel, *Sandwiches for Parties and Picnics and How to Make Them*,
London: Herbert Jenkins, 1953

Beeton, Isabella Mary, *Beeton's Everyday Cookery and Housekeeping
Book*, London: Ward, Lock & Co., 1963

Blackwood, Caroline, and Haycraft, Anna, *Darling, You Shouldn't
Have Gone to So Much Trouble*, London: Jonathan Cape, 1980

The Boke of Kervynge, London: Wynkyn de Worde, 1513

Boulenger, Edward George, *A Naturalist at the Dinner Table*, London:
Duckworth, 1927

Brillat-Savarin, Jean Anthelme, *Physiologie du Goût*, Paris:
Charpentier, 1840

Buckmaster, John Charles, *Buckmaster's Cookery: Being an abridg-
ment of some of the lectures delivered in the Cookery School at the
International Exhibition for 1873 and 1874*, London: G. Routledge
& Sons, 1874

Byron, May, *May Byron's Pot-Luck or The British Home Cookery Book*,
Toronto, London, New York: Hodder and Stoughton Ltd, 1923

Colchester-Wemyss, Sir Francis, *The Pleasures of the Table*, London:
J. Nisbet & Co., 1931

The Concise Household Encyclopedia, London: Amalgamated Press,
1931

Craig, Elizabeth, *Elizabeth Craig's Economical Cookery*, London & Glasgow: Collins, 1934

Craig, Elizabeth, *Entertaining with Elizabeth Craig*, London: Collins, 1933

Cudlip, Annie Hall, *The Modern Housewife or How We Live Now*, London: Ward, Lock & Co., 1883

Davies, Mary, *The Housewife's What's What: A hold-all of useful information for the house*, London: T. Fisher Unwin, 1904

Dinners and Dinner-Parties, or The Absurdities of Artificial Life, 2nd edn., London: Chapman & Hall, 1862

Dods, Margaret, [pseud. of Christian Isobel Johnstone], *The Cook and Housewife's Manual. Containing the most approved modern receipts for making soups, gravies, sauces, etc.*, Edinburgh, 1826

Fin-Bec, [pseud. of William Blanchard Jerrold], *The Dinner Bell: A gastronomic manual*, London: William Mullan & Son, 1878

Francatelli, Charles Elmé, *The Modern Cook*, London: Richard Bentley & Son, 1883

Francatelli, Charles Elmé, *Plain Cookery for the Working Classes*, London: Bosworth and Harrison, 1861

Garth, Margaret, and Wrench, Mrs Stanley, *Home Management*, London: Daily Express Publications, 1934

Hillis, Marjorie, *Live Alone and Like It: A Guide for the Extra Woman*, London: Citadel Press, 1936

Ives, Catherine, *When the Cook is Away*, London: Duckworth, 1928

Jack, Florence B., and Strauss, Rita, *The Woman's Book. Contains Everything a Woman Ought to Know*, London & Edinburgh: T. C. & E. C. Jack, 1911

Kitchiner, William, *Apicius Redivivus or The Cook's Oracle. Containing receipts for plain cookery on the most economical plan, for private families. The result of actual experiments instituted by William Kitchiner*, 7th edn., London: Houlston and Sons, 1880

Layton, Thomas Arthur, *Five to a Feast*, London: Gerald Duckworth, 1948

Leyel, Hilda Winifred Wauton, and Hartley, Olga, *The Gentle Art of Cookery*, London: Chatto & Windus, 1925

Lindsay, Jessie, and Tress, Helen M., *What Every Cook Should Know*, London: Nisbet & Co., 1932

Margolius, Sidney, *Health Foods: Facts and Fakes*, New York: Walker & Company, 1973

Marshall, Mrs A. B., *Mrs. A. B. Marshall's Larger Cookery Book of Extra Recipes*, London: Simpkin, Marshall, Hamilton, Kent & Co. Ltd, 1891

Mayhew, Henry, and Mayhew, Augustus, *The Greatest Plague of Life; or the Adventures of a lady in search of a good servant. By one who has been 'almost worried to death'*, London, G. Routledge & Sons, 1847

Meighn, Moira, *Moira Meighn's Adventure Book of Cookery for Boys and Girls and for Anyone Interested in Cooking*, Oxford: Oxford University Press, 1937

Morphy, Countess, [pseud. of Marcelle Azra Forbes], *English Recipes Including the Traditional Dishes of Scotland, Ireland & Wales*, London: published for Selfridge & Co. by Herbert Joseph, n.d.

Nott, John, *Cooks' and Confectioners' Dictionary*, London: Charles Rivington, 1726

The Official Handbook for the National Training School for Cookery, London: Chapman and Hall, 1879

Peel, Dorothy Constance, *Learning to Cook: The book of 'how' and 'why' in the kitchen*, London: Constable & Co., 1915

Peters, Charles (ed.), *The Girl's Own Indoor Book. Containing practical help to girls on all matters relating to their material comfort and moral well-being*, London: Religious Tract Society, 1888

Philp, Robert Kemp, *The Dictionary of Daily Wants*, London: Houlston & Wright, 1859

Philp, Robert Kemp, *The Domestic World: A practical guide in all the daily difficulties of the higher branches of domestic and social economy*, London: Hodder & Stoughton, 1878

Philp, Robert Kemp, *Enquire Within upon Everything*, London: Madgwick, Houlston and Co. Ltd, 1912

Pierce, Charles, *The Household Manager: Being a practical treatise upon the various duties in large or small establishments*, London: Simpkin & Marshall, 1863

Plumptre, Bell, *Domestic Management*, London: printed for B. and R. Crosby and Co., 1813

Raffald, Elizabeth, *The Experienced English Housekeeper*, London: A. Millar, W. Law, & R. Cater, 1791

Riddell, Robert Flower, *Indian Domestic Economy and Receipt Book*, 5th edn., revised, Madras, 1860

Rundell, Maria Eliza [A Lady], *A New System of Domestic Cookery. Formed upon principles of economy and adapted to the use of private families*, London: John Murray, 1833

Russell, John, *The Boke of Nurture*, edited from the Harleian MS. 4011 in the British Museum by F. J. Furnivall, London, 1577, (reprinted, 1868)

Saxon, Edgar J., *Sensible Food for All in Britain and the Temperate Zones*, London: C. W. Daniel Co.,1939

Self, Jonathan, *Self Abuse: Love, loss and fatherhood*, London: John Murray, 2001

Shand, Philip Morton, *A Book of Food*, London: Jonathan Cape, 1927

Short, [pseud.], *Dinners at Home: How to order, cook and serve them*, London: Kenby & Endean, 1878

Silvester, Elizabeth, *Silvester's Sensible Cookery*, London: Herbert Jenkins, 1920

Somerville, Mrs, *Cookery and Domestic Economy*, Glasgow, 1862

Southgate, Henry, *Things a Lady Would Like to Know Concerning Domestic Management and Expenditure*, London & Edinburgh: William P. Nimmo, 1876

Soyer, Alexis, *The Modern Housewife or Ménagère*, London: Simpkin, Marshall & Co., 1853

Spon, Edward, *Spons' Household Manual: A treasury of domestic receipts and guide for home management*, London: E. & F. N. Spon, 1887

Sylvia's Book of Family Management and Practical Economy, Botolph Press, n.d.

Tegetmeier, William Bernhard, *A Manual of Domestic Economy. With hints on domestic medicine and surgery*, London: Home and Colonial School Society; Hamilton, Adams, & Co., 1880

Thompson, Sir Henry, *Food and Feeding*, London: Frederick Warne and Co., 1891

Timbs, John, *Things Not Generally Known, Familiarly Explained*, London: Kent & Co., 1859

Turquet de Mayerne, Baron Théodore, *Archimagirus Anglo-Gallicus*, copied from a choice manuscript of Sir T. Mayerne, London, 1658

Webb, Mrs M. E., *The Doctor in the Kitchen*, London: George Newnes, 1935

Webster, Thomas, and Parkes, Mrs William, *An Encyclopaedia of Domestic Economy*, London, 1844

Weir, Eric, *When Madame Cooks*, London: Philip Allan, 1931

White, Florence (ed.), *Good Things in England. A practical cookery book for everyday use*, London: Jonathan Cape, 1932

Whitfield, Nella, *Kitchen Encyclopedia*, London: Spring Books, n.d.

Wijey, Mabel (ed.), *Warne's Everyday Cookery*, London & New York: F. Warne & Co., 1929